Being with Children

by

Phillip Lopate

Poseidon Press
New York · London · Toronto · Sydney · Tokyo

POSEIDON PRESS

Simon & Schuster Building
Rockefeller Center
1230 Avenue of the Americas
New York, New York 10020

POSEIDON PRESS is a registered trademark
of Simon & Schuster Inc.

POSEIDON PRESS colophon is a trademark
of Simon & Schuster Inc.

Manufactured in the United States of America

10 9 8 7 6 5 4 3 2 1

Library of Congress Cataloging-in-Publication data

Lopate, Phillip, date.
    Being with children / Phillip Lopate.
        p.   cm.
    1. Creative writing (Elementary education)   2. Lopate, Phillip,
1943–   . 3. Teachers—New York (N.Y.)— Biography.   I. Title.
LB1576.L64   1989
372.6′2—dc 19   89-3547
ISBN 0-671-67680-6   CIP

Contents

I
Digging In

With his work, as with a glove, a man feels the universe.
TRANSTRÖMER

Chapter 1
A Tour of the School

P.S. 90 might just as well be invisible. Most neighborhood people don't even see it. Three stories high, built of administrative red brick, as easily mistaken for a bus depot as a public school, it seems to urge you not to notice it, like a stalled driver who waves the other cars past. A stranger's eye would naturally move away to the blinking neon arrow above the gas station, past the gas station to the viaduct over Riverside Park, to the dark world under its archways, the rusting iron columns, bat drippings, and wet leaves; along the gray string of river to the muscular middle-class buildings facing the Drive, outlined in once-popular staircase style: giants rubbing shoulders uneasily with the indifferent welfare hotels where, sitting on the stoop, a rundown single-room occupant is trying to decide whether to go back in or go out. Go for a walk? See what's happening on Broadway. . . .

With so much to look at, why would anyone want to bother with a low brick box, overpowered by apartment houses, upstaged even by the emaciated trees with fences around them, and a few green leaves? Those trees in front of P.S. 90 are not much more developed than the way they appeared in the architect's sketch, three rapid brush strokes.

The building must once have been spanking new. It must once have been a lightning-rod connecting all the high-minded hopes of parents and community who had to exert incalculable pressure on city officials to get it built.

The cornerstone says: Erected 1950. If you wanted to, you could consider it a modern schoolhouse. Or you could think of it as stylistically congruent with the Korean War.

Taking a closer look at the windows (but why would one want to do that?), you would notice the smiling, bruised construction-paper cutouts of reindeer and clowns which victimize grade schools.

Pass now through the heavy blue doors. A security guard or volunteer is sitting with a sign-in book at the top of the stairwell. If the stranger does not look like a dope peddler or thief, he will be let inside the building proper.

It is here that visitors often lose heart. Such screaming, like the wail of a cattle market, so little spatial clarity, and the sudden darkness, the fluorescent lights.

There are schools that have monitors with sashes to guide the newcomer to his destination; but here, no. Unless someone passing takes pity on you and asks, "Who are you looking for?" By now you have recovered and you see the Main Office, only three steps away.

The visitors are usually of two kinds, parents and jobseekers. They stand behind the gray aluminum counter trying to catch the eye of a secretary, but the secretaries are rarely looking in their direction and so a visitor, learning patience, begins to read a flyer in Spanish and English.

The office monitors, two neatly bloused children, are playing cards.

The older boy has bought a bag of french fries drenched in ketchup and lets the other monitor have some.

Another child sits on a bench with her hand on her forehead. She is turning green. She is "not feeling well." She fills out an accident report.

One of the secretaries looks up from her typewriter and notices you with a smile. The secretaries are warm, congenial women of about forty. They have ready sympathy; they show concern when a child enters bleeding. They seem to accept their lives, or, if discontented and secretly wanting more, they do not thrust their bitterness on you.

The secretaries share a large bullpen but each asserts a proud individuality, a distance from the others, as though thinking: These are not my real friends, though I get along with them, and at night I go home and do something else.

The secretary asks the visitor to state his business. Then she takes a written note into the principal's inner office; and the visitor sits down to wait, next to the monitors, who are suddenly too shy to look at him.

Down the hall are some of the kindergarten and first-grade classrooms.

The kindergarten has a rug and couches and a wonderful big piano. Two girls make themselves comfortable squirming on the couch hugging and kissing each other and laughing and pointing to pictures in a book. Some children are banging into each other for the sheer pleasure of it or sitting alone with colored blocks. The room has an ardent air of giddy happiness just about to break into sorrow. In the corridors there is a freeway traffic of matériel and bodies. The teachers—some young and dungareed, others middle-aged, wearing calico aprons around their stocky waists—pass each other in the halls with frazzled smiles. A shared sense of being overwhelmed, of loose ends piling up, is what they exchange. Even when one of them is not feeling overwhelmed but on top of things, she flashes the other the exhaustion sign as a kind of courtesy.

In the corridor a passionate Spanish boy is smashing wooden blocks with a hammer. Beside him stands a young man—the student teacher—glum, his long hair pulled back in a pony tail, watching with pursed, apprehensive lips and Quakerish frown the boy's demonic enjoyment. The student teacher, preparing any moment to take the hammer away, looks as if he would be happier on a farm. Idealism is written on his face, as on the faces of the missionaries a century ago—but an idealism which has ill-prepared him for the fierce opportunism of the children.

The school has been fortunate in attracting the extra help of teacher colleges which want to make it a showcase for the Open Corridor approach. So it is perhaps a better-off school than most. Visiting consultants give workshops in body movement, ecology, scratch-and-doodle slidemaking, non-violence. . . . There is no lack of stimulation: if children and teachers sometimes walk around P.S. 90 in an anxious daze, it is not because they are "unenriched" but because they are starved for a way to integrate these peripheral excitations into a center that will hold.

On the bulletin boards and behind glass cabinets are featured posters which celebrate ethnic heritage: biographies of Puerto Rican heroes, African papier-mâché masks, essays with "Excellent!" written across them. The art teacher mounts her own colorful exhibits. All these touching efforts at gaiety and decoration fall like dead sparrows against the stony fortress architecture. Try what one might, the place looks bleak. It defies any effort to make it sparkle.

You might even consider this grim, immutable aspect its soul. The school is built in an H shape with one long corridor connecting the two wings. The corridor walls are constructed of rough cement blocks with beveled edges, an anemic green shade. Here the sun never shines. The black linoleum floors and barren overhead lighting call to mind a prison gallery.

Down these corridors the janitor, Dominick, wheels his broom wagon. For him the school is indeed a prison, a fixed quantity of cells that must be traversed without variation from day to day. Each room needs to have its basket emptied, the floors need to be swept, the windows checked in case those jerks left any open. Some teachers made it easier for you by getting the kids to sweep up and keeping everyone inside the room. The rest of the crew, "the wise asses," form the subject of his running monologue. Dominick does not like Open Corridor or any of these "so-called free, let the kids do what they feel like and walk all over you" innovations. His opposition is simple and professional: if you let kids out of the classrooms, you increase the chance of their leaving gum wrappers and junk in the hallway. Dominick is counting the days till his transfer to a conservative school in Queens comes through.

"I don't mind telling you—I'm an old-fashioned guy and I don't go for this crap. Boy, this school used to be so different. You couldn't hear a pin drop when you walked through the halls. Now these maniacs made it so I have to break my back."

As he sweeps he will continue complaining to anyone within hearing distance, and when no one is around, talk to the green walls, pushing his wagon of dirt from room to room, hallway to hallway.

The chief custodian is a different story. He has a neat white shirt and tie, a charming Irish brogue, and stays in his office answering phone calls. If you come to him to get help for a mechanical problem, he will look you up and down with a dubious smile and make you feel like a sissy. This once-over *macho* look must, I think, be part of the civil service examination for school custodians, because I have seen several men in his position deliver it.

After a while, when you get to know him, he is less intimidating, and the teachers use his office with its coffee machine for a hideout. What a difference once you have discovered these hideouts! The teachers' lounge, the custodian's office, the obscure walk-in closets, dressing rooms, supply nooks—all of these zones of privacy must be learned by the newcomer before he can form any true impression of the institution's physical possibilities. The children know most of these hideouts. It is a matter of emotional survival for them to find places in a public school to be alone.

When you come out of the building you notice for the first time the construction ditch across the street, with red flags and mounds of earth the color of mustard seeds. They have been digging up this corner for years and the cars make a sudden swerve around the cracked asphalt pothole. No one bothers to ask why they are digging up the street. It is something that has always been and always will be. In winter on a clear blue day, ice forms around the feet of the dirt mounds, and you have to climb those little hills to avoid slipping on the ice, which makes a fascinating crunch when it cracks. It is almost worth getting soaked just to hear that sound.

Chapter 2
The Change Agents

THE ERA OF THE CONSULTANT

It was inevitable from 1967 onward, with the schools throughout the country troubled about their sense of purpose and the students bored and rebellious, that administrators would turn to experts in entertainment for inspiration. Poets, theater directors, multimedia artists, jugglers, dancers, philosophers were suddenly asked to bring new life to the routine of the classroom. What would result from this chemistry no one was willing to guess. How sincere the invitation was differed from school to school. In some schools the expectation may have been nothing more than a day's entertainment, the way one hires a magician to keep the children occupied at a birthday party; in other cases, the hopes may have gone much deeper. Artists are often sought out, when they are not being ignored, to effect a spiritual regeneration in people's lives which is really beyond their powers.

The almost religious hopes which creativity excites (religious in spirit as well as in approaching the Infinite) may stem from the fact that art is one of the last vocations left with a degree of autonomy and self-sufficiency. A teacher who is not much impressed with the manner of a poet visiting his or her classroom may still feel that the children have gained something merely by being exposed to a person who lives by his self-expression.

I am talking now of a desperate situation. Only desperate people would throw open their school doors and welcome shaggy poets to mingle with their young. Americans traditionally distrust poetry and think it the most frivolous of arts. But the poet has certain practical advantages. He is portable, he is inexpensive, and in some mysterious way he may excite children into writing, which may awaken a taste for reading, which may lead to higher reading scores and happier school boards. Nevertheless, it was understood by schools requesting visiting writers that the poet should not be pressured or consciously programmed toward that end but should be allowed to steer his or her own course. The very innocence of artists about educational matters was considered a potential asset, in that they might be less inclined to duplicate the standard curriculum.

Naturally, misunderstandings resulted; and they resulted quite logically from the initial paradox of wanting strangers to visit a classroom and stir things up and, on the other hand, resenting the turbulence which the passing experts left behind. The errors surrounding these programs were analyzed with rare honesty by Martin Kushner, an arts administrator, who confessed:

> Artists have been dropped into the school like paratroopers onto a strange terrain. Few instructions were given. They had to scout teachers, seek allies, and do the best they could without a great deal of experience. We had many meetings early in the year with the teachers, but these talks were perfunctory. Each artist was simply present in the school to turn kids on, to do his thing, to involve teachers. Indeed, we had selected artists who fancied themselves aesthetic paratroopers and so made their jumps enthusiastically. But how much more we could have achieved with more knowledge of school life and adequately prepared welcome mats manned by school and community people who knew a lot more about what was dropping out of the sky into their laps! We had objectives but they were abstractions. Since no artist can ever really be adequately prepared for a school situation unless he is directly from the community, we know we must be more thoughtful, "up front," and honest about ourselves early with all school personnel. We must state clearly what we are attempting to do—what we believe in. If the administration's point of view differs greatly from ours, then we must either determine whether the difference should exist in the schools and be important tools for learning, or, we have to find another school more willing to experiment.[1]

These misunderstandings are like the ones faced by the WPA—sponsored Writers Project in the 1930s. Nevertheless, the writer-in-the-schools program has suggested at least an embryonic hope of

---

[1] Quoted in *Artists in the Classroom,* Connecticut Commission on the Arts, 1973.

a model for writers to regain a useful role in the daily productive world without relinquishing their identity as artists. Even with the risks attached to such collaborations, no more fruitful experiment could be imagined, since writers need, in addition to a steady income, the emotional nourishment of a workplace, while schools need more poetry, in the largest sense of the term.

The importation of writers into the schools may be seen as part of a larger pattern—the era of the consultant, in which the disinterested expert, who is not engaged in the political intrigues and promotional ladder within the institution, enters the institution, presumably free to put forward a fresh viewpoint. It was a high-ranking official in the Ford Foundation who first coined the term "change agent" to describe a kind of roving catalyst who could go into an ailing institution, size up the problem, and set people moving in a productive direction.

Necessary to the identity of the change agent was that at a certain point he leave. For how else could he maintain his objectivity and his *specialness?* It would dissolve in the bath of the institution; he would be sucked into the petty murk and become just another grumpy, backbiting employee. Even if he kept up his "transformational" ability, this line of thinking went, his continued presence would engender a passivity and dependence on the part of his colleagues. No, the change agent had to leave.

The change-agent concept seems to me the most odiously impersonal and presumptuous imaginable. Yet it sums up the dilemma in which many writers working in the schools are placed. They have been assigned a role of eternally Different, and they can either exploit that, resist it, evade it, submit to it, or subvert it, depending on the particular circumstances and temperament of the writer. In any case, it remains a frame for their actions which they can never ignore.

At the forefront of the movement to bring writers and artists into the schools was Teachers & Writers Collaborative, started by Herbert Kohl in 1966. I joined the Collaborative in 1968, a year that marked the height of discontent with American educational institutions. The school-reform movement had been gathering steam; the first wave of muckraking books by Holt, Kozol, Kohl, Herndon, Dennison, and Conroy had appeared or was soon to appear; and many people seemed to be coming to the conclusion that the American school system was on the point of collapse.

I considered myself part of a second line of reformers, who had inherited the new atmosphere brought about by the impact of the first group on the schools, profiting from the wedge they had made, at the same time as walking into the confusion and mistrust which that initial wave of attack had left behind. The schools had been put on the defensive—which did not necessarily mean that they would transform themselves, only that we were in for a period of much more self-conscious, ambiguous behavior.

The exposé literature had helped to generate an accusatory atmosphere in which many classroom teachers felt vaguely guilty in advance, afraid of "killing the children," afraid to assert a strong point of view because it might be suppressing different opinions. Teachers distrusted themselves, checked their intuitions, became tentative, easily manipulated by children, and, finally, irritated at having to live up to an impossible standard. They had tried; they had bought all the books and taken notes and gone in to transform their classrooms, and their classrooms had stayed essentially the same. And when they went to apply the message of Caring, it didn't seem to be enough. In fact, they had always cared: that was nothing new. Most teachers do care about their children and want good lives for them. A perplexed mood began to develop among certain teachers, which rose to anger at these freedom experts: *the anger of the 70s at the 60s,* for a promised liberation that never came.

Of course it wasn't the fault of the writers for arousing hope. Arousers of hope should not be expected to deliver as well, or no one would take on that function. On the other hand, the critical map of the schools which they had handed down was incomplete. If it showed very truthfully how some children were being squashed by their teachers, it failed to show enough the other instances, the normal everyday resourcefulness with which many classroom teachers meet challenge after challenge and which has to be seen to be believed— a selflessness that is accepted by them as part of their job, like firemen entering a burning building.

But when I began as a writer in the schools, I understood little of the complexity of the classroom teacher's job. I was appalled by the monotony and chained expression that I saw everywhere, and impatient to change all that as rapidly as possible. Naturally I kept getting into trouble. First I was asked to leave a commercial high school for encouraging the students to put out their own (not faculty-censored) literary magazine. Then I encountered censorship problems in a small private school in California, where I also walked into a power struggle between the teachers and the headmistress. I allied myself with the striking teachers and was fired as their "ringleader" (a compliment I always felt was exaggerated). For a while I worked as a roving poet, sent by state arts councils from town to hamlet to make brief teaching appearances in local schools. After that I worked in a high school dropout rehabilitation center in East Harlem, where again I found myself in disagreement with the agency's educational philosophy. The scenario was wearing a little thin. Even I was getting bored with this idealistic young man who enters a school and wins the love of students and gets bounced out because conservative meanies won't understand. Perhaps I was following the reform literature too closely. I knew how to pursue a righteous course which would lead inexorably to a confrontation and my dismissal; I knew how to lose nobly, but did I know how to succeed? There had to be a way to do creative work with students and survive in an institution. I wasn't prepared yet to accept idealistic masochism as the only option.

By now I understood a little more about the power structure of schools: the importance of having parents on your side, the ethnic politics of communities, the district pressures—all those things they never tell writers when they send them on the road to "open up" classrooms. And I was becoming more sensitive to the factor of timing in introducing changes; that is, the humane rate at which people could take in new ideas without losing their personal balance or their loyalty to past beliefs. I had become convinced that it was equally important to develop a base of support for creative projects and to do them in full view of the community, with its approval, as it was to hit upon this or that "miracle" teaching idea.

When I came to Public School 90, I had skills but no community. I was twenty-seven years old. I was tired of being a wandering catalyst; I was homesick for someplace that would receive me and the contribution I had to make. I was very lucky. To find a proper set of circumstances for working today is like looking on the ground for traces of a lost civilization. In my case, I was sent into a public school to do something as vague as "help people be creative." I was responsible for training a whole team of writers to do the same, and for devising a collective mode of operation for which I could locate no precedent. We embarked without a map, without plans, without instructions, with nothing to go on but the good will of the natives.

One final word on the focus of this book. Too often, it seems to me, studies about how to work with children in creative subjects concentrate exclusively on the exercises or techniques of stimulation, making the techniques appear an end in themselves, segregated from the local political, ethnic, and economic conditions in which the teaching will have to take place. The other, opposite tendency is to give full attention to the political and personality struggles of the school without showing in sufficient technical detail how it is possible to carry through a piece of creative work in such an environment.

It seems to me that the tasks which one sets for oneself and the children to accomplish, in poetry, drama, filmmaking, painting, or whatever, grow directly out of the unique local situation in which the teacher finds himself and out of the unique personalities of the children—as well as, of course, the national and global currents affecting the society at large. There is no such thing as a "creativity curriculum" divorced from personalities and social context. For me, this is especially so, because I see teaching as a sympathetic exchange which takes place through the medium of personal relationships. The book thus has two foci: my attempt to find methods by which children could be put more in touch with their creative voice, and the life of the school which hosted this attempt. If the shifting between the two themes baffles the reader, I ask him to bear with me; in my mind, the two are inextricably connected.

Chapter 3
The Agreement

I would love to say that I immediately grasped the opportunity to build something durable which the P.S. 90 project offered me. But the truth is that I backed into it with the lamest feeling of what I was doing. It began in everyone's minds as a kind of afterthought, an expedient to raise money.

The Dean of the Writing Division at Columbia University School of the Arts, Frank McShane, was looking for work-study money for his students. He applied to the New York State Arts Council for a grant to employ his creative-writing graduate students to teach poetry and fiction at a local public school. The grant was turned down. But the Arts Council intimated that if the grant were resubmitted jointly with Teachers & Writers Collaborative—which had more experience sending writers into the school—the request would probably go through.

Columbia University got together with Teachers & Writers, the grant proposal was resubmitted and passed, $6,000 for one year, to be distributed among three graduate students.

No one gave much thought to what effect several young writers teaching in the same school might have on the environment. I don't think anyone had yet conceived of their working *together* as a team. The main idea was to tap an available, enthusiastic, fairly cheap supply of teaching talent by training graduate students to be writing specialists in the public schools.

A line had been provided in the budget for someone to supervise the graduate students, who were officially called "interns," and to act as a liaison between the two sponsors. The Collaborative chose me to be that supervisor. At the time I was still teaching high school dropouts in an East Harlem drug rehabilitation agency. The supervisor post would pay $25 a week, so I don't think anyone expected more than the most minimal overseeing from me—something to allay the funding agent's bureaucratic anxieties. But I was absolutely honored to have been picked by the Collaborative as their trainer. Not knowing exactly what was expected of me, I set up a very formal weekly workshop whereby the three graduate students and I could meet and discuss their progress.

First we were shown around the public school they would be working in by the principal, Edouardo Jimenez, who was eager to have the program. My first glimpse of P.S. 90 made me very uneasy. One of the children had overturned a goldfish bowl and a sad-eyed teacher mopped up the flood, while all these little kids were whining and trying to put the blame on each other. Fortunately, I told myself, it was not necessary to spend that much time in the school. My job as I saw it was to lay a foundation in teaching for the interns, and that could be done as well at Columbia. Besides, I was enjoying the idea of playing at being a university Adjunct Instructor (a title they had assigned me at the last minute so that we could use a room at Columbia).

We met weekly in a graduate-school seminar room. It was a room of corporate dimensions, with a conference table of worn oak and windows barred with heavy iron grates. The belled white ceiling was enormously high. Through the shades and window bars came a kind of mistrustful bony light, that resembled sunlight, though without any of its yellow properties. The interns and I had enough room to sit two chairs away from each other around the conference table.

There was an air of show-and-tell about these sessions. The children's compositions were read as proof that all had gone well. The writers were reluctant to acknowledge difficulties or problems in adjusting. I began to realize that they regarded me as a shop foreman, who could inform the bosses whether they should be advanced or dismissed. Much as I did not identify with that management role, there was some logic in their thinking it.

I assured the three that there was nothing they could do that would get them fired.

But what if the children didn't write anything? they asked. What if they had no papers to turn in?

I answered that I felt no obligation to feed Teachers & Writers with X number of papers per week. We were not working on an assembly line. We were encouraging something as fragile as human creativity. If they did writing with the children, fine; if they did a theater improvisation that disappeared into the air, fine again; if they had a discussion and nothing else, that could be very valuable too. They were free to define the job in any way that made sense to them. I was there mainly to help them with problems and short cuts.

They didn't believe me.

It was as if a hidden curriculum already existed which they thought I was perversely holding back from them—that I wanted them to guess it. Actually, I thought that there was nothing that had gone before in the field of creative writing which they could not immediately supersede with ideas that came from a more personal source. One of the writers went out and bought a popular teaching-poetry manual. All right, use that for a start, I said. But you're a poet; try to teach kids the method you use to write poetry.

I took mornings off from my job at the drug program to "observe" the classes of the three writers. It was a discouraging experience. What the writer did in the front of the room was often completely ignored in the back. There was no sense of common enterprise. I have taught many awful lessons, and I know the dread of seeing everything start to burst apart in front of you. When this happened to the three writers they seemed unable to arrest the momentum, unable to make a sharp personal request or get angry or say what they were thinking: instead they watched the attention spill away from them. Somehow they were locked into the role of the happy-time specialist who came to offer the children some fun. And if the children didn't want it, they felt powerless.

I also saw the regular classroom teachers undercutting their efforts. Sometimes the teacher would reprimand a child who was not writing, just after the writers had finished saying, "You don't *have* to write; only if you feel like it."

Sometimes the teachers threatened to withhold the writers, like a treat taken away as punishment for misbehavior, or belittled the writers by making them seem pathetic. "Now if you don't quiet down you're going to hurt Miss C's feelings and she's not going to come back and visit us ever again!"

Sometimes it was simply the teacher looking bored and opening the windows with a long window pole while the writer was trying to hold the class's attention.

Most of these incidents, I think, were not so much malicious as in the nature of missed signals, misunderstandings that could have been cleared up or prevented if a context existed for the writer and the teacher to form a working relationship. But there was never time. The writer appeared once a week, taught and left—one of a stream of visitors who wanted to "borrow" her class for some reason or another.

Meanwhile the writers were experiencing the culture shock of being bombarded by noisy, disorderly public school life. They felt disturbed, not in control. They were having to face all the anxieties of beginning teachers, without the compensating decision to dedicate themselves to teaching children as a profession.

The sum of it was that the writers were not sure their presence *mattered.* Sure the kids liked seeing them because they were a break in the regular work schedule. But it did not go very deep. And the teachers felt lukewarm about it all.

I wrote four-page, single-spaced critiques of the classes I had observed—evaluations which of course balanced favorable with unfavorable response (when will one ever get tired of that game?)—and gave them to the writers. I wonder how I would have felt if I had received a letter like that. Outwardly the interns took it well; but there was a growing tension in the workshops. One of the writers started skipping the seminar. Her empty chair reproached us. When the group is so small, the absent one tends to dominate. I could not escape the feeling that these workshops were a weekly party at which I was the host. I began to experience that old childhood fear of unpopularity, giving a birthday party and nobody coming to it.

One day it actually happened. None of the three showed up. I sat on the leather couch of the seminar room waiting, reading a campus newspaper. I read the editorials, the football news, the ads. Unfortunately, the paper was only eight pages long. Then I roamed down the hall to the snack bar where they had a machine that made hot chocolate. I was angry.

Never again would I teach a class with three people in it!

Now I was fed up with that lordly seminar room. We had made a mistake by keeping the group anchored to the university. We should have met at each other's houses, or right in P.S. 90. Why didn't I think of that earlier?

It was too late. By late May all three of the interns announced that they would be teaching English composition in colleges next year. Public school was not for them. So ended the fiasco of the first Writing Team.

* * *

There was one moment I look back on from that term with pure pleasure. I was asked by the PTA to give a report at a nighttime meeting devoted to special programs. After listening to the other program spokesmen's panegyrics, I got up and spoke as frankly as I could about the problems we were having. Teachers undercutting writers, writers showing condescension to teachers, the perception of racist behavior, the conflict between educational ideologies which had never been worked out, and the general problem of having outsiders work alongside regular teachers in the school. I told the parents the school was in for some trouble if it didn't integrate its outside services more thoughtfully. I didn't say that my program had had only a mediocre effect so far; that would have been *too* honest. But the parents seemed to appreciate hearing even this amount of candor. I felt a warmth coming from them.

I was beginning to like P.S. 90. It had a promising mixture of whites, Blacks, Puerto Ricans, Chinese, Cubans, Haitians, children of university professors, children of parents on welfare—which gave it a very cosmopolitan atmosphere. I felt more comfortable in the halls; I already knew a few faces; I was no longer so terrified of navigating around the building.

We would be going in again in the fall, with new writers. We had a better idea what we were up against. And we had not yet squandered the stock of good will extended us as creative types. The false start had taught me a few personal lessons about my own vanity of expertise and uninvolvement, which aroused my stubbornness to make it work right this time.

I knew now what I had to do. No more advising people from a distance. I had to quit my other job and teach only at P.S. 90. I had to get right into the center of the work. I had to jump in with both feet. I had to hold nothing back, had to set up a force field of energy that would sweep the others along. There are two ways of teaching: the first is by prescription, the second is by example. I realized now that I believed more in the second way. Somehow I would have to come up with exemplary actions.

The first week in September I made an appointment with the principal, Mr. Jimenez, to get a few things straight and to save us grief later on. For support, I brought along the new director and assistant director of Teachers & Writers Collaborative, Martin Kushner and Steve Schrader. We asked Jimenez for three guarantees: 1) that he would not censor any children's writing that came out of the workshops or was published in a school magazine, should there ever be one; 2) that the school make some financial commitment, however small, to help us pay for the program; 3) that a room or free space, like a large closet, be given to the Writing Team as a base of operations.

Jimenez had no difficulty agreeing to the censorship demand, which surprised me, knowing how sensitive to public pressure other principals were on this issue. He said he was 100 per cent behind our educational philosophy and would stand up for us if we ever got into free-speech trouble. He also pledged a provisional sum of $1,800 in Title I funds for materials, subject to the approval of the committee. The hardest request for him to satisfy was the room. Every inch of space in P.S. 90 was coveted and fought over. But without a headquarters, I argued, we would be reduced to wandering gypsies. Finally he located us a barren classroom on the third floor which he was not sure if he had pledged to some other group—in any case, we could use it for the time being. I accepted instantly. I had expected a closet; this was a whole room. We would set up supplies and establish territoriality, like jungle animals, as soon as possible, so that they wouldn't dare kick us out . . . or if they did, at least we could make them feel guilty about it.

I had to pinch myself to realize that the principal had gone along with all three requests. Of course he was getting a promising program for nothing, more or less; but, even so, he seemed so sure that he wanted us! Jimenez's belief in what we were doing gave me reason to believe. Yet here, as everywhere, a fine tact had to be exercised. We could not afford to let the team become identified in the staff's mind as "Ed Jimenez's boys," under his protection. Jimenez had his enemies.

I spent a week in early September interviewing graduate writing students from Columbia. The four I finally picked were Sue Willis, Tom McGonigle, Christy Noyes, and Charles Self. They represented what seemed to me a good temperamental, geographical, ethnic, and sexual balance. Sue Willis, a novelist from West Virginia, was hard working, experienced with kids—responsibility itself. She was small and from the back, occasionally mistaken for one of the children; but what she lacked in charismatic presence she made up for in conscientiousness. Charles Self, a black storywriter from New Orleans, had been in the Peace Corps in Africa. He was low-key, thoughtful, easygoing, a bit aloof. He had one of those unperturbed personalities that proved to be very popular with the children, especially the boys. Christy Noyes came from well-off New England stock and had a fresh-scrubbed, schoolmarmish quality. She wrote experimental fiction, had no teaching experience, but was extremely eager to try. Tom McGonigle, self-acclaimed "the last of the great Irish drinking poets," added a dash of off-the-wall insanity to the group. There was no telling what he would do. They each would bring a world of exotic experiences to the classroom that would make them novel to these blasé New York City kids. Nevertheless, as teachers in a New York City public school, they were coming in cold. And as graduate students who had as yet published little, their sense of themselves as writers had a certain precariousness.

I begged Teachers & Writers to add one more member to the team, someone whose professionalism and secure identity as a writer would be a counterweight to my authority in the group. They assigned me Maria Irene Fornes, the author of *Promenades* and other off-Broadway successes, veteran of the Judson Theatre movement, a wonderfully sharp human being, who was not only older than I but more worldly-wise. Cuban born, she could also teach the children who spoke Spanish—a big asset in P.S. 90.

We planned to fan out over the school, each writer choosing two classes at first to work with. It would seem as if we had enough manpower, but because there were so many classrooms, the team would be able only to handle the upper grades. This was perhaps for the best since it gave us a common age group and common set of problems. In addition, we had been told that the upper grades "needed it more." The creative-arts emphasis, which was so visible in kindergarten-through-grade three, retreated in four-five-six under the pressure of standardized reading and math tests and the competition for the better junior high schools, so that by fifth grade a child who was accustomed to artistic self-expression was more apt to find himself in a drier, Spartan setting.

The next move was to introduce the new Writing Team to the teachers. The principal called a lunchtime meeting in his office for all upper-grade teachers. I was surprised to hear Jimenez referring to the Teachers & Writers program as an already proven success which was being expanded. If they were satisfied with last term, wait until they saw what we could really do! It struck me that there are no criteria for this work, or else people expect so little of artists in the schools that they tend to indulge us, which is another way of not taking us seriously.

I delivered a short nervous talk in which I stressed that having a writer in the classroom might mean extra work for the teacher and certainly would mean personal adjustments in style. Then I introduced the individual writers. The teachers were enthusiastic, almost all feeling they needed help in creative writing and inviting someone on the team to work with them.

I had mixed feelings about my cautionary talk. Iris Mayer insisted that it went well. She is one of the most progressive teachers I have come across and she had been functioning as a tipster or fifth columnist for our program. She gave me a word of advice: "This school may look very free and groovy on the surface, but don't be fooled, there's a lot of conservative feeling. Nothing from the outside will take root at P.S. 90 unless it's introduced very cautiously and slowly. Better to keep a low profile. If you make big promises first, you'll scare people. Start modest, then surprise them." How sound this advice was I later saw from the staff resentment directed against other new programs which threatened to disrupt the daily school schedule. As for Miss Mayer herself, I think she had her own doubts that we could deliver. She had hosted a writer last term and was not completely impressed. The level of teaching competence at which she operated was so high that an outsider didn't stand much of a chance in her classroom; she would chew us up and spit us out. Maybe this was why she gently suggested I work with her friend Denise Loftin, across the hall, instead of with her.

Chapter 4
Hanging Out

Mrs. Loftin was sitting in jeans and an embroidered smock on a corner couch, instructing two children in reading. I was not immediately sure whether she was the teacher or a school aide—she seemed rather subdued—but I looked around and there were no other adults in the room. I felt a kind of dryness or stillness, like a vacuum. Perhaps this vacuum made certain children extrasensitive to the stranger in their midst. A kid named Jamie engaged me right away in a conversation about monsters. He had some kind of speech impediment which made all his words difficult to understand but he spoke with such juicy enthusiasm that one got the point somehow. A girl named Karen, who was very emphatic, demanding of my attention, pushed Jamie out of the way and began telling me about the weirdoes in her neighborhood. Casually, children nearby started to gather around me patiently and ask my name, and I theirs. I never had to be introduced officially as the Poet. They made me feel welcome from the start—a reflection of their teacher's casual, accepting attitude.

As she walked around the room, checking on work assignments, Mrs. Loftin gave off a warm, steadying, calm vibration, which I can only describe as an inner hum. She was black with an Afro, a stunning figure, which was hard to ignore, and beautiful, high cheekbones. She moved through the school desks as if she were in her living room or had just gotten up from a nap. In her unhurried, well-rooted movements, there was a touch of the sleeper, but her eyes were actually very open; she never blinked.

I had the opportunity to witness a very curious transformation. Suddenly, without transition, she advanced to the blackboard, with her face set in determination, and began to teach a social-studies lesson on Transportation.

Everyone had to face front and pay attention to a trumped-up "class discussion" on fuel, which elicited the usual bottom-squirmings. "Juan, you especially need this," she snapped at a boy. Karen yelled out à propos of nothing in the discussion: "Oh look at that girl; she got a piece of paper stuck to her heinie!"—"Karen, I'm warning you; you watch yourself!" Under her threatening looks and stern disciplinary manner, it was still possible to feel Mrs. Loftin's warmth and easygoingness, but they had been absorbed by an impersonal, detached sense of Duty. It must have been Duty which prompted her to stage this very dull lesson. No one was really interested in the burgeoning list of transportation words taking over the blackboard; least of all herself, I suspect. Who was this list being made for?

* * *

Two days later I walk into the classroom to teach my first lesson and there is cheering and some applause. I've done nothing to earn this popularity but I like it. Three kids in front rush up to me; I start to introduce myself. "We know; you're the poet!" Somehow I realize that I am being watched carefully by the Spanish girls washing the sink in back, by the various in and out groups, to see whom I will favor: the front desk, the whites, the Blacks, the show-offs, the slow learners. One mistake in judgment and they will decide I am "not for them." For the time being, I am riding on a reserve tank of good will because I seem a novelty and a break from schoolwork. A real live poet—something I have to keep reminding myself I really am. The more I try to retain that notion, the more it slips from me. What is a poet supposed to act like?

Where does a poet stand in children's eyes? Not as high as an athlete, maybe above a teacher.

And now the teacher, Denise Loftin, comes forward to tell the class to give me their *full* attention. I wonder where I will locate myself: by her desk, in front of the blackboard, or somewhere completely unexpected. All these desks, these angles of vision, the stage feels wrong. Not my space. And it is the beginning of a struggle to build a comfortable space for myself in someone else's classroom. I start to talk about my background, how I came to be a writer, why I'm here—trying to sound natural. I'm conscious of being too tall: I want to bend in half to reach their level. I incline my head ostrich-like. I move around a lot. I read them a Yoruba poem about a monster God, with lines like:

Ogun has water but he washes in blood
Ogun is the needle that pricks at both ends
Ogun is the death who pursues a child until it runs into the bush
Ogun has four hundred wives & one thousand four hundred children
Ogun the fire that sweeps the forest
Ogun's laughter is no joke
Ogun eats two hundred earthworms & does not vomit.[1]

They like that part. Still, I sense their detachment: where is all this leading to? The teacher steps out to cover a disturbance in the hall. Side conversations begin . . . I'm already losing some of my glamour! Then I pull it all together, WHAMMO, and before they know it I've sprung the assignment I had up my sleeve and yellow lined paper is being handed out. I write topics on the board. Boasts, Changing into a God or an Animal—ideas which don't particularly intrigue me (I wonder why I've started out so impersonally, with someone else's ideas), but you have to start somewhere.

I tell myself I want to get a sighting on their range of interests and writing abilities, though I am also thinking: They better be made to do some work the first time or they'll think I'm a pushover.

So the kids begin to learn the bitter truth, that this poet is merely another in a long series of adult foremen.

I bend down by the desk of one child who is having trouble, to explain the assignment and to help him. I feel relieved to be talking at eye level, one-to-one. Dolores, a provocative, cute-looking girl, keeps interrupting to show me her composition—"Don't let anyone see it!"—and covering it with elaborate gestures whenever anyone passes by. She has written a story about turning into a pig. I know she is testing me because of the line: "I leave shit all over the house." She asks me to read it aloud to the class and I say no, it's hers and she should read it aloud; if it embarrasses her, she should change it.

After a noisy public reading I collect the papers and promise to have them mimeoed by next week. Denise Loftin assures me it went well. "Usually they're *much* more distracted. They liked you."

---

[1] In *Technicians of the Sacred,* anthology of poems edited by Jerome Rothenberg, Doubleday & Company, Inc., 1968, p. 164.

I don't know. I sensed they liked me before I opened my mouth, then I became just another salesman with a spiel to sell.

But I'm delighted I survived!

Over lunch, at the Eat Shop, Denise Loftin and I compared notes on different children. Her class seems skewed toward black and Spanish-speaking children, and I had noticed other classrooms which seemed to have a white, middle-class emphasis. Denise said the reason for this was that the parents were given a choice at the beginning of the year whether they wanted to place their children in an "open" or "more formal" classroom. The white, liberal parents of the Upper West Side tended to select open classrooms. The parents from ethnic minorities opted more for traditional classes, feeling that open education might be soft on basic skills at a time when their children needed a strong foundation in the three R's to crash through the racial barriers. The resulting class registers came out imbalanced. The school administration was caught between its commitment to integration, and its commitment to community control, which promised parents a greater say in the form of their children's education.

The ironic part was that these stereotyped categories were continually belied by the realities of the individual classrooms. I knew certain open classroom teachers who were quite inflexible and devoted to drill work. The only thing "open" about their classrooms was the clearing in the middle of the floor for the gerbil cages. On the other hand, someone like Denise, who listed herself as more formal, tended to be rather relaxed and broad-minded in spirit.

The white parents in her class had been up in arms, she admitted. They claimed their children were being held back academically by being placed with "slower learners" (euphemism for black and brown?). They wanted either to have their children transferred out of the class, or to trade five of Denise's non-whites for five whites in other classrooms. Denise thought such a trade was inevitable. She had already gotten attached to the class as it stood and thought the kids themselves could work out any difficulties among them, given more time. But the parents were insistent, and Mr. Jimenez was eager to bring the crisis to an end.

I asked Denise if she thought her being black had anything to do with the parents' alarm.

"I don't think so. These parents aren't bigoted; they're just worried about their kids' safety. I don't really *blame* them. For instance, Janet's mother is a nice woman; I've known her a long time. She's afraid Janet will get into fights, or pick up street language from some of these kids—"

"But of course Janet already knows every word in the book."

"I wouldn't be too sure. Janet is *very* protected," said Denise.

I thought Denise was being uncommonly fair-minded and disinclined to cry "racism"—more than I would be in her shoes, probably.

Karen, one of Denise's students, handed me a story based on a conversation we had had the first day, and which I had asked her to write up. I could see she was proud of having finished it. The story is pretty harsh, especially when you consider that this is, at eleven years old, the way she sees life. Yet I couldn't help smiling a little at its gruesomeness.

The Lady Around My Block

Once upon a time there lived a lady around my block. She was not nice at all. She had to have a baby so one day she went to town to find herself a husband. She went all over town looking looking looking. So there was a man sitting on a step she said Mr. will you marry me so he was a fool to say yes. So then he went to court to ask could he get married and the court said yes. So when they got married she said give me a child so he did. When the child was born they was so happy when the child was two months old she nailed her on the wall. Happy days were over.

The End

It is almost a truism to observe that some of the most troubled, volatile children have enormous talent inside them. This seemed to be the case with Karen, if I could only find a way to work alone with her, or make her stop bullying the other children. Not a day went by that Karen didn't have two or three tantrums or fistfights; she was bidding hard for the title of class terror.

Karen conned me into overseeing her and two of her girlfriends, Stephanie and Gwen, practice a dance number in the Writing Room for some far-off auditorium performance. The three girls looked like budding Supremes as they went through their motions seriously, with studied arm rolls and hip twitches. I was enjoying the show, vaguely wondering what it had to do with my role as writing instructor but willing to chaperone. Unfortunately, Karen and Stephanie had a furious fight for the position of group leader while Gwen, the only real dancer of the three, watched with contempt. It turned rather ugly as Karen got impossibly bossy and short-tempered, and I had to take them back.

* * *

The second class went well enough, but I was still disturbed about the quality of attention, which declined after fifteen minutes. Of course I could figure out a way to condense everything I had to say into ten minutes, but that was no solution.

The classroom seemed spatially unsuited for holding a large group's attention. It was neither the old-fashioned arrangement of desks facing forward nor the free flow of the open classroom, but a loose confederation of tables. Each of the tables had a separate, social-club personality, with its own peer-group pressure. There were five or six of these large square tables placed at right angles to each other around the room, which meant that no matter where I stood I would always be facing a certain number of backs.

Some children made the courteous effort of turning their chairs around, but others simply continued to face their desks, their pencils, their inkwell, their dreams, their *assigned place,* and to keep their eyes lowered on the loose-leaf notebook, giving no indication whether they were listening or not.

I had the impression at times that I was a madman talking to a subway carful of indifferent travelers. Without that eye contact which registers the transfer of understanding, my own remarks struck me as a manic chain of desperate *non sequiturs,* a crazy plea for attention.

The table arrangement made it easy for the children to evade responsibility for participating and to dip in and out as neutral listeners without necessarily committing themselves to the enterprise. So long as they found me entertaining they would stick with me; otherwise they would change the channel.

I realized I had to find a way to get the students to accept their part in the lesson. They had to take more responsibility for the quality of the experience and stop relying on me as the sole performer. I would probably have to change my style of delivery to work in that space.

Perhaps my concern with the table arrangements was an alibi. I thought of that; but then the quickest way for me to get beyond an alibi to the real problems, whatever they might be, was to fuss with it until it stopped bothering me. By taking the alibi seriously and trying to eliminate it, I would find out the truth one way or the other.

The third time around I tried an experiment. I asked that only those children who wanted to work with me come to the back of the room. The rest could continue their work. A core group of ten arranged the chairs in a circle. With this volunteer structure no one would have an excuse for not paying attention; if he wasn't interested, he didn't have to stay.

The exercise I had prepared was one of my own devising, which promised to generate energy: Hypnotizing Poems. First they were to act out hypnotizing each other, two at a time. Then, once they had gotten the idea, they could write down a list of juicy commands, the sort you gave to some victim who was totally in your power!

I borrowed a gold locket from Roberto to use as a hypnotic pendulum. Roberto and Britt offered to try it first, with Roberto as the hypnotist. Britt was turned into a chicken, made to lay an egg (everyone roared at this innuendo) and worse. I filed away in my mind the information that Britt was a good actor.

The next two volunteers were not nearly as self-assured. Sammy swung the locket, and timid, baby-faced Gregory kept waiting to "go under." It was odd how some kids understood immediately that the game was make-believe, while poor Gregory actually expected to be mesmerized. I whispered to him the trick, and he started rolling his eyes and acting the swoon. Sammy could only think of a few commands, including the chicken routine—the success of the first actors was grasped at again and again.

The next duo came up with some variations and were rewarded with howls by their classmates. A few stragglers, drawn to the laughter, wandered by, including Adiel who was sucked into the excitement. Adiel: a peculiarly sober, phlegmatic kid with thick glasses and a porkpie hat. He started to hypnotize the explosive Karen. He was swinging the locket tentatively, not really sure what the game was about. Karen is not one to suffer insecure males. She grabbed the locket out of his hand and demanded to do the hypnotizing. I had unfortunately already promised the privilege to Xiomara. Karen blew up. I got her out of there before she had a fit.

A few moments later Christine said in a hushed voice: "I think you just made an enemy."

"Oh? Who?"

"Karen!" she said with dread. Christine is a red-haired, freckled girl who listens with wide incredulous eyes to everything that is said around her.

"I'm not worried about it," I replied. I handed out paper for writing. At this point several boys wandered away: game's over. The others stayed. I asked them to think not only of the kind of instructions they had given each other, but of more original, mysterious commands. And, to give an example, I read a few pieces from Yoko Ono's book, *Grapefruit,* which is written entirely in the imperative suggestive mode, e.g., "Watch the sun until it becomes square" or "Keep coughing a year." The kids listened absorbedly, bursting into laughter whenever they could. I noticed Christine especially taking it in with anxious fascination, as if it might possibly contain something against her religion.

After the kids had written their poems they wanted to act them out as we'd done before. So Gregory had to go up to Denise and say that he wanted to share his life with her; Jamie had to stroke my hair; Dolores had to run into the hallways and scream "I love you!" to the first person she saw. I can't say much for the writing as enduring literature, but it was good fun.

Feeling quite happy, I went to lunch with Denise. She was less exhilarated with the experience. She didn't like the way kids kept floating in and out of the fringes of the group. She thought that once they had agreed to join the group they should be obligated to stay and write.

I felt that if they didn't want to write a poem, I wasn't going to force them. And I was reluctant to close the group off to children who didn't see themselves as "writers," either by demanding that they write or by taking only the sign-up group out of the classroom into the Writing Room. Some of that fringe activity seemed to me a

positive thing. Nevertheless, I could see her point about the ragged-
ness of it, which made teaching harder at her end.

I suggested she set up a very definite alternative activity of an
arts-and-crafts nature—anything too bookish might seem punitive by
contrast—and corral the kids into one activity or the other.

"I don't know any crafts, do I?" Denise laughed with coy self-
effacement. "Do I know any crafts? I haven't done anything like that
with them all year."

"I'm sure you can come up with something," I said. My secret
wish was that our working together would force her into more ad-
venturous paths and generate a looser classroom.

Denise was at the point of demonstrating how to make God's
eyes when I came by for my next lesson. God's eyes are diamond-
shaped frames that you weave colored yarn in and around to make
a pretty design. Denise had learned the technique as part of our agree-
ment, from one of the teachers down the hall, and her eagerness to
teach it was beautiful to watch. The kids were fascinated to try it
too—this, their first crafts project of the year.

I had of course prepared my own writing lesson but I realized
I would be an idiot to try to compete with the colored yarn. What
was happening that day was God's eyes.

Outsmarted myself that time!

My carefully planned lesson would keep (what a letdown!), and
I'd just as soon stroll around talking to the kids. The mood was more
relaxed and pleasantly productive than any I had seen in this room
so far. I siphoned off a few kids—Janet, Marissa, and Sammy—and
we started talking about the idea of God having an eye. This led
to the "third eye," which led to my showing them the eye on the
pyramid of a dollar bill, and to feeling the bump on each other's
foreheads (supposedly a test for spiritual insight), which led eventually to their writing a couple of stories. But this outcome mattered
less to me than the naturalness of just hanging out, sitting alongside
one kid after another, letting my hands be used for cat's cradle.

*   *   *

How I needed to cast aside the pressure of proving myself before a roomful of students, and become an ordinary Joe, a pair of

eyes, a passive dope to play patty-cake with, a big giraffe, to tease, or punch, for no reason whatsoever. I had an appetite for soaking in the atmosphere of the school. I would come into Denise Loftin's class on a day off and sit at a desk in my raincoat, like a bum watching the world go by until one of the kids started up a conversation with me, which usually wasn't very long. The easiest way for me to get to know the kids was to talk to them when I had nothing up my sleeve, when I wasn't demanding any work from them.

There was one boy, Gene, who had been singled out by Denise as someone who needed extra help. He was bright, she said, but he hated to work at anything for more than two minutes, and he *loathed* writing, and he had no friends in the class. He was short, blond-haired, with a dirt-streaked face and a dirty football jersey which he wore every day. Through trial and error I got the impression he did not like to be looked in the eye. Sometimes you meet a child whom you have to approach obliquely, like a deer, and stand quietly until he gets a good chance to look you over and become used to your presence.

I sat next to him, looking at my hands for about a minute without opening my mouth. Then I said, still not looking at him, like two old-timers whittling on a porch: "What yer doin'?" "Makin' a drawing." "Let me see it?" It was something ghastly: a man's head being decapitated. "Nice. Looks like a horror movie," I said. "That's where I got the idea." "You like horror movies, eh?" "Yeah!" And now he began talking a blue streak about monsters, and mealworms, and his dog, whom he loved passionately. He talked with a feverish haste, one word falling on the next. We were still conversing through sidelong glances, which would have made an odd impression to a third party; but by the end of ten minutes I had slowly worked around to gazing directly at him, and he at me. It was a start.[2]

I found I did some of my best communicating on the days I wasn't there to teach. The key for me was having enough open, unscheduled time and making myself accessible to the children to fill it. I wanted to be available for their everyday inspirations and small talk. I tried not to let my schedule get so tight that I couldn't noodle around with the kids.

---

[2] Later we became much closer—he never did get to like writing—but I used him in many videotapes and *West Side Story*.

If only there was more slack time in the System! If only regular teachers had more of a chance to be with their children in an ordinary friendly way, to put aside the role of efficiency expert. I knew several classroom teachers who stayed after 3 P.M. just to have a chance to unwind with their students. During the school day these same good teachers would often become harassed automatons who blared out orders like public address systems.

I am aware that most hard-working, full-time teachers didn't have my scheduling advantages and might even resent the suggestion of hanging out. I only wish there were a way to demonstrate by cost-benefit analysis or other means that some of this slack time actually increases educational production. In my case I can swear that the time I spent roaming round the schoolyard and the lunchroom cafeteria led to the children's trusting me more and writing more honestly (as if that were the reason I did it!). In fact I had a little difficulty rationalizing why I was spending so much spare time around the school. I told myself it was an anthropologist's way of gathering clues to the underground culture of children. I told the other writers in the project that listening to kids outside of class time would give them new ideas for writing assignments. But it was pointless to try to elevate to an educational maxim what was largely a question of personal taste. I happened to like being in on the silly conversation of ten-year-old boys in the lunchroom as they made mush of their mashed potatoes. If at first I saw myself as a patient investigator gathering data, in the long run all this jostling with the kids is what sweetened the job, and stayed with me.

> Dolores says to me: "Phillip, I hate you!"
> "Why do you hate me?"
> "I don't! I just like saying that!"
> "One day you're going to make me cry if you say that."
> "You can't CRY; you can only LAUGH."
> "But that seems sad," I said, "never to be able to do anything but laugh. I'm not sure I like that."
> "Well that's TOO BAD. You can't do nothing but laugh."
> There are several girls in Mrs. Loftin's class who relate to me in this flirtatious, sweetly abrasive way. Lilli comes up and smacks me on the arm: "Where's my magazine, Phillip?"—"What magazine?" I ask, slapping her back. "*You* know," she says and walks away—only to return several hours later and smack my arm again.

The kids tease me by matchmaking me with every female in the build-ing. Lately the girls have started the rumor that I love Anna, a tall, quiet Spanish girl in the fifth grade. "How's An-na?" Dolores winks at me. This sends them into hysterics, and the funniest part about it is that Anna is the one student of Denise's whose name I could never remember. She is a silent, inconspicuous child who left so little impression on me that at last I took Denise aside with some embar-rassment and asked her to furnish me with the name of "that tall girl" so that I wouldn't constantly be drawing a blank when I needed to call on her. Maybe the kids interpreted this speechlessness around her as lover's shyness! Anna became one of the five Spanish and black kids traded out of Denise's class to create a better racial balance. I probably would have forgotten her once she was gone if it weren't for hearing "How's *Anna?*" ten times a day. Sometimes I mutter, "I haven't seen Anna in weeks," which is true. Sometimes I answer, "We've never been happier!"

I can do with children what I have so much trouble doing with lovers and friends: I can watch their craziness without being pulled into it. I can take them or let them go. It isn't that I don't care about the children as much. I care about them. But if a child tells me he doesn't want to work with me that day or he doesn't like me any more, fine; I don't feel personally rejected. If he wants to work with me again sometime, good. Meanwhile I can turn my attention else-where.

Maybe it's because I am one and they are many, and they are more focused on me as a source of approval. The balance of power is so much in my favor that I can afford to let them go away from me and come back at their pleasure. I have only to shift my eyes from foreground to background to find some other child who wants my attention, or anybody's attention. But even among the children themselves, they seem to have a greater independence and—if I may use this word for once in a positive sense—an enviable *promiscuity* in their social attachments. There is more of a free-floating affection which settles where it wants to, without the despondency and emo-tional blackmail which one adult so often uses to chain another.

I know that I often feel lighthearted around them, even when there is every good reason not to, and this minuet of teasing and flirtation is the dance I love doing with them the most.

Chapter 5
The Insidious Take-over of the Composition

Walking through the halls one day, I looked into the door glass at Stanley Riegelhaupt's orderly, traditional classroom. I knew Riegelhaupt a bit because one of the writers had taught the previous year in his room. He had a reputation for being strict. He was bent over his register book; he had a crew cut and thick glasses. On an impulse I entered, presented myself to the class as a writer and asked merely if anyone wanted to be in a writing club with me. Fourteen kids signed up. They had no idea what they were getting in for; nor did I.

Stanley seemed pleased that I had chosen to work with his class. He was only disappointed that a boy named Clifford was absent. "This kid's a great writer—well, I'll sign his name to the list anyway. He won't mind." I got the idea that Clifford was the class intellectual. "He writes things that are practically over my head," Stanley laughed. "I have to use a dictionary to understand his compositions. Tommy here's also pretty good," he said, pointing to a boy near his desk, "not as good as Clifford."

It embarrassed me, this praise of one child above the others, and I tried to change the subject, but Riegelhaupt kept returning to it. I later realized that Riegelhaupt had nothing against embarrassing people. In fact, it was his stock in trade.

Riegelhaupt had the loudest teacher's voice I had ever encountered. Children ducked under their desks when they heard that voice; they held their ears like dogs whining at passing fire engines. The strangest part about his voice was that it was not malicious or cruel. Only loud. He seemed to enjoy demonstrating the power of the organ for the fun of it. While escorting his students through the halls he would unleash it, then turn around and smile at the cringing spectators. It did manage to keep his class in line; but only, I think, because they were irritated at the volume, not because they were afraid of him. Once they discovered that underneath that voice he was something of a softie and rather benign, they found ways of getting around him.

Coming into that charged atmosphere as an outsider, it was not always easy for me to know how to react to him. Every time I picked up the kids to go to the Writing Room, he would use my entrance as an occasion for some practical joke. One morning I came in wearing a red-flowered shirt; some kids complimented me on it. Stanley, picking up the murmur, demanded in his loud voice: "All right, class, who has the more colorful shirt on today, Phil or me?" He happened to be wearing an utterly bland tan wash 'n' wear shirt. The kids cried overwhelmingly: "Phillip does!"

"What's that?" he roared. "All right, who wants to stay after school and get extra homework? You should know that I *always* have the most colorful shirts." He took another vote, and this time he won.

What embarrassed me was not the subtle hostility against me but the hostility against himself. But like all Dostoevskyan buffoons, he seemed to imply that his time would come. On another occasion, he took the opportunity to make me blush by announcing to the class that I had just gotten married. As the kids crowded around me, offering handshakes and congratulations, I was covered in confusion and kept trying to tell them that it wasn't true! Finally I had to run out of the room, with a few kids chasing down the halls yelling the news to everyone, and I got teased for days with that apocryphal story.

A love-hate relationship had grown up between Riegelhaupt's students and him, provoked by Stanley's own inclination to self-ridicule. Stanley liked to trade gross insults with his students. But often as not, he was the butt of his own jokes. The room was papered with compositions which told of Riegelhaupt's animal genealogies and uncertain parentage, his lack of wit, his failure at every endeavor, his alleged nasty habits—and on top of each one he had written in red ink, "Excellent!" or "Very Funny, Great Imagination!"

In fact they were not so funny; they were a little hard to take. But the kids liked doing them. He had managed to sell them the idea of creative writing by offering himself as a target. Every week he assigned "Creative writing" for homework, and every week they came back with pages and pages of sarcastic, juvenile fantasies about their teacher.

They wrote two kinds of stories in that class. One kind was the putdown of Riegelhaupt. The other kind was long, episodically plotted adventure stories: about Apollo V space missions, about winning a million dollars and spending it in different ways, about raising a horse to enter the Kentucky Derby, or about visiting the Land of Oz for the tenth time. The adventure stories were patterned closely on library books for children. They took several weeks to complete and the authors kept tabs on each other's progress, boasting how many pages they had done, which sometimes seemed to me their main interest in it all.

The writing was mechanical, in the sense of extending a narrative premise as far as it will go, without making a personal commitment to the subject. It was *facile,* jejeune, bloodless fantasy, cut off from the roots of experience and curiously unadventurous for all the plot. Sure, the kids were getting good practice at sentence-making, agile syntax, and logical transitions. But the price they paid was a loss of immediacy and passion. Their writing was affected by the same blight I had seen overspread other classrooms: the insidious take-over of the essay. By the sixth grade, training in composition-writing begins to color everything, poetry and fiction not excepted: everything starts to sound like a book report. Topic sentences, length for its own sake, impersonal diction, and the whole machinery of expository prose annexes the other literary territories as colonies.

I had divided the fourteen volunteers from Riegelhaupt's class into two writing workshops, Group A and Group B. At first many of the children assumed the workshops to be merely a free period to continue writing their episode stories. They would show me their latest chapter and ask me rather complacently how I liked it. I was in a difficult spot. Stanley had already written his approval in the margin. Nor did I want to discourage them—but I couldn't drum up much enthusiasm, either. All I could hope was that they would eventually get bored with this kind of demonstration and come around to trying a deeper approach.

Many of Riegelhaupt's kids were precocious, academically capable children from middle-class, professional homes, white and black, who were accustomed to receiving praise. They let you know their heritage right away. The first time the famous Clifford put in an appearance, he toured the Writing Room and announced in his cool way that it would make a "good meditation room." Another boy told a story about his parents' summer home in Fire Island and suddenly informed me: "I don't know if you know Fire Island. It's in Long Island Sound."

I confess that I was not drawn to these kids at first as much as I had been to Denise Loftin's. They struck me as privileged, competitive, and snooty. Perhaps I was going through my own form of reverse snobbism—or racism. I could not help contrasting them with Loftin's kids, many of whom had trouble writing a paragraph—but what finally came out was alive with the ache of living. Riegelhaupt's kids, the smarter class from the point of view of marks, had already learned how to pad. My problem here was different; it was not to get them to write. The problem was to get them to feel their writing.

AN ASIDE

It may seem strange for me to be so critical of any children's writing, when tolerance and an appreciation bordering on gratitude are so often stressed in the literature as the proper reaction to a child's written expression. However, there is a great quantity of children's writing that is boring, shallow, unimaginative, unfelt. If one piece in five has vivacity, I feel grateful. Sometimes it is only a single line, or a surprising word, a solitary word, that momentarily leaps from a composition of distracted expediency. How to give recognition and support for that line or that word without fawning over every child's piece—which will only win his distrust anyway—is a discipline we need to begin to learn.

It used to be that children's literary products were ignored. Then the pendulum swung in the opposite direction: they became regarded as "the true poets"—*idiots savants*. A noted authority assures his public: "Children have a natural ability for poetry." This flattery of childhood passes for love of children, instead of what it really is, self-complacency. And it does harm by breeding an expectation, in parents and teachers, that their children are naturally gifted lyricists who have only to be touched lightly for sparkling verses to fall out. Then guilt ensues when this doesn't happen. Why not admit the truth?

Some children write consistently well; most can achieve bursts of beauty; a few never do. The average poetic gift of children is probably no better or no worse than the average adult's gift for poetry.

To believe that every child is a natural poet is a form of democratic wishfulness gone awry. I am not trying to make poetry into an elitist activity; but the fact is that poetry or writing of any quality is hard work. Few children, and few adults, care to work that hard at it. Not everyone has the intellectual resources. *We* can discover virtues or charms in hastily written children's papers from now till Doomsday, but that will not necessarily bring the children any closer to electing the conscious pursuit of that hard road.

It is true, there are miraculous sessions which seem to draw out poetic writing from everyone. A St. Vitus's dance of contagious lyricism sweeps the room and all the children write down beautiful ideas and images. It seems as if they were all latent poets who simply awaited the right pedagogic touch. But then the next week the stimulus may be less "evocative": the results slump; those children who are gifted and inclined to writing continue to write while the others leave it alone.

The teacher who has stumbled on such an open sesame, only to find it close stubbornly a week later in his face, may wonder what he did wrong in not being able to sustain the high level of poetic expression; or may think, If only I could do as good a job as the experts. He should be aware that the experts don't admit their percentage of failure, and they don't publish the lifeless works by their kids. Before getting carried away with inflated expectations of a-poet-in-every-child, we should understand something of the odds involved in producing one good work.

"IN QUEST OF HER BEAUTY"

One torpid morning, when Group A had not the slightest interest in literature, and nothing I said could entice them into writing, and I was considering giving up the profession, I noticed Tommy, who seemed as lost as myself. He was biting his fingernails for lack of anything to do and frowning as the other boys chased each other around the room. I asked him if he wanted to try writing a poem. He said he didn't think he could. And then he looked around unconsciously for Clifford, whose large literary shadow seemed to inhibit him. It had the effect of saying to me: Aren't you asking the wrong one?

I took out a poem in French by Apollinaire and asked him to write down a translation. "I don't know French," he said with understandable perplexity. I said I figured he didn't, but he should look at the words closely and say them over and over in his mind until they suggested some meanings. This is a technique called *mistranslation,* by which someone perfectly ignorant in a foreign language can "translate" it by sound associations, visual similarities and wild guesses. In another situation, with more outgoing children, I would have probably used a direct experiential approach; but with a child like Tommy, who was studious, self-conscious, timid about revealing his feelings, it was better to use a text—an objective starting point outside himself for inspiration.

The poem went:

Photographie

Ton sourire m'attire comme
Pourrait m'attirer une fleur
Photographie tu es le champignon brun
De la forêt
Qu'est sa beauté
Les blancs y sont
Un clair de lune
Dans un jardin pacifique
Plein d'eaux vives et de jardiniers endiablés
Photographie tu es la fumée de l'ardeur
Qu'est sa beauté
Et il y à en toi
Photographie
Des tons alanguis
on y entend
Une mélopée
Photographie tu es l'ombre
Du soleil
Qu'est sa beauté

APOLLINAIRE

Tommy stared at it a long time. I urged him to put down any old idea for the first line; it didn't matter if it was silly or made no sense. When he realized that I was not going to help him with the translation, except in general ways like telling him he could add more words or syllables to make it read better if he liked, Tommy wrote down a tentative beginning. "The town squire's mattress came back to town." I nodded noncommittally. He was not a child given to irrationality of any kind, and I could see he was stretching himself. He kept stealing looks at my face with timorous excitement, not so much wanting suggestions as protection in this strange voyage through unknown waters. He seemed to know instinctively what to do but he proceeded very slowly. "It's weird," Tommy said, "how you could take words in a foreign language and translate them without knowing the language!" I wanted to say Shhh; I was afraid he would lose the spell; instead I nodded and murmured, "It's something like chemistry." Actually more like alchemy, I thought. The poem progressed; at each line he thought of and discarded several options; and after the first two lines (which unfortunately had little to do with the rest), he tried to make everything connect narratively. It was time to pick up Group B, but Tommy wasn't finished yet, and so I decided to let Group A stay in the Writing Room, though they were fooling around. I would have to rearrange my schedule to work with Group B in the afternoon. All these considerations were making me nervous, but I knew it was more important to sit with Tommy and be there for him until he finished his poem. As much for my own sake as for his. How often does one get a chance to be present at the birth of a poet? The whole process gave me shivers. Though the poem as a finished product would probably not convey to anybody else that shiver, I quote it as part of the record.

Photograph

The town squire's mattress came back to town.
Poor mattress fell on the floor.
She photographed the champion broom.
She found herself in the forest,
In quest of her Beauty.
The blankets shone.
Her chair was held up by balloons.

She found people dancing in jars.
As they were dancing they were making
some dough as flat as a plain.
She photographed some fumes from the
dust that rose in quest of her beauty.
She photographed tons of languages.
They entered a melody.
She photographed two lumps of soil
in quest of her beauty.

TOMMY

We went over Tommy's version from the beginning to see if he wanted anything improved. Did he like it? I asked.

"Well, it sounds like a real poem even though it doesn't exactly make sense."

I translated the original Apollinaire for him. Tommy listened with intense interest. Then he said modestly, "I think I like mine better."

"What about it do you like better?"

He thought for a while. "It's more like a story."

* * *

You make those choices: to hold the group's attention together, or go for a quiet moment with one student and let the group thing sag. Sometimes you're too tightly wound and defensive and supervisory even to detect the possibility of a quiet moment. Then something loosens you: a look or a stray remark is thrown at you like a clue, and you take it up.

A boy named Marvin was newly arrived from an all-black school in the South. He seemed stolid and more mature than the other children. One morning he came in late, near the end of a workshop, and sat in a chair with his coat on.

"Why don't you take your coat off?" I said.

He tossed his coat over mine, which happened to be lying on a desk. "Seems like my coat be in love with your coat," he said.

This remark made me turn around. Until he had said that I confess I had thought of him as a dull, "mulish" kid, but now it seemed there was more going on under his slow brown eyes than I had thought.

"Tell me more—how's your coat in love with mine?"

"I can't say, 'cause I don't know much about Coat Love," he said.

Now he really had me intrigued. I asked him if he thought objects, things, had actual feelings. He said he often talked to things that were lying in the street, tires and junk, carried on conversations with them. And now his mother was worried about him—she worked in a hospital as a nurse, she wanted to take him to the "Psych."

I told him I talked to myself, that all writers did, and it wasn't as unusual as he might think. Marvin brushed aside this reassurance with a worried look: "No, she's gonna take me to the Psych. I know something's wrong."

He seemed to want to talk about it, and I wanted to listen. But I didn't feel easy about adopting a therapist's role in relation to him. There had to be a way that he could talk, and that I could show him that his thoughts were not so bizarre or frightening (which I felt pretty certain that they weren't) *through* my ordinary role as writing teacher.

I took him to a far table and sat down with him and asked him to talk to himself as if he were in the street. I would write down everything he said. That way we could make what he said into a poem. "All right," he said skeptically. "Where should I start?" "Start the way you would if you were outside in the street, looking around, thinking to yourself." He began dictating to me. He seemed to be formulating it in his head, consciously editing out certain details and asking me to write down only those that would be good for the poem. At the end of his dictation I asked him what title he wanted to give it; and he said without hesitation, "The Sadness."

The Sadness

Helping my father wash the car
He tells me to get the water
Marvin turn on the hose pipe.
      Turn on the hose
It's on.
All right that's good. Bring it here.

Now we splash the soap on
Marvin run the water on the car
All right that's good. Turn it off.
Now let's dry the car off
Gotta give me some money to go get a soda
Marvin you don't have to help me no more
Here's $5.
I go over to the wall.
Then I start staring.
I look down the street
I look up the street
What do I see?
I see one man coming with a carriage carrying junk
And a freight train running on its lane
There's no kids my size
Anyhow I'm outside
So I guess I'll talk to myself
Well I wish I had a horse
I look down the street and here come a mule.
They start clearing the junk house
So the mule can come and dump his load
I wish I had a darn horse.
I always wanted a horse and Dad know it
But I had to stop being afraid of horses first
Someone said they'll kick you to death
Mom & Dad say when we go down South
We'll get a horse.
And Dad say he'll get him one and me one too
So what am I worrying about
I'll be glad when I go down South
It is so warm there

MARVIN

"It's very good, Marvin," I said when it was done. We were both a little stunned.

I took it to the second floor to show his teacher, Stanley Riegelhaupt, who happened to be in the teacher's lounge on his prep period.

"Marvin wrote that?" said Stanley. "That's terrific!"

"Well he told me what words to write and I wrote them down. . . ."

For all my enthusiasm about the poem, I still felt there was something less "legitimate" about dictated work. Wouldn't it be more useful for him to struggle through a written piece on his own? How much of the final product was shaped by my arranging it into lines?

After the second week's dictation from Marvin, I told him that next time he would have to write it himself. "But it doesn't come out so good as when you write it," he insisted. And it didn't. During the next few workshops, his eyes followed me with a hurt look as if I had betrayed his trust. He understood the trick—the same trick all the other teachers pulled. It was that universal *idée fixe* of adults: to get him to read and write. It wasn't enough apparently that a way had been opened for him to say what was on his mind.

So the weaning process took a step backward: I gave in and he dictated again. Was it the dictation itself that was so crucial to him, or the physical and mental closeness it brought between us? My hanging on to his every word? The next time, he gave in and wrote a page. For the rest of the year we were bound to each other by that first experience, glad when we met in the halls, embarrassed for no reason, as if looking to rediscover that same shock of intimacy.

* * *

Every week I brought in a new writing idea. The kids had come to expect it. I talked to friends who were also teaching writing; I bought materials; I compiled lists. Everything was turning into a writing assignment in my head. I would see a family walking together; we could do a lesson on families. I would get a headache; we could write about sickness and body sensations. The number of potential writing assignments was all too infinite. The night before going into class I would try to convince myself that one idea shone above the rest. I believed in it; I went to sleep on it. The next morning four other assignments seemed equally plausible. I would be riding the bus to school thinking lesson A, B, C, D? Or M? Suddenly I decided it has to be G, G, G . . . !

I am still walking to the front of the class mumbling to myself: G, G . . . or maybe A.

"Let me have your attention please," I would say to Mrs. Loftin's kids. (I had gone back to addressing the whole class.) "I'd like you to quiet down so we can begin."

How many times have I been struck, on uttering the words, "Today I thought we might write about . . .", with the total unreality of my proposition. Why hypnosis and not favorite foods; or odes? Everything seems equally random. And in that split second between the getting of their attention and the telling of what it is they will have to do, as I stare down at thirty pairs of child's eyes, ready to inform me if I have guessed well or badly, how often have I gone dizzy, wishing I could defer the judgment a little longer, and fallen into the abyss between the two halves of my sentence?

Some ideas would catch fire and not others, perfectly as good. Why? Was it my delivery? Or that certain ideas were narrower and less applicable to everyone? Or the mood of the class that day, the weather?

If only I could stick to a coherent plan week after week, a—a curriculum (magic crutch!). But I knew of no writing curriculum that was satisfactory; I would have had to make one up myself. I taught each class only once or twice a week, and the hope of drawing a continuity between the lessons kept getting thinner. When I tried to follow up a successful lesson, often it seemed that too much had intervened for the children in the week between and the idea already felt stale to them. I made attempts to force connections between lessons, but it was mostly for my own conscience. In the end I reassured myself that at least they were getting a "full spectrum" of writing experiences. They seemed to be satisfied with a random approach. But the *arbitrariness* of my assignments continued to gall me.

Rather than always second-guessing the kids' interests, I began asking them to volunteer writing subjects. But when you ask a class point-blank, "What do you want to write about?" the response is usually vacant stares, trivia, insincerity. The kids were still not ready to go without the initial writing stimulus that I brought in each week. Even if they rejected the bouquet, they felt better for having had it brought to them. I was the one who felt uncomfortable. There was something that didn't sit right with my educational philosophy, about programming thirty kids to write in a given form each week.

One day I tried an assignment that fell utterly flat. No relevance to anyone's imagination anywhere. Then I was surprised and moved to see certain children diligently carry it out—not because they were afraid of me but because we had been through a lot and they would humor me this time. They wrote almost out of a desire to make me feel better, with that kindness and childish diplomacy that mysteriously rises out of them. I began to realize I was banking on their love. Behind all the ideas and creative motivators was the unspoken appeal: Do it for *me*.

I was supposed to be teaching poetry and fiction writing to public school children; I saw this as my main job. At the same time I was being drawn to the different children as personalities. I wanted to communicate with them more directly but I couldn't, because the lesson stood in the way. Of course the lesson could be the very medium by which we spoke to each other. Sometimes it was; but sometimes I had the feeling that the lesson was only a *pretext* for us to enjoy each other's company.

The lesson was the tennis ball I hit to the kids every week, and their writing was the ball they hit back. The academic role structure between us was the net. Robert Frost once said that he didn't care to write free verse because it was "like playing tennis without the net." Maybe I'm perverse, but I've always been drawn to the notion of playing tennis without the net. So if the lesson were an indirect and, to some extent, hypocritical means for us to communicate with each other, wouldn't it be possible at some point to drop the pretext? Did we really need it? And if it proved impossible to do without (which I began to suspect it was, since my desires for something else were so vague that I could not imagine what I would put in its place), wasn't there some way to do it without as much artificiality?

What I was really looking for was a way to close the distance between my informal, hanging-around behavior and my regular teaching personality. I didn't want to be two people. It was painful to keep switching.

It was Riegelhaupt's kids who led me to a different approach. By their very indifference to writing games, they forced me to look elsewhere. Ideas that had worked like a charm with Loftin's kids failed to hold them. They had a tendency to use the Writing Room as a playroom. Their reluctance to write was understandable because they were already getting so much "creative writing" for homework.

I saw it would be necessary to remake their whole attitude toward writing, by giving the act of writing a more existential ground. But that might take a long time. . . . Or else find another function and purpose for writing by connecting it like a balloon string to other arts: writing a script so that it could be acted onstage; or writing combined with artwork. Or forget about writing for a while. Maybe they were horsing around so much because they needed it.

I turned Group A loose with magic markers on the drab papercovered closets of the Writing Room, to make graffitti, draw pictures, write messages to each other. I brought in adding-machine rolls for whoever wanted to write Endless Stories; magazines to be cut up for collage poems; fat, colored chalk for the blackboard. With arts materials, the atmosphere became more flowing.

The next time I had Riegelhaupt's kids write monologues and soliloquies for different characters and act them out. Then we combined the characters to make playlets. This led to a few weeks of tape-recorded radio plays: *The Prison Break, The Divorce Court.*

Radio plays are a beautiful form for promoting concentration and discipline. The technical limitation of one microphone focuses the group: everyone *has* to stand close around that microphone. If several people speak at once, the playback sounds like sludge. Whenever anyone starts making noise or jumping around, the others shush him because they want the sound to come out right. Riegelhaupt's kids adored radio plays. At last something had taken hold. I could feel their interest deepening with every advance into drama.

Theater was the activity they were starved for, the form toward which all their playing around had been pointing. The difference between "play" and "a play" is not very great in most children's minds. Theater reconciled their appetite for play with my desire to have them write something collaboratively and work hard at and care about an activity over a period of several months.

The next step was to write an actual play together. I began by having them improvise parts around a form that I always find appealing: the soap opera. Each child was to take the character of someone in a family and make up a disability or maladjustment for that character; or else play a neighbor or family doctor. From the first few weeks of sprawling, sloppy improvisations, we boiled down the best moments into a script, which was written by everyone in the ensemble. The result was our first play: *The Typical American Family with Problems.*

In a sense, I had put off the problem of teaching creative writing by expanding into other arts. It was not until the following year that I felt ready to attempt again a more coherent approach to the teaching of poetry. (See "Seven Lessons.") In the meantime, *The Typical American Family with Problems* was taking off for rehearsals and I was becoming a man of the theater.

Chapter 6
Flying Lessons

The Typical American Family with Problems featured a hypochon-driac mother, who sits on her couch like Madame Récamier with a splitting headache; an alcoholic, blustering father; a mentally disturbed daughter who sweeps with the wrong end of the broom (done with wonderful sobriety by Nina); a whiny, persecution-complex son (Robert); a nosy neighbor (Marvin); a television repairman under the delusion he is a dentist (Clifford); and a demented psychiatrist whom all the family visit in the last scene, played with Groucho Marx, hair-pulling frenzy by Tommy.

The play was a great hit, especially with those classes who sat in the first ten rows of the auditorium; due to the hall's acoustics, those who sat farther back heard nothing.

The most fun was had by the actors, who had spent at least six weeks writing and rehearsing the play. It was gratifying to see certain kids who were usually more introverted and withdrawn, like Tommy, Marvin, and Clifford, letting out some of their exhibitionistic, flamboyant tendencies.

Naturally the rest of their classmates were jealous. Those kids who had not signed up in the beginning of the year for the writing workshops were now feeling cheated. They began badgering me to be in the next play. I realized it would be a good way to do something for them. Though the first skit was hard enough for me to put on, since I'd never directed anything theatrical before, I decided to go ahead and try for one last burst of energy.

My structural problem was this: how to come up with a play that had enough parts for everyone in the class. I thought about it, without reaching any conclusion, and decided to put the problem to Riegelhaupt's kids and see if they could solve it. Together we drew up a list of situations that called for lots of people: mob scenes, birth-

day parties, train stations, hospitals, classrooms, funerals. The one
that appealed to them most as a dramatic possibility was classrooms.
I was happy they had made this choice, since they knew a great deal
about classroom behavior but might have had a harder time with
some of the others.

So, with no one leaving his seat, we reconstituted the classroom
as a "play" classroom. Everything was just as it had been except that
now we had to come up with a dramatic situation. We ran through
a few less than fiery ideas before someone suggested the substitute-
teacher situation. A substitute teacher is sent to cover the class and
the kids put her through bizarre tricks like refusing to give their right
names, bombarding her with paper airplanes, and so on. We began
talking about the underground behavior which children use in con-
spiring to upset adults. Everyone was begging to try acting it, so we
did a quick run-through. It was a more than energetic start. Next
time, I stressed, they should bring about the collapse gradually, sabotaging step-by-step, rather than just indulging in an explosion of noise
and movement which would be theatrically confusing. Five boys volunteered to prepare a script for next week.

The next time my boss, Marty Kushner, director of Teachers &
Writers Collaborative, came along to watch. I called him my boss,
though actually we were close friends. Marty wrote a report of that
day's lesson, and his field notes capture better than my memory can
the sequence of events. (It should be understood that his perceptions
are colored by friendship, and therefore one may take his praise of
me with a grain of salt.)

> When we come in, the class is finishing up a math lesson;
> a cheer goes up as Phillip enters the room. Riegelhaupt says, "Phil,
> we're just going to finish up this lesson and then you can have
> them."
>
> The math lesson finishes. For the next hour, Phil and the kids
> brainstorm to put together the pieces of the script. The script as-
> signed last week is not written. Phil first suggests that the five kids
> who volunteered to write the script go with him to another room
> and work alone, but he suddenly changes his mind because he wants
> the whole class to work. He remarks that many kids came up to him
> before the class to suggest ideas.
>
> "Why come up to me clandestinely with your ideas? Let's talk

about them right here so we can all hear the ideas and share the ideas back and forth."

The kids launch into a barrage of ideas. From all corners of the room they name activities that could be taking place while the substitute tries to teach:

playing jacks
boys scaring girls with a snake
a battery of paper airplanes
an argument that develops into a fistfight.

Phil listens to every idea and gives an instant gut reaction:

That's a terrific idea.
That won't work because . . .
What do you think of that idea? (To the other kids)
That's great. Let's have some more examples like that.
That's a bad idea (a response to some clowning around ideas).

Phil seems to have an urge to drive through any distraction, to get on with it, to create a serious work atmosphere, not by any scolding or moralizing, but by doggedly talking and questioning only à propos the play.

Stefan makes this comment: "When we rehearsed the last play, the rehearsals were always full of noise; we were running around and it never came together, yet when we got up on the stage to perform at the end, everything was perfect." He implies that the rehearsals were not so crucial.

Phil explains that during the rehearsals in spite of the apparent chaos, the points of the drama were being worked out. They were establishing a kind of musical score which would always be there to work from. He demonstrates by walking, saying there are different points in a straight line and that they had to come up with the points so at the end they can walk the whole line. Stefan understands. And the class begins again, furiously calling out ideas.

A girl suggests that the principal walk in with the inspector at a certain moment when the kids are wildly running around the room, looks over the situation and says, "Oh, don't mind them, they're rehearsing a play." Pirandello couldn't have done better!

Phil writes their ideas down on the board, all over the board, in no particular order. Later they will write down the script. A heavy-set boy, Marvin, records all that is on the board in his own order; he acts as some sort of script consolidator.

Someone takes off from the idea of the principal coming in—

he says that everybody immediately gets quiet. Phillip notes that there
are now two very different choices for the kids on the arrival of the
principal: one, that they continue their wildness, and the other, that
they become like little angels.

I'm sitting in the back of the room and start flapping my arms.
I suddenly have the image of the kids as actual angels, all in white,
floating, wisping around the room, in front of an approving principal. Phillip starts dancing around a little, picking up my cue, flapping
his arms; my instinctive suggestion is picked up: the kids come up
with ideas about angels. One boy says, "One kid goes flying up in the
air." Phillip screams, "That's it; beautiful!"

The kids start coming up with suggestions for a pulley system,
to make someone fly on stage. The room is exploding with energy.

A boy shouts, "We'll all have halos made out of tin foil. Then
when the principal comes in, we'll go under our desks and come up
with halos and wings."

Phillip suggests that everyone will have halos but only one person will have wings; he will fly. "And that should be the meanest kid
in the class," another boy suggests.

Stefan, the best actor, volunteers for the flying role.

At that moment the real principal of the school, Edouardo
Jimenez, walks in. The kids start behaving like angels. He walks over
to the teacher's desk, does some business, oblivious to what is happening in class. The kids start joking. Phillip says, smiling and laughing, "You're embarrassing me. That's the principal." The kids laugh
and quiet down a bit.

Never is the entire class involved during Phillip's visit. There
are frequent interruptions; kids come in from other rooms; kids
drop in and out of the discussion. At one point or another, everyone
gets into the act, but sometimes it is just one boy or girl poking
his/her head out from a notebook and making a suggestion. One
silent girl (Nina) suddenly comes up with a great suggestion for doing the scene between the principal and the school inspector *in front
of* the curtain, before they come into the class where the substitute
is teaching. While the curtain is closed, she suggests, the kids can set
up as angels and the devilish boy can get into the harness for flying
up in the air. It's a terrific suggestion that solves a myriad of technical problems and offers a theatrical way of breaking up two scenes.

The class goes on this way, with kids making suggestions and
Phillip responding immediately, saying "Shut up" and "I can't hear,"
when there is literally too much noise or interference for the work

to continue. Every kid's comment on the working out of the play is accepted and dealt with; it is an atmosphere where one feels inclined to contribute.

Riegelhaupt sits at his desk, acting as the disciplinarian to help quiet the room at times. (Phillip sometimes lets the noise take over, then gets the class back, all the time thinking on his feet, his concentration and ability to go with what is given is a superb teaching gift.) Riegelhaupt's quieting of the kids is supportive; it is not the mean teacher shutting up the kids for his own satisfaction, but out of respect for the work that is going on. Riegelhaupt offers to stay after school to help the five boys write the script, which will preserve and arrange the ideas generated by today's improvisations.

* * *

Three separate scripts emerged from the group of boys who had volunteered. Some of the differences between them were dramatic; others stemmed from having looked at the same improvisation but remembered different details. I took the three scripts home and melted them into one.

The Substitute Teacher

SCENE: A regular classroom standing around waiting for the substitute.

(Teacher walks in with Principal)

PRINCIPAL: I'm sure you'll like this class, and what is your name.

TEACHER: Mrs. Zelda Lefkowitz. (Writes "Z. Lefkowitz" on the blackboard.)

PRINCIPAL: Oh, yes, before I leave I must tell you that the kid in the blue is a mental case, and the straitjackets are in the closet.

SUBSTITUTE: Thank you. (Principal leaves.) Good morning class. What do you usually do in the morning?

STUDENTS: Math! Social Studies! Free Play!

SUBSTITUTE: Now let me make one thing perfectly clear. If you want to speak, you MUST raise your hand first. Do you understand?

CLASS:	Yes teacher.
	(Good little girl raises her hand.)
SUBSTITUTE:	Yes?
GOOD GIRL:	I'm the monitor. Just if you need me.
SUBSTITUTE:	Thank you.

(1st Boy raises his hand, drops it before the teacher can call on him and starts talking to his friend.)

SUBSTITUTE:	Be quiet!
2ND BOY:	Teacher, may I go to the bathroom?
SUBSTITUTE:	No, not now.
2ND BOY:	You want me to make in my pants?
SUBSTITUTE:	If you want to, go right ahead.
3RD BOY:	Peowi! Peowi!
2ND GIRL:	(Raises hand, Teacher calls on her) Teacher, what does the Z. stand for in your name?
SUBSTITUTE:	If you must know,—Zelda. Oh I almost forgot, let's sing the National Anthem. (Everyone stands and runs through it in double time.)
SUBSTITUTE:	That sounded more like mumble jumble to me, but let's skip it. On to work!
GOOD GIRL:	We usually start with some math problems.
SUBSTITUTE:	Thank you. What's your name again?
GOOD GIRL:	Liz. I'm the monitor, just if you need me.

(Teacher turns around to write some easy math problems on the board. Meanwhile, two kids start playing jacks, notes are passed, etc. They stop as soon as she turns around again.)

SUBSTITUTE:	Do the math problems I've put on the board. When you're finished *sit still*.

(She sits down at her desk. 4th Boy sneaks around her and erases the problems.)

5TH BOY:	(Raises hand.) How can we do math when there's no problems?
SUBSTITUTE:	There are problems on the board, if you can't SEE THEM YOU'RE BLIND. Now start.

(Looks around.) Hey, you're right. Whoever did that stop it!

(Bad Leader secretly starts passing out battle notes in a systematic way.)

SUBSTITUTE: WHAT is going on?? What is this child's name?

CLASS: Charles! Henry! Tom, Eddie! (One boy starts skipping around, singing:)
Oh my name is MacNamara
I'm the leader of the band

SUBSTITUTE: Sit down! I'm starting a bad student list. (Writes *Bad* on the blackboard. Someone jumps up right away and erases it.)

BAD LEADER: (Yells) PLAN CS 8, you two guard the door. Knock desks down! Front row, get ready, aim fire. Second row now, ready, aim, fire. Air planes released. Fire!

(The curtain closes. Two lookouts are stationed outside, in the hall. From the far side of the stage the Principal and the Inspector come walking slowly on.)

INSPECTOR: What's all that noise?

PRINCIPAL: Oh, the children are having a free period.

INSPECTOR: (Wiping off dust with finger.) Does this school have a custodian?

PRINCIPAL: Yes we do have a custodian, but in a sense we have over 800 custodians, because all the teachers and the children help to keep it clean.

INSPECTOR: 800 custodians, eh? Then how come it's such a mess?

PRINCIPAL: Well the children are encouraged to express themselves. There's a sort of creative mess. It depends how you look at it. For instance that boy over there (points to one of the lookouts who is tossing up a paper ball), he may seem to be playing with a toy airplane, but he's actually solving a difficult mathematical problem.

1ST LOOKOUT:	Oh bless my butt, the Principal and the big Inspector! Warn the class fast. I'll stall them.
2ND LOOKOUT:	(Yells through the curtain opening) Yo! Hey, the Principal is coming with the big I.!!
INSPECTOR:	And what kind of special programs do you have here?
PRINCIPAL:	We have an open library program, a bi-lingual program, a breakfast program, we have videotapes. But most important everyone gets along well in this school. There are no fights and . . .

(1st Lookout blocks his way.)

PRINCIPAL:	Excuse me son.—Let me just take you into one of our classes. Er, not this one. The next one down the hall is one of our better sixth grades . . .
1ST LOOKOUT:	(Blocking his path again) Can I ask you something?
PRINCIPAL:	What is it?
1ST LOOKOUT:	How do you spell Supercalifragelisticexpialidotious?
PRINCIPAL:	S-U-P-E-R—uh listen, we're in a hurry, ask your teacher.
2ND LOOKOUT:	(To Inspector, blocking his way) Want to see a great report? This is all about the sun and the eclipses.
INSPECTOR:	It looks very interesting. How about that sixth grade class—
1ST LOOKOUT:	(Loud whisper) Faint! Faint!

(2nd Lookout collapses)

1ST LOOKOUT:	Oh my goodness, he fainted!
PRINCIPAL:	What's the matter, boy?
2ND LOOKOUT:	(Groans) Mhrirr. . . .
PRINCIPAL:	Nurse, Nurse!—Go down and get the nurse. She'll take care of it. Now let's go in.

(Nurse comes on, drags off 2nd Lookout. Curtain opens to show

the children sitting at their desks, with halos around their heads,
and one boy suspended in air, flapping a pair of wings.)

PRINCIPAL:	See what an orderly class this is?
SUBSTITUTE:	What?????
PRINCIPAL:	(Breaks in) I know how much you like this class but you don't have to go too far into it. . . . We have some exceptional children here. See that kid? He's an angel.
STUDENT:	Here teach, have a donut. (He does this to stop the teacher from telling the principal about what happened.)
INSPECTOR:	It looks pretty good.
PRINCIPAL:	We better be going now, bye. I'll see to it that you get a raise in your salary. (Principal and Inspector leave.)
SUBSTITUTE:	All right class you win. FREE TIME for the rest of the day.

(Desks turned over, one kid staggers out with a noose around
him, murder, chaos . . . Good Girl runs in.)

GOOD GIRL:	I just heard that MR. RIEGELHAUPT is coming in after all. His car got stuck on the highway and he should be here any second!
CLASS:	(Groans) Awwwwwwwwwwwwwwwwwwwwww (Enter Mr. Riegelhaupt)
MR. RIEGELHAUPT:	NO NO NO. All right, shh! Cut it out. You're going to be in big trouble! Now who wants to be the first to stay in the after-school club?

Curtain

For certain, the spectacle of flying would capture the audience.
But at this point I had to admit to myself that I had no idea how
to make anyone fly. I bought a textbook on stage design and read
the diagrams of hoists and pulleys ten times over. None of it made
sense. If only I had been mechanically inclined. Instead, I had to
pray that I would find some good-natured handyman to do it for me.

I called up a few Broadway scenery companies but the price they were charging for harness and rig was beyond me. I was starting to worry. Every day the kids asked when we were going to rehearse the flying. I told everyone I ran into of my predicament, on the faint hope he would know how to solve it.

One day I was riding in a car with a friend, and someone who was driving him, whom I'd never met, and I started babbling about needing to fly across stage. The driver said that it was quite simple to do. He had worked as a stage technician on two off-Broadway plays that used flying. Did I want the character to fly up, down and sideways, or only up and down? I confessed I had not reached that stage in my thinking yet. He said that sideways required a more complicated hookup but it could be done. I begged him to come to my school and show me. He reluctantly agreed.

The stage technician, whose name was John, arrived the next Tuesday at 3 P.M. with several ropes. Stefan and I were waiting for him, alone on the auditorium stage. John, barely speaking, placed Stefan on a desk in the middle of the stage, and we tied two belts around Stefan's waist and shoulders. Then John threw the rope high above the lights and tied one end to Stefan. The other end he tied to his own ankle. John went backstage and set up the tallest ladder he could find. He mounted halfway up the ladder. He told Stefan to jump off the desk, and at the same time he ran down the ladder steps. Stefan sank to the ground. John returned, readjusted the ropes, and ascended to the very top of the ladder. He told Stefan to jump at the count of five; at the count of three John himself began descending the ladder, to gain a headstart. Stefan hit the ground with a soft undramatic thud. It did not seem to be working. This time John went backstage, tightened the ropes, gave Stefan a chair to stand on atop the desk so that there would be more height, and climbed the ladder to the top step and ran very swiftly down. Stefan, about to plummet, suddenly paused in mid-air, hung there, as if he had changed his mind, and started fluttering upward. It was worth everything to see the expression on Stefan's face. Instead of jumping off a desk and falling, he had found himself floating toward the ceiling! Newton himself could not have been more surprised. John lurched him from level to level, controlling the ropes backstage, until Stefan screamed: "Let me down!"

John released him and he came gradually to earth. "Whew! My stomach feels funny."

"Think you can do it for the play?"

Stefan said, shaking his head, "How could this happen to a nice kid like me?"

John said he wanted to test it again. "On second thought, why don't you try it," he told me, "since you'll be doing it for the performance."

"Wait a minute. I thought you were going to do it—"

"Sorry, the play's on a Tuesday. I have to go to Unemployment on Tuesday."

He assured me it wasn't difficult, and I went backstage and tied the rope around my foot. I started climbing the big ladder. There was something wrong in all this. I'm not a coward *per se;* I will do what has to be done (still climbing); I will even force myself to take physical risks when other people are watching and it is expected of me. But the image came into my mind of a World War II movie with Seabees climbing up the wavering rope ladder to get onto the ship, and I had the feeling that I would be the one to fall. I reached the top of the ladder telling myself it would be better not to look down. Stefan was on top of the chair, and ready. I proceeded to go very slowly down the ladder and Stefan drifted down to the wooden floor. It was all very gentle and comfortable and predictable. I think it was all I had hoped for anyway.

"No," John said. He shook his head. "No. This time . . . No. You have to go down the ladder much faster in order to give him lift."

"Isn't there some easier way?"

"Sure there's an easier way. With a winch. But you don't have a winch back there."

"No, we don't have a winch," I said halfheartedly, not even sure what a winch was.

"You'll get the hang of it. Try it again."

I went backstage to my diving platform. I told Stefan I was ready; then I said, no wait a second, and caught my breath. I counted five and said I was ready. I ran down the ladder as fast as I could. I felt Stefan pulling more at the other end, which meant that he had not yet sunk, he was still in the air. Shortly afterward he did sink, however.

"When am I gonna get these things off me?" Stefan asked. "I gotta go home; my sister's worrying!"

"I can't do it," I said to John.

"Well I'm not. I have to be at the Unemployment office. . . ."

"Yeah."

"You almost had it that time," said John.

"Let me try it one more time." I went to my post at the ladder. I waved him over. "Now tell me where I'm going wrong."

"Let's see. . . . You're gripping the ladder with your hands too much. You have to let it kind of slide by your fingers, otherwise you pick up too much traction. Don't use your hands; just use your feet."

"Wait a second! I'm supposed to go down this steep ladder fast as anything without even using my hands? That's too much. I'm sorry."

"Let me show you." He climbed to the head of the ladder and "flew" down nimbly like a leprechaun. If his hands made contact, I didn't see it.

"All right." I nudged him aside and started climbing. If he could do it, I could do it. By now I was prepared to sacrifice my life for the sake of being a good sport. It had been an all-right, decent life. I tied the rope tight around my ankle. "No hands!" I said grimly. Something was very wrong here. I started down the steps without holding on. And Stefan started to go up! His weight was pulling me off of the ladder and, suddenly, I couldn't see why but I was unable to move. I was tilted perpendicularly outward from the ladder in a way that must have looked very funny if I had had a sense of humor at the time. We seemed to have canceled out each other's weights. Stefan hung there; I hung there; I told my foot to move down a step and I sent the message to the brain but the foot wouldn't move. It would not move. For the first time I understood what it was like to be physically paralyzed.

"Help!" John pulled me off just before the ladder fell over. My heart was in my mouth. Stefan had landed safely on the ground by now.

I had found out something. I knew my limits now.

I called John aside. "How much are they paying you at Unemployment?"

"Thirty-seven dollars, but—"

"I'll match it. You do the flying bit, okay? I'll direct the play and see that everyone gets onstage and off on cue. That's enough for me to do." He accepted the offer and we were in business.

The day of the play John came fifteen minutes before curtain, laconic, goateed, and vexed as usual. He confessed to me that he "detested children." I asked him if there was anything I could do to help him set up. All he wanted, he said, was to know where the bathroom was. I tried the backstage bathroom door but it was locked. Then I forgot about it in the crush of other problems. Poor John! Unwittingly sucked into a sixth-grade production. Badly paid, forced to come in from Staten Island to run down a ladder for fifteen seconds, all he ever wanted was to use the bathroom, and even that couldn't be arranged.

Stefan was cracking his knuckles against the curtain ropes. "Don't do that. It makes me nervous," I said.

"What are *you* nervous about? I'm so nervous my legs are like toothpicks knocking together."

We stood there like a pair, he cracking his knuckles, I biting my fingernails.

The auditorium began filling up with fourth-, fifth-, and sixth-graders. The audience settled down and we started the play. Tracy, the girl who played the substitute teacher, did her job well and moved nimbly on stage, chasing naughty kids, getting laughs. My mind was only on the flying. It came time for the two boys to start their scene in front of the curtain; the stage crew rushed the desk and chair on and Stefan took his place behind the curtain as the School Inspector and the Principal wandered on in front. Clifford made a wonderfully insolent Inspector, not too different from the real ones I have seen. Robert was suitably distracted and ebullient as the Principal. The tricky part was for the flying rig to be set up and Stefan's lift-off to take place *just at the moment* that the scene in front had ended and the curtain pulled. And now it seemed that something had gone wrong with one of Stefan's belts. "The belt! The belt!" he kept crying in a whimper. I ripped the belt off my pants and substituted it. Everyone was flapping his hands around Stefan in desperation and panic, like frightened ducks. Stefan scrambled onto the chair. "What happens if he doesn't—" Tommy started to ask me.

"We have to pull the curtain anyway," I said fatalistically.

John started down the ladder and Stefan was suspended, bent

in two, dangerously close to the ground. "Drop him," I said. "Try it again. Get him back on the chair." We still had two more seconds. I could hear the dialogue in front of the curtain coming to an end. The Principal and the Inspector were already parting the curtain. And Stefan was still on the chair. Stefan jumped, the curtain was pulled all the way; Stefan was aloft with half-a-second to spare! There was an enormous roar from the audience. A roar of ecstasy such as I had never heard at any gathering. Flying had taken place, on the stage of Public School 90.

True, I caught myself thinking, it was only up-and-down flying, and it would have looked better if we could have made him move sideways. . . .

The rest of the play was pure relief. Stanley Riegelhaupt came on at the end and gave everyone a big laugh by bellowing his lines. Stanley was tremendous in the part he loves best: Mr. Riegelhaupt.

The cast took their bows. I went backstage to bring out our unsung hero, John, but he had already left. I never saw him again.

Afterward, the whole school was buzzing. "That was really wonderful," a teacher, Mrs. Lipton, said to me in the halls. "I could have died laughing when that kid started flapping his wings! And you know, it gave me an idea. Next year I want to put on *Peter Pan* with my class. The kids are so excited about it! And there are lots of opportunities for flying in that one."

I had a shudder envisioning ten ladders backstage, with ten of us running up and down while everyone who had ever wanted to play Peter Pan sailed from every end of the stage, smashing into each other.

I said sure, we could think about it for next year.

II
The Adults

Chapter 7
Relations with Teachers

From the start, everyone had had big plans for the Writing Room. It was going to be something sensational, with a different aura entirely from the typical classroom. At an afterschool meeting about how to fix it up, seven teachers and two parents joined the writers—nine people who had no particular stake in the room's improvement but were simply responding to a neighbor's call for help. We encouraged anyone with a decorating itch to think grandiose. The proposals ranged from an indoor Buckminster Fuller dome, to a 1950s-type clubhouse with a pingpong table, to a waterfall with adjoining Mexican hammock, to a combined science and art Learning Center. The teachers seemed to like imagining zany things for someone *else's* room, even though they would not have dreamed of having them in their own. A sign of the times. There were so many deschooling ideas in the air, in teacher's magazines and popular books, that no one was startled at the wildest suggestions because they had already encountered a similar idea in print, although no one took them quite seriously either.

At the end I asked, in my best chairman-of-the-meeting manner, what system we could devise to ensure a follow-through and a division of tasks.

Monte Clausen, an open classroom teacher who had been around the school much longer than I, quipped: "Probably none."

Still, Margaret Trabulski volunteered to bring in curtains, Denise Loftin offered to organize a painting squad, Leo Gelber, an excellent carpenter, said we could call on him for help. I came away with the impression that the good will and faith of some public school teachers are unkillable, even in the face of the most harassing conditions.

While waiting for a master decorating plan, we continued work-

ing with small groups of children in the big, barren, echoing room.
A few metal schoolchairs and, later, some stuffed antique settees donated by parents did for furniture. The window curtains were given
to us but never got hung. No geodesic dome was built. No tent
pitched. No hammock strung. No collapsible room divider added.
Nothing but groups of children and us, busy interacting.

Sometimes, in spite of our attempts to stay out of each other's
hair, there would be a dramatic improvisation in one corner of the
room, and a quiet poetry workshop in a second, and a conference
between a writer and myself in a third.

We had gotten used to working together in that Spartan space.
After a while we couldn't bear to embellish it! For improvised plays,
the emptiness was convenient: the kids could fill it with their imaginations.[1]

Someone had donated a shocking-pink nappy rug, which lent
a touch of homeyness to the room. The kids could now spread out
on the rug and write, if they were bored with chairs. They had a
perfect right to find the most comfortable position for themselves to
write. But write they did. We had to abandon the clubhouse notion
when we realized we ourselves wanted the kids to work seriously and
intensely; and it wouldn't do for the Writing Room to get the reputation of a lay-about place.

Keeping the room clean was a problem. So many groups used
the room that it was difficult to get anyone to take responsibility for
it. And even when a writer (usually it was one of the women writers,
I must add) swept up at the end of the day, it was back to its old
seedy self twenty-four hours later.

There were rumors that the library next door wanted to take
over the room; that they were going to bust through the wall to expand their facilities. Mr. Jimenez warned us that we needed to rally
more schoolwide support. We were not making ourselves *visible
enough,* in his words. But we held on; we fought for our piece of
land. In the end they left us alone. Maybe Irene Fornes was right

---

[1] Now, when I visit a learning center or "enriched" environment, which
are all the fashion, crammed with parachutes and glass display cases and sand-
boxes everywhere you step, I start to get a headache. I wonder if all children
really like this busyness, as EDC and the materials-oriented educators seem to
assume, or if the thinking process is sometimes better served by a degree of
austerity.

when she said: "No one will ever take the Writing Room from us. It's so ugly, who would want it?"

One cold morning I came to school to teach and discovered the front door locked! I got the cleaning lady to let me in and asked her what was the holiday. It was Martin Luther King Day. No one had told me. . . . I decided to go upstairs anyway, since I was already out of bed, and straighten up the Writing Room.

The room looked tossed about as usual. The pink rug had crushed crayons and gum wrappers sticking in its mane. I turned the rug over, letting clouds of dirt fall; and then swept, putting books away, folding aluminum chairs, humming to myself. I was thinking of other times I had stayed late at an office just to feel that possessiveness and mental quiet. The pleasure of being in your place of work when everyone else is gone . . . I stood back to inspect my cleaning job: the "after" of before-and-after. It looked pretty much the way it had when I began. But it was ours.

* * *

Out of the corner of my eye, I had been watching the writers teach in the Writing Room and the classrooms, and I knew generally who was doing an effective job and who seemed unconnected. This brief, peripheral style of observation suited me more personally than the formal "observations" that had been a trauma for the first seminar group. The daily contact between us took some of the sting out of the apprenticeship situation. I might see them teach an uninspired workshop, but then the good days canceled that impression out, for both of us. Most of what I saw the other writers doing, in fact, was very exciting.

The writing team met now on the average of once a month. We rotated from one member's house to the other. The meetings were occasions for us to get together socially (which we never seemed to have time for during the workday), to gossip about careers and writing. But sooner or later we would get down to business.

I had no desire to use the meetings to flush out *mea culpa* confessions of bad performance. On the contrary, they were intended to give us a sense of group strength, and to let each writer realize that his struggles in the school were not as isolated as he might think.

They were occasions to share successes and new techniques, and to take pride in ourselves as a productive unit. But they were also, I hoped, opportunities to air problems and doubts in a relaxed, supportive atmosphere, with people in the same boat.

What surprised me was that those writers who were doing the most consistently conscientious teaching expressed the most confusion and uncertainty at meetings. The ones who were relatively ineffectual either kept silent or boasted. Of course an explanation for this is not too hard to imagine, but it still surprised me.

No matter what order of business we started from, we soon arrived at a point of shared anxiety. Again and again the issue was brought up, whether it was better to work with the whole class at once or take small groups into the Writing Room. It seemed to be a common experience that relationships with children in small groups were more personal and satisfying, yet the writers felt guilty about neglecting the other part of the class. How were you supposed to work with seven kids only, they asked, when you saw twenty other kids needing it as much?

From my point of view, I said, the dilemma was a false one. The project was intended to accommodate any number of different teaching styles. If you want to work with a lecture situation, work with a lecture situation; if you want to work in small groups, work that way. What counted was the richness of the contact between the children and us, not bulk numbers reached. What we as writers could give the kids (because we were freed from some of the babysitting responsibilities that the regular teacher had) was precisely an experience of a different quality. We could give them a taste for higher standards of concentration and craftsmanship. We would be fools to forfeit our privileges and our freedom for the *self*-inflicted burden to meet quotas. We simply had to trust that sooner or later we would work our way around to reaching all the children in the class and giving them a worthwhile experience.

My answer dispersed the uneasiness, temporarily, without attacking it at its source. The writers seemed to be implying that if you were really strong enough or charismatic, tough enough, you could take on a whole class. Maybe some early class disturbances had driven them to working with small groups prematurely, more from a sense of inadequacy than from choice. In which case they would have to go back and try it again, no matter what I said. But

I felt it would be a mistake for us to concentrate on techniques of Classroom Management in order to get thirty kids to sit in their seats at a ritualized signal, like a good regular teacher. It would be defeating the whole point of why we were there.

There were other nagging issues that kept coming up, questions for which I had no simple answer—which meant to me that the right questions were being asked. What if a child kept crumpling up and destroying his own compositions? What did you do about a child who never wanted to write, week after week? Should you ever try to force him? Do you correct spelling mistakes and grammar when you type up the children's work for mimeographing? Should you try to get the children to edit and rewrite? Was it a good or bad idea to read your own poems to the class? If you saw a classroom teacher hitting a child or saying horrible things to a child, should you stand by or intervene? What did you do about reading aloud a piece in which one child made fun of another in a way that might hurt his feelings? What about racial remarks in a story—should you censor them or discuss them?

Significantly, most of these problems involved questions of tact or personal relations, rather than of writing curriculum. They pointed to the delicate line we had to walk as outsider-insiders in a public school. With each question, I discussed the advantages and disadvantages of different courses of action; I explained what I had done in a similar situation, but insisted that every situation was locally different. A lot depended on the specific classroom, the teacher and the child; and the background of the writer. The writer had to do what felt right to him at the moment the incident came up. The only way to find out was to go on instinct, experiment, and make mistakes; and not be so hard on yourself when you made the wrong move.

As for prodding or goading children to work, some people seemed to feel that the less you tell your students what to do, the better, but I didn't agree. Both intervention and non-intervention have their rationales. The art of teaching is in knowing when a student is best left alone and when he is ripe to receive your help. The moment of ripeness is different in each student.

I took this pluralistic position not because I wanted to be nice— indeed, it would have been more reassuring and "nicer" in some cases to have laid down strict guidelines. But for me there had never existed a sure-fire method for teaching children. It had always been trial and error, arising from the demands of each situation.

The meetings succeeded in building a kind of clarity. We usually left the discussions feeling stronger and more eager to continue. But there were times when the cloud of unresolved anxiety never quite lifted. Dealing with anxiety in public is peculiar in the way it differently affects individuals. Some people are relieved to have their doubts spoken; the mere acknowledgment of their uncertainty is enough for it to begin to go away. But with others, the confession of one anxiety leads inexorably to another and another, like a pinball bouncing from light to light, until the sympathetic listener wonders whether to take each of these worries seriously and try to solve them one by one; or whether all these doubts are only the complicated disguise of a larger lament, which is inexhaustible and so private that you can do nothing about it.

After a meeting sometimes I found myself, from the strain of having had to be so reasonable and so mature, lost in the personality of an older, problem-solving, benign, and slightly pompous bore who had taken over my brain. I liked him, in some ways, better than myself. But he was threatening to take me over.

Of the team, only to Irene Fornes, who had become a confidante, could I confess how absolutely tired I felt, how little sense the whole thing made to me sometimes. As for the others, I was worried that if I showed them my own lapses of faith it would scare them. Perhaps I was wrong about that. But my faith in Irene was unshakable. What a pleasure it was to watch her with the Spanish children, improvising a play and moving them by the shoulders to show them where to stand or how the vampire bat should fly around. She could create a theatrical stage anywhere. But even Irene complained that it was draining her—more so than working with adult actors. She had the idea that her personality wasn't right for children. I told her I thought she was doing wonderfully. She had to stay. She was my ally.

In December, Christy informed me that she was quitting. She said she wanted to devote her full energies to writing. The job at P.S. 90 had fragmented her, taken up too much of her mind. I was worried about the effect her leaving might have on the morale of the team. And I was angry at her for abandoning the two classes of children. Why couldn't she serve out the year and then quit? I wanted to know.

What galled me the most was that Christy had been doing a first-rate job. If she had shown no aptitude for the work, I could have understood it; but no, her lessons were exceptionally well-planned, the children liked her, the writing she was getting out of them was beautiful, and suddenly . . . it was as if she had had enough of that experience.

I couldn't help taking her defection as a personal rebuff. Anger has a way of dredging up racial stereotypes: and this time an unexpected fury against upper-class Wasps broke out of me. Goddamn bluebloods! A month or two of work in a slum school, then bye-bye!

I asked her if she would reconsider teaching out the year. She kept saying I could easily find a replacement just as good. For some reason, this modestly intended statement infuriated me even more— I imagined that she was belittling the job. I was torn between giving her a real piece of my mind and coaxing her to stay. But there was no way Christy would let her resolve be changed. She said that she didn't really need the money and, anyway, it had only been "a loose verbal contract."

I asked the group if they might be able to recommend anyone to take Christy's place. Sue Willis suggested Karen Hubert, a friend of hers at Columbia graduate school who wrote interesting short stories and had had several years' experience with troubled children. I was very impressed with Karen when I met her; she had a sensitive and honest personality and was willing to struggle. It was clear that she would find her own way in the school.

Karen took over Christy's classes in January. After a fragile turnover period, during which Christy's old students showed their loyalty to their first writing teacher by giving Karen a hard time, Karen blended in smoothly and became a valuable member of the team.

THE TEACHERS' LOUNGE

The teachers' lounge had the air of an ocean liner. Several leather deckchairs leaned out from the wall. From time to time someone shifted in one of these chairs or groaned, thinking aloud of something she had to do, or talked to the person next to her, both staring straight ahead like passengers looking at the identical body of water.

Time had been made to slow down here, so as to get the most out of coffee breaks. When you entered this room you went into a kind of suspended animation where the metabolic processes were reduced. But in spite of this dazed atmosphere, the promise of something raucous happening was always close by. There was a large table in the center of the room coated with durable orangish resin, like the surface of a pingpong table, and those teachers who had not yet plopped into the deckchairs were finishing their bag lunches, usually having a "friendly argument." And Stanley could be counted on to turn any statement into an outrageous *double-entendre*.

I would wander in after a morning's classes, to grab a Coke, sometimes to conduct a little business with a teacher or find out in a subtle way how the writer assigned to her classroom was faring. The older and more traditional teachers would be unwrapping their egg-salad sandwiches with great dignified unconcern. When I first began coming in, they addressed me as a visiting specialist. They asked me how to get good writing from children, or showed me a composition they were especially proud of. I would give some advice, but my ears were straining to catch the funny story someone was telling across the table about buying a corset: that was the conversation I wanted to join. I put in my two cents' worth. There was a flicker of shock on some faces, as if to say I had not yet received the right to participate. I kept joshing for all I was worth. Let them think me a clown—just so long as they abandoned that ceremonious tone with me!

They came to regard me eventually as harmless.

I had the giddy sense that I was watching the backstage personalities of my own grade-school teachers. I still felt like a child around them, but now I had the disguise of a man's body which allowed me to sit in their midst. It was as if I could relive my school days from a more privileged ringside seat.

I loved sitting next to the older women teachers who were the physical embodiment of the "battle axe" type that used to terrify me in my youth. It was a strange experience for me to lose my ancient fear of them, by seeing them at their most relaxed. Then their common sense and their survival humor would emerge. Who knows how many bureaucratic regimes and changes in educational ideology they had weathered?

I particularly liked watching Mrs. Jacoby, who had a solidity about her most ordinary actions. Even if the educational Establishment had gone completely haywire, she knew what she was entrusted to do with the children. She would talk about her Willie with the confidence that she could contain his hot temper. She knew he was a good boy. She would show me the dreadful snowflake poems she had elicited from her class with the same certainty. She had always believed in the value of Creative Writing. Of course it was nice to have a writer assigned to her class (McGonigle), and his methods were very different from hers so the children could have a chance to compare, and sometimes she felt the writing she was getting from them was even more sophisticated than the things he got, but he would find his way, and the children seemed to like him. So placid was she in her conviction of her own competence that later, when the class made some beautiful videotapes with McGonigle, she was only happy for them. A strict traditionalist was the way she described herself, but she had a courteous hospitality toward new ideas. Nothing could alter her very much; on the other hand, nothing new could threaten her either.

At bottom she enjoyed children and wanted them to have a good time, after their work was done. The one area of pleasure she always condoned was food. Every year she ran a Food Fiesta in which she and the children and parents prepared a banquet of dishes from the United Nations. Then she pulled the great teacher coup of the year. McDonald's had taken over the franchise of a local restaurant on Broadway. The kids of P.S. 90 were swept with McDonald's fever and watched the progress of the store renovation with unconcealed excitement. On Grand Opening Day, with flags and streamers festooning Broadway, Mrs. Jacoby took her class to McDonald's and bought each child a Big Mac. Out of her own pocket. She had the good sense to know what really mattered to them and the heart to follow it up.

One day the teachers needed a fourth for bridge and invited me to play; another time I was invited over to Leo Gelber's house after school for drinks. Each of these casual acceptances of me into the normal lives of the teachers made my heart swell.

One morning, Denise told me in passing that there would be a lunchtime birthday party for three staff members whose birthdays fell that month. Why didn't I stop by? Again, I was like the new kid on the block, excited to have been asked. The party was in Margaret Trabulski's room—"at Mother's," as she was affectionately called by her younger colleagues. The desks had been pulled together to form one long table, and each staff member took a seat in front of his paper plate and soda cup. Denise had baked a delicious rum cake. Everyone was joking about getting plastered from the cake.

An elderly teacher, who was one of the birthday girls, was asked to cut the cake first. "Age before beauty!" she announced. In honor of the occasion, she said, she had a funny story to tell. The gathering quieted down. I was utterly shocked when I heard this prim woman launch into a dirty story, one which moreover satirized the teaching profession—and I admit I liked her a great deal more for telling it.

"Once," she began, "a man visited his friend, who happened to be running a—let's call it a 'house of ill repute.' 'How is business?' the man asked his friend. 'Well I'll tell you, only the third floor is showing a profit.' 'How come?' 'Well on the first floor, I have ex-telephone operators, and when I put my ear to the door I hear them saying, 'Sorry, your time is up.' Then on the second floor there are the former models, and all they ever say is, 'Please, you're messing up my lipstick; you're messing up my hair!' But on the third floor where I've put the schoolteachers, I hear them lecturing their customers: 'You'll *do it and do it again* until you get it right!' "

I had come to my own conclusions about the teachers based on first impressions. But these impressions were being continually jolted as I witnessed some surprising turnabouts, or learned of a personal detail that made the teachers suddenly very real. The fact that one had just lost a brother, that another moonlit as a potter, were not the kind of things I could anticipate. Then another six months might pass before I found out one more intimate, revealing fact about that person.

A place of work is the ideal milieu to learn a person by infinitely slow degrees, since one is faced with too many people to want to probe them all simultaneously. The work day is filled with colleagues leaving little dust trails of hints about themselves, then clouding them over, or allowing the mechanical succession of tasks to erase the trails for them. At school I felt surrounded by the riddle of other teachers' personalities—a mystery which here I could tolerate quite comfortably, discovering a little more from time to time, like checking a row of pots on a stove heating to a slow boil for no one knows what purpose.

THE THREE SISTERS

Around this time the young teacher clique began eating lunch in the guidance office instead of going down to the teachers' lounge. I found myself doing the same. We were attracted to the new atmosphere in the guidance office, which had developed with the recent addition of two staff members, Toni and Milly. Along with Judy, the guidance counselor, they formed a triumvirate of three lively women in their early thirties, intelligent, professional, and psychologically quick. It was a triumvirate which incidentally mirrored the school's ethnic population: a white (Judy), a black (Toni), and a Puerto Rican (Milly). Not that they were unaware of this fact. Much of their humor consisted in good-natured racial putdowns. They were like three sisters who loved and teased each other. Sharing an office, they kept up a manic stream of wisecracks like the patter in a 1930s screwball comedy.

Toni was the teacher trainer, Milly was in charge of bilingual programs, and Judy handled guidance, but they switched off and shared jobs. All of them were at the beck and call of the principal, who fed them work, which meant that there were occasionally slack times. Teachers on their "prep" periods would go there for a smoke. Iris Mayer would waltz into Room 307 and fling off her shoulder bag and put her feet up on the desk. Denise Loftin would duck in on her way to the bank. Then someone would wonder wasn't it time to call out to the Eat Shop for lunch? Milly would volunteer to buy cottage cheese, bread, and bologna at the grocery store. Or Toni and Judy would plot to get up a lunch party at a fancy neighborhood bar.

What amazed me at lunchtime was the skill with which the teachers hit upon topics which were of interest to the group—neither too personal nor too abstract. They were masters at it. I remember conversations about unusual murders, union fringe benefits, buying a car, the intelligence of dolphins. Favorites were those which pointed to a common human foible, like not being able to get off a chair after one martini, or not being able to pass up a piece of chocolate cake while being on a diet. These alluded to the tip of the person's anxieties without exposing the dark stuff.

In this setting Margaret Trabulski was a diamond. A large, affable woman in her early fifties, with teen-age children and a liking for younger people, she had a genius for raising issues which pretended to be controversial but which actually offended no one. She insisted on knowing what the group felt about such and such— euthanasia, say—but with so good-tempered a manner that the others treated it as a joke.

I liked Margaret Trabulski as well as anyone. How could you not? Every time I met her in the halls she had a big grin and a "How goes it, Phil?" Then she would nod and smile, no matter what I said. Her eyes shone alertly and her head looked about like an eagle's, but the smile was not always completely . . . à propos. I suspected she was a little hard of hearing, though I was never able to confirm it.

* * *

"How are you doing, Toni?"

"Worse than evuh." That was the way Toni would start, two months into the job. She was tired; she didn't want to be here; she wanted to go home to bed. Then she would remember something nice that had happened to her. Oh yeah, an actor friend of hers had given her two tickets to the preview of *Uncle Vanya*. "That was nice," she would say slowly, and her face began to wake up. Though she was black, her accent had traces of Yiddish and Croton-on-Hudson. She wore an Afro, theatrical blue eyeshadow and false eyelashes, and five or six bracelets on her wrists, which she moved about with limp, campy gestures. It was as if she were daring you to call her affected. But she wasn't in the least affected: she had simply accepted costume as the only way to hold together the disjointed sides of her. Large-bodied and timid, brash and fragile, a black woman who got along easily with whites, she seemed to straddle too many worlds for her own comfort. And she landed in the public school factory like so many other gifted, divided people, because she needed to earn a living.

I had asked too many questions. Suddenly, from nowhere she would say:

"Leave me alone. I'm going out of my mind with these reading scores!" (This to her friend Judy.)

"*You're* going out of your mind!" Judy said. "I've been trying to read this sentence for the last half-hour and I can't manage to focus."

"Well that's different. You're just—ill."

And back to the insults. It was their favorite game: who was crazier, who was more neurotic.

A competitive lethargy had stolen into their bodies, like adolescents going through physical change who spend hours leaning against a car; only here the slowing-down agent was not chemical but institutional. I thought they had grown disaffected because so little of their work originated from themselves. They were carrying out someone else's priorities, not their own, and they resented every second they gave to it. The less work they had to do, the more harassed they seemed. At the same time, they seemed unable to rope off an area of work that made sense to themselves, and that might have protected them from the make-work. As long as they did not initiate their own projects, the principal gave them clerical tasks or used them as pinch hitters during prep periods.

Once I saw Toni take over the direction of the chorus for graduation. She stood in front of the children, and raised her arms, and the most beautiful language of hands I have ever watched came out of her. You could literally see the notes being written in the air. As she conducted the kids, her hips, her skirt, her bracelets, everything swayed to the rhythm. The senior class had no choice but to sing beautifully.

Wasn't it possible for more of this vivacity to emerge in her work? The three sisters were missing a great opportunity, it seemed to me. As marginal, auxiliary staff, with sketchily defined responsibilities, they could potentially do anything they liked with groups of children or staff members.

I had thought that their discontent arose from their being incompletely integrated into the heart of the school—the classroom—where the real action was taking place. Yet it was the same with many of the classroom teachers. Complaining had become a way of life. "I'm getting out of here. I can't stand it any more. This place is falling to pieces." When it was learned that one of the kindergarten teachers had been admitted to medical school, the teachers swarmed around her like convicts wishing an envious farewell to one of their own. "Gee, you must be so happy. You're leaving. I bet you never want to see the inside of this place again."

This attitude struck me as a bit melodramatic. After all, P.S. 90 was not a prison. It was a fairly stimulating, free-wheeling school where most teachers could teach pretty much the way they wanted. Certainly it had its failings and its administrative constrictions, but these were *nothing* compared to some of the Gothic schools I had seen in my travels. I knew several teachers elsewhere who would have given a lot to be placed in P.S. 90.

All this, I think, was understood by the teachers; but they could not stop complaining. The griping had outstripped the objective conditions which may have originally given birth to it and had begun to live a life of its own. It was a plague—people would get together and infect each other. The poison seemed to me a protective defeatism which excused them from any failures beforehand. It was a way of holding each other down, as in high school, where it is considered bad taste to study for tests, so that any studying must be done on the sly.

At one extreme were a handful of teachers who walked about in a fog. Like sleepwalkers, their lives were elsewhere. At the other end stood a half-dozen teachers who were among the best I can ever hope to encounter: totally engaged individuals, lively, resourceful, productive. Yet even they considered it bad taste to like their job or admit they had ambitions relating to it.

I began to suspect that my more optimistic attitude left a distance between many adults in the school and me, however cordially we accepted each other. Their prevailing vision of work was as something self-demeaning, to escape from. However much I would sympathize, or remember jobs in which I had felt exactly the same, it was finally a vision which I could not accept. I was frankly able to satisfy my need for activity and personal expression through the opportunity of this job. P.S. 90 was the proper arena for my talents. I could not have imagined any situation more desirable to hold at this time in my life; they could have easily imagined another one.

* * *

I wanted to believe that the reason for my pleasure in work and their discontent with it was a matter of personalities. The truth is that there were certain advantages in my job over the average teacher's that I kept forgetting. I could come and go according to my own schedule, without punching a time clock. I did not have to stay in the school full time. I could work with smaller groups of students and was absolved from the debilitating responsibility of keeping track of thirty children always. Nor did I have legal and medical responsibility for them. I was even allowed greater leeway in terms of keeping discipline. I was not under the thumb of an administrative bureaucracy. I did not have to toe the line to receive salary increments or tenure. (On the other hand, many teachers would have been horrified with the economic insecurities of my situation. Writers earned a salary of $4,000 to $8,000, tops, a year. We looked forward to no seniority, no social security, no paid vacations, no fringe benefits, and the constant threat of unemployment if the next grant didn't come through.)

On balance, however, we were freer. I did not have to deliver higher reading and arithmetic scores, or fill out attendance sheets, or put up with organizational interruptions. Most important, I had an attractive subject to teach. Even if it was as vague as creative expression, it was something I believed in, and that the kids liked as well. I had a craft, a specialty, to impart. And I had received ego-satisfaction outside of the school through publications of my own work. My writing was always something I could fall back on, an alternate life, which many of the teachers didn't have.

All things considered, it is a wonder that the teachers did not hate us. That they continually gave the Writing Team help and friendship is a tribute to their durable sense of fairness. Only once did I hear one of the three sisters make the impatient outburst I had been waiting for all along:

"I'm sick of seeing all these *disgustingly creative people* around here!"

At first I tried to overlook my special situation. I needed to believe that what I was doing could be done by any classroom teacher. "But of course we don't have your freedom . . . !" That voice seemed to cheat me of all my achievements. I wanted to be considered like every other staff member—except, perhaps, a harder worker. The more I saw what advantages I had, the more I struggled to eradicate them. I would come in five days a week, early; I would prove to the teachers that I could work as long hours as they did; I would help the kids with their fractions; I would watch a teacher's class when she went out for a smoke. . . . No use! All these attempts to assume the normal teacher's responsibilities simply got translated into more freedom for myself, since I had voluntarily accepted them.

It was foolish for me to think I could erase the distinctions between their situation and mine. I had pushed that as far as it would go. Better to respect each other's differences and to realize we performed separate functions.

Chapter 8
The Principal

They say that the principal sets the tone for the school. Maybe that was why P.S. 90 had such a dramatic, restless, progressive atmosphere, with a special knack for discontent.

Edouardo Jimenez had come up the hard way. He had been an idealistic classroom teacher who had taken his ghetto kids on trips around the city, even on Saturdays. He had stood with the community against the teachers' union in the complicated 1968 New York City school strike, had been roughed up by police. He had fought the good fight so many times that when he was suddenly promoted to Community Principal in the wake of the city's decentralization troubles, he still carried himself with the attitude of an underdog, a boxer who is willing to take and give punishment in a losing cause.

It must not have taken long for his satisfaction in having the new post to give way to discontent. He had that kind of pressing idealism which is admirable from a historical distance but hard to live with day by day. When teacher morale was going smoothly, he brooded about the "dead weight"; when some of the staff dead weight was gone, he brooded about racial prejudice; when the ethnic minorities were not being slighted, he brooded about reading scores; when the reading scores were riding high, he was upset about the directives of the district office. Discontent was his gasoline. It kept him from sinking into the complacency he so much dreaded, but it also kept him from feeling pleasure when something good happened.

Jimenez was brilliant at snaring extra programs and side benefits for the school. In addition to the Writing Team, he had visiting consultants in bilingual education, music, environmental studies; he made deals with local museums and universities. He was astoundingly open to the possibilities and rich resources of big city life. Nor have I ever come across a principal so enlightened about the value of the arts in education. He was Teachers & Writers' strongest defender and best friend.

On the other hand, Jimenez's importation of outside programs and personnel to supplement the curriculum was symptomatic of his lack of faith in his classroom teachers' ability to handle the job. He could be very hard on his staff. In this sense, his external relations, or should we say his foreign policies, were often stronger than his domestic relations.

Occasionally I would see him pacing around the first floor as if he had been locked out of his office: bedraggled, scowling, like a refugee in his own school. One day around Christmas time, when the whole school was celebrating, I went up to him and invited him to a staff party on the third floor. He seemed so alone, like an outcast. Jimenez reacted as if I had disturbed him from an intense revery.

"No. Thanks. Maybe later," he said.

It was always incongruous to see him at a festive gathering. He did not seem to know how to go about relaxing. His brooding eyes would take in the room, the guests, and then he would corner anyone who would listen. Some of his staff took the opportunity to snub him socially at annual parties. This tactic seemed cruel to me; but I realized later that those who felt they had suffered at his hands could not easily turn around and make pleasantries.

There were days when it was definitely unwise to run into him. Then the word would go out: keep away from the Main Office. Even we of Teachers & Writers, whom he was more tolerant of than anybody, were not immune from his moods. At such times he could not resist the itch to intimidate.

He would come across me in a stairwell. "What have you been doing for the Brotherhood Essay Contest?"

"What Brotherhood Essay Contest?"

"You don't know?" he glared. "The NAACP is sponsoring a contest for the best essay on brotherhood and every class is expected to participate! If Teachers & Writers can't keep apprised of this sort of thing, all I can say is, I'm dismayed. Maybe you're spending too much time with the kids and not enough time with the teachers. Maybe we have to look into this question; maybe we need to take a good hard look and evaluate your relation to staff. You may be boxing yourself into a corner where no one's communicating with you. . . ."

"I didn't know because I wasn't here on Friday. Now I know," I said tamely.

I would walk away muttering to myself that anyway I didn't believe in Brotherhood compositions and all that positive brainwashing rot. It was a misuse of Teachers & Writers to put us on such a job. We needed to maintain our autonomy—and besides, he wasn't even my boss. Next time I would tell him that to his face.

Yet, the next time he was either friendly or there were too many people around. I decided to be ready for him if he ever yelled at me again.

When he did attack, it always caught me off guard. I was too fascinated watching him to think of good responses. His eyes would shoot off acrimonious sparks; he was not to be tampered with. You don't stick your fingers into an electric fan.

It was easier for me to listen silently and then go ahead and do what I had planned to.

On the few occasions when I defended myself solidly, he took it very well. In fact, he changed his whole tone. I had the impression that people who responded weakly or weepily brought out the worst in him, while a strong, defiant response made him relieved.

A complex man; when all is said and done, I was (and am) very fond of him. I admired his energy and his larger-than-life sense of destiny. He seemed to see himself as a lonely Castro battling the corrupt, sluggish forces of reaction. And on some strange level, I accepted his self-definition and thought of myself as his loyal lieutenant.

I admired his integrity and his impatience for social justice even as I wished I could tell him that it was necessary first to love people as they were before you could change them.

At three-thirty, after a very long day, we would be standing alongside each other on the front steps of the school and he would stare out weary-eyed, like a captain on the deck of his ship, in Conradian isolation. He had a largeness of build and a largeness of purpose that seemed to set him further apart from the people passing in the street. At such times I liked to imagine that I enjoyed a special relation with him; that I was rather like him; that we were two of a kind.

* * *

I knock on the principal's door. Jimenez gestures that it's all right for me to come in; they're having a meeting. "Sit down. It's our usual crisis situation. Maybe after you hear what's happening you won't want to work at this school." I take a chair to his left, facing all five of the teachers. I don't exactly feel good about being on the boss's side of the desk, but since I'm not strictly a teacher either (and enjoy basking in Jimenez's power), I stay there. The five teachers include two young Spanish men who were hired to teach bilingual classrooms, one young black woman, and two young white teachers who have been trained in open-classroom methods. They are five of the original eight young teachers hired by Jimenez, who are now in danger of losing their jobs. Because of the citywide excess of licensed teachers, the union and the Central Board are trying to force P.S. 90 to get rid of these eight and hire teachers from elsewhere with more seniority: a procedure called "bumping." But Jimenez and the PTA want to hold on to the eight because they are young, relate well to the kids, and fit better into the educational atmosphere of P.S. 90, which is experimental, open corridor, bilingual. It is doubtful that the teachers with seniority whom the city wants to foist on the school would be as congenial to the P.S. 90 style.

At stake also is the right of a principal to hire his own staff. But the immediate crisis is saving the eight young teachers from getting "bumped"; this is why Jimenez has called the meeting. What a performance he gives! He does literally all the talking. I am looking into their eyes all the time Jimenez is speaking to them. I can't tell whether behind their impassive expressions they resent the one-way direction of communication, or whether they accept it as the normal terms of a briefing. They are there to learn what plan of action is open to them; he knows all the legalities, the political ins and outs, they know nothing. He goes over the territory once in broad terms. Their best hope is a legal suit: at least they can stall the Board; maybe they can get an injunction. But they will need more than one plaintiff, because one plaintiff alone will lose heart. He'll decide it's too much of a sacrifice or move to another city, but if there are a few plaintiffs, they can give each other mutual support. And, if they win, they will have struck a blow for teachers all over the city. That's the way it always is, he says; a few stick out their necks and everyone benefits. But think it over . . . decide carefully if it's something you personally feel you want to do . . . if it's worth the battle for you. On the other hand, you'll be protecting your jobs so you have nothing to lose and everything to gain. Think about it. (Looks from face to face.)

No one seems to be backing out.

He starts to explain that he went all through this last year on the supervisory level. He and a black principal were filing a suit together and one man would get discouraged and the other would call him up and give him a boost. "Again," Jimenez says, "our greatest weapon is the court ruling on the underrepresentation of minority teachers. No one can replace you (he points to the Puerto Rican men) or you (to the black woman) or any of you for that matter," he says for the white teachers' benefit, "because you two are trained in open classroom procedures and we need you here. P.S. 90 will just have to take the vanguard position once again in this fight—as we did with supporting the Vietnam Moratorium last year. . . ."

Jimenez goes over the same points again and again but there is no way of cutting it short because each time he adds one more fact, and people are so hungry for facts that they have no choice. Nevertheless, his voice begins to have an attritional effect; teachers start slumping in their chairs, looking at the door. He is careful not to encourage too much hope. I can't escape the suspicion that he loves these situations where his back is to the wall—where he is telling everyone the grim realities of all the forces pitted against them. His particular form of strength flourishes in the nicotine weariness of late afternoon. He addresses the teachers from behind dark sunglasses—which I find astonishing. If he is taking the trouble to frame a defense campaign for them, why the impersonality of not letting them look in his eyes? But this is the paradox of Jimenez: always fighting for the good while his personal interaction style is alienating the people who should be his allies.

At the end of the briefing he asks, "Any questions?" There are none. He sets up another meeting for them with a lawyer. Then he says, by way of good-by, *"Muchissimos gracias."* A nice human touch . . .

Gomez and Nestor, the two bilingual teachers, linger behind, along with me. Jimenez says to them: "I made the point before one of you came that the Board has no intention of giving the bilingual qualifying exam this year. So you're particularly vulnerable. They can hire someone who knows three words of Spanish if they want to."

"Yeah," Gomez says in a bitter voice. "The bilingual teachers they want are named Rosenberg and Ginzberg."

"Careful," says Jimenez. (I stare at some papers on the desk, too embarrassed to meet Gomez's eyes. And to think I had thought he was so nice on the basis of his Zapata looks!)

"Don't say anything stupid you'll regret later," Jimenez continues. "We need all the allies we can get. I don't care if they're Italian, Jewish, Polish, or Greek. I'll take support in this fight even from people who are my enemies on other issues. So be very, very careful what you say." He goes on to repeat this in about five different ways, backtracking and covering over until Gomez leaves. Jimenez expresses pragmatism a little too much for my taste, rather than attacking the latent anti-Semitism; but I am amazed at the rapidity with which he did confront it, whereas I hadn't managed to say a word!

Afterward we are alone. Jimenez turns to me and says: "Don't you think I was right about that remark by Gomez?"

"You were 100 per cent right," I answer. "Look—I happen to be Jewish. I was disturbed by what he said. And I'm supposed to be on his side."

Chapter 9
The Writing Team

Around this time I became conscious of another potential problem the Writing Team faced. The team was overidentified, in the minds of the school staff, with me. Secretaries would address organizational details to me, which was only natural. But it went further than that: administrators, parents, and teachers seemed to have trouble remembering the names of the other writers, so that we were often referred to as "Phil Lopate and his crew." I am sure I did my share in promoting that imbalance. I have a tendency to grab the limelight and accept credit for work which is only partly mine, without remembering to mention the names of coworkers.

Nevertheless, my own self-aggrandizement would not alone have led people to equate me with the project. I was also more visible than the others, since I went to PTA and staff meetings more often, socialized with the teachers, and knew everybody's business. I had started attending the lunchtime staff meetings because I wanted the teachers to form a different impression of us than creative butterflies who, wrapped in poetical mist, flitted into their classrooms, sprinkled excitement, and then left them to pick up the pieces. I wanted the teachers to see that we were not merely renegade activists of the Imagination. We shared their concern for the kids as whole human beings. We wanted the school to run effectively and sanely as well, because we had a stake in it too.

Whatever shock waves of politics were running through the school (district superintendent—federal requirements—ethnic—reading scores—Union—vandalism—parent factions) would eventually affect the writers and the job we were doing. The writers had to look beyond the narrow problems of teaching literature. Only when they understood the school as a *totality,* as a living organism going through continuous stress and change, would they be able to make a powerful impact on the institution. But this awareness implied more work. Or, more precisely, a vast extension outward of the definition of their work, to include not only teaching writing lessons but immersing oneself in the environment.

What I was asking for was essentially a commitment and dedication to public-school life. Sue Willis and Karen understood. Irene did, too, though she was reluctant to become as involved. Tom and Charles were likable but elusive.

Charles had other things on his mind. He was a married man with a family. He was picking up extra money any way it came. Charles had to fight to find time to write. I could hardly expect him to give up his evenings to attend a PTA meeting.

The time commitment was easier for me to make because of my personal circumstances. Maybe it would be better if I spelled these out. I was not a family man; I lived alone. I had been married for six years, and divorced, and was going through a period of random dating. To be blunt, my relationships with women were a mess. One affair after another would start up, promisingly enough, only to dissolve in my hands from the excessive demands I placed on it, in one sense, and from not taking it seriously at all, in another, followed by a period of stubborn isolation during which I "threw myself into my work." The somewhat manic energies I brought to the job may have been connected to my dissatisfaction in the other realm and my need to obliterate that pain from my thoughts.[1] Not only work calmed me: even the word "Work" began to have a mystical attraction for me, so that I would tramp through the streets thinking to myself, "Work! *Arbeit!* The Work!" until I felt more at peace. And when I was not teaching I was writing—poems, stories, articles. It was a fertile time for me, the one profession stimulating ideas for the other; work progressed everywhere, so long as I did not feel too troubled at the thought of not being in love.

It interests me that in some other written accounts of teaching experiences, the involvement with the kids seems to coincide with the author's decision to marry and raise a family. Herbert Kohl's *36 Children* and George Dennison's *The Lives of Children* both end with

[1] Or again, it might have had nothing to do with it. Someday the book will be written which plots the two energy curves of work and love, and we will be able to see what the correspondences are. A day-and-night diary . . .

their heroes getting married. James Herndon was already married when he went through the experiences in *The Way It Spozed to Be*. With these writers, their commitment to *communitas* naturally leads to the mature task of building a family, of making a harmony between work and personal life. I can't say the same for myself. My personal life was anything but harmonious. All those sober, responsible, root-taking attitudes had been transferred over to my job, which in effect I had married.

I could hardly expect everyone to feel the same degree of work dedication that I did; I was at a unique juncture in my life history and could give everything to the job. Yet the time had come in the team's own evolution to decentralize some of my authority. But I was still unwilling to give up responsibility to someone who was not as truly committed to the work. This was the dilemma: I sensed that if I did not loosen my hold, the members would never assume greater responsibility and they would drift away like the first group. They would rightfully resent being kept in a subordinate, apprentice position. Every final decision at that time was made by me, from the room schedule to the type face for publications. Clearly it would be healthier for us to spread the authority around more. But how could I bring myself to give up any of my authority when I was not yet sure of their competence and interest, when I didn't trust them enough? In the meantime I stalled. We talked about sharing the power. Oddly, none of the writers seemed as impatient to solve this question as I was. They had gotten used to a top-down structure. I, on the other hand, had strong egalitarian leanings and could not reconcile my one-man governing of the group with my politics.

When it came down to a choice, I was a protector of the project before I was a democrat. It struck me that the relinquishing of responsibility to those who were not prepared for it, or had no wish to take it on, would be doing violence to the project. Whether this was the familiar casuistry of rulers, or the most sensible course open to us, we put aside talking about finding a new governing structure for the group.

A better balance emerged gradually. It was not anything I could have engineered with sudden generosity, whether I'd wanted to or not. In time, some of the writers saw what tasks needed to be done and asked if they could help me with them. I was surprised and touched. Their request for more responsibility had come as an offer of help, when I had been expecting a *coup*. I had not anticipated the changeover to occur in this way, and I gratefully let them do some of the work that had been piling up on me. From this start we began learning how to handle projects together and how to ease each other's work load. We began to function, in small ways at first but gradually more confidently, as a team of equals.

* * *

I was beginning to think that all was for the best, when I received my second shock. This time Irene told me she was quitting. She had received several professional offers to work with theatrical troupes—in Paris, in Cincinnati—and she had to accept them for the sake of her career.

That was understandable, I said. She could go on a leave of absence.

Irene looked downcast.

Now she admitted that she did not feel comfortable doing the work with the children. "I feel—like a pretender," she said. "Every time I go in, the night before my stomach is a nervous wreck. And when I get off the subway to go to the school, I'm afraid. I don't know why. But that last block I walk to school, I'm shaking all over."

Her terror was visible as she spoke. Nevertheless I tried to talk her out of it. She was doing such a good job. . . . I needed her. . . . I couldn't do it alone. . . . She could take as long a leave of absence as she wanted; she could have any schedule she wanted; she could name her own terms.

"That's very sweet of you," she said. "Only it would be fooling us. I'm just not cut out for this kind of work. The children take too much out of me. I have nothing left for my plays. Besides, I'm accustomed to a certain level . . . of success, and with children it's something entirely new for me to learn. I have to start like an amateur, and I'm too old to start like an amateur." Irene smiled her charming smile.

This time I did not feel like ranting about lack of commitment or dilettantism; I was too fond of Irene for that. She was my favorite. No, she had to go her own way. It was becoming clear to me that this work in the public schools was not easy or suitable for everyone.

We made no attempt to find a substitute this time. The team

would stay as it was. The group had absorbed its second casualty; it was still rolling, still finding interesting solutions to the problems of generating creativity. In a paradoxical way, I felt closer to the team than ever before, now that we had survived the one loss I thought would be irreparable.

Chapter 10
Videotape Diary

Over the Christmas vacation, the Teachers & Writers team had met with Media Equipment Resource Center (MERC), which agreed to lend us a videotape setup—one ½″ Sony portapak, one TV monitor, a videotape camera, a tripod—for the rest of the school year. As our part of the arrangement we would hire a MERC student technician who would supervise the use of the equipment and teach videotape to the kids. The equipment would be available for use by the writers of the P.S. 90 team, the kids, and interested teachers.

We were still in the dark as to what we would do with the equipment, but we knew we wanted to experiment with videotape, to see what effect it would have on the classrooms, whether it would generate more or different kinds of creative writing, whether it could reach kids who didn't like to write. I myself wanted to learn videotape for selfish reasons: pleasure and curiosity. The writers received some basic instruction from Jaime Caro, MERC's very helpful director, and we were ready, more or less.

Videotape proved to be vastly more engrossing and popular than I had anticipated, and I spent the rest of the year doing nothing else with Denise Loftin's class. My whole mode of operating in the classroom and my relations with the kids changed after the introduction of the machinery, which pushed me into working with smaller groups on independent, longer-range projects. I was grateful to get out of that rut of delivering a different, unconnected writing lesson every week. It isn't that I abandoned creative writing, rather that I became interested in how to take the written word one step further—from script to another medium—and by doing so, convince the kids of the immediacy and practical application of their written ideas.

The diaries I kept at the time provide a hasty but physically accurate account of the sheer surge of adrenalin which the videotape drew out of everyone.

JANUARY 6

First day back after vacation for me. I wanted to rehearse a play for the coming of the videotape next week. Where to begin? The kids made everything easy. Their class had been studying conflict situations in social studies. Britt and Ricky said they had a great idea for a video play, all about how a fight starts. This chimed in well with Adiel's schoolyard play of several weeks ago, which I'd been hoping we could expand on. "OK this morning I'll work with one group—Adiel, Britt, Ricky, Roberto, Francisco, Juan and some girls. . . ." "Ooo—ooo!"—"Karen and Virginia. And this afternoon we'll rehearse the play that Maria, Marissa, etc., wrote." Gregory and Jamie: "Hey, why can't we be in it?" I'm ready to apologize but Denise Loftin says forcefully: "I told you to finish writing your play, didn't I?" The right tack—lets me off the hook. "Yes, you guys write a play and we'll videotape it."

March into the Writing Room. Britt takes over and starts spinning out a plot, telling everyone what they're going to be. Even Karen the Terrible falls into line. Unfortunately, Adiel's script hasn't a chance in the whirlwind of Britt's extemporizing. Adiel appears to take it phlegmatically, with characteristic resignation. I could force them to adhere to Adiel's schoolyard plot but I'm also curious to see what Britt will pull out of the hat. Which becomes known as:

*The Gangsters and the Girls—*Two girls are walking along discussing how their mothers never let them have any fun. Britt strolls up and tries to make a pass at one of them (Karen). She shakes him off and the girls enter a bar. "Johnny Walker Red," they say. The bartender, Ricky, won't serve them because they're underage. Britt, who has followed them in, gallantly insists that they be given the drinks. Ricky refuses, says he'll lose his job. Britt punches Ricky, and Roberto and Francisco jump in on Britt's side and somehow Ricky and Adiel chase away the three men, but not before Britt has threatened to come back and kill them. Meanwhile the girls are

thrilled at men fighting over them and decide to throw a party for
Britt, Roberto, and Francisco. Britt and his gang decide to rob an
old man to buy tuxedos for the party. . . .

At this point I had the feeling that the improv was disturbing
another writer, who was working with her group at the other end
of the Writing Room. So we moved down to the auditorium, which
was packed with little first-graders eating lunch. All of them screaming. I took my group into the makeup room behind stage. The
makeup room had its own bathroom and the kids rushed to use it.
The toilet kept flushing by itself, but I paid it no mind.

We arranged a few chairs to simulate a living room, and everyone started improvising the teen-age party scene. This was obviously
a scene they wanted to act; yet, compared to the high-octane action
of the first part, nothing was happening! Stilted small talk, a little
embarrassed dancing to imaginary music. It suddenly occurred to me
that the kids might not actually know how these parties went, though
the need to play out this courtship game which was on their minds
was very strong. Hence the shyness. Roberto and Adiel were getting
restless in the background of Britt's and Karen's flirtation, but like
true partygoers, they remained watchful, pretending to eat potato
chips. Just as I was casting about for some way to make the scene
more dramatic ("A fire?" suggested Roberto), the water from the
toilet lapped under the bathroom door and flooded the makeup room!
At first the kids wanted to go on improvising—all except Virginia,
who said plaintively, "I don't like water." "Don't pay it any attention," Britt said. "Now wait a second." I finally found my voice. "This
is serious. Go and find the custodian, Francisco; tell him what happened." Adiel went too, bringing back the martyred janitor Dominick
who sees his life as a losing battle against the forces of dirt. I took
one look at Dominick's face and hustled the kids onto the stage.

Leo Gelber, the teacher, was on the stage apron entertaining
the kindergarten kids with some weird pantomime. Suddenly the curtains were pulled behind him and we had sealed off a rehearsal area.
At this point the drama took a turn into violence and pathos. Britt
was shot by the bartender on his way home from the party. His
friends gathered around him. He asked for his girl, as he lay on the
ground. "I can't die," he whispered to me. "I'm the hero."

"No you die," I told him.

I wanted a death scene.

"How does it feel to be dying?" I asked. Britt's eyes fluttered upward, revealing the whites. Leo Gelber came backstage to see what was happening. Instinctively I held him back from the action, as if to say, "Don't interrupt their play." But he said, "I want to play too; don't push me away."

"OK, you be the doctor." Perfect for Gelber with his goatee. He laid his ear on Britt's chest. "I don't think he has much chance."

"What are his odds, Doctor?"

"Ninety-nine out of a hundred he won't last." Karen began wailing. So Britt died. Karen died soon after of a broken heart, Francisco and Roberto died avenging Britt, and Ricky was arrested. They wanted to keep it going but it was already after the lunch bell and I was meeting a writer for lunch.

JANUARY 12

This was our first day with the actual videotape. We got there at nine-thirty and the kids were so excited trying the camera that we stayed with them till 3. J.T. Takagi, the MERC technician who will be working with us, did a beautiful job of putting the video tools into the kids' hands right away, instructing without intruding too much. J.T. is seventeen years old, Japanese, a freshman at Antioch College who is spending this term at a work-site; next term she'll go back to Antioch. She's pretty calm and the kids liked her. I began relying on her right away. We taped *The Gangsters and the Girls* first thing in the Writing Room. Only it is no longer called *The Gangsters and the Girls:* Karen appointed herself the announcer and renamed it *Karen's Show!*

The first two takes didn't register when the kids forgot to push the camera button. Just as well, because we needed to rehearse. The scenes took place in different corners of the room, and when it was finally taped the action rolled on in one continuous camera shot with the cameraman scurrying to keep up with the actors who shifted from corner to corner. Both the kids on camera and the actors tended to want the show to keep going at all costs, which gave the tape a sprawling ship-tossed look. Sound was also a problem. Partly because the sound man was wiggling the mike a lot, partly because the room is large and hollow. We may have to shoot against corners more instead of placing the camera in the middle of the room and panning across empty space.

Juan was adorable in the play. Despite his not knowing much English, he delivered his few lines with sober dignity. "He is dead," he says when Britt gets shot. At the end of the tape everyone came forward to take bows in front of the camera; Britt, emceeing, said, "Here's Juan, a man who always helps everybody out."

We took the machinery back to Denise's room and the class gathered around for the replay. They had been working with incredible concentration for an impressive stretch of time; the teaching assistant said she wished Karen would devote that kind of energy to math. Everyone was very pleased with the tape. Yet they had a curious reaction of blaming the cameraman for all the missed action and rough edges, when actually it was the setup that was to blame—the fact that it was a filmed *play,* not a televisually conceived story. It may take them a while before they understand the need to break the action into shorter, more selective camera setups.

All during the day, different kids came over and thanked me and J.T. for bringing them the equipment. They're not like other kids that age, so spoiled that they take those benefits for granted. They seem so touched when someone goes out and does something for them. Maybe that's why I love working with Denise's kids so.

JANUARY 14

We decided to split the remainder of the class into two groups. I would take Maria, Marissa, and the other girls who were doing a beach-blanket play and rehearse them once without the videotape. J.T. would take a group of kids who fitted into none of the main cliques—kids who are very often left out of things, the quiet ones.

The girls in my group had written a charming script about romance and jealousy at the beach, *The Double Daters.* Not only was the script a pleasant surprise, but also the fact that the girls had gotten together all week and had managed to stop arguing long enough to write the play and type it themselves.

Once we were in rehearsal, certain tensions developed. Stephanie (black) thought Christine and Maria (white) were having everything go their way. Maria said: "You weren't even supposed to be in it!" Somehow the last scene in the car had been written in such a way that only the Julie-Christine-Maria-Marissa clique were given parts. I made a fast suggestion to stave off tantrums: let Stephanie, who played a waitress, ask the four if they could give her and her friend a lift home. Maria was resistant. Stephanie said: "What's the matter? You think we're not good enough to ride in your snooty car?"

Both sides were eventually placated and rehearsals went on, with the girls rolling around the pink rug and hugging each other to get into the mood. They were insistent on having no boys—they will play all the boys' parts themselves. The girl-girls will wear dresses and the boy-girls, dungarees. A wedding scene is planned for the end.

My belly was still burning from a confrontation I'd had with two sixth-grade boys who came in and started wrecking the Writing Room. After asking them politely three times to leave, I had to throw them out bodily and they shook their fists. "We're gonna get you. I'm telling my brother." "Yeah, we'll see about that," I said.

J.T. told me her group had gone well. Saul, Soypathe, Irilia, Wendy, David, and Robin, usually *very* shy, had worked out a story with a detective and a murder which they would videotape next week. J.T. was proud and had obviously enjoyed working alone with her private group of kids. She senses the danger of being treated as a kind of technician-machine for everyone else's projects, when she has creative ideas of her own she would like to try out.

JANUARY 19

What a devastating day! And I thought it would be so easy. All we had to do was shoot the two plays we'd rehearsed last week. The introduction of the videotape equipment again created a great stir. J.T. took the group she had been working with last week into the yard to tape. I told Maria's group to make titles for the beach play, while waiting for J.T. to get back. Roberto and Ricky wanted to do a war movie, so I worked with them on a script—Gene and David joined in, adding a few comic touches to the script—but Ricky was hurt. "We wanted this to be serious." A serious play about how we defeated the Krauts in World War II. The idea was so hopelessly dull that I let Christine take me away to settle a dispute about some costumes.

As for myself, I had a case of media overstimulation—too excited and jittery to concentrate on anything. I felt like a ringmaster tossing lions into separate rings. I had divided the work so totally that, like the classic administrator, I had nothing to do myself and felt ill at ease.

Maria's group wouldn't stop quarreling and yelling. I hustled them into the Writing Room to get ready. We were all succumbing to the mad pressure of accommodating too many groups of kids, too many productions in one day, simply because we didn't have the will to say No.

"How did it go?" I asked J.T. when she returned.

"You can't believe how crazy it was down there. These same kids who were so well-behaved in the classroom, they went haywire when we got outside. Everything distracted them. Fire engines, some punks—the tape itself looks fine. It came out really good."

"Good." On to the beach play. They rehearsed their lines; Stephanie was ultra sullen. When it came time for her to say "Shame on you, Hon," she merely said "Shame on you" and the other kids turned on her, yelling "Hon!" We videotaped anyway and the acting was very stiff. The kids were rather dismayed with the results, though they couldn't put their finger on what was wrong.

The camera had recorded everything—our embarrassed pauses, our whispered stage cues. ("You're supposed to go over there!") We felt ridiculed by it. It had shown us exactly as we were—no, not exactly, but in a puny cardboard facsimile, like a diorama which makes every bush look silly. It may be significant that *The Double Daters,* which started out with a much tighter, better-written script than *The Gangsters and the Girls* or the little people's *Murder Story,* was the least alive of the three videotapes. Its own precision of dialogue inhibited the sort of casual, offhanded freshness that videotape celebrates.

We watched the tape of J.T.'s group at lunch with several teachers. I had not seen the *Murder* tape yet and it turned out to be unintentionally hilarious. Everything takes place within the same enclosed *play space,* very, very much like the space of little children's make-believe in their backyard. People on the phone who are supposed to be separated by miles are sitting next to each other. "Indoor" scenes take place outdoors. At one point the detective asks "Where's the body?" and the camera pans downward no more than a foot away to pick up Wendy lying placidly dead on the ground. It's so funny and unexpected to see her there, right by their feet.

While Gwen is pretending to stab Soypathe, Margaret Trabulski remarked to me, "I see you agree with the Commission's Report that says TV violence doesn't beget violence. It's an arguable point." I didn't know what to answer. Did she want me to tell children to stop pointing their fingers as guns?

We took the equipment back to MERC at three. I was exhausted. I'm still trying to process the strange experience of seeing the kids' plays on tape: how the rough edges, the imprecision and invasion of extraneous sounds and offstage details ate away at the dramatic verisimilitude of the fantasies being portrayed. I'm learning the hard way about the peculiarities of videotape. I had thought of it as a kind of 16mm or Super 8 with instant playback. How wrong I was! I remember seeing some Super-8 films Miguel Ortiz's sixth-graders had made. They had the fresh naive flavor of early silents —a closeup of the barking dog, the titles spelled out in pebbles on the ground. In contrast, videotape seems a shockingly sophisticated medium which delivers more information than its users intended or bargained for. In the Super-8 films we laughed more with the kids, as creators; in the *Murder* videotape we laugh more *at* them.

J.T. and I got into a rather defensive argument/discussion with Scott Morris, a young video expert and MERC's second-in-command, who said the problem we were running into was that videotape isn't suited for dramatic fiction, that it's used best in capturing the flow of "documentary reality." Scott also said the videotape *experience* at its core is not especially in being taped and seeing yourself on tape, but in operating the camera. That is, videotape is a perfect extension of the way you see and move, a record of each person's particular style of vision. To prove his point he showed us some documentary footage of an antiwar demonstration his workshop members had taken, which looked to me like every other documentary of a demonstration.

MERC director Jaime Caro disagreed both with Scott and us. He thought videotape was about *feedback*. And what we were going through now (self-criticism) was part of that feedback process. Scott suggested the kids videotape the rehearsals and the setting up as well as the dramatic action of the plays.

My nineteenth-century armor was beginning to clamp into place.

If feedback was the message of videotape and the recording of documentary material its cardinal use, then good-by Carl Dreyer, good-by transcendental art. I realize that in poetry I have final control over the work. I can change one word and put it next to another until eventually I can say I stand behind this poem. Videotape seems to demand more of a wise passivity and a surrender to the "cosmic flow" of which I'm not sure I'm capable. The takes tend to go on and on because—unlike a Super-8 camera whose button usually has to be held for the duration of the shot, thus building up a physiological anxiety and the desire to get to the end of the shot—the video camera's button need be pushed only once, and you can walk away and leave the building and the camera will go on filming moronically in whatever direction it was last aimed.

Actually, all of these theoretical points worried me less than the fact that Loftin's class and I had already become interested in plays. I hated to give those up, especially since dramas were so much better at bringing in a larger group of kids as actors and extras than documentaries. Persuasive as Scott's arguments were, there could only be one cameraman at one time, and what was I going to do with all those other kids if we did nothing but documentaries? J.T. and I insisted we were going to stick with dramatic work for a while longer and see what happened. Maybe we'd be pioneers.

Bruised, J.T. and I retreated to a coffee shop. We agreed that we would try documentaries soon. Taking up Mrs. Jacoby's request to tape her Food Fiesta seemed a good place to start. Maybe we could also have kids do five-minute portraits of everyone in the school, pairing one kid with one subject, or letting groups of kids tail and interview different subjects.

JANUARY 25

The Double Daters is almost filmed. It's good, if a little stiff; it reflects the character of this particular set of girls. The videotaping definitely benefited by being broken into smaller shots. The girls were seized with a perfectionist itch: wanted to do scenes over and over. The acting got a little sharper. Tammy was an excellent camerawoman.

There was some sabotage at the start that ruined our first takes. Stephanie was so infuriated because she couldn't hold the mike (I'd promised it to Dolores who had no acting part) that she stood in front of the camera and wouldn't move. I told her there was no reasoning with someone who blocked the camera—either she moved or was out. Xiomara unwisely pushed her toward the door. Two minutes later Karen—who wasn't even in the play—charged in to beat up whoever had touched her friend Stephanie. I got them both outside (telling J.T. to go ahead with the shooting), and in the corridor, with Stephanie weeping against the door, I explained the situation realistically to Karen. Karen said: "Oh. You didn't tell me *that* part, Stephanie. If she won't co-operate give *me* Stephanie's part." A little bit of friendly double-dealing. Then she changed her mind and decided the best bet was still to beat up Xiomara. In the end, miraculously enough, Karen went back to class; Stephanie returned to the Writing Room and worked smoothly with us for the rest of the day.

By that time, Dolores was having a terrible time. Having come into the room to be given a part, she kept begging the girls for something to act and the girls with characteristic clubbiness rejected her. I found little things for Dolores to do, but she was still miserable. Finally I confessed to her, "I wish there was some way I could make this day better for you. Isn't there any way you can stop being sad?" Later she handed me this little note.

> Philp
> I sorry for what I did. Is just that I got so mad.
> > Goodbye
> > Dolores

I love the melodramatic "goodbye." I keep coming back in these diaries to the emotional upheaval which is almost the genius of Denise's class. Sometimes after a stormy crying thing, I'll just feel dazed, as if someone had punched me in the stomach. I wonder if the kids know that that's the way to get to me and are exploiting emotional displays?

FEBRUARY 1

Decided to teach Loftin's class something about the grammar of filmmaking. This in order to get them thinking more ambitiously in terms of visual effects, and beyond the single-take syndrome. Denise Loftin wasn't there, and the substitute wasn't there mentally, but I raised my voice above the din and grabbing a piece of chalk wrote down:

CLOSE-UP
MEDIUM SHOT
LONG SHOT
CUT
PAN
ZOOM
TRACKING SHOT
FADE
DISSOLVE
FEEDBACK

As I defined each one, J.T. would demonstrate it with the camera and the kids would look at the result in the monitor. We even tried a stop-frame gimmick with one person pretending to be in a car and advancing a few feet with each cut. Some kids were still running around. I was yelling information at them, the scene was getting more and more manic, the goody-goodies shushing the others. I refused to give up, wanting them to "learn something"—there are times when learning is not a spontaneous "doing" activity and ya just gotta shud up and lissen—unwilling also to give them a lecture on behavior because I remember how I was in school when the substitute came in. I told them it would help if they mapped out their shots beforehand by drawing a shooting board, with each shot labeled as long, medium, etc., and the figures sketched in and the dialogue underneath. Very sophisticated concept, storyboards. I was sure no one got hold of the information.

A miracle. That afternoon Roberto brought me the first of two scenes of the war movie he had been working on. His shooting board was full of the terms and effects we had discussed that morning, with lucid little drawings that were worthy of a professional.

Jamie and Gregory wandered in at three, while we were packing up the equipment. I suggested to Gregory that he do a video script of his story, *Sir Launcelot Dubernickle*. Gregory was very excited, and J.T. showed him her own shooting scripts from an oversized black notebook she carries around. She ripped out a few blank pages for him, which was enough to get him started.

FEBRUARY 2 / PORTRAITS

Denise got everyone quiet to listen to us, so I realized a speech
was in order. I said we wanted to collect a library of videotape portraits on people in the school. Everybody knew what a portrait in
painting was like. What is a portrait in words?

"Description?"

"Good. Description, or biography, or autobiography. But how
do you show what a man is really like on film?"

"You don't just ask him questions," said Julie, "because he'll
probably lie. You have to spy on him."

This seemed an interesting idea. How do you find out the truth
about a person? If you think he's lying, maybe you can ask him more
questions and trip him up. David made the interesting point that
people have a special way of talking to an interviewer for television.
He called it "microphone language." Just as the discussion was trick-
ling out, Leo Gelber walked in. "Ah, our first victim!" I said. I asked
him if in fact he would consent to being interviewed.

"Why not? I'm a ham. Can I make it up or do you want me
to tell the truth?"

"I'd prefer you tell the truth."

"Then it can't be as funny."

"Why not? Reality is pretty funny."

"Not in my case. It's sad—tragic. If I'm going to be interviewed,
I need an easy chair," said Leo, and he left to fetch one from the
Writing Room.

The girls were all atwitter to ask him personal questions. I recommended that they write down, say, ten questions. One of the kids
had a brainstorm and suggested we put the chairs in a row facing
Gelber, like a panel. Ricky came up with a proposal to introduce
Gelber in front of a hand-held curtain and then pull the curtain aside,
revealing Leo in his easy chair smoking a pipe. A homey touch.

The easy chair was a stroke of genius because it changed Gelber's whole bearing and created a special dramatic set in the room. As
we were hooking up, Denise gave the kids a strong talk reminding
them the best way to interview was to *listen hard.* Talk naturally and

if you see the person is starting to get on to something interesting, *pursue it*. Don't just ask the next question on your list.

Almost all the questioners were girls. They came up to me giggling and showing me their lists, with items like: "Would you climb the Rockies for Mrs. Rubinger?" and "Do you see other women behind your wife's back?" The boys were either operating the equipment or tensely keying up for the war movie. Roberto was worried I might break my promise and spend the whole day on this "gooey stuff." Odd how quickly everything gets sexually polarized in this group.

The interview began. Leo Gelber contributed so much by being verbal, gracious, expansive, and patient. Even when the same questions were asked twice. He also helped the kids sharpen their questions. When one girl asked, "What do you think of Mrs. Loftin's figure compared to others?" he answered: "That depends on whom you want me to compare it to. If Raquel Welch, that's one thing. If Mrs. M— (a large staff member), that's another."

They asked him about teaching and he was quite candid—said he almost quit last year when he had a sixth-grade class but this year he was much happier as a cluster teacher. The only questions he didn't answer were his age (which the kids guessed—thirty-six) and the saddest thing that ever happened to him. Denise noted that the kids were really probing and trading information: for once they didn't care if *they* were on camera. A break-through, of sorts. She suggested that all future interviews take place in that easy-chair corner. Clearly part of the success of the event came from its spatial clarity—Gelber in the chair, the kids facing him in a row, camera to the front, sound man at Gelber's feet. The pleasures of structure. Leo was exhilarated at the end. "When's my next screen test?"

THE WAR MOVIE—ADVANTAGES OF OUTDOOR SHOOTING

In the afternoon we took the boys out to film the battle scenes in the snow. Marissa, Maria, and Xiomara begged to come along and learn how to operate the cameras; later they were given parts as Red Cross nurses. Riverside Park was lovely and moody and could well have been the Black Forest. Wherever we pointed the camera it turned up a gorgeous picture. The snow was falling throughout the film, a light snow, not sticking, and to the right was the West Side Highway.

I had given them my pup tent to set up as part of the war maneuvers, hoping that this task would be a perfect vehicle for video-tape (fusing real-time documentary processes with the dramatic: influenced by Scott Morris' ideas). The kids hadn't a clue how to set it up. Neither did I! I'd just gotten it as a gift—but I didn't tell them that—said we would shoot them trying to figure it out. After two unsuccessful attempts, they finally found soft marshy ground and got the tent to stand. Roberto, Britt, and Ricky were eager to start the fighting scenes; some of the other kids were just trying to keep warm. I had an easy feeling about everything. So nice to be outside on the first snowy day. This is certainly one of my biggest highs of the year.

Even so, there were casualties. David refused to go down the little hill because he was sure he would slip on the ice. And Britt's saying "Come on, it's easy!" didn't help any. Poor chubby kid. I remember what it was like for me as a boy, those times when jumping three feet seemed an impossibility. I tried to help David with the neutral "scientific advice" that there was more traction going down sideways, but he looked at me like: If only life were that simple! On top of everything, David had brought his two magnificent toy machine guns for the war movie and in the midst of shooting decided that the other kids had only let him have the General part to use his guns. He walked off the set sobbing and I ran after him. Coaxed him back with a mixture of sympathy, persuasion, and—as a last resort I realized I had one more ace—adult command. It seemed that he had purposely set up a situation to be exploited. But then, I keep seeing that even on the best days school is a Darwinian struggle in which some kids learn how to take the limelight and others to be extinguished in the corner.

The battle scene played itself out against a fieldstone parapet which the kids used effectively. Britt, the German-black sentry, was knocked on the head and "dropped into the ravine." There was much shooting and wounding in the legs. Fighters fell in long pan shots with the casual indifference of Godard's death sequences. The snow turned everything poetic. We played it back in the classroom for Denise at three-fifteen, still shivering, and even the retakes looked breathtakingly cinematic.

I think location shooting with interesting backgrounds is the best way to enrich that boxy blandness of the videotape image.

FEBRUARY 8

This was a lovely day. Just so full. We knew we would have to divide the video time between Mrs. Loftin's class, which was to do another portrait, and Mrs. Jacoby's Food Fiesta. But as soon as we entered the building, the girls from *The Double Daters* ran up to us saying Stephanie's mother had lugged her portable organ in to play the wedding march for the final scene. Naturally she was going to be furious if we couldn't film her today. We agreed we would tape it during lunch. I took the girls into Assistant Principal Hardwick's office to rehearse. Maria and Marissa sat on top of Hardwick's desk (he wasn't there) and called their mothers to tell them they couldn't go home for lunch and would their mothers please bring their costumes in? So nonchalant . . . Christine, looking out the window into the yard, thought we should film the wedding scene under the white wooden arch that does look like a canopy; then afterwards for their honeymoon they could climb over the fence to the swings! I thought this was an ideal image summing up their status as children playing adults.

"But what about the organ?" asked Maria with that fretful concentrated look of hers. "How can we plug it in outside?" "We can't, unless we plug it into the clouds. Let's just intercut the two scenes and shoot her first inside." Some of them grasp the idea of intercutting and shooting out of sequence; some don't. Just then a kid from Jacoby's class ran in saying there was an emergency: J.T. didn't have a take-up reel. Listen, I said to the girls, I may be gone for fifteen minutes but we'll definitely do it during lunchtime. Meanwhile, rehearse your scene! "We will." But they seemed more worried about the costumes than the actual play. One thing these girls don't need to do is rehearse a wedding scene.

In Mrs. Jacoby's room, J.T. and the kids and several adults were gathered around the videotape pack like a nativity scene. Mrs. Jacoby was dressed up for the Food Fiesta and everyone was smiling. But there was no take-up reel. J.T. apologized for forgetting to check the set. I looked around for a likely errand boy, and slowly it began to dawn on me that I was the one. "If you take taxis both ways," said Mrs. Jacoby, "it will only be twenty minutes." But I had no money! I borrowed $5.00 from Mrs. Jacoby and hurried out.

Gritting my teeth in the taxi . . .

At eleven-fifteen I was back and entered Mrs. Loftin's room to do another portrait. The wedding scene girls were pulling at me because they didn't know how they were going to videotape *and* eat their lunch. They would be too late for the lunchroom. I said that I would buy them lunch. Since I was entirely broke I deferred that organizational decision till a later hour. The decision that was right upon me, like a Great Dane sticking his paws on my chest, was, *Who* would we use for our portrait? I made a quick scouting trip of the floor and all the teachers were chicken. Finally the assistant principal, Claude Hardwick, agreed to be interviewed as soon as he was finished with some pressing business.

While waiting, we watched the Gelber interview, and I discussed with the class two problems, one technical, one thematic. First, how could we set up the scene to avoid panning across so much empty space and so many non-involved faces to get from questioner to subject? Tammy came up with a good spatial idea. Have the kids divided into two smaller groups on both sides of the person, and the camera back more, facing all. That way the camera would have to pan only an inch from one side to the other, as compared to the old way, in which sometimes the camera had to do an 180-degree pan before it picked out the face of the questioner.

Second problem: How could we dig deeper into a person's life? It wasn't enough to ask them whom they would like to date. What are the important things in a man's life? We made a list on the board: LOVE, WORK, FRIENDSHIPS, CHILDHOOD MEMORIES, MONEY, HOBBIES, POLITICAL VIEWS, FEELINGS, DREAMS OF THE FUTURE.

Claude Hardwick appeared, looking handsome and sartorially dressed as usual, in a herringbone three-piece suit. He is remarkably young for an assistant principal—twenty-six, black, hip, liked by almost everyone, including myself. Perhaps because of his position, the interview began very stiffly. The kids spoke too softly to be heard. Claude was not being very open either; Denise Loftin and I, with our foreknowledge, had to drag out of him the admission that he is an accomplished musician. After the usual questions about various teachers' figures, he started warming up, saying how he liked to put on the stereo after work and drink beer. He admitted that he thought someday of changing fields. Then someone asked him: How come he got so angry in the lunchroom? And Julie wanted to know: How come he didn't listen to the kids' side of the story?

Could you be more specific? said Hardwick. Julie cited an incident about lunchroom passes in which he had assumed she was lying and "I wasn't lying; I was right and you were wrong." Hardwick stated his memory of the incident, which was quite different. David wanted to know if he believed in the slogan "Respect your elders." "No I don't," Hardwick said. "Not unless they merit your respect." I could see beads of sweat break out on his forehead. Hardwick was being very honest (if defensive) in answering, and they kept circling in on the issue of punishment. They had a real live AP in the hot seat! Someone asked if he had ever gotten into fights, fistfights, with people his own age. "Yes, on occasion. I try to stay out of them because I'm quick to lose my temper." Did he ever have arguments with Mr. Jimenez, someone asked. "Yes." "Did you ever win one?" "Yes . . . occasionally."

The kids were getting an inside look at power in the school. We ran out of time, but everyone agreed this had been a great interview. Gelber, who had seen part of the taping, said: "They seem to be learning a great deal from this. What it is exactly I don't know, but . . ."

Lunchtime: we ran to fetch Stephanie's mother for her organ solo, "The Wedding March." She is an impeccable, stately woman who plays the organ cautiously, picking out the notes one by one. The girls had their coats on, ready to zip out to the yard for their scene, and they stood perplexed as we taped what must have been the most drawn-out molasses performance of the wedding march in history. Everything takes its own sweet time.

Then down to the yard. A snowy wedding. Everyone was freezing. Emily made a fine priest. Christine dropped the ring in the snow. I got a chance to be the cameraman. The girls ran over to the fence, the grooms lifting their brides over it as a "threshold" and then tearing off to the seesaws and swings. End of *The Double Daters,* thank God.

We went off to lunch at the pizza parlor. This was the nicest part of the day. Maria and Marissa had managed to get their hands on some money, which helped pay for Xiomara, Stephanie, Christine, Virginia, and myself. We ordered seven burgers and cokes, everyone feeling so relaxed and adult to be sitting in a restaurant on schooltime. The girls were talking about their summer experiences. Finding jellyfish, ants, crabs, the blue ocean in Puerto Rico. I was temporarily too tired to speak and enjoyed the privilege of eavesdropping on their conversation. It was lovely sitting in that bright snack bar with the sun coming across our Formica table. But we had to get back.

Back to find that Tammy and Julie were hurt because they had missed going along to the pizza parlor. So I sneaked them in with me to the Food Fiesta. All I had to do was tell Mrs. Jacoby that they hadn't had any lunch. She's really very kind. The room was packed with kids, parents, educational dignitaries, stuffing themselves with the incredibly tasty ethnic dishes which the parents had prepared. Posters from many lands and a pious statement on the board that you can take the first step toward understanding people by learning to love their food.

A very warm, cluttered, happy feeling in the room. And in and around people's feet some kids were conducting interviews while others were watching the monitor. Mr. Jimenez liked being interviewed. From a technical point of view the footage was sloppy; but somehow the videotape's presence had enhanced the effectiveness of the Food Fiesta without usurping it. Mrs. Jacoby was pleased.

At three o'clock we trooped back to Denise's room and collapsed on the couch. Now that she's stolen our chair from the Writing Room, Denise has set up a lovely little relaxed corner with couch and throw rug to go with it. Dolores and Britt and Robin were doing instant plays for us, just showing off the way kids do. Dolores put on my white winter coat and pretended to be a very snooty rich lady. Britt did an imitation of me. "Here's Phillip." He came bopping in with a big smile, acknowledging non-existent applause, and then said: "Today we're going to do a film about . . . a film about . . . now let me see . . . what was I just thinking?"

We played back the wedding scene and it came out surprisingly well. Then about fifteen minutes of Hardwick. We were totally zonked out, watching telly at three in the afternoon.

FEBRUARY 16 / *Sir Launcelot Dubernickle*

It never stops being good. We spent all day today on Gregory's *Sir Launcelot Dubernickle,* in which Sir Launcelot saves a lady from having her brain transplanted by the Mad Scientist and his brainless assistant, Igor. Denise Loftin asked "Can I work the camera?" in a voice like a little girl, and since she was so keen to be in on it and couldn't leave her class unattended, her solution was to move the whole class to the Writing Room (which had become our Hollywood). I was afraid we'd have a hard time keeping the kids quiet during takes, but it wasn't bad. The overseeing was shared by J.T. and Denise and myself; whenever one got distracted with a kid's personal problem, the other two pushed the show forward. It's "child's play." The kids do most of the work. (Sometimes I wonder what it is I do. Mainly hover and watch.)

What a funny play! Gregory had written and drawn a shooting board, but the improvised dialogue fleshed it out much further. They tied up Soypathe in a white sheet and a ball of twine and put her next to the operating table with its wonderful collection of colored bottles and a battered, broken doll's head in a strawberry box. Jamie explained to her: "I am going to transplant your brain into this head with the help of these chemicals." He elaborated a great deal of pseudoscientific explanation, then said "Is there anything you want to say?" and pulled off her gag. On the first take she had absolute stage fright and finally managed to say No. The second time, I had given her a pep talk about making things up even when you forget your lines, which I doubt she understood, because Soypathe is often in a fog. This time Jamie pulled her gag off and she looked at us for help. Karen, standing behind the camera, made a horror-scream pantomime and Soypathe let out a scream, only five seconds after it should have come: NO! DON'T DO IT! Then he put the gag back on. Jamie turned to the coffee machine, which was supposed to be a computer, and as he leaned down to throw the brain-transfer switch he quipped: "Which would you like? Coffee? Hot chocolate? Or chicken soup?"

Gregory was waiting off-camera, having Wendy see if his mask was on straight. Strange to say, though Gregory had written the script, he had no interest in controlling the production. All of his intensity was concentrated on his entrance (in cape and mask) as a superhero. It amused me that he had given Jamie much the *longest* part, taking for himself the heroic but very brief and dull role of Sir Launcelot.

When he finally did jump in, he was fairly static, throwing Roberto (Igor) off him and then standing wistfully with his hand on his hip as Roberto (twice his size) struggled up and tried to ready himself to look shattered by the next rude push. CUT! I took Gregory aside and told him to punch, make a fist. Use the uppercut and—giving him the opposite advice that I usually tell them when they're going to film a fight—whispered in his ear that he should really punch hard. Take 2 was a lot more roughhouse, with Gregory jumping on tables and flying at his opponents' necks. In fact, when the shot ended it was discovered that Jamie had a bleeding nose. He lay quietly for a few minutes on the couch while Dolores applied her grandmother's sure-fire method for stopping blood—a penny on the forehead!

With Jamie stretched out, we filmed the flying sequence where Sir Launcelot, having rescued Soypathe, flies away with her. I was curious to see how they would solve the problem of filmed flying in technical terms. Personally, I had no idea how to do it. Someone suggested that the two get on top of the supply cart and we wheel it around, shooting them only from the waist up. A very surreal calm effect. (So what if the ceiling is in the frame?) Then the cameraman suggested that we mount the camera sideways to give it more the illusion of flying horizontally through space. Denise was pushing the wagon; she kept telling me, "This play's really going good."

Strange that it is good, with such an unlikely cast. The largest speaking part taken by a kid with a partial cleft palate (Jamie), the superman played by a fragile, polite boy who doesn't fight, and the captured girl so befuddled she even forgets to scream. Most of Jamie's speeches still come out as if he has marbles in his mouth—even though we did hide Wendy under the table with the mike—but it doesn't matter much because the set is so convincing and the motif so familiar. As Jamie goes twaddling on about chemical formulae and telepathy and memory we watch because of his beautiful aplomb. It was particularly spellbinding when Jamie wrapped Roberto's head slowly with a surgical bandage or extracted the brain (a sponge) from behind his ear. *Any physical task, done with concentration, seems to have a compelling hypnotic effect on videotape.* This is something for me to remember: if mundane tasks like wrapping a bandage or putting up a tent can be soaked up by the video camera and given a kind of obsessive density, it may be a way of regaining some of the monumentality which movies lose to television by the smaller image.

Roberto made a fine slobbering Igor. I told him privately to repeat like a dumbbell everything Jamie told him, so that the audience would have double the chance to understand. "Now pick up the girl," Jamie would say. "You mean you want me to pick up the girl?" Roberto answered, etc.

MARCH 1

Today we robbed a bank! Irilia and Wendy had come up with a play about some thieves who try unsuccessfully to rob a bank. They had planned to shoot the bank scene in the Writing Room but I thought, Why not try a real bank? It was a record 73 degrees and a natural for taking the kids out of the school. The streets were teeming with street-corner men in a good mood. Wherever we set up the cameras they watched with curiosity, discreet enough not to harass us with questions or jump in front of the camera.

We took our band into the huge Greek Revival savings bank on Amsterdam Avenue and asked if they would co-operate in letting the kids "pretend to hold up the bank." Xiomara explained, "It's for a school project," and looked the picture of innocence. The account manager, still dubious, thinking perhaps this was a novel way to pull a heist by using child accomplices, and not liking the looks of my dungarees, phoned the school to verify. The principal himself had to give the word that there was such-and-such a person as me working at P.S. 90. By this time J.T. had already set up the tripod. A burly, friendly black guard was smiling into the camera for test shots. When the account manager got the go-ahead, he asked an old teller lady to perform in the film. We were ready to roll.

Juan and Francisco and Soypathe went up to her, thrust a toy gun above their heads (they were too short to come up to the window), and said, "This is a stickup. Give us all your money." The old lady answered brilliantly: "We don't do business that way. Guards, throw them out!" At which point the kids get tossed through the door.

We had to take the scene over because the lady was acting so nonchalant that she continued working her adding machine during the dialogue, drowning out everything. I asked the lady and the guards if they would do it one more time, this time with the mike on the counter ledge. Here I learned that people, who are quite happy to appear in a film, grow slightly chagrined when faced with the technical demands of filmwork—getting it right. This time the shot went off perfectly, the camera panning across the hollow Greek-columned spaces of the interior as the guards rounded up the kid-robbers and ejected them. In the background Muzak was softly playing.

I had the feeling that a few bank tellers were sorry to see us leave. One friendly guy behind a cage detained me: "Will this show be on 'Sesame Street?'"

"It might," I lied.

"Pretty good. When I went to school, all we had were the four walls to stare at. Take it easy."

MARCH 15

Today we made a videotape documentary about the school lunchroom. I'd wanted a change of pace from fiction-fantasy and thought it would be good to focus on the lunchroom, since everyone knows that's a problem in the school. Plenty of action guaranteed. I warned the kids a few weeks earlier that we would be taping the lunchroom, and we discussed the best way to get across the nature of the problem (chaos, overcrowding, awful food) and the possible solutions. This morning we brought our camera down at ten-thirty, before the onslaught, to tape the cafeteria ladies preparing the meals. We got amazing footage. The interviews with the ladies were hilarious, because the interviewees were so bad-tempered and sour:

KID: Do you like working in the cafeteria?

LADY: What a stupid question! (Wanders out of camera range)

KID: Why is it a stupid question?

LADY: (Returns) I said it's a *stupid* question because you think I'd be working here if I didn't like it?

KID: (Timidly) How long have you been working here?

LADY: I don't see how that's any of your business!

2ND KID: Do you think the kids in this school are nice or bad?
LADY: You're one of them yourself, you should know! I seen
            you coming up here asking for seconds.

One lady actually held a tray in front of her face like a gangster
being photographed. Denise Loftin tried to explain that this was not
going to be shown anywhere; it was just a class research project. No
dice. The lady refused to lower the tray.

Assistant Principal Glass didn't want us filming inside the lunchroom once the kids had arrived because it was "an illegal situation."
Overcapacity. We waited till the principal came by, interviewed him
about the lunchroom, then moved the camera in, using Jimenez's
proximity as a shield. It was total anarchy, hand-held camera at its
purest! That's to say, at a certain point the controls went; I lost contact with the camera crew and it was every man for himself. The eaters
were singing, rolling on the ground, play-fighting, yelling, playing
cards, some of it typical lunchroom behavior, some staged for the
camera. Fifteen minutes later we reeled out of there and sat down in
a stairwell to catch our breath. I decided to stage a self-criticism session (videotaped) about how they thought the filming went. "Awful!"
said Maria. "Disgusting," said Marissa. Why? "Because they were
just showing off for the camera, they weren't being real," said Robin.
"Well then it was a documentary about how people respond to having
a camera around," I said bravely. "That's just as interesting as a documentary." They didn't buy it. They didn't seem very upset, either. We
had had a good time.

Viewing the tape in the classroom, I was impressed with the
flavor of the one continuous take. It *was* an excellent record of the
way the eye and body of a cameraman respond to crisis situations.
The raw picture of institutional life reminded me of Fred Wiseman's
brutal documentaries on mental hospitals and high schools. I was
more than pleased with the results: perhaps because it was my brain-
child; I had conceived it and pushed it through. For once I wasn't the
patient midwife of one of the students' scripts. The kids, on the other
hand, took an immediate dislike to the tape. They couldn't stand
the wobbly camera work, the poor sound, and finally hooted it off the
screen. I suspect they also couldn't stand an accurate picture of the

squalor in their lives, which they know all too well and would instantly trade in for a superman plot.

MARCH 23

Our big problem so far is screening. We have made so many tapes and don't know what to do with them once they're made. They disappear into boxes. The kids and I rush into a new production. The pressure to shoot is great. Since we only have one portapak deck, and you need a deck to show tapes on as well as to shoot them, we have to decide which takes precedence. We usually end up doing a new tape. All that beautiful footage, I wish we could leave it with the kids in a corner to look at again and again. They need more passive viewing time to digest and analyze what they've done.

*   *   *

We found a partial solution to the problem of displaying the video-tapes by arranging for a local cable-television station to give us a half-hour program slot a week to broadcast tapes made by P.S. 90 children. Since the program was on a public-access community chan-nel, air time cost us nothing. The program gave the children a cul-minating goal to aim for, and the parents who had cable TV a chance to see the shows as well. We were moving out into the community. Of course it put a strain on us to come up with a half-hour edited show a week, but we did not start the series until we had enough of a back-log of finished tapes to enable us to continue working at our own sweet pace.

Chapter 11
The Spicy Meatball

By spring, the Writing Team had reached the point of gathering up the material worth saving and taking it a step further, into the light of day. For seven months, stories and poems had been collecting in our hands. We now had a substantial body of good student work, and we turned our attention to putting out a school magazine.

The name of the magazine had already been selected: *The Spicy Meatball*. Riegelhaupt's kids had made it up and had chosen it from a field of more staid titles, like *Our Writing,* with my coercion and approval. They also did a funny, tape-recorded commercial for the new magazine which was played over the public-address system to drum up contributions from children we had not been able to reach.

The meeting at which the writers assembled to choose the contents of the first P.S. 90 literary magazine took place in a pioneering spirit. We had in mind the start of a tradition which we hoped would last, and so the first issue had better be good.

Naturally every writer had his or her "must" pieces. None of us wanted to disappoint the kids we knew; everyone was trying to be objective; and then there were stories that seemed fairly humdrum but whose inclusion would mean so much to a particular child that human considerations outweighed literary ones. With all the compromises and committee dealings, the final selection came to one hundred large, packed pages.

The contents of *Spicy Meatball* were typed on a big-lettered electric typewriter for easy reading by children, and Karen Hubert and Sue Willis did the paste-ups and layout. Meanwhile we had found a non-profit printer (government subsidized), The Print Center in Brooklyn, who would do the magazine offset at minimal cost. We decided to do all the collating by ourselves to bring the price down further. We would use the kids as "volunteer" sweatshop labor. I selected for the cover a glossy still from a monster movie, showing Godzilla attacking Rodan, which came out nightmarishly murky if arresting. We still had so much to learn about printing. But there was something very fulfilling and magical about the making of a printed object. Even when things went wrong, with excruciating delays, it was wonderful to get involved in the picayune, grubby, ink-stained mechanics of seeing a magazine through the press, and to lavish finishing touches on the presentation. Selecting the best type face and the weight of stock, picking an eye-catching photograph for the cover, deciding whether to center the titles or print them all flush left—these minor, fetishistic refinements constitute the secret hedonism of magazine editing.

The rationale behind the magazine (which turned out later to be true) was that children in the school would have a greater incentive to write once they saw that there was a market for their compositions. We were appealing to precocious writer's vanity. Children want glory as much as anyone: they are eager to have work that they care about distributed to the larger world, and will keep pestering, When is it going to be shown? When is the magazine coming out?

But beyond the incentive argument, I think we as young writers felt another reason for publishing the children's writing: justice to the written word. There is justice in the celebration of effort and merit. Good writing deserves to be seen, and seen properly, by others.

Our layout reflected a desire to present the children's work with the integrity that the little magazines give to serious verse and fiction. The decision to exclude children's drawings from the first issue, while leaning perhaps too much toward the severe, was made with the object of playing down the cutesy, illustrational aspects and letting the writing stand on its own merits, in a clean, undistracted format which children's writing so rarely receives.

It disturbs me when I see a teacher, who has gone through the trouble of eliciting strong writing from his students, proceed to dash it off on blurred purple rexograph, using double columns to squeeze eight poems on a page. The eye has nowhere to focus; everything runs into everything else; the effect is of a bargain basement flyer. White space around poetry is essential for it to breathe. So is uncluttered design necessary for prose. As a good painting cries out for something better than a shoddy frame, so good children's writing requires that extra moment's attention to detail which will give it a suitable setting.

Putting out a good-looking collection of student writing at the end of the school year might seem to many classroom teachers an impossible undertaking. Yet it is not very hard to do, from the standpoint of modern printing technology, with the wide choice of offset, xerox, mimeo, and letterpress. What it mainly requires is consideration for the feelings of each written piece—which is another way of saying, valuing the work properly.

Ten cartons of free *Spicy Meatballs* were driven to the schoolhouse one warm morning and given out to the classes. An hour later every kid in the school had one. The reaction to *Spicy Meatball #1* was instantaneous and enthusiastic. We had a tradition on our hands.

Chapter 12
The Hustle: A Cautionary Tale

> *Children! children! form the point of all.*
> *Children & high art.*
> *Money in the bank is also something.*
>
> JOHN BERRYMAN

The Goodgold Fund had millions to give away. It made me giddy to think about it. Walking around the place was like being inside a bank vault with all the safes open, and you could take any amount you wanted and no one would stop you, provided you thought of the right words to say to the guard.

Marty Kushner and I were told by the secretary that Miss Nevermore would be out in a few minutes. I noticed a sumptuous art magazine and showed it to Marty. He whispered that Evelyn Nevermore, the Fund director, was considered something of an expert in arts education. That was our field—we were in! Our training grant with Columbia would be expiring soon, and we needed money to keep the program alive next year.

The secretary asked us how we would like our coffee. By this time Miss Nevermore had appeared; and so the coffee was brought into the inner office on a tray, along with powdered cream and sugar. The cups were plastic—not as fine as I had expected. On entering the wonderful world of the Rich, I half-expect everything to be rich, down to the last detail; it came as a disappointment to know that they drank out of the same plastic cups I did.

Evelyn Nevermore shook hands with us and told us to be seated. The chairs were brought around in a semicircle. The director leaned forward with a pad and ballpoint pen in her lap. She was a small woman in her middle thirties; soft round features; glasses; well-tailored clothes; and a sunken way of sitting, with her shoulders curved around her chest.

"Suppose you start by describing your program," she said to Marty, "though of course I'm already familiar with some of it."

Marty Kushner sketched an overview of the different schools Teachers & Writers was working in and the history and philosophy of the organization. His manner in speaking to her was orderly, forceful, and oddly neutral for him—careful to stay away from any self-praise. Then he moved on to a description of the P.S. 90 project. Every so often he would ask me for a detail. That was when I noticed something peculiar about Evelyn Nevermore's note taking. She seemed to have a prejudice against any but numerical information. No matter how important an idea was, she would let it brush by; but if I said that I worked with fourth through sixth grades, she would write down, *4–6*. If I said the school had three floors, she would write down *3*.

I noticed also that any emotional enthusiasm was discounted as irrelevant, or even worse, a *faux pas*. Now I knew why Marty had been shying away from value judgments. If I said anything like, "The kids had a great time doing the show," she would get a look of withdrawal and distrust, as if to say, That would have to be verified.

Evelyn had a nervous habit of clicking her ballpoint pen while listening. She threw in a question at regularly spaced intervals, but it was the kind of random "intelligent question" a person makes to demonstrate he is shrewd and no easy fool; the kind one dredges up from a preoccupied brain at a party when asking someone what he does for a living. Her attention would stray and then she would click her pen again and ask another question. I had the feeling she was bluffing. She was no expert in education; I doubt she had been inside a public school in the last five years. And now she was possibly way over her head, making decisions that involved hundreds of thousands of dollars in fields she knew little about. She seemed tough in the way a frightened person can be stubborn and tough if pressed.

Eventually Evelyn turned to me and asked me to describe some of my teaching experiences. This was obviously the lead-in for the humanistic stories I had been brought along to tell; a kind of comic interlude in the proceedings. I was a bit dry getting started, but after a time I warmed to the attention. I told anecdotes about different children. She started smiling indulgently and she seemed to relax. Marty was enjoying this part; his quick wit bounced off my lines. I became more zany in the telling, I started to embellish with vocal imitations and who knows what. Suddenly everyone was roaring, we were holding our sides. Evelyn allowed herself a joke and we laughed all over again. The walls were throbbing with a sickly sense of relief. For a moment I sensed something flirtatious pass among us. We were three young people, after all. It was as fugitive as a pout, and then it disappeared.

And all at once the laughing stopped. We were back to being petitioner and banker. Now the intermezzo was over, the heavy, third movement began: the getting down to business.

Miss Nevermore told us that frankly she thought we had made a good presentation. She liked the sort of creative emphasis we had. The only problem was that two other arts organizations who were also doing interesting work in the schools had applied to the Goodgold Fund. And according to her guidelines, she was only allowed to fund one arts-in-the-schools program.

"If you don't mind," I asked, "if you don't think it's a breach of confidence, could you tell us who the other two groups are?"

"I see no reason why I can't reveal the names. One is . . ." she looked through her bulging manila folder of grant proposals, "the Films by Youth Foundation. . . . And the other is Free Video."

When I heard Films by Youth, I jumped up. "But we're already working with Films by Youth through MERC at P.S. 90! They lent us a portapak. I know Gerard Duggan; they've been wonderful to us. There must be some way we can combine our proposals."

"Yes, I was already thinking along those lines," said the executrix, in a cooler voice. This was her idea; I was not to anticipate. Now she turned to Marty Kushner and addressed him, top-level officer to top-level officer, with the proposal she had had up her sleeve all along.

It would be easier from her standpoint to combine the proposals, she said to Marty. The trustees would permit her to fund more than one arts group if they submitted a joint proposal. Of course quite a bit more money would be involved. It might be more sensible to make it a three-year, $250,000 application. The funds would be shared among the three groups, of course. For purposes of simplifying the grant they could be merged into a "superagency." The Goodgold Fund would sponsor and be the fiscally responsible agent for this superagency. Having the three groups under one umbrella would also cut down on administration and overhead costs.

All this was so much more money than we had dreamed of that for a second we were speechless.

"It would be difficult to handle the diplomatic relations," Marty said cautiously.

"Yes, but we would work that out."

"What I mean to say is, the directors of each agency might object to losing some autonomy. And to taking their orders from a foundation."

"But I don't intend to run the show. I see my role as a—matchmaker at the early stages," Evelyn said. "To bring you three together and then withdraw. I also thought that, since Teachers & Writers is the oldest and most established of the three groups, and has the best track record in the field, you people would be the ones to administer the project." She looked straight at Marty.

"I've got to think about that," he said with a nervous laugh.

"Of course there's still a lot to be worked out. We have to agree on the sites," said Evelyn.

"What sites?" I said.

"It would have to involve a number of schools in one area."

"Well, what's wrong with the upper West Side of Manhattan?" Marty suggested. "Phil's already built a strong base at P.S. 90—and we have writers going into a junior high and another school in that district. We could run a district-wide program with writing workshops, film workshops and teacher training, open to all the teachers in the district," Marty said, warming up to the idea. "And we could get cooperation from the District 3 office to give the teachers in-service credits."

"That sounds possible. . . ." She scribbled *Dist. 3* on her notepad.

We were suddenly all on our feet.

"It's been a pleasure talking to you two," said Miss Nevermore. "And finally meeting you after all our correspondence. . . ."

"Yes, it does make a difference, face to face," Marty said.

She promised to get word to us in a week. Meantime, she would try to set up a summit meeting with all three groups. We shook hands, and the elevator took us down to the muggy, grungy, earthy, un-air-conditioned street.

"We made it!"

"Gimme five!"

"Whoopee! She thinks we got a great track record!" cried Marty. "We're asking for thirty and she starts talking 250 Gs!"

"What do you make of the superagency idea?"

"I don't like it," Marty snarled. "It's a pain in the ass. That's big league paperwork. Teachers & Writers—it's a small outfit, see? And we gotta stay small! I'm here to see that we stay small. Because if we stay small we trust each other, and we can make decisions fast."

"But what are you going to tell her about the superagency?" I asked.

Marty suddenly looked disturbed. "Listen, I'll try to get money from them for workshops, and I'll tell them . . . I'll tell them anything they want to hear. But we'll use the money to keep doing what we believe in, for as long as we can get away with it."

*   *   *

Two weeks later Marty called me. The pot had been sweetened to $90,000 for Teachers & Writers alone. That was the figure that Nevermore had advised Kushner to apply for a two-year period.

"So, that's good," I said encouragingly.

"Yes, it's good."

"Then why do you sound so sad?"

"She—seemed concerned that you were getting too wrapped up in P.S. 90. She said she was worried that the P.S. 90 teachers would become dependent on us, that we weren't making adequate preparation for them to carry on after we were gone. Evelyn is concerned about the replicability of the project. She says, quote, 'We're not interested in funding anything that can't be replicated. Can it be done in Omaha?' "

"Sure it can be done in Omaha, if you get the right people."

"Forget about Omaha," Marty said glumly. There was a silence on his end. I had never heard him talking so slowly. "I think she wants . . . you to pull out of P.S. 90 by the middle of next year and go to another school in the district. Start that up the same way."

"Screw her! I'm not going to do that!"

"Don't get annoyed at me; I'm just reporting her end of the conversation. She asked me to ask you for a timetable of withdrawal.

When did you think you could start to phase yourselves out of P.S. 90."

"I don't like the sound of that phase yourselves out. This is not a military operation. Do *you* agree with her?" I demanded.

"Obviously I don't agree with her or I wouldn't be having such a hard time making this phone call. . . ."

"I'm sorry. It's just that I get suspicious. What does she mean, she's not interested unless it can be replicated? How do you replicate an act of love? Can you replicate a—a surprise, or a child? We're not prefabricated parts that you can plug into any system. We're unique. We're poets! The hours I spend working in this school are worth spending in and for themselves—not merely as a prototype for mass production."

"I know this; calm down."

"Look, she wants us to spread into this district, that district, don't get bogged down at P.S. 90, proliferate. What for? I like this school. I want to stick around. What's the sense of pulling up roots and starting the same program over again, back to zero, having to win the trust of a whole new set of teachers and children? It isn't as if we're about to run out of material. There are 800 kids in that school. I could stay there for ten years. Tell her that. Tell her it's my life's work. That should scare her. They want a traveling salesman. Johnny Appleseed. I'm sorry. I don't want to convert vast numbers to poetry; I want to build a sensible work-life for myself. Tell her there is no timetable. We're just beginning to scratch the surface. We're only now finding out the extent of the work in all its spin-offs. Tell her any estimate of a deadline would be sheer hypocritical bluff."

"I'll figure out something to tell her," Marty said, sounding worried, and hung up.

The meeting was in the Goodgold conference room. Leaders of the four organizations had arrived by ten o'clock. I already knew Gerard Duggan and Aline Smith of Films by Youth, Marty Kushner of course, Evelyn Nevermore, and her secretary. The only stranger was Marsha Applebaum, the director of Free Video, who looked very much at ease behind a conference table, leaning over this one with her long hair pinned in a loose chignon.

I wandered over to the coffee-maker, a stainless-steel urn with a red electric eye. There was a jar of Cremora next to it and some butter cookies with jam fillings. No sandwiches or rolls. I had the feeling I would never eat well at this foundation. I stood in front of the plate-glass windows, tinted cinnamon brown, and looked out over Park Avenue. The center of the American Empire. Tablets of solid turquoise and black glass reflected each other's dark-edged profiles on enormous, smoked cocktail glasses, under a diffused smarting sun. I couldn't turn away; it was so dramatic. I was also anxious to delay the moment when I would have to focus entirely on the meeting at hand.

"What's he doing?" Gerard Duggan said with mock annoyance.

"He . . . often does that," Marty answered.

"I'm sorry, just looking." I took my coffee over to a seat, a bit annoyed at myself for playing the fool, which I had vowed not to do.

The meeting got under way slowly. We were feeling each other out: three little arts agencies who maybe had no real desire to be hitched together, but who were just hungry enough to go along with the plan. Not only their salaries, but the payrolls of all their workers might be picked up for another year or two if they were just cool enough to show the woman at the head of the table that they could co-operate with their neighbors.

Evelyn looked different to me—stronger than the last time when we had had that tête-à-tête squeezed into her office. The enforced distance of the conference table was more her element. "I think we should get down to basics," she said.

Everyone scrambled to it. We each took a turn at guessing what she might have in mind by basics.

"I think we ought to define what our goals and evaluation procedures are going to be," said Marsha Applebaum, "because evaluation comes very high in my list of priorities."

Gerard Duggan agreed that certainly, nothing could be more important than evaluation, "but first you have to have a program. And you have to know who is going to be in charge of that program. First set up the basic structure, then comes evaluation."

I noticed that Evelyn wasn't talking any more about putting Teachers & Writers in charge of the superagency because of "our great track record." That proposition had fallen by the wayside; dead; finished; it would be bad taste to bring it up in front of the others.

The needle swung back and forth between the speakers like a ouija-board dial; only, here, the force guiding it was not a mysterious power but the shades of approval and disapproval that could be read on Evelyn Nevermore's face. Everyone's eyes were on her. Whoever had the floor may have tried to deliver a point to the whole group, but at the end of his speech his eyeballs gravitated, involuntarily, to Evelyn. She kept a basic poker face—though there were moments when she frowned slightly. Her eyebrows traveled a fourth of an inch downward as if the sun were bothering her; and then it was astonishing to see grown men and women backpedal in midsentence, changing their policies at the lowering of an eyebrow. It must have been fun for her. In this moment alone, her face was scanned more intently than Garbo's, and hearts rose and fell when she parted her lips to speak. Sometimes she merely wet her lips. No words came out. She said less and less, until it reached the point that each of her statements, even the most incidental, was searched for hidden clues. A few casual words of doubt would occasion a half-hour dispute among the three groups, each attempting to clarify his position.

In spite of the need to demonstrate concord, the groups were beginning to assert differences and to line up by position. Marsha Applebaum introduced a series of proposals which I found hard to accept. First she stressed how important it was to set up a structure that would "enable" the school system to take fiscal responsibility. (*Enabling* was a big foundation word that year.) "We can't just come in with these goodies," she said. Evelyn Nevermore nodded several times. Seeing that her idea was the right one, she went on to build a long speech about different federal sources of revenue: Title I, Title III, etc., etc. Then she argued that we needed a full-fledged evaluation unit, with an outside evaluator, and one third of the budget to go to documentation and evaluation. Finally she insisted that we take six months before putting the program into operation, to come up with a design, and that we be given "planning money" for this preliminary stage.

I felt in my gut that I could never work with Marsha Applebaum. It was not that any of her ideas was so bad in itself as that, together, they were completely inimical to the Teachers & Writers style. They suggested a very cut-and-dried bureaucratic approach to an arts program, which, to my mind, required a more alive, improvisational attitude. As I say, it was a difference in styles. The director of Free Video was not even necessarily pandering to Nevermore's foundation viewpoint by using the current jargon; but she saw the world in the same terms, as a fund-raising administrator—not as an educator.

Marty and I both argued strongly that the money should be spent on more workshops and materials. For instance, we didn't need planning salaries; we were already getting paid to run the program, and that included thinking and planning; why be paid twice for the same job? As for evaluation, I didn't see why we couldn't evaluate ourselves as we went along. Most outside evaluations were expensive and ended up in a file cabinet anyway where nobody read them. . . .

I saw immediately I had said the wrong thing. Evelyn looked down at her coffee cup, dismayed, while Marsha beamed.

"I don't understand," I continued. "Who is this evaluation for? If it's for the school, they haven't requested it. If it's for the foundation, why doesn't Evelyn herself come up to the school and check it out."

Here Marsha repeated in firm language that we must have an outside evaluator. Evelyn looked relieved, as if Marsha were protecting her, like an older sister. From what? I wondered. Unless it was from having to confess her inability as an evaluator and her ignorance of public schools in general. . . . Marsha would bring her the evaluation reports and all the information she wanted and she would never have to leave this office.

It was hard for me to understand why the meeting was going in the unpleasant direction that it seemed to be taking. I had the feeling that everyone was rehearsing from a script which had been given out before I came, but the pages of the script were scrambled so that the speeches did not follow each other logically. Gerard Duggan and Aline Smith of Films by Youth were trying to occupy a middle ground between Free Video and Teachers & Writers; they were still hoping to pull out a compromise. Gerard expressed most concern about who would head up the superagency. He returned to the question of choosing a project director through all the twists and turns of argument. It was then that Marsha Applebaum unveiled her final suggestion. The leadership should not come from any of the three groups, she said; the Foundation should choose a totally neutral outsider.

Gerard was opposed. "How will we find a stranger acceptable to all three groups?"

"To me," I injected, "the people who are most involved in the thing should run it, not someone who's 'disinterested.' This isn't the Commissioner of Baseball, after all—"

"You probably think you should be made the project director," Marsha retorted.

"Why not?" I said.

"Let's be sensible," said Gerard. It was becoming like a poker game: three sit down to play; by the end of the game, two get up together. I had the strong feeling that Films by Youth was leaning toward Teachers & Writers. I decided to give them a push. "I want to bring up a question that's been on my mind from the start," I said. "Won't Films by Youth and Free Video duplicate each other? Films by Youth does video; Free Video does video; what is it that one does that the other can't do? Why do we need two media organizations in the program? How many videotape cameras can a kid hold in his hand at one time?"

"That's not the point. Why do we need writers, for that matter?" Marsha snapped. "You know, our grant was submitted to the Goodgold Fund last November, so if anyone's the latecomer, it's you."

"Now wait a second," Gerard held up his hands. "Let's not have this develop into bad feelings."

Aline Smith agreed. "Let's keep the discussion on a non-personal level."

I blushed. "Who said personalities? I don't understand why we need two film organizations. It seems like an unnecessary overlap. Marsha was the one who inferred that I meant her organization should be cut. I didn't say anything about Free Video. It could be Films by Youth."

"As long as it's not Teachers & Writers," Marsha said bitterly.

The meeting broke up shortly after. Another meeting was proposed for sometime "next month." I stole one last look at Evelyn Nevermore's face. She looked depressed.

The feelings between Marsha and myself had grown so acrimonious that, although we rode the elevator together, we immediately parted on the sidewalk. Gerard and Aline joined Marty and myself, who were headed in the opposite direction. The four of us shared impressions of the meeting: Aline and Gerard made it clear that they were much closer to Teachers & Writers' way of thinking than to Free Video's. It was a good sensation to have allies. We decided to sound out Evelyn on the possibility of doing the program with only our two groups. There was something conspiratorial and even fratricidal about this arrangement. At the time, though, I had no second thoughts about it; the meeting left me with the sweaty feeling of having traded low punches at close range. I felt winded but on my feet, and it was exhilarating. I was acquiring a taste for dirty fighting.

Fool! If only I had known that at this very moment the game was over. I had been outmaneuvered, knocked out cold, and didn't even know it, and was still rejoicing at the sport of it.

A LETTER FROM GODARD

Evelyn's unhappy expression at the meeting's end left a disturbing influence on me. She had been the center of everyone's maneuverings; she had seemed to enjoy it; and yet at the end, she appeared deflated. I had not gauged properly how much of her own ego must have been invested in the setting-up of this superagency, and how disappointed she must have been when it did not come off. The creativity of her administrative job was in "matchmaking" and originating superagencies. We had stepped in the way of her creativity, and that was not going to be good.

Nevertheless, I was still reasonably confident that we would get some money out of the Goodgold Fund, for three reasons: 1) Justice —we deserved it. 2) We were on the side of the majority, which held two thirds of the original organization votes. 3) Evelyn continued to make statements indicating that "our chances looked very good."

One day I received a letter from Paris. The address and the handwriting were unknown to me; the writer signed his name Jean-Luc Godard.

I thought it was a practical joke from someone who knew that Godard was one of my idols. I did not dare think otherwise. But after my heart stopped pounding, I read the letter and realized it was in fact from Godard.

Dear Mr. Lopate
My comrade Gorin spoke to me of your video-films. I'd like very much to look at them and make you and the little ones who cre-

*ate them some proposal for showing them in Paris. I'll get in touch
with you when coming to the N.Y. film festival.*

*Yours
Jean-Luc Godard*

Now that I thought about it, the letter made perfect sense. It
so happened that a French film director, J. P. Gorin, had been visiting
the States. Gorin was a friend of a friend, and I had showed him some
videotapes made by the kids. Evidently he had gone back to France
and told Godard about them.

This is not the place to go into the effect of illumination which
Godard's movies—*Breathless, Contempt, Bande à Part, My Life to
Live, Pierrot le Fou,* etc.—had on me and many of my college genera-
tion. Enough to say that the letter appeared to me as a divine con-
firmation that we were on the right path, a message from God
(Godard) to keep working. I sent off a Xerox immediately to Evelyn
Nevermore at the Goodgold Fund.

This at last was ammunition of an irrefutable sort!

At about this time, however, communications between Teacher
& Writers and the Goodgold Fund began to slow down. Marty would
call up the Fund and Miss Nevermore would have "just stepped out."
Letters sent to her received no reply. Marty did not want to make a
pest of himself: there is an etiquette, after all, in these solicitations,
and one tries to avoid incurring the anger of the benefactor by too
many approaches. But in the few times that he did speak to her, he
got the impression that Evelyn was now leaning toward Free Video.

It all began to make sense. Marsha Applebaum and Evelyn
Nevermore belonged to the same genre, the same class. I saw them
in my mind's eye and realized they wore the same kind of suits, as if
they'd bought them at the same dress shop. It had to be questions of
style—invisible communication—sexuality. It couldn't be educational
criteria, because we ran the best arts program of its kind in the country, or so I had thought.

I still had the fixed idea that if Evelyn Nevermore could only
see the program in operation, and the good feeling between the kids
and us, and the beautiful serious productions they were making, she
would have a change of heart.

Even now, I hoped that we would get *some* token amount from
the Goodgold. After all, they *told* us we had the best track record.

They even encouraged us to double our request, which was a good sign. Why would they have led us on for so long if they had no intention of making a small donation? And besides, they had so much money to give, it wouldn't hurt them to give some of it to us!

On such naïve wisps were my steady hopes based. A woman who had raised tens of thousands of dollars for Harlem cultural organizations gave me some advice: "You have to learn how to do the Foundation dance. Each one has to be handled in a different way. Some of them you coddle; with others you throw a picket line in front of their offices."

We had obviously done the wrong thing with the Goodgold Fund. I was beginning to grasp the full, terrible meaning of the adage, Don't put all your eggs in one basket. If Goodgold didn't come through, the program would die and everyone on the Team would lose his job.

I told Marty to arrange at all costs for Evelyn or someone from the Goodgold to come to the school. Miss Nevermore said she didn't quite see the point of it. Her tone was becoming curt.

It had finally sunk in. *She was going to make a decision about our future without ever having seen the program she was judging.*

There was something unthinkable in this. I wanted to force her to set foot inside P.S. 90, whether she had already made up her mind or not. I wanted to force her to confront the mistake she was making.

I arranged a showing of videotapes and Super-8 animation films in the Writing Room and invited teachers, parents, school officials, kids. Marty saw to it that Evelyn Nevermore and a woman from the New York State Arts Council would come. It gave us an opportunity to stage an end-of-year celebration of the kids' work, as well as demonstrate community support. Jimenez, Stanley Riegelhaupt, and Margaret Trabulski took it on themselves to give eloquent, outspoken testimonials for the Teachers & Writers program. Everyone loved the films. The good feeling in the room would have impressed anyone with the eyes to see it.

I wanted Miss Nevermore to dare tell me right then and there that she would not be funding our program. Instead, she said that she would be sending her decision to us "in the next couple of days," and she retreated in palpably nervous haste. Marty whispered to me: "Leave it alone. Her mind was probably made up long ago."

I was torn between feeling angry, disappointed, and pleased with the way the reception had gone—proud of the school community for rallying around us. My feelings of gratitude for the teachers suddenly broke out of me. As Denise, Margaret, and I were talking in the stairwell, on our way out of the building, I said impulsively, "I want to stay because I like the people here. You're my friends!"

"That's not a reason," Denise patted my arm. "The main thing is that you're good for the kids and they like the program and you do valuable work—that's the main thing."

Even they did not understand. Was it entirely beside the point to want to stay in a place because you felt at home?

The letter came. The Goodgold Fund had regretfully turned down our proposal. The reason given was that the school administration had not been willing to make a large enough financial commitment to the program. Another school, P.S. — in the Bronx, had pledged twice that sum for the Free Video project; and so the Goodgold money would go there.

(Films by Youth, by the way, was not to get a cent.)

This harsh testament had no effect on me. I was finally prepared for it. But Ed Jimenez was incensed, since he was the one being blamed for the result. What did she mean, the school wasn't financially behind the program? Of course it was! He would write another letter to that effect. He knew that other principal—"That guy doesn't have any more public moneys to spend than I have. Either he's lying or she's lying. We'll go over her head. We'll get her fired! We'll get statements of support from all the congressmen and councilmen in the district. Public pressure can reverse her decision—"

Leave it alone, I told him. It was too late.

*   *   *

My experience with the Goodgold Fund was not unique. Every day, worthwhile organizations struggling to stay alive find that their proposals have been turned down for some smooth-sounding reason having nothing to do with the program's worth. If the program has already been in operation, many foundations don't want to fund it because they can't take credit for starting it. If the program conversely is brand new, they don't want to take the chance. Or the foundation has already funded something in that locale. Or they are no longer interested in supporting "services," they want to support basic change. They have a million rationalizations for all their moves which change from one year to the next, and what bothers me is that people actually swallow the foundation logic and hop to it.

When you look more closely at the system of rationales which may be called "foundation-think," very little of it stands up. Consider the myth, for instance, that the community should take up the funding. Where is the community going to get the money, if not from federal funding or local taxes? The federal government asserts that more of the burden should be picked up by the "private sector"; the private foundations pass the buck back to the local government, and the starving organization is left running in between these self-righteous giants. This grand pretense on the part of the foundations, of pious seignorial withdrawal before the self-governing community, hides the fact that it's all the same money. Under the interlocking corporate-public economy which we have now, the charade wears increasingly thin.

But a much more basic myth to consider is that the foundations are benevolent, philanthropic institutions who do you a big favor by giving you money. Now I don't want to seem ungrateful or to bite the hand which on occasion feeds me. But the fact is that the private foundation as an invention was taken up less for philanthropic reasons than for a means of circumventing estate taxes. However idealistic certain titans of industry may have been, the foundations they started are now run according to marketing principles which consistently clash with idealism; and this contradiction is what causes so much of the confusion and pain.

Foundations operate as investors, speculators. They give you a certain amount of money to go into business with, "seed money," and you are expected to use it to stand on your own two feet. Even when your organization is non-profit, you are expected to raise fresh money somehow and become independent. By refusing to give *continuing* support to small non-profit organizations, the foundations condemn many of these experiments to a premature death, and others to a life of constant, uneasy hustling.

Here is the voice of cold foundationese, supplied by a Richard Taft Association Report:

> Only a well-planned development program, carried out on a continuing basis, can provide an arts organization with reasonable assurance that it will have the funds it needs each year to support its

operations, although the source of funds themselves constantly changes. If arts organizations really value continuing support, they must realize that they will have to devote as much effort to fundraising as to their artistic efforts. . . .

Funding sources should never be approached for "emergency" funds to "tide them over" to keep from disbanding. Funding sources always want to know that they are supporting viable organizations.[1]

What this means is that every cliff-hanging, local arts agency has to sprout a professional public relations arm to stay alive. The tendency is to become preoccupied with writing grant proposals and chasing down leads to contacts rather than giving direction to the program. What a horrible waste of energy! When you multiply that fund-raising apparatus by every social welfare agency in the country—community health services, drugs, social services, educational, conservational, etc. —then you get a better idea of the enormity and the duplication and futility of the hustle.

*   *   *

I can only conclude that the economic support for the kind of work I do is based on a misunderstanding. The funding agent wants the population to be exposed to the arts on as broad a base as possible: the artist, who is not temperamentally a traveling salesman, wants to engage with people in the joint making of art as deeply as he engages in the making of his own art. The true artist knows only one thing: investigating to the depths.

The private foundations, posing as social revolutionaries, maintain that it is more important to reach the largest number of people in order to transform backward areas. Considering the sources of foundation money—big business and millionaire families—one may be permitted a doubt that these foundation people are sincerely Kropotkin anarchists interested in community control. What they are doing, in fact, is transferring marketing philosophy to art. They are concerned with selling art to a clientele, the general population, which must develop a hunger for art through tantalizing exposures. The con-

---

[1] The Richard Taft Association Report, 1969, prepared for the New York State Arts Council (unpublished).

sumer must develop an appetite for culture and "eat" more and more art. The funding agent, however, is not concerned very much with the quality of the involvement between artist and learner—that interface that they are so busy setting up—or, let us say, they are only concerned with the documentation of that experience insofar as it can be used for annual reports and public relations. Surface evidence, slide shows, photographs of smiling classrooms take precedence over the experience itself. How could it be otherwise? In order for it to be otherwise, the foundation officials would have to leave their glass towers and see for themselves the work they are considering funding —and I don't mean once-a-year visits either—which would mean they would possibly even be drawn into participating in the work. They might lose their objectivity, which is at present based on ignorance. My main criticism of funding agents is that they stay too far from the action. They cannot know intelligently whom to fund because they don't have an idea what is really going on at the different worksites; and so they ask to be lied to. They reward the best proposal-writers, the slickest salesmen, the appearance of a few statistics; they hedge their bets, giving big grants to organizations that offer a "name" as a front man; they force organizations to distort their real purposes and change priorities like hats; they encourage a climate of lies. They make beggars of us all.

POSTSCRIPT

Late in August 1972, Teachers & Writers Collaborative learned that it had received a basic operating grant from the New York State Council on the Arts to continue its programs. We were saved. My own program would have to be reduced, since there were barely enough funds to cover the writers in the other schools, much less field a full team at P.S. 90. The new austerity budget would allow us to pay for two writers two days a week and myself on a schedule of three and a half days a week. J.T. had, to my regret, returned to college. We were back to three people. Sue Willis, Karen Hubert, and I comprised the team that would start the new school year—at this point only a few weeks away. We would have to double up on

III
The Big Show

Chapter 13
The Big Show

You're never alone,
You're never disconnected.

JETS' SONG

* * *

I never wanted to do *West Side Story.* In October some kids approached me to help them put it on, and I said absolutely not. I had plenty of writing workshops to give, I wanted to settle into a calm unfrenetic teaching year, and, besides, who needed another production of *West Side Story?*

"Hey, I got a great idea. Watch this, Phillip," said Britt.

"Watch what?"

"Come on; I'll show you. Take us into the Writing Room." Britt was tricking me; he may have just wanted to get out of Math. In any case I bit. He signaled to his friend Luis, who had been trailing along behind, marking time, looking at the walls. Luis was a new boy in school, transferred into the sixth grade from parochial school. He had a fresh energetic face, a chunky build, tough but still soft, with pinchable dimpled cheeks, and a bouncy way of moving, as if ready for anything, and I took to him immediately.

"Okay, watch this."

I closed the door of the Writing Room and drew the curtains, not knowing what to expect.

"Come on Riff, you yellow-bellied chicken!" said Luis.

"Nobody gonna call me that," said Britt. He twisted Luis's arm backward but Luis quickly broke away and hurtled Britt against the blackboard. Slowly, Britt wiped his face, got up and kicked Luis in the chest, sending him smash across our homemade couch.

"Hey, watch out for the furniture," I said.

Luis rose to his feet, carefully pulled an invisible object from his sock and started testing the air with it. Britt's eyes registered fear. He looked toward a corner of the room (where his invisible pals were) and caught the "knife" they threw him. "I'm ready for you, Bernardo." They circled around each other. With a balletic thrust of his foot, Britt kicked the weapon out of Luis's hand. And returned to a formal Kung Fu, fist-ready position. Luis, dazed, felt around the floor for his knife and stood up with a mean look. Just at that second a voice distracted Britt: "No, Riff, don't!" (Britt himself said the line and then looked around as if in surprise.) Luis rammed forward; Britt doubled over, clutching his stomach, fluttering his pupils upward so that only the whites showed, sunk onto the ground; Luis backed away, horrified; Britt's legs trembled together and all the life went out of him. Then he jumped up with a jack-in-the-box smile.

"Well, what do you think?"

"It's pretty amusing," I said.

"So will you do it? Will you help us?" asked Luis. He had such an appealing, winsome face it was hard to turn him down.

"No."

"Aw, gee!"

"So we don't need him," Britt said indifferently. "We'll do it ourselves. We been doin' it by ourselves till now."

"I think it's more valuable if you do it by yourselves," I said glibly. "You'll get more from it."

"See ya." Britt started to leave but I couldn't let him get by so easily.

"Who else is in the cast?"

"Xiomara, Willie, me, Luis, Virginia, Roberto, Gene, Scottie, Vicky, Janice, who else?"

"Dolores," Luis helped him out, sullenly.

"Dolores, yeah, Yolanda, Teddy, Seth, Jerome, the other Willie, Richard—"

"Richard ain't in the play." Luis objected.

"Yes he is. He's one of the Jets. *My* boys."

"No he ain't! If Richard's in it, I'm quitting!"

"You know Richard is in it. You were there the day it was decided," Britt said.

"Oh no I wasn't!" Luis stomped his feet. "If Richard's in it, we're finished, 'cause he doesn't know how to be serious."

"Well, I'll see you guys," I said. "It looks like you have your work cut out for you."

* * *

I have always believed that my intuitions should be trusted. My hunch was to stay out of *West Side Story*.

In the first place I didn't like the play. It seemed to me a dated, sentimental, condescending view of inner-city violence by a Lincoln Center tuxedo crowd who had no real understanding of life in the streets. That sophisticated kids like Luis and Britt, who grew up rubbing elbows with real Upper West Side gangs, should believe in this romantic *kitsch* for a moment was incredible to me. One would think they would laugh at it.

My judgment of *West Side Story* was all the more sweeping as it had no experience to contradict it. I had not seen the Broadway or the movie version. I had simply heard the songs on television, read the ads, and come to my own unswervable conclusions. The tendency to be most snobbish about a popular phenomenon one has never actually experienced is hard to resist. Anyone with an interest in movies or plays has to develop a nose for what will please him in advance if he is not to spend his life chasing from one rave hit to another. I had already sized up *West Side Story* as a part of the culture I felt no obligation to explore.

Second, it was obvious that it would be a backbreaking job to put on such a show with children. They knew well enough how to stage hand-to-hand fights; but what about memorizing lines, acting, singing, choreography, orchestra, costumes, sets? It would take a very experienced theater director to pull it off. My entire background in the dramatic arts was a few skits put on the year before with sixth graders. It would be suicide.

My third reservation had to do with Britt. We were tied to each other by a curious affection and mistrust that was not in the usual adult-child relationship. When I first met him, he was a fairly timid, down-on-his-luck kid. Unable to concentrate on schoolwork, poorer in reading and mathematics than his intelligent responses suggested, he was an agile, moody, jumpy black kid who I thought might enjoy some acting. As it turned out, his mother was a professional actress and had given him a few pointers, added to which was his natural gift for mimicking the emotions and gestures of adults in any standard dramatic situation. I used him in a few videotapes and he was excellent. He seemed to have the knack of externalizing an encyclopedia's worth of responses—including certain ones that it was doubtful he had ever experienced, like the pain of a divorced husband or a worker being fired from a job. He was light years ahead of his classmates in this respect and knew it. If any Hollywood talent scout had seen the videotapes, he would have said: "That's the one." Yet there were many times when I thought other kids acted more convincingly than Britt, if acting is the kindling of an emotion inside oneself and bringing it to the surface. His dramatic gift was not the Stanislavski reliving method but one based on pyrotechnics, a memory for other actors' grimaces. I suspected that he had that hollowness which some say is in all actors, and which in his case drove him to feel alive only when he was performing.

His first successes gave him a bit of a reputation around the school. He began showing a different personality: more dynamic, ambitious, bossy, always showing off, lording it over younger children. He had a scheme for a gigantic videotape which he would star in, write, and direct, with my help. *The Cowardly Cop* was an epic based on the superblack flicks like *Shaft,* and it differed from our other productions in having many more plot twists, naturalistic locations (fire escapes, empty lots, etc.), and technical innovations (freeze-frame, first-person narration, complicated montage sequences). He edited the final version himself, on big Sony 3650 editing tables downtown. When he was finished with that, he immediately began writing a script for the sequel.[1]

Britt was brimming over with new stunts to try. Slow motion, manikins, God knows what. As soon as he saw me he would run over and clutch my arm, "Yo, Phillip, I got a great idea!" like one of those comedians cornering a booking agent in Milton Berle—Betty Grable movies about Broadway.

It got so I had to wave him away to pay attention to other children. "But, Phillip, I *gotta* talk to you."

"Not now, Britt. At lunchtime."

---

[1] He was a classic proof of one of our theses, often expounded but rarely tested: that involvement in dramatics would lead to writing scripts, which would lead to better reading skills and higher reading scores.

"But this is important!"

It was always important. He didn't see how resentful the other children were becoming. The word was that Britt had me in his pocket. "How come you've got to spend all your time with Britt?" they asked. I didn't have to; Britt just made it look as if we had a special deal cooking. Man to man, adult to adult, not like these other—punks.

We were, in fact, two of a kind. Drawn together by a love of improvising, rehearsing, and a tendency to drive ourselves until we dropped, we had more than a touch of rivalry in our collaborations. I was as critical of him as I was of myself, and often for the same reasons; and he did not spare me. But how his eyes flamed when he saw me! It could have been affection—on the other hand, it was more a look of pure egotism. When Britt saw me, he saw his name in lights; he saw all his daydreams realized, all his pet schemes turned into star vehicles for himself, that one, that only, remarkably cute kid. He was con artist enough to realize that he could not do it alone. Here was I, necessary adult, keeper of the keys, able to spring him and his pals from classtime, able to reserve the equipment and the auditorium; and, on top of that, strangely, chumpishly fond of *play.* Ordinarily I accepted cheerfully that undercurrent of exploitation— they were not only using me, I was using them for my own purposes. But with Britt I began feeling myself turning into an instrument of *his* will. He had moments of treating me like a wonderful robot sent to do his bidding.

No, I didn't want to be sucked into any more of Britt's productions. First it would be *West Side Story,* then the sequel he had planned to *The Cowardly Cop;* there was no end to it. I was pleased that we had helped to "unleash" his creative potential; but, as Dr. Frankenstein thought to himself, enough is enough.

*   *   *

"How's *West Side Story* going?" I asked from time to time, not without a twinge of regret.

"Oh, fine, pretty good," Britt would say.

The others had a different story. Gene told me they could never get all the actors together to practice, and when they did, rehearsals were a shambles. "Lots of kids already quit."

"Why?"

"Mostly because *Britt* always has to be such a dictator. And Vicky and Xiomara's the same way. Everybody wants to be the Big Chief," he said disgustedly. He looked right at me.

Gene was one of my favorite kids. It made me sad to see him sad. A pint-sized, sandy-haired boy who compensated for his smallness by wearing football shirts with shoulder pads to school every day, he hung around with the bigger boys and took a lot of lumps from them, but never stopped telling them what was on his mind.

Gene, Britt, and Roberto were best friends. They went over to each other's houses after school. They played tricks together; they quarreled constantly. I could never get over the surprising racial balance of the trio—one black, one Puerto Rican, one white—which is more common in war films than in city life. They had their racial prejudices, but they were united by an antagonism to school authority, to sissyness, and to anything that stood in the way of their emerging manhood.

During school they hung around our Writing Room, using it whenever possible as their *de facto* clubhouse. Gene had even constructed a secret cockpit out of the cardboard furniture. Gene had a passion for disappearances, privacy, the anonymity of closets, and climbing to high places that were difficult to reach. It was not surprising to look up and see him on the roofs of bookcases. "What are you doing up there?" asked with genuine alarm, was a question that would make him happy as a monkey.

Roberto was the largest, strongest, and beefiest, a bull of a kid. He loved to play-attack people like a monster. Sergeant Rock became his other ideal. The contradiction in him was that he drew like an angel and was fascinated with costume designing! Sylvia Ashton-Warner has written that there are two vents in children's minds, the creative and the destructive, and when one is widened the other will diminish. Roberto was the exception to this very sage rule. He would get up from a lyrical painting and bash a child on the head. The destructive, the creative, had no trouble coexisting in Roberto's sense of things.

None of the three had much patience for sitting at desks and doing schoolwork. Gene had the best academic skills. I would not be surprised if he shared his homework in return for some of that masculine bonhomie the three exuded when they were together. Gene took a few more joshing blows than the other two, and he got very sensitive to being playfully abused or threatened.

It was interesting to watch the way they worked out their urge for physical contact and touching, with their fear of homosexuality. One time I saw Roberto go into his Wolfman number and cuff Gene playfully on the arm. Playfully but hard. Gene socked him and pulled away fast, with tears in his eyes. "No, that hurt!" He yelled: "That's the last time you put your hands on me, Roberto!" and slammed the door behind him.

"Damn, what do he got to be so temperamental about?" Roberto said. He seemed genuinely puzzled. He seemed to be surprised that that fun bit of collision he liked to have with people actually caused pain.

Britt was the sparkplug, the star of the trio. Gene was its conscience: at least the one most apt to be honest about his feelings. Roberto set the group standards for masculinity.

There had been an incident during the class's camping trip, that no one could put out of their minds: Roberto had accused Gene of fraternizing with the girls too much, playing girls' games and, in effect, turning into one. He wrote about this episode, boasting of this threat in a story that was later published in *The Spicy Meatball:*

> One day when we went to Goddard-Riverside Camp, my friend and I were sleeping in the same room. Then two days later he started to act like a girl. He was hanging around with the girls and picking flowers. Everyday he'd bring the girls in my room and start playing catch with the daisies, jumping on my bed, and dropping petals all over the floor. So I came in the room with Ricky's knife and the girls left. I told my friend that this knife could kill him instantly and threw it at him. It stuck into the wall. He was ready to cry. He said, You could get in jail for this. I told him Maybe I will, but if you bring the girls in the room I'll really stab you.

> —ROBERTO

The part he left out was the aftermath. Gene ran away in the woods, where no one could find him, and Roberto felt so guilty that he wept and punched the cabin wall with his fists, and cried: "Why did I have to do that? Why did I have to open my damn ugly mouth?"

Eventually the two made up and went back to doing things together. There were still some guarded feelings. But by November the three were again so inseparable that their friendship posed a threat to quiet in the halls. The idea was raised at a lunchtime teachers' meeting of splitting up the trio for purposes of school discipline.

Denise Loftin, their teacher, was against it. "I'm the one who has to put up with them all day, and I don't see why we have to break them up just because they're roaming the halls. If they're friends, they'll find a way of sneaking out of their different classrooms and meeting anyhow."

Judy Gorman, the guidance counselor, was unsure. She remarked that their friendship had many destructive tendencies. "Particularly Gene and Roberto—that relationship would take a lot of work on our part if we decided to leave them together."

It seemed strange to me that we adults were presuming to "guide" a kids' friendship one way or the other. I said I knew that there were marriage counselors, but I had always thought friendship problems were to be left to the friends concerned, for better or worse. Maybe I was wrong. Judy was looking at it from her professional point of view: the way to deal with an emotional problem is through counseling. The proposal, in any event, was tabled. The three boys would be permitted to remain in the same classroom.

*   *   *

Every day brought new reports of defections from *West Side Story*. The cast was finding it hard to follow orders from the four-member junta of directors: Xiomara, Britt, Luis, and Vicky. There was no clear leadership, no point of view. By early December, Britt was discouraged.

"I'm just about ready to give up on the *whole thing*."

"Don't talk like that," Luis pleaded. *"West Side Story*—it could be beautiful! We've been doing it for months."

"So what?"

"So what?— If you want to quit, go ahead, man. I'll do it alone."

"See now, if Phillip here would help us out . . ." Britt said.

"Phillip can't do nuthin'." Luis scowled.

"That's right." I nodded genially.

"Nah . . ." Britt took a long theatrical pause, staring at his fingernails. "Phillip could do it. Only he don't want to do it."

"Why don't you want to do it?" Luis demanded.

"Because *West Side Story* is corny," I said.

"No it isn't," Luis frowned. He had to figure out a way of deal-ing with this irrationality of mine. "Can't you just come down to one of our rehearsals and tell us if we're doing it right?"

"That I can certainly do. I'll be glad to watch one of your re-hearsals."

"Well all right!" he grinned.

You must understand that what was involved here was not adu-lation of me as a director but the realization that they needed an adult to pull things together. The Kingdom of the Children had fallen apart. This I saw clearly in the afternoon rehearsal, where I took a very pas-sive role. Everyone screamed at once, quibbling over details that looked to me very small, no greater spatial clarity emerging at the end than at the start. I had come armed with pious ideas about the value of children doing the direction by themselves, making their own de-cisions through conflict and compromise, etc., but what I saw was that the production was on the brink of collapse. If someone did not step in, all the hopes and rehearsal time that had been put into it would be swept away. Nothing would be left of their *West Side Story* except demoralized bitterness and the accusations among each other for not being able to transcend their noisy ways and tempers—that is to say, their childishness, which, being children, they had every right to.

*   *   *

My refusal to do the production did not sit comfortably with me. It violated a mental rule I had formulated long ago, the Golden Rule, let's call it, of Motivation: If children seem to hate and resist what you're teaching with a passion, leave it alone; but, conversely, if they express a clear preference, desire, fascination for some activity, especially one which involves hard labor, then you have discovered a learning situation which can turn into a gold mine.

Nevertheless, I could not make up my mind. On the one hand was the kids' blatant motivation and their need for my help. On the other was my first hunch, which had admittedly been getting cloudier —and hunches, like anything else, do not have to be treated sacro-sanctly—but which still seemed to me validly self-protective. Of

course no one minded my taking on an impossible task; I had to look
out for myself.

A few days later the principal's deputy called me in for a chat.
It was about Roberto. Several parents had lodged complaints against
him for terrorizing smaller children in the halls. It was necessary to
keep him out of further trouble at all costs.

"They tell me he likes to hang around you," Louise said.
"Couldn't you find some way to keep him occupied? By making him
your monitor or putting him in a—a show or something?"

"Well, as a matter of fact," I found myself saying, for something
to say, "I was thinking of putting him in our production of *West Side
Story.* . . ."

"That's just the sort of thing I meant."

On such tiny conversational embarrassments are major commitments made. "We're doing a mammoth version of it," I said, warming up, crossing the Rubicon in a big way.

"That's just what I meant," said Louise. "And that should keep
him busy for a long, long time."

                              *   *   *

We would start from the beginning, scene by scene. I assembled
the original complete cast in the auditorium.

"All right, how does this thing begin?"

Luis was trying to get everyone quiet, telling them how I had
agreed to "help us, so Phillip's the boss; what he says goes." A handful of kids, not too impressed with this information, continued to chatter away as they always do when released from the classroom; and
the chorus of those demanding quiet swelled and equaled in noise
those who were ignoring the order. The policing kids were so self-
righteous in their calls for QUIET that they had no idea they were
causing half the ruckus. I listened to this antiphonal chorale roll from
one side of the stage to the other, like searchlights sweeping the Berlin
Wall. After about five minutes of impassive spectating, I cleared my
throat: "All right, how does this thing begin?"

It began with Britt coming out onto the stage alone, looking over
his shoulder, snapping his fingers impatiently, and doing a pantomime of rolling dice. He was flawless in his execution. It made sense
that the actor with the least stage fright should set the scene. He was

soon joined by other members of his gang, the Jets, who noodled around raggedly pretending to be happy to see each other. After their hand-slapping ceremony, Chino (a Shark) strayed onto their territory and was menaced by the Jets. He left and returned with his boys, the Sharks, led by Luis. The two gangs started swinging. All this was performed with sure theatrical instincts. "Then the cops come on, break up the fight, they leave, and that's when we sing the Jets' song," explained Britt.

"So sing it!" I said.

"We can't, without the record."

I didn't see why they needed the record, but the performers were quite insistent. "It won't sound right without it." Someone volunteered to go get the record, another to borrow a phonograph, and we took a break in rehearsals until they came back, heroic, having cadged a Walt Disney portable record player from one of the more malleable kindergarten teachers. These kids knew where every crayon was hidden in the school. The portable had no volume to speak of but the girls turned it to the loudest and the Jets began their song. In fact, only Britt was singing. The others were shuffling and hiding behind the record sound.

"Can't hear you, Gene."

"I don't know how to sing loud," Gene shrugged.

"Well I can't hear any of you." Now I understood why they needed the record so much. It allowed them the illusion that they were performing *West Side Story,* in its original fullness and polish. The *West Side Story* they loved was syncopated, proud, tight. They were holding on to the record to prevent themselves from seeing how unprofessional they really were.

Yet that cruel knowledge must come out if we were to create our own show.

I asked to see the next scene. This turned out to be the ever-popular Dance in the Gym, which called for the entire cast to be on-stage. Finally all the bit players had a chance to do something. They jockeyed for positions, paired up into boy-girl partners, started to dance, blushed, danced, giggled, guffawed, broke up. So far as I could tell there was no scene. It was like taffy. "Let's do the gym scene," certain kids had been pestering me since the beginning of the rehearsal. Now that they were in the middle of it and embarrassed by the dating implications, I began to hear "Let's do the fight scene!"

"Yeah, the rumble!" On to the rumble. That would salvage every-thing.

This was the same scene which Luis and Britt had showed me in the Writing Room. Both gangs stole onstage and surrounded their leaders, who performed a magnificent ritualized duet that held the attention of everyone. The cast was justly proud of this scene, so tense, so controlled, so well-thought-out. Some of its grace and dignity must have derived from the original Jerome Robbins ballet, a little came from the TV show "Kung Fu," but whatever the source, the movements held together and didn't need to be touched or im-proved in any way.

I took stock of what we had. The fights were excellent, but you need more to a musical than fights. The whole Romeo and Juliet plot was non-existent. The gym scene was a mess. Several of the actors had a good hold on their characters. The first scene could be knocked into place with a little emboldening. Total: three and a half, maybe four scenes had been started. The rest was unknown territory.

* * *

We began meeting once a week, rehearsing those four scenes, my idea being that we would get them down "cold" and then move on to new material.

I had already decided to wean them from the record player. What would take its place I had no idea. An orchestra? Where would I get an orchestra? A combo of teen-age rock musicians? Perhaps some staff member could play piano and would step forward out of the shad-ows when we needed him. . . .

Meanwhile, we would concentrate on dramatic acting. The prob-lem was that I had no idea how the story went, moment by moment. I would get everyone quiet, then whisper to a child next to me: "What's supposed to happen next?"

I would tell someone what to do and be corrected: "That's not the way it goes, Phillip! He's supposed to tell her to leave!" It was not the kind of direction that would inspire the cast's confidence in me. I gave orders, but they were purposely vague, lacking hard detail. I took to yelling "Next!" "Come on!" "Let's get on with it!" as my only directions, watching for any visual clues I could pick up as to the action and meaning of the scene.

It might be a good exercise for theater majors, in the subtle art of deduction, to have them direct actors who know the script without the directors' being familiar with it. Myself, I don't recommend this method of working blind. It made me the most grouchy and least knowledgeable of anyone in the play.

Rehearsals were scattered. The miraculous crystallization they had expected from my participation did not take place. We were floundering. I had begun to let them down.

Well, what did they expect? I told myself. I never wanted to do *West Side Story* in the first place.

It was unlike me that I did not get myself a copy of the script. But as long as I was under such emotional reluctance about the project, I would drag my feet, neglect to take the necessary steps, blunder along, refuse to acknowledge how much labor and forethought were really required. I was punishing them for making me accede to their demands. I was sabotaging the project by not giving it my best attention.

I began to get an insight into the mental life of a mediocre teacher. You start off with an ambitious six-week-project idea, the kind they're always writing about in teacher magazines. Hopes are high; intentions are good. But it does not quite catch fire as planned. You feel the energy drain out of the brain first, then the hands; a delicious letting-go takes over, like the pleasure of deciding to lose at tennis at precisely the moment when focus is becoming hard to keep. The pleasure of failing is in its termination of uncertainty. Then the alibis come rushing up to help: the group was too large; it was too early in the year; it was too late in the year; the parents didn't help; nobody helped; they were too young, too wild; their home lives are peculiar.

I put it to myself: Why did *West Side Story* give me such reluctance? Maybe it was that I didn't think of the idea first? No, that was making me out to be too petty. I often started out with other people's ideas. Maybe it was that it was too hard. I would have to go underwater for a few months; I would have to submerge myself, live, eat, become *West Side Story*. Yes, but hard work had never scared me before. Maybe, and this was the one I liked least but that seemed truest, I did not see how it could bring me any glory. If we were putting on a new show, improvised or written entirely by the children, people would say: How clever! How original! What a good writing teacher he must be! But *West Side Story* was old hat, and all I could hope to do was mount a playable but pale version of a Broadway hit, like one of those schlocky summer camp productions of *Hello Dolly!* or *Jack and the Beanstalk.* If I toiled to the limit, I would be serving the children and I would be serving faithfully the authors of the show, Arthur Laurents, Leonard Bernstein, and Stephen Sondheim, but I would not be serving my own vision, because *West Side Story* had nothing to do with the way I saw the world.

There. At least it was out on the table. I saw no prestige in it for myself. No gravy, nothing but the chance to be a Good Samaritan.

Precisely because I had defined it this way, I became intrigued with the idea of doing something which didn't interest me in the least, and doing it well, purely as an act of service. Like Albert Schweitzer! All of us have fantasies of being selfless. I decided that the time had come to act on mine. Added to this was the habit of work pride—the knowledge that I would be very down on myself if I did a sloppy job and would feel better if I gave it an honest try.

I have dwelt on these doubts at some length because I think that unwillingness, and the struggle with unwillingness, is a major part of creative work. I have often enough found myself balking or mysteriously marking time until my reluctance had its full say. It seems to me that good work requires a recognition of one's resistance to a task, and then either eliminating the obstacle or else refusing to do the job altogether or, what is probably most difficult, living with the obstacle.

It is not that my doubts magically went away by examining them, but they did become tamer, more familiar, almost—accommodating.

*   *   *

Shortly afterward I went hunting for a paperback of *West Side Story.* I found six copies in a downtown store and bought them all, deciding that night to read it. Laurents' book was no pinnacle of dramatic art, but it had its moments. Actually, I found it rather riveting in spite of myself. The shape of the drama began to take place in my mind. I saw how we could prune it to twelve scenes and still retain the play's dramatic arc. And keep most of the musical highlights. My adaptation went something like this:

First scene—The Jets are hanging out and a Shark, Chino, strays into their territory. The Jets rough up Chino. He returns with his gang and the Jets and Sharks go at it until Officer Krupke and Lieutenant Schrank intervene. The Jets sing their song of pride—"When You're a Jet." Tony (the hero) enters. Riff invites him to rejoin the gang. Tony says he's trying to break away from all that and keep an honest job. However, Riff talks him into going to the dance that night.

Second scene—Two Puerto Rican girls, Maria and Anita, are sewing their dresses for the dance. Maria is the sister of the Shark leader, Bernardo, and Anita is Bernardo's girlfriend. Maria complains that she is bored and wants some excitement; her brother watches her too closely. She begs Anita to lower her neckline "just a little." Anita won't, but Maria tries on the dress and loves it anyway. Bernardo and Chino come to escort the girls to the dance. Chino is Maria's date, though it is clear that she is not attracted to him.

Third scene—In the gym. The two gangs hostilely eye each other. A feckless older man named Gladhand tries to get them to make peace through a square dance, but the two gangs stay unfriendly. Then Maria and Tony see each other: it's love at first sight. They start to embrace when Bernardo, furious, sends his sister home and challenges the Jets to a rumble. Tony wanders off while Riff and Bernardo are arguing.

Fourth scene—The lovesick Tony is singing to himself: "Maria, I just met a girl named Maria." He comes across the object of his dreams. They play a love balcony scene, and sing the duet "Tonight." This part, I thought, could be played in front of the curtain (meanwhile stagehands would be changing scenery) as Tony walks along the apron and comes upon Maria peeping through. She can be standing on a concealed chair or platform, for the balcony effect.

Fifth scene—Anita and several other Shark girls argue about the relative virtues of the United States and Puerto Rico. They sing the satiric number "America," ending in a joyous dance.

Sixth scene—The War Council. The two gangs meet and lay down the terms for the rumble. They are just about to catalogue all the weapons they will use when Tony, hoping to prevent bloodshed, challenges them to a symbolic contest—"Your best man against our best man, bare hands." All agree.

Seventh scene—The Quintet (as the kids always referred to it), a big production number in which all sing about their hopes for the night: the gangs violent and triumphant, Anita sexy, the two lovers tender.

Eighth scene—The rumble. Bernardo tries to provoke Tony. Tony will not fight, so Riff steps in for him. Riff is just about to stab Bernardo when Tony pleads with him to stop. Bernardo, taking advantage of this momentary distraction, kills Riff. Tony avenges his friend's death by stabbing Bernardo.

Ninth scene—Maria's bedroom. Chino comes to tell her the bad news. Maria is worried that something has happened to her lover, Tony. Chino, enraged, spits at her: "He killed your brother!" Chino leaves; Tony arrives; Maria tries to push Tony away but she loves him too much and forgives him the murder of her brother.

Tenth scene—The remaining Jets come together and sing the humorous song, "Officer Krupke."

Eleventh scene—Tony asks his boss, Doc, for some money so that he and Maria can go away. Doc tells Tony (incorrectly) that Chino has killed Maria.[2] He gives Tony some money to leave town, but now Tony only wants to die.

Twelfth scene—Tony goes looking for Chino, begging to be shot. "Kill me too!" he yells. He suddenly sees Maria, who *is* alive, and goes running to her, but at that same moment Chino steps out of the darkness, takes aim, and shoots Tony. He dies in her arms. The entire cast gathers around them. Maria threatens to kill them all—"Now I know how to hate"—but breaks down, throws the gun away. Tony is lifted onto an ambulance stretcher and carried around solemnly in a funeral procession, which ends with the cast sitting on the apron of the auditorium stage (as I pictured it), singing the mournful finale, "There's a Place for Us."

The original had a dozen more transitions, but we would still have quite a lot to handle. I had the inspiration of collapsing two adult roles, Gladhand and Doc, into one, and giving it to—myself. Why not? I needed someone in the cast who would follow my orders. I was ham enough to want to be onstage like the others, and it would give me a good excuse to keep an eye on them during the gym scene. The kids accepted this addition to the cast without much surprise.

---

[2] There was still the problem of how Doc gets the mistaken impression that Maria has been killed. This is explained quite clearly in the book, but it involves Anita being sexually molested. This would never do in an elementary school production. All I could hope was that in the confusion and pathos of the final scenes the audience would overlook this enigma.

We began going through the play scene by scene, the actors sharing the six paperbacks and reading their lines stumblingly from print. These were nearly all children with poor reading skills. Some of the 1950s slang was already dated. (Who says "frabba-jabba" any more?) I tried to get them to improvise more natural choices but they were loath to take that freedom. The text was sacred. The Spanish children especially had a funny desire to hold on to that stilted dialogue, as if it were synonymous with being professional and mature. Sometimes they were very charming when they delivered a "I cannot tell" or other formalism that would never have crept into their speech. I was tempted to let this dignified clumsiness flower. A *West Side Story* with Velasquez courtliness, the Infanta Maria and her playmates . . . But no, that would never work.

I knew I would have to type up a script just for us, adapting, condensing, and modernizing. The thought of how much work it would take stalled me, but the paperbacks were no substitute for a playing script. So long as they had the books in their hands they would feel dishonest whenever I told them to skip several pages. "Why can't we do that too? I remember that part from the movie!" How to make them understand that they did not have the stamina or experience or the budget to put on a three-hour show? Once they got excited they had so little sense of practical limitations that we might as well have put on Wagner's *Ring* cycle. Their lack of knowledge gave rise to a hope that anything was possible—a beautiful rainbow hope that I felt powerfully tempted to satisfy. Let them learn about limits later. This time we would go for broke.

Or was I the one who thought nothing was impossible, and they the skeptical, but loyal, troupe following after me?

We seemed to alternate in our powers of faith.

* * *

The actors, with a few exceptions, filled their parts exactly. I was struck again and again by the psychology of the children's choices. Britt made a fine ironic Riff, leader of the Jets. Luis was all sincerity and passion as the Sharks' commander, Bernardo. Our spitfire, our Latin bombshell, Dolores, was an ideal Anita—the girl who sings "America." I would have perhaps wanted her for a bigger role, because she sang and moved with such electricity, but this one suited her and there was no sense tampering with a good characterization. Chino, the Shark rejected by Maria, was actually played by a Chinese boy named Scott (apparently the kids took the name Chino literally). I had filled in the few remaining parts with type-casting: a chubby, blustery kid named David made a perfect Officer Krupke, a tomboy was recruited to play the Jets' reject, Anybodys, and so on. We were doing fine except for—except for our two *leads,* Tony and Maria.

Tony and Maria were played by William and Xiomara, brother and sister. This rather incestuous casting had come about long before I entered the play, and I accepted it without anticipating the trouble it would cause. The trouble surfaced the first time we started rehearsing the love scenes.

Xiomara was a year older and several inches taller than her brother. When they first meet, at the dance, they have an exchange which goes something like:

TONY: You're not thinking I'm someone else?
MARIA: I know you are not.
TONY: Or that we have met before?
MARIA: I know we have not.
TONY: I felt, I knew something was going to happen. But this is
          too much—
MARIA: My hands are cold. (He takes them in his.) Yours are cold
          too. (He brings them to his face.) So warm. (He starts
          to kiss her hands. Then moves to kiss her lips. But Ber-
          nardo steps in . . .)

Willie, twelve years old, was not too happy about having to speak these moony lines of devotion to his older sister. Nor was Xiomara a model of patient reception—tapping her foot, gritting her teeth in front of the company. When he gazed up into her bossy, irritated face, he went flush red with sweat.

"What are you lookin' at me like that for?"

"Damn, *Junior*"—she alone had the right to call him by that family name—"just say it already!"

"How I'm gonna say it when you makin' me crack up with them fish eyes?"

I had to bite my lips to keep from laughing, because there was something piscine about Xiomara's brown bulging eyes. "Look, you're playing a role. Get into your roles. Start again."

"Haven't I met you somewhere before?" Willie said sweetly.

"I know we have not. . . . My hands are cold."

"I'm supposed to say, 'I *knew* something was going to happen,' dummy."

"All right, just go ahead anyway," I told them. "From 'My hands are cold.'"

"My hands are cold," said Xiomara, looking indifferently over her shoulder. He took them in his. "Yours are cold too," she muttered. He brought her fingers to his lips. Titters. Whistles. *Oh, Willie! Willie gettin' off on his own sister!*

"I can't do this! She's making me crack up." He threw her hands away and bolted.

"Willie, don't blame Xiomara— They're the ones who made you embarrassed." I glowered at the cast. "I blame the rest of you for scoring a cheap laugh at Willie's expense. *West Side Story* happens to be a love story. You knew this when you chose it. Now you're either gonna be babies about it—'Ooo, Ooo, Willie and Xiomara'—or you're going to shut up and let them play their scene."

That seemed to have an effect. I realized I would have to work with these two alone, though, to get them to relax.

How had it come about that brother and sister were doing the Romeo and Juliet roles? My guess was that both had wanted to be in the play, and both were respected members of their circle, capable of demanding major parts. Xiomara wanted to be the star; but she came from a strict family and would not have felt right playing love scenes with a boy when it might be whispered he was having a romance with her. Willie, in the grand tradition of Spanish brothers, was watchful of his sister's honor. And so the only solution was for him to take the part.

Thus, protection of a sister from other men, the convention on which the tragedy of *West Side Story* turns, had entered our local school production, transfigured it, and in a certain sense subverted its original meaning. We might as well forget about the theme of the doomed love of two young people from opposing ethnic groups, with Xiomara and Willie both being Spanish and everyone in the school knowing it.[3]

---

[3] I was surprised no one else commented on this. In fact the children had cast the show in such a way as to blur all racial lines. The Jets were composed of four Blacks, but also one Puerto Rican, and one WASP (Gene); the Sharks

Whatever motives had led them to this arrangement, the machinery was beginning to turn against them. They were clearly under a strain, acting with each other in public. Willie would be bugged at Xiomara, but it seemed more to convince the others than to injure her. There was no getting around the warm family affection they had for each other which was beautiful to see, which had probably never given them any trouble in their lives until this peculiar circumstance had made them embarrassed about it. Like rabbits caught in a trap, they stumbled, struggled to get free; their efforts only tightened the teeth. Worse, it was a trap of their own making. Willie, who loved to blame the person nearest him, got a puzzled look on his face whenever he realized this. I felt he was heroic in his attempt to work it out. Still not admitting to anyone or to himself the source of his discomfit, he began to accept his twelve-year-old's cross with stoicism. Irregularly, he would revolt against the pressure with a sudden flare-up.

Xiomara simply withdrew her energy from rehearsals. She carried herself cross-stage like a sick moose. She looked at the ground, she folded her hands over her knees so that her center of gravity was even lower, and delivered her lines in a cross mumble to her shoe buckle.

"Xiomara, if you're going to put so little of yourself into it, why bother? . . . Don't you want to be in this?"

"I don't feel like it today, Phillip. I'm tired. I'm no good; I'm not an actress! You should get someone else."

I was tempted to agree with her. Xiomara was just not the ingenue type. A prematurely maternal face, full of character, more Medea than Maria. But who would I get to replace her? Maybe transfer Dolores to the Maria part, and find another Anita? I felt like a heel having these thoughts, especially as I was approaching Xiomara to comfort her. She was sitting balled-up in a metal folding chair.

"What is it, Xio? What's the matter? Tell me; I'll listen."

"Nothing! Just go away from me. I'll be okay in a minute."

"You're sure?"

---

counted three Spanish, one Chinese and one Jew (Seth). Whether this mingle-ment was wise foresight on the children's part (I would not put such prudence beyond them), to forestall the "play" gangs from developing real racial ani-mosity, or was the result of indifference toward the racial theme, as in choosing up sides for punch ball, I can't say. All I know is that it did cut down on the potential racial tensions during rehearsal.

"I'm all right! Just let me take care of it—you mind?"

I wandered into the wings, where Virginia, sour-faced, tough, scowling, always-right Virginia was fiddling with the ropes. "Do you know what's the matter with Xiomara?"

She shrugged. "I think you said something that hurt her feelings."

* * *

There were twenty children in the cast—including a number of the most notorious characters in the school—and always a few hangers-on. Word had gotten around the school of our rehearsals, so that now lower graders I had never seen before, on their way from the bathroom, would stand in the back door of the auditorium and gape.

"Hey, you ain't supposed to be in it. Make them get out of here!" Virginia yelled.

Roberto, the enforcer, would start up the aisle to crunch heads.

"Roberto, get back onstage! I'll take care of it." I spoke to the little kids in a huddle, telling them that the cast wasn't ready yet and they were "shy" about letting anyone see it till it was ready. The little kids turned obediently and left.

After they had gone, I put it to the group. "What would be so terrible about having a few visitors in back? It might make you used to dealing with an audience."

"Naw, we don't want any of those little punks around," said Gene.

"They ain't supposed to be here." Virginia pulled a long face. She had the sourest expression whenever it was a question of extending a privilege of hers to others. She was equally put out when she suspected being cheated out of her just deserts. I have never heard a child say "How come I didn't get any?" more sullenly and unthinkingly than Virginia. She was the original Deprivation Kid. She had taken it upon herself to be a sort of traffic director for the show— "You're supposed to be on the other side!"—which was actually quite valuable because it kept everyone honest. Virginia was not much for finishing her schoolwork, but this show had awakened in her a sense of responsibility and discipline. I had never seen her work so hard.

This particular bunch of kids had a natural pull toward dramatics, which was obvious from their tendency to "act out," as psychologists say. Roberto, Richard, Virginia, Seth, Willie, Vicky—what a crew! Any one of them could shatter a classroom's peace. They made a practice of shrugging their shoulders at any adult's threats of punishment. In a perverse way, I was proud to have so many troublemakers under my wing. The price I paid for this pride was having to repeat every order three times, the third time at a murderous scream.

I got used to the idea that on days I directed *West Side Story* I would leave school with a sore throat.

Of course I dreamt of developing a style of quiet authority that made all the kids obey instantly, so that I needn't speak above a murmur: that blend of karate master and veterinarian. Wouldn't it be nice to have them eating out of your hand? *They say so-and-so, that guy who used to be in the Marines, has all the toughest boys crazy about him. . . . He's what those kids needed all along. Some say it's in the voice; some say a quiet, firm, competent hum he gives off, an inner peace. . . .* In any case, I didn't have it!

What I did have was a large tolerance for noise. But even I was getting sick of it. Ten minutes into rehearsals there would start the distractions from the actors who were *not* in that scene, a shift of attention from stage center to the curtains and the wings, which I came to think of as the Revolt of the Bit Players. Gene had climbed up the steampipes and was resting dangerously in a nook twenty-five feet above us. Seth was making a pest of himself by punching actors from behind the curtains. ("Stop that!") Richard had discovered the world of water pistols. Roberto lay in ambush for the weaker boys in the cast. Yolanda and Wendy took to gossiping, and Vicky and Janice, who had had a decisive voice in the original production (before I came in) but whose acting parts were actually quite small, contented themselves with criticizing the stars and predicting disaster for the show.

It seemed as if two rehearsals were going on. One group was practicing a scene; the other was using the loose rehearsal milieu as a cover to hang out, gossip, play jacks, roam free, and learn a little more about the opposite sex—all very sensible desires with which I sympathized, but they happened to run counter to my goals. I could get on my high horse and scream at them to be good; the results of such lectures, a chastened obedience, tended to fade in half an hour. Besides, it was not a problem of virtue but of structure—not that they were bad but that they had nothing to do, and only angels could be expected to sit with their hands folded watching two actors get their lines right. I am told that even in the adult world of show business, bit players, though they don't climb steampipes, chatter away and have to be shushed.

How to keep the secondaries occupied? This required some thinking. I understood their enormous need to unwind and to socialize, especially since there was so little opportunity for that in school. I could see their attraction to being with kids from other classes. The beauty of this production was that the cast came from four different classes. They had formed their own band which was all the more natural for having resisted and transcended the artificial barriers of classrooms—those bureaucratic impositions that have so little to do with the true friendship lines in a school.[4] It was thrilling to watch them interact. I would be lying if I said they were all friendly; what they had was even better than friendship, a sense of society, a sense that they belonged together, that they were cut from the same cloth.

The problem of disciplining the cast seemed to be mixed up in my thoughts with a reluctance to bust up their society. Yet something had to be done about the bit players. The solution was simple. We would rehearse the play scene by scene, using only those actors necessary to the particular scene. When their scene was finished, I would return them to their classes and pick up the next bunch. In short, no full-cast rehearsals till the week before performance.

Not everyone was happy with the new policy.

"Hey! Aren't you going to take *me* down?" shouted Luis.

"No. Only the Jets today."

"But you haven't called for the Sharks in—weeks! It's not fair!"

"Tough. I never said I was fair."

---

[4] What begins as a convenience of the school system, the division of students into units of thirty, ends with our believing that the children have chosen each other. We tend to exaggerate the importance of the isolated classroom as a miniature society, as if all of a child's friends and enemies were contained within its walls. Actually, even when friendships are made within a classroom, the next year the unlucky pairs get split up according to new racial or intellectual balance requirements for classrooms, with the result that by sixth grade a child may find his social circle fragmented in several rooms. The outgoing kids become adept at finding excuses to pay visits to their friends. The more passive kids must wait for their teacher to be sick and their class split up, to have a short, nostalgic rendezvous with former classmates.

"Aw man! I thought you were a friend. I want to rehearse!"
"No."

It was a liberation. All I had to do was be mean. I would refuse to give way to that egalitarian pressure to include everyone. No more drifting, cyclonic, Russian rehearsals.

We would take *West Side Story* apart scene by scene, like a Swiss clock; we would analyze each line and movement; we would work *small*.

* * *

The decision to limit rehearsals coincided nicely with the completion of a typed script. And I, by putting that extra labor into typing and adapting, had come that much closer to thinking the production my own. Copies were distributed to all the members of the cast. Having the words to keep gave them more control over their own performances. They could study their parts at home. They could grasp the exact order of scenes. For the first time they understood the parameters of the production.

I took a bunch of girls into the Writing Room to practice the "America" scene. "We're not going down to the auditorium?" "No, not today." We arranged the chairs in a small circle. I asked them to read their lines—not to get up, not to act them out—just to read them in a normal voice.

You could not have imagined a calmer and pleasanter afternoon. They were behaving like professional actors, smoothly reading through a new play. All that was lacking were plastic cups of coffee and filled ashtrays. They made jokes, certainly, but the humor was easygoing and didn't take away from the concentration. If anything, it helped.

The second time around we added vocal shadings. By the third time we were ready to stand up and begin moving through it. I had them think about their spatial relation to each other and how the dance might be staged. They were embarrassed singing the song "without the record," but they got through it twice, tittering and dancing in stamp-stamp flamenco rhythm. The dance-work looked almost ready. I felt we had definitely hit on the right rehearsal method.

"That's all," I said. "You can go back to class."

"Why? We weren't being bad," Xiomara pleaded.

Her guilty conscience took me by surprise and gave me an inkling of what a child's life must be like. "On the contrary, I thought you did beautifully. It's just that it's three o'clock. You have to go."

*   *   *

We still had no music. No volunteer from the teaching staff, paraprofessional, or parent had materialized. One teacher told me: "If it gets out that I play piano, they'll never stop pestering me for assemblies." She was right. Besides, who would cover her classes during rehearsals? I finally accepted the reality that we would have to hire someone. I called the music schools around the city and listed the job with their employment counselors. It seemed to me that we could manage with just a piano accompaniment; but it would have to be a professional, and we would have to pay a minimum of $7.50 an hour. I asked my boss at Teachers & Writers if we had the money to cover it; Steve said something about "Sure, within reason. . . ." I chose to ignore the troubled undercurrent in his voice. "I knew you would understand what a necessary expense this is," I said. "Look, I try to be generous. . . . Just go easy, Phillip," he added apprehensively.

Two days later I received a call from a young Juilliard student named Alban who said he was already familiar with the *West Side Story* score from accompanying a production in summer stock. I said great, he was hired, and if he came down to the school that afternoon we would handle the final details. Alban arrived carrying a black reed case and the piano score. He was a sensitive, small, darkly handsome, aristocratic-fingered musician who for all intents and purposes could have been the young Alban Berg penuriously applying for a position as a dance-hall medleyist.

I was delighted to see him, so desperately did I need help. "Have a seat. We'll be through in ten minutes and you can get a chance to see . . ." He looked distastefully at the cardboard chair as if it might collapse under him. Luis broke away from the others and asked him in a cheerful, curious manner:

"Who are you, Mister?"

Alban replied: "I don't know why I have to respond to that."

"This is Alban," I said. "He may be helping us with the piano."

"Oh," Luis said, looking a little stunned. "Great!" and he wheeled back to his place in the war council.

We were rehearsing the war council scene and the rumble. Having both gangs in there was a pain. I had my usual logistical difficulties getting the secondaries to remain in place. On the other hand, it was encouraging to see Gene helping Richard with his lines. The "gang" was taking care of its own. I kept stealing side glances at Alban: his intense scholarly air was very attractive. I liked the idea of working with him. He seemed a bit uptight, but that would pass. A moment came when the dramatic action jelled; they had gotten the outline of the scene, and there was no point in overrehearsing them. I was tentatively satisfied. Rehearsal was over; several of the kids gathered inquisitively around the visitor.

"What's in there?" Willie pointed to the black clarinet case. Alban seemed horrified that he might break it. I had forgotten the fear some adults have around children.

"I bet I know what that is," said Luis, trying to get a closer peek at the pale blue score.

"What is it?" I intervened, to save Alban embarrassment.

"*West Side Story,* right?" Luis answered with pride.

"Good guess. Now leave us for a few minutes. I want to talk to this man. Or maybe I should introduce you to the cast before they leave."

"No. That's—not necessary. I mean, I'm not doing it."

"You're not going to play for us?" I was feeble with disappointment. My head felt a little dizzy.

"I'm sorry. I just can't do it under these conditions. I had no idea it would be with such young children," he said rapidly and nervously.

"I see. . . . Well—so you're not going to help us after all?"

He winced; there was no need of me to make him keep saying it! "Can I ask," I said, "what you mean by 'these conditions'?"

"Disobedient. I'm used to a professional standard of conduct. I don't have the patience for this kind of—I'm sorry."

"I see. . . ."

"The *West Side Story* score cost me $5.00. You can buy it from me or I can return it."

"No, I'll buy it." I handed him a five-dollar bill absent-mindedly. He took it and rushed from the room.

I felt very blue. Luis asked me what was the matter. I told him it was too horrible to talk about. Then I told him. "We're back where we started: no piano." Luis said damn! and punched something or other. I went home to brood.

Was it really that chaotic? That an outsider would throw up his hands in horror? If I hadn't liked him, I would have thought: "He's a schmuck" and that's that. But I kept blaming myself: maybe I should have picked an easier scene, with the girls, like "America." No, sooner or later he would come up against that unruliness. . . . I knew I ran a loose ship. But I had been feeling that in and around the distractions the work was getting done. All along I had been seeing *progress,* tiny cohesions, tiny advances to celebrate. Was I only deluding myself? Would someone experienced in children's theater work have been able to perceive the trembling order arranging itself under the surface mayhem, or would he have taken me aside and said "It will never work"? There was no higher authority I could ask to tell me whether I was doing the right things. Common sense told me that if I persisted long enough it would end up being the right thing. If I gave in and let them perform it prematurely, it would be the wrong thing.

As usual, no use looking to the skies for a sign.

The next morning the sting was taken out of my sulk by a cheerful Irish voice on the telephone who agreed to play for us and "loved kids." Mrs. Maureen McGuire, a mother herself and a graduate student in piano, arrived full of pep, ready to begin. She was a substantial, hefty woman who tilted a little forward on high heels: not the type to be frightened by children's questions; if anything, she might do the intimidating. "There's a strange lady waiting for you in my office," Toni said. "She scared me out of my wits!" No matter. As long as she could play the piano.

I took Xiomara and Willie down to the auditorium and we worked on their solos. Mrs. McGuire told them when to sing, when to take breaths, "and when you go up for that long note, make it an *A*—'To-naaaaaaat'—right, because if you hit it as an I the voice will tighten up—'Toniite'—see, sounds ugly, jars the ears, but the other way you can hold it, Naaaa, and they'll hear it as *tonight* anyway."

"How do you know all this?" I asked, fascinated and awed.

"I'm an opera singer as well as a pianist. I give vocal lessons," she smiled.

The expert had arrived and was going to take care of everything. I floated toward the back of the theater, a hundred pounds lighter in spirit. For the first time in longer than I could remember, I knew the cool pleasure of watching a rehearsal without having to be in charge. I saw Willie's funny habit of holding his right wrist whenever he started to sing: like a ballast preventing him from flying up. I saw his frustration whenever he missed a line and thought that maybe the long rehearsal process would be teaching this hot-blooded kid some habits of persistence.

Fortunately Willie was proud of his sweet, soaring alto and liked to show it off. Not so his older sister Xiomara. The moment of truth had arrived for her. She mumbled and swallowed her notes. "Louder!" Finally she let go. I knew now why she had been so resistant to singing *a cappella*. Xiomara was tone deaf.

A musical show with a tone-deaf star and brother and sister playing romantic leads! This was shaping up to be some *West Side Story*.

But when they sang their duet, "Tonight," there was something heartbreakingly pure about it. The strain of trying to sing together emerged as a pristine romantic earnestness which produced just the right effect.

The first- and second-graders ran into the auditorium with their brown lunch bags just as we were finishing our practice. They were all admiration and wild eyes. The middle-aged paraprofessional lady in charge of watching the lunch period commented to me, "That sounded much better. When will it be ready?"

"Oh—another month or so."

"What's happening?" asked Mrs. McGuire.

"It's ten to twelve," I said. "The little kids take over the auditorium for the first lunch shift."

"What do we do?"

"We go to lunch."

At a nearby Middle Eastern restaurant we discussed the children. "Willie will make out all right," she said. "He has a good strong voice and just needs to push himself a little on the high notes. But Jemina—is that her name?—"

"Xiomara. . . ."

"—is completely tone deaf."

"Is there anything we can do about it?"

Maureen McGuire sighed. "You can get yourself a new Maria if it's not too late for that."

"We can't." I explained that the cast had been chosen long ago by the children themselves; and I liked the idea of working within that frame, like the "given" in a geometry problem or the structure of a sonnet. But Xiomara was irreplaceable for another reason. I tried to make the point to Mrs. McGuire, and as I did it became clear for the first time in my own mind.

Xiomara was the queen. No matter that she sang or acted wood-enly; she made herself felt. She was respected and sought after by children and staff. It was not easy to put my finger on the source of this popularity. She was not particularly sweet: her greetings were frequently abrasive, like "What's the matter, ugly, don't you say hello any more?" But she cared enough about the people around her to intrude into their consciousness and stay there until they realized they were staring at a live human being. Xiomara insisted on being treated as real. She had more maturity than the others, and her maternal side came out in many emergencies, from calming Willie's temper to tak-ing responsibility for Virginia's tears. The kids recognized her maturer development by making her their star, Maria. If she was not the best actress in the school, she was probably the best person to hold the cast together.

In the afternoon, the auditorium was being used by an African dance troupe. Even the lunchroom was packed with classes watching our P.S. 90 cable television show. Unwilling to give up as long as Mrs. McGuire was there to work, I found another piano, in the bi-lingual classroom. We wheeled the instrument past the dazed teacher and her thirty kids ("We'll bring it back in an hour; no problem!"), and down the second-floor corridor, parking it in front of the gym-nasium. There it created quite a stir among the classes using that facility. The Jets were gathered around the piano and Mrs. McGuire, who made do with a child's chair as a stool.

Mack the janitor was shaking his head, growling about its being against regulations. I could see why the custodians thought we were nuts: it was a crazy thing to do.

Nevertheless, we rehearsed "When You're a Jet" and "Officer Krupke." The Jets' song sounded strong. But Mrs. McGuire was getting annoyed at Rudy, who sang the melody of "Krupke" all wrong.

He seemed obstinately unable to correct the fault, though she hit the note over and over and asked him to repeat it. Finally she turned to me and muttered that it would take six years of vocal lessons to get him to sing right. All the while Rudy was twisting and turning and longing to be off with his class watching TV in the lunchroom—which was the real reason for his failure, I thought—but I had wanted him to know that he didn't know the song. Rudy is a bright, mercurial Dominican kid who, because he is so quick at certain learning processes, doesn't want to stick with anything he can't succeed at immediately. At length I let him go and suggested privately to her that she teach him to play the melody on guitar. "Believe it or not, he's an excellent musician." My hope was that he would make the connection between the guitar note and the vocal one.

At the end of the day Mrs. McGuire said, "I must tell you something."

"What?" I said, dreading bad news.

"I just have to tell you, you're so nice! The kids hang all over you. You're so patient with them."

It's true I had been oddly patient lately. I didn't know why. Couldn't seem to blow up at them for their childish tricks.

At last my stubbornness with *West Side Story* is bearing fruit, I thought. The compliment of an outside witness made me serene. I walked around the rocks of Riverside Park and was stunned by the openness of the world on this atypically warm winter day, with the Hudson River catching splashes of sun; I was soaking in the warmth like a bear.

*   *   *

This euphoria lasted for several days, or up until the next bad rehearsal.

I had expected that the piano would solve most of our problems; when it didn't, I was nearly ready to throw in the towel. A diary entry bears witness to this reaction:

FEBRUARY 15

Devastating rehearsal. For the first time I am thinking that

WSS may be simply too difficult to do. There are some mountains too steep to climb. The kids have an awful lot of scenes, an awful lot of lines to remember. We rehearse a scene and go on to the next, then we come back to the first a few weeks later and they've forgotten whole chunks of it. With videotape it was so much easier! We could shoot a scene until we got it right and then forget about it. It was in the can, we didn't have to think about it any more. In theater nothing is ever finished. I feel like a man holding a bag of wet sand and the bottom is wet and it's leaking. That's what theater means to me.

* * *

Like the thought of suicide, "which gets many a man through a bad night," I was comforted by the idea that I could give up the project if it turned out to be humanly impossible. What the criteria for human impossibility were never got straightened in my mind. I toyed with the idea of doing the whole show on videotape, a scene at a time. Then fortunately I came down with the flu. After a few days of lying in bed, I was ready to resume work.

One morning after the other kids had left for lunch, Xiomara and Dolores hung around the piano, looking over Mrs. McGuire's shoulder at the score. Though they were not very fond of her as a person, they kept being drawn to the piano and her fluent skill with it.

"You know what I like?" said Dolores. "That song that Anita sings. 'A boy like that, who killed your brother . . .' "

"That's the prettiest song in the whole show," agreed Mrs. McGuire, playing a few bars of the melody.

"See that, Phillip? We can never sing any of the *good* songs!" cried Dolores pettishly. Everything Dolores said came out with a flourish. I was putting some chairs away, not paying much attention to her Carmen act. "What's the matter now?"

"You're the matter! We can never sing the songs we want to sing. No! Only the ones *you* want. Everything has to be *your* way."

"Believe me, I don't even know that song. How does it go, Maureen?"

She sang it for us, in that full-throated operatic style that the children made fun of behind her back.

A boy like that   who killed your brother!
Forget that boy   and find another!
One of your own kind,
Stick to your own kind.

A boy like that   wants one thing only,
And when he's done   he'll leave you lonely!
He'll murder your love,   he murdered mine!
Just wait and see, just wait, Maria!

It had a very dramatic, oriental melody, I thought. "That's not the way it's supposed to go. Watch," said Xiomara. She advanced on Dolores, poking her finger in anger, all sharp, staccato sounds, clipping the ends of her words; it was perfect.

"That's wonderful, Xio. Maybe you should play Anita and have Dolores take your part, you do it so well."

"I *know* how to do it, Phillip," Dolores said disdainfully. She shook her hair out and waited for the pianist's cue, with the composure of a *prima*. Her version was more melodic, though it lacked some of the passion and resentment that Xiomara's had.

"Good, Dolores. But more fury. Xiomara, show her again how you did it." Xiomara repeated her blood-thirsty performance. Then they went through the duet from start to finish. After Anita's venom, Maria must fend her off with a melody of ingenue softness and sweetness, and some high C's that I feared Xiomara would never hit. Mrs. McGuire was busy transposing the keys downward.

"Can we do it?" they asked me.

"If you can learn the words, it's yours."

They clapped their hands with excitement.

"When are we going to put it *on,* Phillip?" Dolores demanded, pouting.

"Let's say about a month."

"You always say that—'a month'!" She started walking out of the auditorium in a huff, then turned around with a pixyish smile. She was trying out the whole repertoire of feminine enticement on me, and I had to admit that I found her irresistible. I would have loved to give her a big hug—not entirely motivated by fatherly feelings.

She had my number, that girl. She could flounce, she could sulk, she could stretch out vowels in her peculiar misguided imitation

of a movie star; I found her entirely charming. It gave me a lift just
to see Dolores.

"A month! We've been doing this since last Octo–ber," she
chided.

"It needs more work," I said.

"But you said it would be a month a month ago—in Jaan—uary."

"This time I mean it."

* * *

Our ship was drifting closer and closer to *West Side Story*,
guided through endless fog by the vision and shared recall of the kids
who, unlike me, had a perfect, a Platonic conception of West Side
Storiness. In the middle of a song, Britt would suddenly see among
the empty rows the way the actor had done it in the film. His body
would jerk into expressive movement. But these apparitions were
also getting in the way of our production.

"What are you looking at?" I asked. "There's no movie out
there. You're trying to remember how *they* did it and it's slowing
down your reaction time. Forget the movie. Look at your other actors. Interact. Don't be thinking about how they did it; the feeling
has to come from *inside you at this very moment*." I felt incurably
jealous of their attachment to the old show. "Look, that was someone
else's *West Side Story*. This is a whole new production. Maybe ours
will be better!"

"How's ours gonna be better?" Britt shook his head.

"It could have more life to it. Theirs was slick. They had a two-
million-dollar cinemascope budget. But if you put real feeling into
your parts, ours could have more life."

"Sure, we know," said Britt and Gene. They had the original in
their heads and they were frustrated at not being able to duplicate it.
The distance between their envisioning of the scene and the way it
came out was mystifying to them. They had become self-conscious
of their amateurishness, paradoxically, just at the moment when the
show was starting to come to life.

Because they had seen *West Side Story* whole, and had ingested
it whole, they had assumed that it would come out of them in a totality, like a Homunculus with a life of its own. What they had trouble realizing was that the wholeness had originally been constructed

from thousands of tiny, petty details. Some of them were already beginning to grasp the truth, that the torrent of feeling which was *West Side Story* had to be glued together piece by piece. This was a significant moment in their education, when they realized how much those entertainments that had appeared seamless, had been assembled through step-by-step analysis and mundane work. Or to put the matter another way: a contradiction in dramatic art (even more so, film) is that it leaves the impression of an emotional cohesion while its production processes are fragmented in the extreme.

The kids would have still preferred to do the unabridged *West Side Story*. In their eyes *West Side Story* was a Classic, not to be tampered with, in precisely the same sense that the Greeks view *Antigone* or the English *Hamlet*. I had come finally to appreciate that their respect for the original was a very promising thing, the closest feeling they had to that fondness for imitating certain models which is at the root of a love of culture; and it deserved to be nourished with all the support we could give it. They had a fine sense of loyalty, finer than my own. Of course it was easier for me to be disloyal, since I had never seen the original (and now was afraid to, in that it might influence me too much).

So far I had taken few liberties with the plot except to condense it, but the change I was about to make was of a more controversial nature.

Luis knew all the parts in the show. One day I heard him singing "Officer Krupke" to himself in a rich, mellow voice. It was a shame Luis had no solos. Rudy, who did little for the song, had gone to the Dominican Republic for two weeks. It would be a dirty trick, I thought, but suppose I were to give the song to the Sharks? After all, the Sharks had no songs and the Jets had two. We could push "Officer Krupke" way up in the program to Scene 6 (before Luis/Bernardo gets killed), where it seemed to belong dramaturgically anyway.

I told the cast my idea. Luis was thrilled. The majority thought it was worth a try. But the Jets were horrified.

"But that's a Jets' song!" Gene protested.

"You can't give that song to the Sharks. You gotta be losing your mind," Britt said kindly. "What's wrong with you, buddy? 'Officer Krupke' has always been a Jets' song."

"It's sick!" Gene said. One would think from his face I had suggested an act against Nature.

For once Roberto did not side with Britt. A Shark, he kept
silent.

"They wrote it for the Jets; let's keep it for the Jets," said Britt.

"The Jets already have a song," I said, firmly.

"So? So what? That's the way they wrote it in the first place."

"Look, Britt, Rudy can't sing and Luis does it beautifully."

"I should never have asked you to direct this thing. I should
have gotten my mother to direct it." Britt turned his face away. "This
thing is gonna be a disaster. Yeah. We're gonna be the laughing-stocks
of this school."

I glanced quickly at the faces of the cast to see if they were demoralized by Britt's words. They were listening hard, expression-
less.

"Pessimism is a little out of place in someone your age," I said
quietly.

"I don't care. If this was my mother doing it, these kids would
listen. She'd get these kids to sit quiet. This way they be runnin'
around, nobody listenin' to orders—"

"Let's get this straight. I'm not your mother. Your mother I'm
sure has her way of doing things. I have mine. Both methods work.
Someday you'll appreciate what a great privilege it was to work with
me," I said, walking away and leaving him muttering mutinously to
his pals.

*   *   *

Why did I need this heartache? They think I'm an iron man.
I was rushing my guts out and all they could do was criticize me,
make fun, abuse me. I was sick of it! I began ranting to my colleague
Karen Hubert. They don't appreciate me enough. They take me for
granted. They just want me there as an authority figure to rebel
against.

"They appreciate you more than you think," Karen said mysteriously.

"How?" I demanded.

"I happen to know. I've heard things—you'll just have to take
my word for it. They appreciate you, believe me. And if they don't

know how to demonstrate it well, or you can't feel it enough, that's
—regrettable."

Maybe yes, maybe no. Karen was so fair-minded about things,
so understanding, I felt ashamed of my rabidness. "But they take me
so much for granted!" I repeated.

"What's . . . behind that statement? What are you trying to
say?" she asked carefully.

"For instance, they talk fresh to me all the time. They tell me
'Shut up.' They would never say shut up to their other teachers."

"But you've encouraged them to be informal with you. To call
you by your first name. I don't know; it seems to me you have a very
good relationship with them, from what I've seen. They may not be
afraid of you but that's something you've wanted as well. And what
you have with them is . . . much more satisfying. You can pull things
out of them that other people can't."

My rage was already diminishing. Unwillingly, I felt it going.
"And another thing: I'm hoarse! I can't police them backstage and
watch the rehearsal in front. I don't know how to be physically in
two places at the same time."

"Maybe you should try working with a smaller group . . ."

"I know that! I've done it. But there are some scenes that
call for lots of people."

"Well . . . I can understand your problem. You're doing it all
by yourself. Nobody undertakes a production of this size without
an assistant director."

This comment came as a complete surprise to me. I had never
thought of it! No wonder it seemed so difficult! I felt doubly sorry for
myself but also sweetly vindicated.

Karen Hubert and I had worked together for two years. I had
been her supervisor, had advised and helped her through many shaky
moments, and now she seemed to be offering the same support to me.
I knew she was too busy to be that assistant director, but perhaps
she could videotape a few rehearsals, which would give the actors
valuable feedback and Karen a role or an excuse for being there.

That afternoon, the pianist being ill, we practiced the non-
musical scene where Chino comes running in to tell Maria her brother
has been killed. It was so funny to see Scott, who comes up to
Xiomara's shoulders, trying to get her attention. Scott is a very seri-

ous, good-looking kid from Taiwan, but evidently not Xiomara's type. She gave him an incredibly snooty look. Then she started wandering downstage, farther and farther toward the wings, doing the leaded anchor thing with her shoulders. The two of them seemed eager as possible to be through with the scene. I stopped the action: "You're rushing it. Look, he comes to your room and you see he's got a dirty face, all cut up, so you start to take care of him, bring him over to the sink—"

"What sink? You see a sink, dummy?"

"To your dresser, then. Toward the back, okay? Wipe him off with a cloth." I started pacing across the stage, demonstrating the positions as I talked. "You're worried, Xiomara, but not too worried because you're happy to be in love and you don't believe anything bad can happen. Scott, you're the messenger with bad news. You'd rather not have to say it; you know something terrible has happened, so you're torn in two. You try to explain, but she doesn't want to listen; you know how it is when you try to explain something to someone like your mother or a teacher and her attention keeps wandering. She's too much wrapped up in her fantasy of Tony. If she keeps wandering away, you follow her, stay on her toes; this frustrating part should last as long as possible, to build up the tension. Then suddenly, Xio, you start to wake up. You realize something really bad *has* happened; and now Scott gets tongue-tied, and you have to pull it out of him. That's where that line comes in: 'If you say it fast, it will be easier.' But he can't say it—and all you can think is that something has happened to your beloved Tony, Tony. 'Is it Tony? Is he hurt?' And, Scott, you're so pissed off at the cruel joke that she's worried about that *Jet,* that enemy, Tony, Tony, the guy that stole your girl, the guy that killed your best friend, that you spit it out at her like a rotten tooth. HE KILLED YOUR BROTHER. Right?"

"Come on, let's get it over with. I hate this part," said Xiomara.

"Why? It's a strong dramatic scene. Why don't you like it?"

"It's so mooey; it's so mooky; it's so ucky. Let's just *do* it."

"Okay, get in place. Remember, make it up as you go along, improvise, stretch it out. Forget the lines in the script, make up your own—"

"Come on, Phillip. We don't have all day!"

They began. The dialogue was longer and fuller and more natural. But again the physical movements made no sense: they would approach each other and reel away like sprayed cockroaches.

"They're embarrassed," Karen whispered to me. "What can you do?"

"You can make them do it until they lose their embarrassment. Okay, let's try it again."

"Again?!"

I jumped onstage. This time I wanted them to stand quite still and face each other. "Don't take a step. Keep looking at each other."

"Please." Xiomara made a face.

"I don't want to look at *huh*," Scott retorted.

"You're actors. You're supposed to make something electric happen between the two of you, search each other's faces for clues—"

"We *know,* Phillip," Xiomara said.

"If you know, then why are you running around the stage like windup cars?"

They were silent.

"All right, let's do it one more time. And on that last line, Scott, give it everything. Slap her hand away. Get real angry so you can feel it in your stomach. You know how you get angry and your stomach burns?"

"Yeah," he said stolidly.

"Make it burn."

We practiced it again. I loved this scene. I was feeling powerful like a Stanislavsky. They were doing quite well looking into each other's eyes until right near the end, when Xiomara broke down giggling. "Finish the scene!" I yelled.

"He killed your brother," Scott shouted and bolted furiously.

"That was good and loud. But you ran off so fast that it's like you're scared of her, not angry. And the last words, 'your brother,' get swallowed up in the curtains. Stay there. Say the whole line. He—killed—your—brother. Count a second. Then leave."

I took Xiomara off alone and told Karen in the meantime to coach Scott.

"Okay, Xio, what's going on?"

"I can't help it, Phillip," she smiled. "When I say, Is it bad?, he says, 'Werry bad.' Then he goes, 'He kill yo blother!'" We both laughed at this rather racist imitation. "And I don't know, I can't hold it in."

"Do you not like acting with him?"

"It's not like I don't like him, Phillip, don't misunderstand, it's just he says things that come out so funny-sounding!"

"Don't you think Spanish accents sound funny to him?"

"Maybe. Not *that* funny."

"Look, Scott has been showing a lot of courage in this. It takes guts to act opposite you, when you're giggling in his face. Be sensible, Xio. . . . If you do it right, we can forget about it. If you do it wrong, we'll have to rehearse it till you're sick to death of it."

"I'm already sick to death of it."

This time we started with a prop. Xiomara, sitting on a big chair, humming to herself. The run-through sponged up everything good and bad that had happened in the previous takes, every contradictory hint I had given them. (I was surprised how much they had been listening.) Xiomara began drifting away from Scott, Scott moved away from Xio, then Scott remembered to pursue Xio, then Xio remembered to look into Scott's face, and I heard him say 'Werry bad,' and she looked at the floorboards, and at the end he slapped her hand away with true anger and screamed his line.

"It's ten to three. Can't we go up to our class?"

I was debating whether to run through it one more time.

"I—don't—think," Karen Hubert said cautiously, "it's going to get any better."

"Okay, you can go." They left. We folded up the video equipment. "I'm curious," I said. "What did you say to Scott when you took him aside?"

"I said: 'This is the moment when you discover that the girl you thought you were in love with is a real bitch.' "

"Wonderful!" We locked the equipment upstairs. I was still fishing for a positive response. "How did you think it went?" I asked.

"Well. Very well. It's a difficult scene for them to play. . . . I imagine it's embarrassing because they have to pretend to feel very grown-up emotions that they've never experienced."

"Sure it's embarrassing. The closer we get to the emotional romantic core of the play, the more self-conscious they become."

"Still, I think you did very well with them. You took them to the limit. I would be surprised if they could go any further with this particular scene."

"That's where we differ. I think they can make it a lot better."

"When are you going to put it on, by the way?" she asked.

"I've been resisting a deadline, because of all the hysteria that unleashes. Probably sometime before Easter. I don't think I can hold them together much longer."

*   *   *

The pianist was already waiting in the auditorium, bright and early. I rushed down the hallway quickly gathering my troops. They were scattered in four different classrooms. As soon as their regular teachers saw me, they made a joke of unloading them. "You want Willie?" Miss Mayer said hopefully. "Here, take him. Keep him. Bring him home with you, adopt him, just get him out of my hair. He's driving me nuts. Come on, Willie, here's this nice man come to make a star out of you."

Willie showed me his script of *West Side Story*. He had pasted a fuschia-colored star on the front page and written his name and in big letters: THE STAR.

"Are you sure it's okay if I keep him out?" I asked her.

"I'll even pay you to take him out," she said. We both smiled; this was more cynicism for show than an expression of her true feelings. "No, really, I think it's the best thing that's happened to him all year," she said in a low voice.

Next we paid a visit to Monte Clausen's room across the hall. *"West Side Story?"* he asked. "Good. Richard, Seth, Jerome, Billie, take your coats with you. You'll be gone the rest of the morning. How's Richard? Has he been acting up?"

"Not at all. Richard has been co-operating a hundred per cent. The other day he even filled in for Britt when Britt was absent." I went on to brag about how well he had read the lines, in spite of his reading handicap and the mockery of a few others.

"I'm surprised he subjected himself to reading aloud in front of a group. He usually won't do that," said Monte, thoughtfully pulling on his mustache. I wondered how he secretly felt about this advance of Richard's. My competitive feelings toward Clausen had led me to imply that I could *involve* Richard better than he could . . . that ugly game teachers play with each other.

"Richard hasn't been any trouble," I reiterated.

"What about the others?"

I took him aside: "Seth can be a pain in the ass. He goes around mimicking Superfly, strumming a make-believe guitar, defying me for show."

"He can do that," Monte agreed. "He's essentially a good kid. He listens, but you have to take him aside from the others." It was good advice; now we were even. I thanked him and left.

Only one teacher, Denise Loftin, showed any reluctance about letting her children go to practice. The largest portion of the cast came from her class, and every time I arrived to take eight or nine away I had the uneasy feeling of gutting her classroom. Sometimes Denise held them another fifteen minutes to complete a math or spelling lesson; other times she only sighed, but the sigh was audible enough for me to ask her about it.

"I miss them when they're not around," Denise admitted. "The room feels lonelier. Especially those kids. For all the trouble they make, they're the ones that give the class its flavor."

It had been easy to guarantee the teachers at first, when we rehearsed only once a week, that *West Side Story* would not be much of a drain on their children's time. But now as we neared the final stretch we were having to meet rather more often, and there was no way of disguising the fact.

It was a while before I realized that my entire waking life had been expropriated by *West Side Story*. I was a happy zombie, a willing drone to an ideal. So skeptical at the beginning, I paid by ending up one of the worst fanatics.

First the songs got to me. The piano had given a bounce, an underrhythm to rehearsals. The song numbers became the heart of the production, which they need to be if a musical is to work. I found myself humming "Maria" or "America" or "Tonight" or "Krupke" or "A Boy Like That" in school corridors, in the street, in the shower, waiting on lines. They would take over my brain for hours, like a commercial jingle that gurgles away until you have to beg the Powers to be delivered from it. Still wrinkling up my nose at the lyrics, I would thrill when I picked one out from the Muzak in a coffee shop —"Shh, listen; it's 'Maria,'" I'd say midsentence to a friend, who'd look at me with sympathetic pity. Those songs, I had never noticed before, they were everywhere, on the radio, in the elevators. Was it all just coincidence? I felt my whole life about to sweep off the sidewalk. I understood that moment in movie musicals that had always seemed most ridiculous to me as a boy, when the hero and heroine, who are walking normally down the street, suddenly burst into song at the top of their lungs. How could they make the transition from normal speech to serenade without a flicker of self-consciousness? Now it seemed to me that they could if they were overtaken by something majestic and allowed themselves to give in to it. The melodies of *West Side Story* were constantly on the tip of my tongue. It would of course be self-indulgent to bore my friends with these medleys; so my only relief was at rehearsals where I could indulge my melodic obsession legitimately and to my heart's content.

Every song was preceded and followed by straight dialogue or little dramatic interludes. I was grateful for this alternation which created tension and made the release through song more delicious. Something as obvious as this strategy, which I had known all my life, the way one knows a million things sitting on one's behind in a theater, was raised to an iridescent truth by the experience of actually doing a musical show. I had stumbled on the great biological reflex of the American musical stage: dialogue, song; contraction, expansion; systole, diastole; Helen Morgan in *Show Boat,* the mother of us all. I had a flash of what it must be like to be one of those devoted Judy Garland fans, whose only happiness is in the bosom of the Musical, a world which may be sentimental but at least delivers surfeits of emotion.

At night, and I'm not exaggerating, I became insomniac with the throb of the Jets' song in my ears. That insistent locomotive energy, it had to run its course, there was no stopping it:

> When you're a Jet you're a Jet all the way
> From your first cigarette to your last dying day
> When you're a Jet if the spit hits the fan
> You got brothers around, you're a family man!

What was it about this one song that wouldn't let me get to sleep, that was so exciting me?

> You're never alone, you're never disconnected!
> You're home with your own
> When company's expected, you're well protected.

That was it! I must have bought into the heroic fantasy some-where along the line; I must have thought I was a member of a gang. Never to be disconnected, never again to wander listlessly through cities that weren't mine, never to put up with an office job that meant nothing to me, never to turn back into an invisible person, never to be separated from the living juice that only the others could give me. Home-free, *connected,* a member in good standing with the commu-nity. I think I understood now why the kids had such a special feeling for *West Side Story.* Weren't they attracted to the same guarantee of belonging? And when you added to this security the spice of danger and reckless fight, the dream was irresistible.

* * *

A show date had to be set. We would definitely perform *West Side Story* in two weeks' time. I went so far as to reserve the audi-torium for a couple of morning assemblies from Mr. Glass, the assist-ant principal.

"It might be nice if you put it on in the evening for the parents as well," he suggested.

"That would be fine with me."

"I used to work in a school which was famous for its shows. They played them at night and everyone in the community came. It gave a very nice tone of pride to the school . . ." said Mr. Glass.

I did not dare tell him that the production might as easily turn out a shambles as a success. We still had never run through it from beginning to end; and I had no way of knowing whether the kids would pull together in time or not. "Of course," I said, "we would need a better acoustic setup. The sound doesn't carry at all."

"It's true. The acoustics are lousy."

"You can tell the kids to talk louder till you're blue in the face —and they do it, they shout, but you still can't hear. That auditorium is built like a swamp that sucks all the sound into the first ten rows."

"Well, we might be able to get you a microphone," the assistant principal said, frowning.

"Then there's the lights. Most of them are broken. We have no color spots."

"That's easily fixed. I know something about lights. I used to be in charge of stage shows at a summer camp."

"You do know lights???"

"Sure, we used to put on some great shows. . . . They were mostly skits, but still and all the kids had a nice time," he said, drifting off nostalgically.

"Uhm—where does one get the lights?"

"You can go down to Forty-second Street and rent a portable-light setup very cheap. . . . Wait a second, I think I have the catalogue here."

He produced it from his desk. I looked over his shoulder at the illustrations; I could barely contain my excitement or desire to exploit him. Instead of subtly leading up to it, as I had planned, I blurted out my thoughts:

"The truth is, I know nothing about lighting. I would love it if you'd help me. Could you—could you go down with me this afternoon and advise me on what to rent?"

"This afternoon?" he said, shocked. He pinched his chin where a goatee was starting to grow. He seemed tempted, but he didn't like being on the spot. Glass was quite an intelligent man, formerly an art teacher, who had drifted into administrative work through a strange circumstance: it seemed he had a friend who was taking a course to prepare for the Assistant Principal Exam. The friend had asked Glass to come along with him to class one day, and Glass, out of curiosity, tagged along. He became moderately interested in the course and stayed, while his friend dropped out; at the end of the term he took the Supervisor's Exam and passed it. The pay was good, and he had a family to support. But he never was as happy in the new job as he was teaching art. He dropped hints to me that he did not identify with the role of assistant principal, which in an elementary school is taken up largely with disciplinary problems, lunchroom duty, and dissatisfied parents. He did his job well, I thought, but he was trapped in an official mask for which he occasionally expressed his distaste by a very distant look in his eyes and a contraction around the nose, as if he were smelling something sour. Yet, bureaucracy so reshapes those who come in contact with it that even his opposition to the job assumed a bureaucratic form: evasiveness, an unwillingness to be put on the spot.

I sensed he wanted to help out with *West Side Story*—as a favor to us and for the fun of it. He seemed caught between the opportunity to get away from his desk and the danger that it might entangle him in unforeseen man-hours. Perhaps he also felt it was beneath the dignity of his office to become something like my technical assistant.

It might well be that these thoughts did not race through his mind, but in any case he finally answered: "This afternoon is no good. All you need to do is order a follow-spot, it's very simple."

"I don't even know what a follow-spot is. And you do. Please."

"I could go down with you Friday afternoon . . ." he considered.

"Friday afternoon's fine."

"I would have to catch my train around four, but if we left here promptly at three we could make it."

"We'll take a taxi," I said.

That Friday afternoon the assistant principal and I taxied down to a theatrical-supply store near Times Square. As we leaned over the counter discussing our "needs" with the salesman, I had the heady feeling of being on a holiday. It *was* a holiday—from the hierarchical boundaries we respected in school. The novelty was even greater when Ted Glass and I went into a greasy-spoon donut shop for a cup of coffee.

"That follow-spot looks terrific," I said. "For twenty dollars a week it's a steal. Maybe we can do the whole thing with just the follow-spot, from the projection booth, and not even bother with the house lights."

"I think you're going to need some house lights," he said knowledgeably.

"You're probably right."

"This evening performance should be a very good thing in terms of school and community relations. It will give the kids a real sense of accomplishment to put it on in front of the parents. This may well be the start of a yearly tradition at P.S. 90."

He had that one idea about tradition in the back of his mind. I wondered what it meant to him, personally. Myself, I wasn't thinking about the years ahead; all I wanted was to survive the next two weeks.

* * *

"I don't have a white dress, what am I going to dooooo?" demanded Xiomara. Always when I was talking to three other cast members.

"Wear another color dress," I said briefly.

"I don't have any dresses for the part! *Don't you understand—*
all my dresses are miniskirts!"

"Then wear a miniskirt."

"They didn't have them then!"

Her fidelity to the "fifties" was priceless. With all the anachro-
nisms in our show, was this one more going to matter? I know: as
Maria she felt she should look more virginal.

Every day for the next week Xiomara wore a different dress,
each time asking me if it was all right for a costume. Each time I said,
"That one would do fine."

"Are you sure? But it's dark blue!" Xiomara cried.

"I can see that."

"It has to be white!"

"Borrow a white one from Dolores!" This solution was less acceptable to her vanity than any of the others. Eventually Bette Korman, the art teacher, helped her decorate her blue dress with a special
white collar, and that solved the problem of the dress.

The next crisis was not long in coming. I learned from the other
children that Xiomara would not be in the evening performance.
Something about her father.

"Is this true, Xio?"

"If you put it on at night, you have to get someone else. My father won't let me go out at night."

"Even if he escorted you?" I asked.

"You don't understand. My father's not interested in my schoolwork. He's not one of those fathers who comes to see his children
perform. Don't make it more difficult for me, Phillip," she said with
sad maturity. "Just take my word; he'll never let me."

"What about your mother? Wouldn't she like to go?"

"Oh, my mother—my mother would love to go! My mother could
come during the day. But my mother doesn't think it's right to leave
my father in the house alone at night."

"Maybe I could phone him—"

"Don't. You'll only make it worse. You better get someone else,
my voice is terrible anyway."

There has to be a way out, I thought to myself. I spoke to the
school family worker. She said she knew the family and the father
was indeed a hard, stubborn man. But she would pay him a home

visit. The next day she told me he had agreed to come to the performance.

We were rehearsing Friday afternoon when July Gorman, the guidance counselor, came into the auditorium with dark rings under her eyes, looking "like ten volumes of Dostoyevsky." Preoccupied as I was, watching Xiomara and Willie go through the love scene, I asked her if something was the matter. She had just gotten the news that Xiomara had been turned down for Hunter Junior High School, an elite public school that gave its students better college preparation than the notoriously wretched junior high in the neighborhood. We were standing toward the back ten rows of the auditorium, and Xiomara was onstage, still unaware of the bad news awaiting her. I asked Judy not to interrupt her just yet.

Judy looked inconsolable. "There's no justice. It could have changed her whole life. Hunter could have made a big difference." She added with a pained smile, "And *I* wanted her to get in."

There was something so poignant about the simultaneity of Xiomara acting onstage a short distance away, and my knowing already that she was in store for a disappointment. How would she take the news? I hate to admit it, but I was more concerned just then about its effect on her performance than on her future.

* * *

Meanwhile, a crazed killer was on the loose on the Upper West Side. Charlie Chopoff, the popular name he had been given, had already mutilated and stabbed a few young boys, not far away from P.S. 90. His face—or a police compilation sketch of it—was hung in every shop window. The kids in school jabbered about him constantly. The boys especially talked of him so often that he took on the shape of a perverse folk hero, half-monster, half-outlaw. They ran out of the backstage bathroom yelling, "Charlie Chopoff!" That damned killer had inconvenienced my life in more ways than one. Now I had to arrange for adult escorts to be provided every child in the evening performance.

However, the Charlie Chopoff scare was only a mild shiver compared to the jitters of stage fright. A week before our opening, the terror began to surface. Short tempers masked cold feet. One fight after another broke out, like firecrackers in a line.

Richard, whom I had been thinking all along was a good kid struggling along, misunderstood, the victim of bad press, Richard finally gave us a demonstration of his famous temper. One afternoon, with no provocation that I could see, he began smashing auditorium chairs. What stuck with me was the nihilistic swoon in his smile: no anger like the others, nothing but the clear joy of destruction that a tornado must feel.

It took several adults to subdue him.

Next, a fistfight broke out between Willie and Janice, who happened to be working the videotape camera. Some remarks passed between them, and Willie, his anger boiling over, took after Janice. I had never seen such blows. They had to be held apart by their arms. Xiomara was the only one who could quiet her brother. "It's not worth it, Junior; you'll get into trouble!" I told Karen Hubert to take Janice away. Karen, out of inexperience, escorted her to the door and let her go up the staircase herself. That was a mistake. Willie tore out after her and everyone ran through the doors to see the fight.

Let them go, I thought. I had no more stomach for rehearsing. It turned out I hated violence: I had never really known that about myself. You think there is something thrilling and Dionysian about violence and then two people start pounding each other's flesh and it looks so crummy and shoddy.

I told Mrs. McGuire that rehearsal was over.

Roberto was very critical of me. "Damn, Phillip, you shouldn't stop rehearsing just because of that. These kids are like everyone else. They run to see a fight. When the fight's over, they'll come back."

"I don't care if they come back. Rehearsal's over because *I'm* discouraged; *I* can't work." I told the few who had stayed to go back to their classes. The pianist started to pack up the score, but hesitated. Roberto and his group refused to leave. Just as I did not humor their discouragements as an excuse to stop work, so they were not humoring mine. What occurred was very interesting. They started to practice "Officer Krupke," and naturally I watched; then most of the runaways came back, and we rehearsed "A Boy Like That" and "America." It turned out to be a very productive morning.

Picking up the pieces was the only pedagogical method I had to go on during this last hectic week when everything fell apart and came together again at least a dozen times. Certain children made it easier for me by unobtrusively assuming responsibility. Jerome, who was nobody's teacher's pet, saw to it that the gangs lined up in a V so as not to block each other from the audience. Britt led the Jets onstage with such verve that they were a little timid to go on without him. Virginia plugged up the holes in the "America" dance, clapping her hands, stamping her feet to keep the girls moving. And Roberto (not Luis, who was too engrossed in his solo to pay attention) held the Sharks' team together in "Officer Krupke."

Roberto had become involved in every aspect of the production. He found an old tire for the Sharks to roll back and forth onstage, to give them something to do with their hands before Krupke enters. He and Gene located an aluminum cot to use as Maria's bed, and as Tony's funeral bier in the last scene. He helped paint the scenery. He designed costumes. He had ideas about the lighting. If only he had stopped there! Roberto took to sitting on a chair facing the stage and cracking his belt for a whip. "I'm the director," he snarled. His excitement had a way of turning animalistic. Swinging his arms to look like a gorilla, he picked up the camera tripod with a threat of bashing Karen or me.

"Put that down," Karen said with real annoyance. "I don't relate to being hit over the head with a tripod."

"You've got to take a more delicate approach with women," I teased him. "Suppose you were on a date."

"I don't want to go out on no dates. I just want to get *down* with a woman. And she better do what I tell her to."

That was Roberto. As valuable as he could be on the technical end, the next moment he would do something that made me wonder if it was worth it.

He had gotten into a particularly raw, nasty mood during a dress rehearsal, turning light switches off and on, fooling with the curtains and disobeying orders ostentatiously. There was a strange situation brewing backstage between him and the girls that I didn't quite understand, but from time to time I heard a girl cry out, "Cut it out, Roberto." I went behind the curtains and told him if he didn't stop bothering the girls he would be dismissed from rehearsal. He seemed not to like hearing this. As soon as I had gone frontstage and told Maureen to begin playing the music again, Roberto yelled out, "Phillip is a faggot and he don't wear no underwear." For some reason this random taunt got under my skin.

Like, who you callin' a faggot? I ripped open the curtain to see him advancing on Dolores.

"Get out."

"I ain't leaving this auditorium."

"You're leaving all right. Come on. You're through for today."

"Gonna make me?"

"I'm gonna make you. Get out."

"I'm not leaving no matter what you do to me."

"I'm not kidding with you, Roberto. GO!" I started dragging him down the stairs. Everyone was watching us now. There comes a time, I thought with a lump in my throat, when you can't back down. I pushed him. He pushed me. I pushed him. He pushed me. I shoved him hard. Tears in his eyes. His hand went up to his neck. "You broke my locket." A sigh went through the cast. "He broke it." "Roberto's gonna tell his father." I sensed that popular sympathy had turned against me. It was absurd, an accident.

"You broke it and you're going to pay for it!" A great childish blubber broke out of him, so different from the tough guy of a moment ago I could only be relieved. He was crying like a baby. At last he had a focus of outrage for all that frustration he had been feeling.

"You better fix it!" he said. Suddenly he was no longer in big trouble; in fact, he had the upper hand.

"I'll fix it; don't worry."

"It's gonna cost you two dollars!"

"I'm not worried about the two dollars." I almost smiled. "We'll get it fixed during lunch. Meanwhile, I want you to go out of the auditorium and go back to your class." He turned his face away to ignore me. I started escorting him by the elbow and he pulled away.

"Don't you shove me."

"I'm not shoving you. Move by yourself and I won't have to touch you." At the head of the aisle I told him I wanted to speak to him in private for a moment. I was working up to an apology.

"I don't want to talk to you!" he said and slammed the aluminum door going out.

Just as well. I turned to face the cast, who were all onstage, waiting silently. I wondered what the pianist thought about me. I felt we had just undergone the most serious threat to the show since the beginning. By hitting him I had committed a cardinal error. It would endanger all of us, if his parents were to press charges. Looking into their faces, though, I saw they attached no such importance to it; they seemed to regard it as in the nature of school life.[5]

We continued rehearsing. Ten minutes later Roberto was back. He took a seat morosely in the first row. I preferred to ignore this infraction and go on with the scene. Maybe I was doing the wrong thing again by letting him disobey me. Consistency is all very nice, but how was I going to manufacture the self-righteousness to eject him again when I had expended all my anger? I did what I felt right; I let him stay. He jeered at the actors from time to time, not much.

At the lunch bell I asked Roberto to stay behind alone for a moment, before going off with him to the jeweler's. I told him that I was sorry for breaking his locket, and sorry if I'd hurt him. But it had been absolutely necessary that he leave the auditorium when I told him to. "You were really getting out of hand."

"How did you know I was doing anything wrong?" he objected.

"You were fooling with the lights; you were bothering the girls."

"But did you see me?"

"Not only did I see you, Roberto, everyone was coming to me and saying that you were bothering them. And to be honest about it, I was angry when you called me a faggot. I really don't like that, you know? I'm human. My feelings get hurt too."

Roberto nodded. He seemed much more subdued and open to reason, with no witnesses around.

We went to the jewelry store to get the link soldered. Willie was excited because he knew a Dominican jeweler who would do it for less. "This guy knows my family," he said. Willie did all the talking in Spanish and we were charged a mere $1.50. Roberto looked considerably relieved that he would not have to explain to his father how the locket got busted. In no time he was confiding in me his plans for the weekend. We went into McDonalds and ordered some Big Macs, sat back, and had an easy lunch. Who would have guessed that an hour after the incident we would be on such good terms?

Perhaps with a kid like Roberto, drawing the line is a sign that you care for him. Dolores told me later that Roberto had been coming out of the dressing room in the morning with his zipper open, and

---

[5] The pianist *was* a little shocked—not, it turned out, because I had pushed Roberto, but because he had dared to lay a hand on me. She had no trouble supporting my action, even if I did.

"his private parts showing." That was going pretty far. I began to understand why he kept asking: "But did you see me?" Much as he may have wanted to escape detection, he seemed to be demanding a punishment by his provocative stance.

Puberty had hit our sixth-grade cast. It was late March and the Rites of Spring were being performed backstage. The girls teased the boys, then ran away and shut the door. The boys tried to force open the door and invade the girls' dressing room. To do what? It was never clear. Once they were inside they would fall back. There were struggles to get in, to get out. Virginia and Yolanda refused to rehearse their dance "in front of those dirty boys." It seems the boys were sitting in the front rows and trying to stare up their dresses. Their modesty would have been more creditable if Virginia and Yolanda had not had such spicy mouths. In any case, I spent an amazing amount of time protecting their offended virtue from the boys, and separating the two sexes.

How much of this flirtatiousness would have gone on without the show I don't know, but certainly the backstage of *West Side Story* proved an ideal, fecund culture for it to develop.

We had found a separate dressing room for the boys, a little-used, almost secret room one floor above the stage. For a while the boys resented being shut off in this obscure corner. Then in exploring it they discovered a metal ladder behind one of the closet doors, which led to the roof above the stage. Gene and Roberto took me up there: it was pitch black except for the rows of house lights which glimmered underneath us like a city seen at night from an airplane.

Virginia's voice and those of the other actors could be heard beneath us. It was fun being up there, eavesdropping on them. Gene giggled. "I wonder if they can hear us."

"Shh," I whispered. "Don't distract them." I had remembered suddenly that I was the responsible adult. It was probably illegal for us to be up there (though the metal walkway felt structurally sound enough to me). "Let's go down." I knew it was too attractive to forbid their exploring it, so instead I cautioned them to stay on the catwalk. "I don't want you hurting yourself or something. See all that wiring? And if you miss your cues up here, I'm really gonna have a fit."

"Don't worry; we won't."

As I climbed into the dressing room, Jerome walked in with a message for me.

"Uh—Phillip . . . the piano lady's crying."

The piano lady—they never could seem to learn her name. Maybe that's why she was so sad. I rushed down the steps wondering what would be the best way to approach her. She had seemed such a hearty type the first time I'd seen her; and then, little by little, she had started looking haggard, resting her head on the keyboard between numbers, her eyes always a step away from tears. And now she was crying, which I could plainly see as I entered the auditorium, with the children surrounding her but keeping an uncomfortable distance.

"Is there anything wrong?"

She smiled up at me and her face was like sunshine behind clouds. "Nothing. I'll be okay." She seemed glad to have an adult around.

Her green eyes were very badly red. I knew she had been having trouble with her contact lenses. "Is it your lenses?" I gave her an out.

"No. This time it's not my lenses."

"What's the matter then?"

She blew her nose into a Kleenex. "Oh, I'll be all right!" she said in a giddy way that indicated quite the contrary.

"Is there something I can do?"

"That bastard."

"Who?"

"My husband," Maureen said between her teeth.

I don't know what collapsed in me, but I was not in the mood to hear this story; I wasn't in the mood to sympathize; the kids were waiting for our tête-à-tête to be over; we had less than a *week* to put this thing on; everyone had his personal problems; I paid her by the hour to play the piano, and I goddamn wanted her to play the piano! I counted to ten to calm myself.

"Maureen—do you think in a few minutes you'll be ready to play? I have to know, because otherwise I'll send the kids back. . . ."

"Oh, I'll be all right."

"Fine." I walked away as she flattened out the score. "All right, everybody get back onstage. We're going to practice the finale. Vicky, that means you too. The song is 'There's a Place for Us,' Maureen."

* * *

The tempo picked up. By now we had two stagehands, Tammy and Kelly, who were very fussy and responsible and kept complaining to me that "the actors are touching the props!" We had also added a reliable curtain puller, Bob; a makeup girl; ushers. Children begged to be given odd jobs in order to have a part in the production. *West Side Story* had become a kind of Juggernaut that all the kids wanted to jump onto at the last minute.

I had no shyness any more about asking staff members to help me organize traffic and matériel. They understood that I was not making the request for *myself* but for this larger cause, the Show, which had come to symbolize the pride of P.S. 90. Yolanda's mother voluntarily sewed matching bolero skirts for the girls in the "America" dance. Toni Farrington, our reading teacher, led the cast chorus in the final ensemble number. Everyone in the Teachers & Writers team pushed aside other commitments to help: Karen, to run the follow-spot from the projection booth; Sue Willis, to oversee backstage; Bette Korman, to help the kids design scenery and costumes. Now that we were in full rehearsal, it was no longer possible to work with small groups: everyone had to be backstage for his or her entrances. Problems of maintaining order (and I use the term in its most free-swinging sense) increased geometrically. I needed adult bodies to occupy the girls' dressing room and prevent assault or quell tantrums. Toni, Sue, and an officer in the PTA, Ellen McIntyre, took turns being policewomen—an unglamorous but critical function. Bette Korman kept some of the boys busy by having them sew gang names on the backs of their jackets. The Sharks were cutting and sewing red felt letters onto their denim or white zipper jackets, while the Jets were using a lively aquamarine material.

Now the boys went around the halls in their colors and insignia, walking tall, as if they were actually members of rival gangs or clubs. The distinction between theater and life kept thinning to a pencil line.

Denise Loftin dittoed up tickets for the evening performance ($.50 adult, $.25 children), and the cast members went around the classrooms and the neighborhood cajoling and selling tickets. As a big favor to me, Denise kept track of the receipts. (I was too nervous to fidget with quarters and dimes.) Her class also painted a bedsheet with the words WEST SIDE STORY and the date and time of the evening performance, and we hung it from the first-floor windows as a banner. It was very noticeable. Monte Clausen and I, having gone through all sorts of trouble to hang it symmetrically, were standing back on the sidewalk, admiring our efforts, when Clausen turned to me: "Hey, wait a second. What kind of paints did you use for this?"

"I think she said tempera."

"Great! You're going to have a very mushy sign if it rains. That thing's going to look like tie dye."

"What can we do about it?" I asked him. "Can we spray it?"

"Sure, spray it! You know how many cans of fixative that's going to take? And even then it's doubtful." He looked up at the sky; my eyes followed his. There were storm clouds gathering. Gray, pregnant clouds, swollen with water. "At this point, I think your best bet is to pray."

God, see to it that it doesn't rain for seventy-two hours, or, if it does rain, that the colors don't run. . . . I didn't mind adding this to the long list I was already giving Him on the subway down to Lafayette Electronics to pick up an omnidirectional mike. Only a miracle could pull us through. Two days before performance and we still had never run through all the scenes consecutively. The ending had been practiced only once or twice. And they were still coming up to me begging to have this scene or that scene added. They were crazy. That follow-spot was a beautiful invention. For $20 we get a machine that has red, blue, amber, green, and white and can open to half the stage or narrow to a facial close-up. It's all coming together. But he's right, the color lights alone make everything a little dim and down. We need them and the house lights, but it would take a lighting genius to figure out how. I have to stop thinking about *West Side Story!* . . .

*   *   *

The day before opening I came into Denise Loftin's class at ten o'clock to collect her kids and they were so happy they burst into applause. Only Virginia made a mean face: "We been waiting and waiting for you all morning. When are we going to *practice?*"

The whole crew ran through the halls and down the stairway to the auditorium. Rehearsal began in an unusual way. Britt and Willie collided like outfielders and hurt their heads. Britt refused to go onstage. "He did it on purpose," Britt said, rubbing his head.

"Get on that stage. Come on," I said. I was talking all in mono-syllables. My impulse to nurse their bruised heads (for genuine or social reasons) had been worn through like a frayed collar. The naked, instinctual me was coming out.

I yelled; I screamed; I lifted children through the air. I wanted them to move from scene to scene—snappy—get those transitions sharp.

Roberto, always the technical expert, stopped in the middle of singing "Officer Krupke" to call for a blue spotlight.

"You going to do that tomorrow? You're an actor!" I cried. "Stop directing the lighting crew!"

Dolores, who had been so eager to rehearse, did her familiar number of walking around the back of the theater in her winter coat like a lady bored at a gambling casino.

Out of the clear blue sky, Britt said to me: "You remind me of a poor man. Helpless."

"Why do you say that?"

"Because you're always trying to get everyone to listen and they won't pay attention. I can't explain it. You just strike me like a poor man," Britt shrugged.

I told him to save his pity; I was doing what I wanted.

Eventually the kids calmed down and we ran through most of it. There was wonderful energy in the dress rehearsal. Loud voices: they remembered to do that. While they were not always as good at facing front, I decided it was better for them to relate strongly to each other as characters and sacrifice some articulation than to make them self-consciously turn toward the audience. Their interaction *with* each other within scenes was fantastic, better than many professional actors I've seen. I only wish we could have gone through the whole thing once.

We would put it on first for the little kids. Gullible first-, second-, and third-graders, they would more likely be impressed.

And we could learn enough from our mistakes to correct them in time for the Thursday night show. That was our crucial test. Then on Friday we would face the most difficult audience: the older kids, the classmates and peers of the actors.

It went well today!

Still no flyer gotten out to the parents.

I'm connected to the great flow.

Fingers crossed.

*   *   *

The first time we were able to do *West Side Story* from beginning to end was before an audience, on opening day. I had posted signs listing the order of scenes on the dressing-room doors. I wanted to give a pep talk for everyone, like Henry V's inspirational address to the troops, but this ambition was denied me when they wouldn't quiet down long enough to listen. And anyway, they didn't need one. The kids swarmed over the stage and started rehearsing songs by themselves. Suddenly they had regained the drama and blood and passion of *West Side Story;* they had regained their original inspiration.

Britt brought in a tube of red dye which he fastened to his belly for the death scene. The boys were more wrapped up in the red dye than in what I took to be more important matters. Tammy was giving the girls elaborate eye makeup in the dressing room. All this attention to decoration was no doubt a way of quieting their stomachs.

And the usual punching from behind the curtains, so much so that the curtain resembled a sea full of waves.

And finally the moment came when the classes started filing through the aluminum doors, down the aisles, and my heart sank and I wanted to say, Go back, it isn't ready; but nothing could hold them back now, the hordes.

"They're here!"

"Will you tell Richard that it's my job to open the curtains?" complained the curtain boy.

"Bob is the only one to touch the curtains," I said numbly. I could barely open my mouth, I was so frightened.

"And the first scene you want the back curtain open and the

front curtain open, then you want the front curtain open and the back curtain closed?"

We went over his cues again.

Meanwhile David was very upset because he couldn't find his policeman's stick.

"Use this." I bent down and handed him a chair leg that happened to be lying on the floor, a casualty of some actor's rage against furniture.

"But it's *curved*," David whined.

"Use it."

I could sympathize. How could he feel like a policeman with a chair leg for a billy club?

A moment later he came back. "If you find my regular stick, will you tell me? This stick isn't any good."

I took him aside. "Listen, use the one you've got. And don't talk to me any more about that stick!" I said ominously.

Britt would save us. That was all I could hope for. The Jets were in place. Everyone was in place. "Don't push!"

"Good morning boys and girls. . . . We have a special treat today," I heard Mr. Glass's voice boom unreally over the auditorium. He came backstage. "I made the announcement. Do you want me to stay out there and keep them quiet?"

"No, I can do that," I said. "What I really need is someone to operate the stagelights." Glass rolled up his sleeves and got down to business. He had a kind of dour expression but was intensely involved.

I gave the signal to Mrs. McGuire to play the overture. Then Britt strode on. As soon as Britt got the audience's attention, I knew we were in the clear.

I can't say what the first performance looked like because I was too busy chewing my nails. I remember holding kids back or telling them to go on, but in a sense I was unconscious. Everything was going so well my mind shut off and I was transported to that region of icy happiness.

They tell me that children were weeping and even Mrs. Banta had tears on her face when Tony died. Virginia too—she who knew all the artifice that went into it. I had forgotten that *West Side Story* would be an affecting experience. When we picked up the cot with

Willie lying on it and circled the stage and came and sat on the apron one at a time, until we were all seated together, and sang "There's a Place for Us," it did seem sad and impressive, even to me.

We were in trouble only once. It came during the start of the second act. As the gangs moved onstage for the Quintet number Willie felt a shove and yelled, "I quit!" He ran out the side door and up the staircase toward the gym locker room. I chased him up the stairs, knowing that I had to get him down onstage in twenty-five seconds. The gangs were already singing "The Jets are gonna have their way to-niiight." I caught up to him on the staircase. What's the matter? He pushed me. Who. Richard. You've got to go on. No. I'm sorry he pushed you, but you can't quit in the middle. Please, come on. Okay, but next time I'm quitting for good.

It was all done in shorthand, his rebellion, my coaxing and insistence, the form honored but streamlined as we were both so conscious of the secondhand piercing our guts. He gave in and ran downstairs through the stage door to arrive onstage just as the pianist was cueing up for his sweet "Tonight" solo. Not a second too late, not even out of breath.

As I walked up the auditorium aisle at the show's end, I spotted two friends, Bob and Sylvia. They were dancers whose opinions I trusted, and I asked them how they thought it went.

"Great," said Bob. "Fabulous. It held my interest throughout."

"How about the dancing? Should we change the choreography?"

"The dancing's fine, man. Leave it alone."

Sylvia seemed to have some unspoken reservations. "You don't agree?" I asked her.

"No, I thought the kids moved very freely with their bodies. It's just that we were sitting far back, and you couldn't hear some of the lines. Other than that—"

"Other than that it was tremendous," said Bob, with characteristic generosity.

"Hey, Phillip, why don't you introduce us?" Britt came over.

"Sorry, these are my friends, Bob and Sylvia. And this is Britt, Luis, Roberto, and Gene."

Britt looked from Sylvia's face to mine and back again with his cunning leer. "So this is your girl friend. . . ."

"No, these two are married," I explained. Bob and Sylvia laughed politely.

"So what did you think?" Roberto asked them.

"I thought you guys were great," Bob answered.

"We really enjoyed the whole thing," Sylvia added.

"See what I mean?" Britt said to me. "I told you we would come through."

"What do you mean, see what I mean? You told me it would be a disaster—"

"Yo, Phillip. We want to put it on in the afternoon for the other kids," said Roberto.

"Yeah, we come to ask you if we can put it on this afternoon," Britt said.

"No. You're putting it on tomorrow and the next day."

"But we want to put it on *today*."

"You're going to get hoarse. Don't make me work harder than I have to," I said.

"We're the ones who do all the work. You just give orders."

"Now I don't do work!" I turned melodramatically to my friends for support.

"Then we'll put it on without you," said Britt. "Come on, fellas. We know what to do."

They started running toward the stage to rally the remainder of the cast. I yelled after them: "How are you going to sing without a pianist? Britt, Roberto, if you put it on this afternoon, I'll break both your legs!"

No fear of that. They would wait till tomorrow evening. But I knew they wanted to keep doing the show to hold onto their momentum. It was no longer a question of ducking schoolwork. Their everyday world was pallid next to this all-consuming theater world. It was painful to have to return to being ordinary school children. Xiomara begged to rehearse in the afternoon, and when I told her I couldn't because I had to make up the program notes for tomorrow evening, she said: "Couldn't I help you do the printing?" "No, Xio, I have to take it to a Xerox shop and they'll print it for me." "So, don't you need someone to fold it?" "I could use help folding it, sure. But that won't be for a while." "Come to my class and ask for me," she said coyly, making me promise.

Later, as I was sitting in the main office typing up the program notes, the principal saluted me.

"How's our impresario, Sol Hurok?" Ed said with a grim smile that meant trouble.

"Okay. It went surprisingly well."

"So well," he retorted, "that I lost my assistant principal for the cabinet meeting."

"I'm sorry about that. It's my fault."

"I'm saying you have to consider the totality of the school and not just *West Side Story*. Ted Glass was down there the whole morning. He *said* he was just going down to see if it would start all right. Our cabinet meetings are held only once a week. He may have missed out on some important information. I'm saying for you to keep him down there the whole time—"

"Now you know I don't have that kind of power," I answered smoothly.

"I'm not sure. That atmosphere can be pretty seductive." Suddenly Jimenez must have thought better about making an issue of it, because he did one of those gracious about-faces that always surprised me. "How would you like to produce our cabinet meetings? Or stage our Title I luncheon meetings?" he said good-naturedly. "Maybe we can even find some money in the budget to hire you as an entertainment director. I'm sure the meetings would draw better attendance."

*   *   *

The next morning, staff members stopped me in the halls with compliments. Several lower-grade teachers who had been in the audience told me how much they had loved it and that the children were so inspired they were making storybooks based on *West Side Story*. These copious praises began to weigh heavily on me and I felt a turbulence and anxious desire to get away every time a new person started.

The whole experience demonstrated how off-balance I became from success. I needed to keep a sense of proportion and to hold my ego in place. "You are a mere speck in the universe," I told myself, not too convincingly.

Seth's mother, who was also a second-grade teacher, told me

how fantastic she thought the first performance had been. "I'm coming again tonight. Seth told me last night: 'You know, Ma, we couldn't have done it without Phil. There isn't another teacher in the school who could have gotten us through it. Phil understands us. And we put him through so much trouble in the beginning. But he had an idea how it would look and that's why we stuck with it.'"

No kidding! I thought. After all the lip that brat had given me, I was surprised he had come to such a warm independent judgment. Of course he would never let on to *me*. But it was nice hearing it from another source; and, come to think of it, he had shown many signs of maturing during the last few weeks. I told his mother, naturally. Then somebody said Mr. Glass was looking for me, and I departed with relief.

Ted Glass was in the yard, overseeing the play groups. It was a slightly chilly day and I had run out in my shirtsleeves; from a distance away I could see him among the jungle-gym bars, surveying the concrete playground for possible trouble. He was wearing a mustard-colored corduroy jacket with black elbow patches, and a narrow wool-knit tie. As I came upon him, he had one arm comfortingly around a very little black girl with tears streaming down her face.

He sent her off with her teacher and turned to me. "I wanted to speak to you about ironing out some of the snags in yesterday's performance. Now I think you have a good production and you've managed to make the kids stay in character which is the most difficult part. I don't know—you say you have no theater background," he said doubtfully, his gaze continually roaming the schoolyard as he talked. He had that radar-scan mannerism that seems chronic with principals and assistant principals. "But I think you can use the time profitably between now and tonight by tightening some of the mechanical details. Curtains, getting the scenery on and off faster, coordinating the lighting cues between the projection booth and backstage—for instance, the blackouts should be sharper." My face must have sunk at that moment because he reassured me: "I don't mean to take away from the value; what you've got is very good. It's just that these technical things shouldn't detract from the performances which are the heart of the show."

I nodded. He was right of course; only, I was unprepared for anything but high praise, and I suddenly felt as if I'd been punched in the stomach. Then I remembered, he had his own problems.

"Listen," I said, "I hope you didn't get in trouble for helping us yesterday morning."

"Oh, that. That part doesn't bother me," he made a dismissing gesture with his hand. "If I ever let that start to worry me . . ."

"Anyway, you'll be there tonight?"

"I might be a little late. But I'll try to get there before the curtain goes up. Seven-thirty, right?"

"Seven-thirty, yes. Thanks a lot!"

There would be a full rehearsal that afternoon. Glass's suggestions were weighing on my mind. I was torn between a responsibility to perfect it—iron out the kinks, pick at it, tighten the little nuts and bolts—or let it come off the way it had yesterday. Basically I liked the show. It was more important that they retain some spontaneity for the evening performance. Besides, there was a point of diminishing returns with them after which it did not get better. The kids would improve and then slide back to old habits like turning away from the audience, almost as a determined gesture to retain their amateur status. "We're not professionals, Phillip!" Xiomara told me more than once. It was true; they were doing it for fun, not Broadway.

In spite of these reservations, I went ahead with a full-scale dress rehearsal because it was expected of me. And how I wished I hadn't. It was very demoralizing. Instead of getting tighter, the show unraveled like a ball of wool.

The tension of whether we could do it or not had dissipated with yesterday's success. What could ever replace the cohesive terror that had cemented our opening performance? I had never faced this problem before, in the couple of one-shot productions I had directed last year. It was a new phenomenon: the problem of "the long run."

Everything was conducing to make me uneasy. The good mood from this morning's compliments had disappeared without my even noticing it, nibbled away by tiny anxieties. Many of the kids were not going home after three but would be hanging around school till curtain time. Maybe they were telling the truth that their homes were too far away; maybe they liked the pajama party aspect of lolling backstage. In any case I would have to babysit from three to seven. Then a group of tough older kids from the local junior high school had sneaked into rehearsals, drawn by the mesmeric flame of *West Side Story*. They demanded to be let in free tonight. My sixth-graders were frightened of the older kids. Visions of Altamont fistfights danced in my head. Something malevolent was in the air. I couldn't put my finger on what, but it was a grr-rrr, a buzzing of scattered energy. Somehow I felt it was up to me to set the right tone and to hold everything together by the force of my concentration.

"Leave those curtains alone!" I shouted.

Gene pulled me over to a quiet corner backstage.

"Come 'ere; I want to talk to you."

"What is it?" I bent down to Gene. He came no higher than my stomach.

"I want to ask you something."

"Ask me," I said tiredly.

"I'll do anything you say. I'll sing loud, I'll face the audience, but we've got to make a deal."

"What's the deal?" He seemed to be stalling before saying it, and I was in no mood to play guessing games. "Come on, tell me."

"Just cool down! You're way too nervous."

"Right." I put my arm around him. I laughed. I kissed him. He was taking care of me. The kid saw right through me and he understood me and he was giving me his protection. It made me secure as nothing else could have.

"Let's go out and get a Coke," I said to Karen Hubert. "Someone else will watch them for a while." As we left the auditorium and headed for the front doors, briskly before anybody could stop us, I said to her: "I finally put my finger on what was wrong with today's rehearsal. . . . It was *me*."

Xiomara, licking an ice cream cone, ran into us on the front steps. "Where *you* going?"

"Out to get a Coke. Gene told me I needed to calm down."

"That's the truth! The trouble with you Phillip is that you hold in your anger too long and then it comes out too much."

"What else is wrong with me, Xiomara?" I asked this snotty twelve-year-old with amusement.

"Your face!" she cried.

"You should talk."

"Drop dead."

An hour later, calm, detached, my head cleared, I re-entered the school building, thinking, Let it be. Whatever the Gods had up their sleeves was fine with me.

In the auditorium Dolores, Virginia, Yolanda, and Xiomara were playing an unusual game: leading the smaller boys by the neck around the aisles like pet dogs. It was a very interesting glimpse into their future relations with men. After watching these dog-master teams go round and round for five minutes, I started getting dizzy.

"Don't you think you should give him a chance to relax, Dolores? Save some energy for tonight."

"No. This one doesn't get tired!" she said and continued leading Scott around the hall.

How would I get them to conserve their strength? Children are great energy squanderers. If they feel a burst they spend it immediately like a nickel at the candy store. Then they're grumpy and tired. This is their beauty: they let their energy rule them. "Hey, remember in kindergarten," I said, "when you took a nap in the middle of the day? This may sound corny, but it's nap time. Go to sleep. Rest. Lie down for a few minutes."

Several of them obeyed, to my surprise. They spread their jackets on the wooden stage as mattresses. Willie said, "Lie down here with me, Dolores."

Dolores walked over to him and took a stride over his prone body, fanning her skirt flamenco style.

"I can't watch this," said Karen, clutching my arm. "I'm too embarrassed."

"But do they see it the way you do?"

"I have no idea!"

"And yet, for all her provocativeness, none of the boys asks Dolores out."

"Of course. She's too formidable."

The technicians began arriving. The apprentice who would be videotaping the evening's performance, the ticket takers, the ushers, the stagehands . . . everyone was asking me questions about where to hook up the microphone, how was the public-address switch turned on, questions that an electrician might be able to answer but not me. I tried telling them everything I knew; then I tried bluffing, which meant going with them to the switchbox and holding their hands while they fooled with one thing or another, and commiserating if it didn't work. It was obvious I knew *nothing* about the wiring of the building. Yet people insisted on asking me more and more of these questions because I was identified with *West Side Story,* and it seemed natural to them that everything should go through me. Only a few insightful people, like Xiomara or Karen, took care of problems without asking me. The others passed on their anxieties to me until I started feeling like a switchboard dangling with loose prongs. Finally Mrs. McGuire said that she had forgotten to bring an extension cord for her piano lamp and where did I keep the extension cords?

"It's getting to be too much; I'm getting depressed," I said, and walked like a prima donna across stage away from her.

How did these words come out, I wondered, and not the ones that were on my lips: What's the matter, you don't know where to find an extension cord? A big girl like you? Do I look like a hardware store? You think I carry extension cords in my pocket?

Somehow she got both messages; she didn't bother me about it again. Later on, I noticed an extension cord had found a way of being attached to her reading lamp.

It was time to go out for another Coca-Cola. I left Sue Willis in charge of the group. "Remind me to buy some flowers to present to the leading ladies," I said to no one in particular.

At six-thirty, when I returned, once more relaxed and equable, several kids frantically pulled me inside the building.

David gave me the running report. "Where were you? We've been looking for you for a half-hour! Virginia quit. Yolanda's quitting. Everybody's screaming. It's going to be a failure."

"No, it's not."

"If only they could be made to have *order!*" said David. That funny word. I thought how fitting that he should play our Officer Krupke. I went backstage to the girls' dressing room, confident the problem could be handled. Xiomara and Dolores were leaning by the curtains, their cheeks fire-engine red and their lips glossy with lipstick. Their hair and their eyes were shiny black. Dolores had on a very mature white brocade dress. "How does our makeup look?"

"Beautiful. Both of you look sensational." I had never seen them so grownup and womanly, and it startled me.

"You should talk to Virginia."

"I know." I knocked on the dressing-room door. "Open up. It's me." Yolanda let me in. She was the first to speak.

"I'm quitting. If Virginia quits, I swear I quit." I looked at the pink velvet ribbon in Yolanda's hair and shrugged. She'd never quit. She wanted that applause. Virginia was another story. She was slumped over in her deepest sulk, wouldn't lift her head. I would have to coax her. "What's the matter Virginia? . . . The boys were bothering you? I told Mrs. McIntyre to come back here, so from now on there'll be a lady in the dressing room at all times. Yolanda, could you go and get Mrs. McIntyre? She's standing in front of the stage." Yolanda left and Virginia and I were alone. "Virginia, you can't quit. You're too important to the show. I wouldn't mind if someone else quit, but you hold that 'America' group together. They'll fall apart without you. And you wouldn't feel very good if you let them down. Think about it. We need you. What do you say? Will you do it?" I tried to look under that chin and mouth which were so low; I didn't know whether the answer was Yes or No.

"Yeah, I'll do it."

"Thanks, Virginia. I really appreciate this."

Just then sounds of a new fight broke out. "I'll speak to you later," I said. Gene was stalking down the aisle, toward the doors. "He's leaving for good," Scott told me.

"Well let's catch him!"

Scott, David, and I chased down the corridor of the basement, catching up with Gene just as he was about to reach the exit. He had every intention of leaving the building. I could tell by his face, by the tears in his eyes that he was serious. I blocked his path.

"Let me by. I'm not coming back. Roberto called me a faggot for the last time. A whole year he's been calling me a faggot." Gene pulled loose and hurled himself toward the door. I had to cut him off again and back him up against a wall, without hurting him. Gene was so swift and hard to stop that it took all three of us to impede him. We surrounded him like a body cushion, which frustrated him even more. "Let me go, Phillip. I'm not playing with you."

"Calm down first."

He burst into tears. "A whole year he's been calling me a faggot. I'm not a faggot!"

The parents were already coming in that exit to buy tickets. I was conscious of not wanting to make a scene. But I couldn't very

well shush him. What could I say? Banalities. "Look, faggot is a
name. People call each other names all the time. You know it's not
true. It's like insulting each other's mothers. Saying, 'Your mother's
a whore' or 'you're a bastard, bitch, idiot, schmuck, dumbbell.' . . .
They're just words. Words people use to get under each other's skin.
You know the truth about yourself. You know it's not true. Why
do you let a name bother you when you know it's not true?"

"It would bother you too if somebody called you a faggot for a
whole year!" He pulled away again. He ran for the door; his face was
hot and red. I saw that my speech on names wasn't working. It wasn't
working because it wasn't true. Of course names hurt; the same one
had hurt me. I would have to come up with something better. Meanwhile there was the problem of edging him toward the wall and con-
taining the noise. It dawned on me that this was not going to be an
easy persuasion like Virginia. Gene *could* get stubborn and leave.
He had only a small role, I thought rapidly, but that wasn't the point.
His desertion would have a very bad effect on the cast. Besides, I
liked Gene too much to see him beaten and driven wild by a false
accusation, a doubt. And what if he did actually have homosexual
feelings? So what? What insanity, to be dominated by such a false
standard! But I sensed this was not the time to preach acceptance
of homosexuality. Gene wanted no part of recognizing those feelings
in himself.

"Listen to me." He looked away. I thrust myself purposely before
his eyes. "LISTEN to me. When Roberto calls you a faggot it says
something more about him than you. You know what's inside you.
You know you're a man. This is the truth. When somebody calls
you a faggot, it's because he's insecure. He's insecure about his
manhood. I'm giving it to you straight, as if you were an adult. You
think because Roberto is so big and tough he doesn't have doubts
sometimes that he's a man?"

Gene looked confused. "But he keeps on calling me a *faggot*
and I don't have any friends any more and I can't make friends."
Tears were streaming from his eyes: years and years of childhood
loneliness that suddenly seemed too much to pretend weren't there.

"We you friends," Scott said. "You got lotsa friends."

"Yeah. We're your friends," David said gingerly. Gene brushed
them away like moths.

"See what I mean? You have plenty of people who like you," I said.

"Right? Roberto's been calling me a faggot in front of the whole class. In front of everyone?" Gene demanded of Scott.

Scott nodded sadly.

"But then why do you let goddamn Roberto be more important to you than *me*, than us?" I said. "If you walk away it's us you're hurting!"

"You hurting us," Scott picked it up.

"And then YOU"—Gene pointed to me—"you had to go ahead and print that story of Roberto in *The Spicy Meatball* about him calling me a faggot. And everybody knew."

"Your name wasn't even in that story," I said defensively.

"But *everyone knew!*" It was out in the open now: his long held-in distrust of me, the hurt I had inadvertently done him. Now my guilt was added to the stew. I felt terrible. If there is such a thing as Karma, my Karma was catching up with me. "Look, I'm sorry if that upset you. . . . All I can say is that that happened a long, long time ago."

I returned to the earlier argument. Name-calling was projection. I could see the idea was just beyond him; in a few years what I was saying would probably click. For now it slowed him down, which was all I wanted. We were starting to wear Gene down. I reminded him how much work we had put into the show, how much tonight meant to us, to everyone. Walking out on the show was not the way. "You don't have to make friends with Roberto," I said. "It's fine if you stay away from him. Tonight is not the time to settle this." Really, that was the truth of it. We did not have the time or the professional skill to untangle their relationship. "All I know is one thing," I let myself say it. "The show must go on."

"All right, I'll do it. But if Roberto calls me one more name—that's it. I'm walking out and I'm not coming back."

"If Roberto calls you one more name, I will personally make him a cripple."

We re-entered the auditorium fifteen minutes before curtain time. Several rows near the front were already filled by parents and families of the actors. Roberto and Britt saw us enter. They were sitting with their feet up in one of the back rows, looking moody and tense. I suspected they realized they had made a mess of it. I left Gene and went over to Roberto.

"I just want to say that Gene has agreed to come back. But you had better not call him a faggot or any other name, so help me."

"Then tell him to stop calling me Fat Boy," Roberto sputtered. "You think I don't know I'm overweight?"

Somehow I had to laugh. Everybody had his misery. "I don't care what he calls you."

"A whole year he been calling me *Fat* Boy."

"Tough," I said sarcastically. Roberto knew it wasn't equivalent.

Britt said: "We should go up to him now and apologize. That's the only way he'll stay in it."

"But what happen if he don't accept our 'pologies?" said Roberto.

"I don't know what, if he won't accept our apologies," Britt shook his head solemnly.

"He'll accept them," I said. "It's okay to apologize, but after that I'd rather you stayed away from him. Give him a lot of space. Walk away if he calls you a name. Just . . . don't go too near him; he's very upset."

"I don't need to go near him," Roberto muttered.

Mrs. McGuire arrived in a white formal gown with an astounding plunging neckline. She had dashed home to change and now bobbled down the aisle, explaining that she was so overdressed because she had a tenor recital to accompany immediately after the show. I thought her satin gown gave a perfect touch of bawdy elegance to the evening.

Customers were jamming the ticket tables. Five minutes before curtain we had a sellout. All five hundred seats were filled, and people were standing along the back. The largest turnout in the history of P.S. 90! Ted Glass showed me a black stick he had gotten for the switches so that they would go off simultaneously. "A sharp blackout," he said, his eyes twinkling boyishly.

"Britt quit," Tammy ran over to me.

"What?"

Willie confirmed the rumor. "Britt said he wasn't going on until his mother showed. And his mother didn't show up."

"Impossible. She must be somewhere in the audience. Where did he go?"

"I don't know, back toward that door somewhere," Willie pointed to the dressing rooms. "Maybe he ran into the street."

"I'll go look for him. Meanwhile, tell Mrs. McGuire to keep playing the overture." I ran backstage. I opened the door that led onto the street. All was quiet, down to the river. The street was chilly and fogbound. He wouldn't go out there, would he? How would I ever find him if he left? I decided he must still be inside the building. The staircase to the boys' dressing room was unaccountably dark. I started climbing along the bannister by touch. I got to about the third stair when my knee struck a person.

"Ha, ha! Fooled ya!" Britt said and slipped away from me, angling toward the stage. Now I understood: each one of them had had to see if I would run after him. Well, it was a dirty trick but at least he was safe. I had no time to get indignant. I moved onto the stage.

"Ladies and gentlemen, welcome to tonight's performance of *West Side Story*," I said, addressing the noisy mob, which suddenly stilled itself. It gave me a start to notice the junior high tough kids in the front row; I nodded to them to be cool. "As soon as everyone's seated, we'll be happy to begin. We hope you enjoy our production of *West Side Story*. We take this story very seriously, and we hope you take it seriously too." I don't know why I had to add *that!* I went through the curtains, muttering to myself. Glass was ready to kill the houselights. Karen was ready in the booth with the follow-spot. (They communicated with each other by means of a phone.) The pianist was ready; Britt was ready; the two gangs were ready; the curtain man was ready; the girls were ready. It began.

I was afraid to look. The audience showed their appreciation for every gesture. They oohed Britt's pantomime; they laughed at the way Anybodys wiggled her toosh; they applauded warmly after the Jets' song. I had never seen a more receptive audience. I sensed the actors were holding back vocally. Terror constricts the larynx. But the audience gave them its most quiet attention, and soon the actors were holding forth. I could feel the spotlights bathing their faces blue. Why was it so much more dramatic than during the daytime performance? Of course—no daylight to vitiate the colors. It looks good, I whispered to Glass. He nodded. We were afraid to say anything, to jinx it. From the truncated perspective of my position, I watched a sliver of the play through parted curtains. I wished I could have been in the audience. One thing followed another. "Officer Krupke" got roars of approval. The love duet between Willie and Xiomara also came off well. I suffered through only one embarrassing moment when Willie went up for a high note and his voice failed to go with him. No note came forth. He looked around at the pianist and the audience in surprise, as if someone would hand his voice back to him like a rubber ball. It was just the sort of thing that always happens in juvenile theatricals, but I was chagrined at the audience's patronizing laughter. This is no cute kiddie show!

Britt, feeling superconfident, began improvising bits that I had never seen him use. During the gym scene he introduced Tony (Willie) to every Jet in the cast. "What's he doing?" I asked. Britt saw my consternation and flashed me a smile. "Get on with it!" I whispered. Britt was taking his time, like Walt Frazier slowing down the ball. The audience loved it. He was lapping up their adoration.

In the second act, when I came onstage to act my little scene with Willie—a bit I loved, because the script called for me, Doc, to slap him in the face—the spotlights blinded me. I fluffed my lines! I had never expected myself to clutch. Willie helped me out of the jam, and I gave him the play money, slapped him (meekly), and got offstage quickly. I left with a new appreciation for the courage of these kids, to face those lights and those strangers!

Xiomara's performance impressed me the most. She had passion during the scene when she pounds her brother's chest, yelling "Killer killer killerkillerkiller!" All Willie could do was stand there taking it. And in the last scene, when Xiomara picks up the gun and cries, "Now I know how to hate!", it sounded so real that I had to bite down on my cheeks to keep from laughing or crying. I wonder why that intensity made the audience giggle too. Were they embarrassed at the melodramatics—or at the raw truth of it? The same thing happened with Scott. He had finally listened to me and produced a "He killed your brother!" that came shrieking from the gut. Some people laughed. If only they knew how far he had come to be able to give out those words with so much feeling. The audience seemed more at home with Dolores's pose-taking and Britt's cool professionalism.

All the actors were given ovations when the curtain went down. I had them stand in a line and step forward as I called their names.

Certain children seemed afraid I would forget their names: their faces were pitifully anxious and smeared with makeup and sweat. At the last name, Seth stepped forward and introduced me, and I took my bow. I gestured to the pianist, to the lighting crew, the stagehands; one only had to point somewhere to get people clapping their hands together. When it ended I drifted up the aisle accepting compliments.

Dozens of people whom I knew and half didn't expect to come were there: Maria Fornes, J.T., my father and mother, sisters, friends, writers, teachers. Swirling around. I let the crowd push me wherever it was moving.

I met Britt's mother, who was very sweet. Everyone was in a good mood. The principal was standing at the exit door, saying good-by to parents. He looked relaxed and expansive. "To be perfectly candid, I envy you," he said to me. "For being able to get so close to those kids." He must have been fond of me to admit that. I don't know why, but I had wanted his approval very much. Meanwhile a father was waiting for his daughter, who seemed to have gotten lost in the rushing crowd. "Did Christine come out yet, do you know?" he asked me. We all went searching for Christine. Calling "Christine! Christine!" in the hollow hallways until she appeared.

"How did you like it?" I asked a friend, who had not said a word.

"It was fun," he answered. "The best part for me was the fight between the two gang leaders."

* * *

I knew I had forgotten something last night. The flowers for the leading ladies.

I woke up Friday morning and walked out to a florist's to buy a bouquet. No point in mentioning tiredness; I was buzzing with fatigue.

"I want a bouquet. . . . I'm not sure what kind," I said.

"What's it for?" asked the florist.

"To give to some actors," I said, after blanking out several moments.

"A presentation bouquet." He showed me carnations and roses and I chose red carnations. Somehow they made me think of Spanish girls, Xiomara and Dolores. They were very pretty.

"Usually we make these up for evening shows, not in the morning. What's it for, a school?"

"Yep." I watched him trim the stems. He broke off the ends and then in one deft motion wired the stems so that they would stay in place. He arranged them fanwise.

"What kind of play is this?" he said without taking his eyes off the flowers. He was a white-haired, slender Irishman and knew his job well. I wondered if he was making conversation just to be gregarious or because he was lonely.

"*West Side Story,*" I said.

"Oh yes. Just about every school does that," he chuckled. I could have killed him. Didn't he know there had never been anything as big as our production in the history of the theater? "Every other day you hear on the radio some college is doing it. That's a darn good play, *West Side Story,*" he said. "I remember when it opened—twenty years ago. We get a lot of requests for theater bouquets, you know. From Lincoln Center. Vivian Beaumont, the Opera. We had a girl come in here yesterday . . ."

I wrote on a plain white card:

> To the cast of *West Side Story*
> from
>
> A Secret Admirer

I gave the flowers to one of the secretaries in the Main Office to hide until the proper moment. Assistant principal Glass walked in. "Glad you're here," he said. "We have to make arrangements for the final performance."

We counted up the classes who had not seen it yet. Sixteen. But the auditorium only seated thirteen comfortably.

"You're going to have to give another performance for those three classes."

"Maybe there are enough kids absent so that it will even out," I said desperately.

"Not a chance. And if you leave those three teachers out there's going to be hell to pay."

"I guess you're right. Dammit!"

"You're better off doing it on Monday. You should have planned this well in advance," he said. Why was he taking this peculiar tone with me? Where was our shirt-sleeved camaraderie of yesterday?

"I'd rather get it over with today. Let me talk to the kids," I said. I walked upstairs and told them the bad news. They took it professionally. We could put it on in the afternoon. No one liked that idea. Their cast party was scheduled for the afternoon and they couldn't bear to give that up.

"Why not have two shows in the morning?" Scott suggested.

"Yeah!"

"Your voices are going to be shot," I said.

"We don't care."

It was nine twenty-five. We could start the first show at ten and cut the intermission out; it would be over by eleven. Then have the theater emptied and the new kids come in. Figure eleven-twenty. We could be done by twelve-thirty. It was tight.

"Set up the scenery for the first scene," I said vaguely and ran out to find Assistant Principal Glass.

"They've agreed to do it twice this morning. . . . Okay?"

"No, it's not okay. Where are you going to put the little kids who eat lunch in the auditorium?"

"There's only about forty kids. We'll put them in the Writing Room, in the lunchroom, anywhere."

"It's easy for you to say, stick them in the lunchroom. But those kids are my responsibility. If there's an accident, it's my fault. That means setting up two extra tables in the lunchroom." His face narrowed and became pinched around the nose. The holiday was over.

"Can't we keep them in the auditorium during the play?" I asked.

"When are they going to eat? Be reasonable. You'll do it Monday."

"They can eat while they're watching the show," I said.

"They can't eat and watch the show. Besides, they've seen it once. You'll do it on Monday and that'll be the end of it."

"We can't do it Monday." I was ashamed to tell him the reason: If I had to live with *West Side Story* three more days, my nerves would go berserk. "We can't do it on Monday; the pianist is going away." Mentally, I sent her to the tip of South America. "She has to play in South Carolina."

He looked as if he didn't believe me. "Then sometime later in the week, when she comes back."

"No. She's busy. She works at Juilliard. She's a professional. She plays for opera singers."

Mr. Glass started to shake his head.

"You asked me to compromise! I got the cast to agree," I said. "We'll do another show for those three classes. Now you compromise. . . ."

"It's not a question of compromise. You have to do it for the whole school."

"Look, two performances in the morning, we'll do it for everyone." And I walked away. "Okay?" I turned around.

"You're being very unreasonable. . . ."

Unreasonable! Let *him* try to hold that cast together another week.

I ran back to the auditorium. The kids had casually set up the street props. I was proud of them. Maybe they didn't need me any more. . . . Meanwhile, the microphone was dead.

"Roberto told me to tell you the microphone isn't working," said Luis.

"Thank you."

Karen said: "Phil, the microphone doesn't seem to work."

"There's nothing we can do about it."

Dolores said: "The microphone—it's not on!"

"You'll do the best you can."

The kids breezed through the first performance. Their voices were a little ragged, but their timing was impeccable, like Frank Sinatra and the Rat Pack. If anything, the show seemed to me to be getting a bit too slick.

"That was the best one yet!" the prop girl marveled.

"You think so?" I didn't agree. I went to the front of the stage during the changeover in audiences and called the whole cast together. Which was never easy. Still hoping for one more chance to give my rousing Henry V speech, I appealed to the other adults to quiet them. "Listen," I croaked. "Hey, shut up! I gotta tell you something." It got a tiny bit quieter, so I proceeded. "That performance we just did was very smooth. But it was a little lifeless, a little dead. I don't think you were into the feelings enough. Now we've got one last performance. Let's give it everything. There's no tomorrow. This is it. Don't hold back. I want some soul! I want emotion!" By this time the new audience had begun to arrive. So much for Shakespearian orations. We ran behind the curtains; everyone was pushing, kidding around. "Come on, Richard! We can't pull the curtain until you're offstage." Richard laughed. Richard was in a very funny mood.

The final show had more *energy* than the penultimate one, I'll say that for it. It was jumping with wayward surprises. While Britt, arms spread, delivered his Jet solo, Richard turned his back to the audience and began shooting a soda can into the garbage pail. Then he remained onstage after his scene and I had to pull the curtain to shoo him off. He went into one of his "Don't you touch me" rages and I decided to give him a wide berth.

But by now Vicky wouldn't move off the stage rim during scenes. "Get off of there, Vicky, *please*—the audience can see you."

"I'm not in anybody's way."

"Vicky—get away from the curtains."

"You shut up."

"Oo, all I can say is if you were my size I would knock you flat," I gestured with my fist. Suddenly I heard myself. I sounded just like them! Not only had I taught the children, but it had been "a mutual learning process" (as educational textbooks say) and my mind had gone into twelve-year-old orbit.

The kids were making noise on both wings. Now that the pressure was off them and the show no longer a novelty, backstage life began to take on a yeasty exuberant independence.

"You got some nasty boys back here," Vicky smiled.

"They be pinching the girls' behinds. Cut it out, Richard!" said Janice.

Fortunately I realized that there was nothing I could do any more to hold it together and so fell into a cheerful state as I always do whenever I come to that conclusion.

Now a rumor started that Dolores had quit. I found her and asked what was the matter, but she wouldn't tell me. Another girl filled me in. It seems that right after the "America" number, which she executed superbly and with great poise, just as she was bowing to the audience and exiting to their applause, she ran into Britt, who said: "I heard you just got your period."

This remark utterly shattered her. She was no Miss Prim so I wondered why, of all things, that would send her over the edge.

Maybe it was that she was high and opened-up from the applause and the reference to menstruation soiled her triumph. Maybe it was Britt's sly undercutting digs which finally get to a person. I persuaded her to go on again for one last scene, the duet with Xiomara: "A Boy Like That." It was crooned so weakly that I could barely hear them three feet away. At her last note she stalked off saying, "That's all." She had managed to quit like a star, after finishing her last scene.

Willie, seeing that things were not going well, withdrew conviction from his performance midway. Nevertheless, he took the immense hooting that greeted his and Xiomara's love scene with dignity. When Xiomara placed her head on his shoulder and said, "Promise you'll stay with me," the upper grades went nuts.

By the time Willie and I came on for our little scene in front of the curtain, it was *West Side Story* frontstage and backstage. "You better quit it 'fore I knock you upside your head." "I'm not taking that from no black nigger," we heard from behind the curtain. Then a door slamming—"I quit!"—and something that sounded like a pile-up. I begged the audience's indulgence for a minute and stepped behind the curtains. Now I made myself fierce. "We have ten minutes more to go! Can't you stop arguing for TEN MINUTES?"

"No, Phillip. You don't know what these boys are doing," Xiomara said.

"Save it for the party," I muttered and pushed them into the dressing room, making sure Toni kept the boys and girls separated, and came onstage again. Willie was thoroughly disgusted. He gets disgusted easily. "They messed it up!" We managed to rush through the finale and did a ragtag funeral procession with everyone giggling as they carried Willie's body on a cot which split down the middle. We slumped onto the apron of the stage to do "There's a Place for Us." I think there were only about three people singing. The rest were battle weary.

I didn't care. I was so happy it was over. And that last show was exciting in its own delirious way.

Sue Willis put it well: "Without the last show I would never have realized what a miracle the first three were."

Toni Farrington presented the red carnations to Xiomara and Dolores. It gave the cast a nice final lift. The girls were pleased. They kissed everyone on the cheek, even me.

Later I saw Roberto walking around with a red carnation in his hand, like Ferdinand the Bull.

* * *

Nothing was left but the party. The teachers whose children I had worked with were kind enough to buy the refreshments during lunch. They had set up the potato chips, sweets, Hawaiian punch, and paper cups on a long table in the gymnasium, and were chatting pleasantly with each other, as I could plainly see by looking through the window of the gym door.

When I came in, a peculiar awkward formality fell over them as soon as they saw me. They stopped gossiping and pulled themselves straighter. I wanted to say, continue, don't mind me, but it was too late.

"On behalf of Denise, Monte, and myself," said Iris Mayer, "and Margaret Trabulski, who was very sorry she couldn't make it but wanted you to know she was in on it—"

"And because you took a large chunk of kids off our hands, including some of the worst," quipped Monte.

"And because you did a great show," said Denise.

"We would like you to have this tiny token of our appreciation. . . ." Iris handed me a box and I opened it hastily.

"What a nice vase!"

They burst into giggles. I turned it around. "Oh, a bottle of wine! Excuse me, I spoke too soon." I was mortified. My face went absolutely red. Well, that sort of mistake must happen to everyone in his life. . . . They accepted the fluff gracefully. I kissed each of them on the cheek, Monte wincing, of course.

"We figured you'd need it. Go home and get plastered," said Monte.

"Oh I will." I was terrifically touched. Why were they being so nice to me? Would I have bought them anything under similar circumstances? "It looks like really good wine."

"It's from Margaret Trabulski, too," Iris repeated. I tried opening it to offer them some but my hands weren't getting anywhere.

"You need a corkscrew for that," Monte said gently.

Denise stirred herself. "Hey, it's late. We've got to pick up our classes from the yard." They started making their way out.

"You mean you're not going to stay for the party?" I said, suddenly very lonely.

"Nah, we've got to stay with the other kids. We'll send the kids from the cast down to you in a few minutes. Have a good time," said Denise. They seemed not too sorry to leave.

"Well, come down for a few minutes if you have a chance," I said to all of them.

"We will. . . . Have fun."

They were gone. I was alone in the enormous gymnasium behind a table of party candy, feeling rather foolish. The sunlight was streaming through the window gratings and playing tricks with the scuffed-dull, wood-panel floor. I noticed motes of dust floating through the light, light that fell in arcs just beyond the wall benches and then diffused over the great space.

Presently the girls started coming in. Yolanda was very excited.

"We're gonna teach the boys the meringue!"

She set up the record player with a stack of 45s. Kim, a timid blond girl who was not so sure she knew the meringue and had joined the stagehand crew at the last minute, went to work seriously on the chocolate malted balls.

"I like the kind that get your hands all red."

"Red hots. We've got some."

"Yippeee!"

"I hate those," said Virginia. "They burn my tongue off."

Now the whole group rushed into the gym. The girls went over to the record player and the boys grabbed for the basketballs and immediately divided into two teams. Yolanda and Virginia had looks of disappointment on their faces. They would have a hard time rounding up the boys, much less dancing with them. It struck me as funny how these same boys who had had sex on the brain a short time earlier had redirected their energies. Either the gym was too connected in their minds with one thing, basketball, or the dark of the curtains had given them a courage that folded in open air.

The boys stampeded over to the eats table before everything was gone. Britt began organizing a circle. "Circle, everyone." He wasn't having much success. "Let's go, circle. Circle for Phillip." I was frankly amused at the trouble Britt had getting them to listen. He'd been telling me for months how I can't control them; now let's see how well this joker does.

"Circle for Phillip; come on everyone." They crowded around me.

"Phillip, this is for you from all of us," Britt said, gesturing around him with his unbeatable smile, "for helping us with *West Side Story*. Congratulations." He handed me a brown bag signed by each of the kids. "Three cheers for Phillip; let's go everyone." Britt conducted them through the cheers. "Yaay, yay . . ."

Inside the bag was a Billie Holiday record. (How did they know?)

"My favorite singer! Wow. Thanks so much, everyone. I love you."

Karen came in and I showed her my presents.

Did I forget to say that I was happy? I was very happy. My cup was brimming over.

Dolores taught us how to do the meringue. The kids were as usual fascinated to see their teachers dancing.

Somewhere in all this a fistfight broke out between Willie and Britt. Roland Warren, the security guard, separated them and I didn't think much about it. But five minutes later a monitor came from the principal saying I was wanted in his office. I left Karen in charge; I was feeling so jacked up that it was easier for me physically to respond to a crisis than to relax and party.

Willie was suffering in a leather armchair too big for him, up against the wall, and Ed Jimenez had on his humorless expression. Ed looked very tired. He had bags deep as welts under his eyes.

"We have a very serious situation here. Willie said he was going to bang Britt over the head with a chair. There have been racial remarks. Willie claims Britt threatened 'to knock the Spanish out of him.' I don't know; they're acting very much like people in *West Side Story*. I'm a little disappointed. . . ." Ed looked at me significantly. I recognized that administrator's tendency to distribute vague dustballs of guilt wherever they happened to stick.

"You can't blame this on *West Side Story*," I replied.

"I don't know. Willie, has this ever happened before with you and Britt? I don't mean arguments, but have you ever threatened to hit him with a chair?"

"No," Willie said morosely. (What else would he say?)

"I wanted to get Britt down here, but I'm afraid this thing is going to escalate and have schoolwide community repercussions."

Ed was exaggerating. I liked him very much, but he had a habit of anticipating race riots at the drop of a hat. "I'm not even sure we can bring the two together in one room," he added.

"You can bring them together."

"Where is Britt now?"

"He's in the gym."

"Another problem is that I don't know if I can trust Willie to stay down here alone."

"I'll stay with him," I said. The principal left.

Willie and I were silent. I gave him some time to catch his breath. The kid's eyes told me that he had spent his anger and he probably felt afraid and uncomfortable about being in the principal's office.

"What happened?" I asked nonchalantly.

"See I was playing basketball and Britt came in and started taking the ball away from me. I told him to get out of there. He's always thinking he's *bad*. So then he told me he was going to knock the Spanish out of me. But then everybody told me it was Roberto that said it. But Roberto was outside getting a drink of water! How he supposed to say it when his mouth is full of water?" Willie demanded of an invisible gallery. "And I didn't like that because it was an insult to my people. So then Mr. Warren came and held me down. And while he was holding me down Britt punched me. That ain't fair! That's just like Britt. Britt likes to hit on people when they're down. The way he was picking on Gene. Everyone's afraid of Britt, but Britt just acts like he's tough by talking himself up. I'm gonna tell everybody in the school not to be afraid of Britt because he's nothing but a bully."

He had run out of his first breath. I decided to take not the ethical approach but the pragmatic one.

"Let me ask you something. Did you ever get in a fight with Britt before?"

"Yeah, I did!"

"Who won?"

Some seconds went by. I knew the answer anyway; it was common knowledge.

"*He* did," Willie said with disgust.

"What makes you think you can take him now?"

"I been watching him. I know how he fights. Plus I'm stronger than I was last year."

I laughed.

Ed Jimenez walked in with Britt and the security guard. Britt was in remarkably self-assured spirits. Either that or he knew how to disguise his fear.

"Now we've got all kinds of stories here," Ed began. "Willie tells one story; Britt has another version; Mr. Warren saw something else. All right, when did this start?"

"Around two o'clock."

"All right, Willie, you go first."

Willie proceeded to tell his story. He was a little less impressive this time. Meanwhile Britt was watching his face with disdainful amusement. Never once did he contradict or cry out: "That's a lie!" No, he let Willie bumble over his words as if to say: Let this fool have his time on the stage, and then watch what I do.

The principal was trying to pin down the exact details, the order of events, the angle of a punch. . . . I knew where Jimenez was headed: a compilation of data and hearsay, an exercise in Rashomon point of view, a bureaucratic approach to anger that seemed so tired and heavy-handed, given the actual two boys. We would never be able to reconstruct the moment; that was *lost;* all we could do was satisfy our adult appetites for legal procedures, a waste of time. I was being carried along hypnotically by the logic of the investigation and Ed had just asked Britt to tell his story, when, before that superlative actor had a chance to seize the stage, I decided there must be a way to cut through all this.

I asked permission to interrupt. It seemed to me, I said, that these boys had committed a million follies and aggressive acts in the last weeks of rehearsal. Why concentrate arbitrarily on this one? They had been together long hours; they were always getting in each other's hair. Furthermore, both were very powerful, respected kids in the school with followings of their own. This incident was all part of a larger fight for top dog. Now we could go into the minutiae of this incident or we could try to figure out a way for them to live together for the rest of the term. If *West Side Story* did accentuate trouble, it was in the sense that they were both stars, and maybe they couldn't stand the applause the other got.

"You *are* like two actors," Jimenez concurred. "You're really putting on a great show and you should both get Academy Awards. Trouble is, the other kids might egg you on to turn acting into reality. A lot of kids in this school wouldn't mind seeing Britt get his lumps. They want Willie to fight you. Same goes for the kids who want to see Willie get his. They'll try to get a fight going. And you'll oblige because you like to put on a good show. But it will be your blood on the street, not theirs."

Both boys smiled at his directness. I was pleasantly surprised how easily he had abandoned the evidential approach and fallen in with mine. "So what do you think we should do?" Ed asked me, his eyes almost closed. "Excuse me, this comes at the end of a very tiring day."

"The two of them should maybe get together alone and talk it out. Tell each other what bugs you about the other. But don't always do it in front of everyone so that your allies make you fight."

"Well that's what I was trying to do! I tried to tell the guy"—Britt shrugged—"what was happening, but he wouldn't listen."

"Don't call him the guy," Jimenez put in. "You know his name— Willie."

"I told Willie I didn't say anything but he's the kind of guy— 'scuse me—that has to destroy. He smashes things. Makes him feel good," Britt observed.

A lot more was said back and forth; I was rushing them because I wanted to get back to the party. Finally Jimenez asked: "How do you feel about this now, Willie?"

"I feel like I got a headache sitting in this damn chair all afternoon."

"What do you think we should do?" Jimenez asked everyone.

"I think they should both go back to the party"—I stood up— "and stay out of each other's hair."

"I'm not sure I feel safe about that. We haven't called in the other kids yet and seen how it's affected them."

"Let them be allowed up to the party. I think they'll behave. If I'm wrong, I'll take the blame," I said.

Ed agreed to remand them to my custody. Luckily, there was no further trouble.

When we returned to the gym, no one was playing basketball any more; everyone was dancing. The tide had turned in the girls' favor and those who had not managed to ensnare a partner were chasing the available boys around the floor, hunting each one down in packs.

Dolores had been teaching the smaller boys how to grind. It was Scott's turn. She placed him against her leg and moved his leg very slowly and methodically against hers. "You have to get closer, Scott," she said, initiating him cheerfully into the Mysteries. Our temple priestess. Scott came just up to the point where he would have gotten buried in her womanly bosom. He refused to come any closer, but he did not pull away either. He took it like bad-tasting medicine that you knew in the long run would be good for you.

Poor Bob was harder to catch. He had to be surrounded by Virginia, Yolanda, and Susanna after a chase that covered half the gymnasium. Then he was dragged to the dance floor; my heart went out to him.

By this time Britt had found Vicky and they were dancing slow and sexy. Britt looked around with a grin every other second to see if anyone was paying attention to their hot performance. Vicky seemed a willing partner to his narcissism. "Come on, Phillip, why ain't you dancing?" he asked.

"I danced already."

Mack, the custodian, brought his pushbroom in and shook his head.

"I hope you gonna clean up this mess," he said.

"We will."

"All this junk under the benches better be out of here by three-fifteen."

It was close to three. I organized a clean-up squad and we scooped up the largest part of the clutter into big garbage cans. It was really over, the show, the effort, hard to believe . . .

I went upstairs to get my coat and belongings. When I stopped by the second floor to take one last look at the gym, I watched with envy. They had thought up a new game. Several girls had consented to stay behind to be part of what looked like a Cattle Run. The girls were given seven seconds' headstart to run, after which the boys tore across the gym floor after them and it was every man for himself.

IV
Seven Lessons

Chapter 14
The Balkanization of Children's Writing

When I first began teaching creative writing to children, I was frightened enough that I ran to the library to read everything I could on the subject. I discovered that there was no serious criticism of children's writing as a branch of literature. But there were books of methods; and the more I read these books, the more my skepticism increased. Each seemed to be founded on an absolutely different version of what children were like or what constituted good literature.

I came across manuals dating from a century ago to the present, on teaching children to write. The oldest books appear to have featured piety and holiday verse. A manual dating from 1872, by John S. Hart, is especially fascinating because it makes a point of encouraging whimsy. Its wonderfully copious list of writing suggestions includes: Rural Happiness. Moonlight at Sea. Religion Tends to Make One Cheerful. The Duty of Confessing One's Faults. The Difference Between Beauty and Fashion. The Rainbow. Evils of Public Life. The Ever-Varying Beauty of the Clouds. Dreams. The Uses of Ice. What Kind of Popular Amusements are Desirable. Modes of Burial. A Visit to Greenwood Cemetery. A Visit to the Cave of Aeolus. A Ride Across the Atlantic on a Cloud. Gossipping. Nursing Sorrow. The History of A Pin.[1]

At that time, creative writing and, above all, poetry were clearly seen as vessels for the reception of elevated moral attitudes. Some fancy was allowed, of the doggerel-limerick variety. Children confess wanting to play hooky or go fishing—the stuff of *Our Gang* comedies, innocent amusements, reflecting perhaps the fondness of an adult remembering his golden youth, more than the actualities of child-

[1] Excerpted from *A Manual of Composition and Rhetoric,* by John S. Hart, LL.D., Philadelphia, 1872.

hood. Local banks put out advertising newssheets which occasionally included a column of children's verse. The state would sponsor a contest on a broad ideal, like "The Value of Commerce" or "The Purpose of a Good Education," and award prizes to children who wrote the "best" compositions supporting this philosophy.

This historic phase in children's writing could be called the era of the "Goody-Goody" and the "Cute," which has survived intact to the present day. Indeed, it may still be the dominant approach.

Most children's verse in the 1920s and 1930s was still written with rhyme and meter. For two reasons: 1) the innovations of Whitman and Pound and the modern school continued to be resisted by schoolteachers as not really poetry; 2) children's first introduction to verse usually occurred through rhymed jingles heard in the street or at school. The use of rhymes as a *phonics* device to teach reading reinforced the idea of poetry as something that had to rhyme. Little children are in fact drawn to rhyming as a nonsense game. But the influence of jingle phonics readers kept them (still does) at a cat-bat-rat level of poetry that could not keep step with their more complex thoughts.

Then writers like Flora Arnstein began calling for the introduction of free verse into the curriculum. In her pioneering book, *Children Write Poetry* (1946), there are many examples of children's poems in a new mode: condensed diction, jagged and irregular lines, sound that is based more on alliteration and onomatopoeiac imitation of nature, and subject matter of a pantheistic bent. The influence of Imagism and Carl Sandburg is very strong in poems by her students:

> The dismal foghorns are sad today.
> They are crying so drearily, so mournfully.
> What is your sorrow, foghorn?
> Have you lost a friend,
> Or are you just moaning all your troubles
>   To the world?[2]

This is a very specialized and—I don't know what to call it—Impressionistic idea of poetry. Evocation of mood, the elements, the eternal

[2] *Children Write Poetry,* by Flora Arnstein, Dover Books, p. 179.

ebb and flow, with each detail softened and generalized to the point that it loses its particularity. If the poems in Arnstein's books seem dated to me, it is probably because I am willing to trade some of their gossamer timelessness for a few hard if perishable facts: this man named John, that detergent box of All, a town called Paterson New Jersey.

Elwyn Richardson's classic, *In the Early World,* shows New Zealand children putting their ears to the ground and writing about the sound of grass. Here the stress is again on natural detail, delicate haiku phrasing, and a shying away from large resolution:[3]

> I lie in the long grass
> Watching the long, thin power pole
> Through the tall seed headed grass

Poetry and *quietness* are made synonymous. New Zealand may simply have children who are more quietly civilized, though I doubt it. These children were taught to use poetry only as the record of still moments.

Coming into the present era, the sound of children's poetry breaks into louder, brasher, more colloquially urban possibilities. Now the claim begins to be made that we are getting the unadulterated version of what children are like, not the prettified way that adults would have them. One collection actually calls itself, with prophetic stateliness, *The Voice of the Children.* The writings of children are suddenly accorded the ethnopoetic dignity of a lost tribe whose songs have been discovered, the veneration reserved for naïve art, and the political sympathy for an oppressed and inarticulate minority which has begun to learn to speak. So much of this appreciation is long overdue, and just; but few bother to question the representativeness of the children's voices. What is missing is any perspective in clarifying the collector's prejudices, the range of the sample, the methods of collection, and the degree to which it is possible to generalize from the results.

On the contrary, parents and children are promised nothing less than the hidden, secret world of children—the me nobody knows. The books sell well. Some are packaged more as Christmas gifts, coffee-

---

[3] *In the Early World,* by Elwyn Richardson, Pantheon.

table charmers, to leaf through at idle moments and feel a smile brought to one's lips.

The most exciting breakthrough is Kenneth Koch's *Wishes, Lies and Dreams*. Fresh, colorful, zany, chatty, funny, poignant, sweet (sometimes to the point of preciosity), these children's poems reveal a verbal dazzlement and imagination that can transform distances and objects at the stroke of a pen.

What Shall I Chartreuse?

Oh green, yellow, orange, pink, red, black, brown,
What shall I chartreuse today?
I could chartreuse with brown and gold,
Or I could red John in the nose. What could I chartreuse?
I put a green croak in Pinky's bed, what shall I chartreuse?
I could put a silver yeow on teacher's chair
What shall I chartreuse?
I could ooze the blue toothpaste in Dad's face. What shall I char-
    treuse?
What could I chartreuse if I got a paint brush?
Oh, oh I just wasted the day on thinking on what I shall chartreuse
But I could always think of something to crown yellow tomorrow.

CHARLES CONROY[4]

Poetry is approached here as a game, with certain rules: here the rule is obviously to put a color in every line. Children emerge as playful and vivacious, but, even more, as "naturals" who express themselves off the top of their heads very much the way modern poets do. This is a grain of truth in this premise. Take down the mumblings of a kindergartner, as Armand Schwerner once did with his son babbling at the bathroom door, and you may get a product uncannily close to the feel of a contemporary poem. This is because both children and many poets of the new school are attracted to chanting, to free wordplay, to sudden changes of scene, to hypnotic repetition in a Gertrude Steinian mode, to simple diction, to cataclysmic visions stated with present-tense certitude.

This said, there is still something mechanically induced about

---

[4] *Wishes, Lies and Dreams,* by Kenneth Koch, Chelsea House, p. 210.

the hip, modernistic surface of many of the *Wishes, Lies and Dreams* poems. A good example is the Swan-of-Bees assignment, which asks children to think of an object being made of some entirely different material (e.g., "A blackboard of moons/A swimming pool of doorknobs"). This method is a fail-safe pedagogic machine for the mass production of surrealist metaphors; but it is a silly gadget for all that. What Kenneth Koch did was to perform a brilliant act of analysis on the body of modern poetry and on his own poetry. Many of the hallmarks of the avant-garde style—long free-verse lines, all-inclusive dream catalogues, collaged effects, exotic place-names and European vocabulary, madcap humor, sound poetry, synesthesia, collaboration poems—were translated into easily understandable game formulas. Koch was so successful that the poetry written by his Lower East Side schoolchildren has a remarkable similarity in flavor to his own poetry. Koch belongs to what is commonly called the New York School of Poetry; and so, by persuasion, do all his students at P.S. 61!

Stephen Joseph's *The Me Nobody Knows* is slanted in a very different direction. Children come across here as angry muckrakers, frustrated, unable to think about anything but their neighborhood. They write from a tell-it-like-it-is, 2 x 4-foot mental cell, overlooking the lot with broken glass.

New York

New York is a dirty filthy place to live. It is full of dope addicts, pot smokers, speed and LSD and nothing is being done about it and I think it is disgusting the way the kids are losing their lifes from sniffing glue. I just think it is disgusting.

FRANCES[5]

What is amazing is that the children who wrote the stories in *The Me Nobody Knows* live in a neighborhood very similar to the one around P.S. 61, where Koch taught. Had the teachers been switched from the start, I would not be surprised if the above-quoted Frances wrote about zeppelins and Alaska, and Charles Conroy wrote about drugs.

Two other interesting collections by ghetto youth, Bill Wert-

[5] *The Me Nobody Knows*, edited by Stephen Joseph, Avon Books, p. 130.

heim's *Talkin' To Ya* and June Jordan/Terri Bush's *The Voice of the Children*, reflect the pungent influence of black and Puerto Rican contemporary poetry. The youth's revolutionary political sentiments, drumming rhythms—even their spelling mannerisms like "u" for "you" and their splayed syllabification come right out of the style of Sonya Sanchez, Imamu Baraka, David Henderson, Victor Hernandez Cruz, June Jordan, Felipe Luciano. . . . Most of these writers have worked at one time or another as visiting writers in the public schools. David Henderson made no bones about importing this influence:

"The best way to teach black kids to write is to bring in large doses of

Gwendolyn Brooks	Langston Hughes
Don L. Lee	Nicholas Guillen
Sonya Sanchez	Mari Evans

These are contemporary poets, from them we can get to the great heritage of black literature. From the particular and familiar of contemporary black poets and writers we can capture the enthusiasm of the young student and really begin to teach."[6]

Somewhere off to the side, in this Balkanization of children's literature, were Richard Lewis's anthologies, gathered world-wide through a grant from UNESCO. Lewis expresses a debt of gratitude to Elwyn Richardson, and his poetic taste shows the same respect for the understated haiku touch. In *Miracles,* we meet the child who looks out the window at the rain, solemn, struck with wonder, without much sense of humor. Lewis's next anthology of verse I found very moving. *There Are Two Lives* is a collection of poems by Japanese children, taken from the ordinary, domestic perceptions of being human:

The Western Movies

My father always watches the westerns
on TV.
He opens his eyes wide,
with a cigarette in his mouth.

[6] Quoted in Teachers & Writers Newsletter, vol. 4, issue 3.

> He watches TV,
> dropping the cigarette ashes
> in the fireplace.
> The cigarette becomes very short.
> He holds it with his fingers
> until it burns his fingers.

ITO HIROHIKO, *age* 8

I cannot resist quoting another of these poems, a lovely bit of child erotica.

Teacher

> When I hugged my teacher from behind
> I couldn't touch my hands.
> Teacher, you're too fat!
> My hand touched your breast.
> It was soft like a sponge.
> Teacher, let me touch your breast again.

KOBAYASHI TERUO, *age* 7[7]

Here, I had felt, was the real inner voice of children in writing. These poems were filled with the daily hurts and hopes of childhood; I recognized my own youth in them! The diction was pure, the thought unlabored. But by this very purity one comes to sense the paring, influencing, modernizing adult hand. The poems are *too* whole. Their poignant closure reveals a feeling for time, solitude, loss, and the passage of time that has more to do with adult taste than children's.

It is unnecessary to belabor the point. We have already been through the Child as Christian moralist, the Child as Nature-worshiper, the Child as avant-garde poet, the Child as muckraker and social realist, the Child as right-on revolutionary, the Child as astute psychological observer of daily life. Every aesthetic stance has had its analogue in a collection of children's writing. Just as Paul Klee seems to have needed children's painting as a reference point and precedent for his art, or Picasso the tribal sculptures of Africa, the

---

[7] Both poems come from *There Are Two Lives,* edited by Richard Lewis, Simon and Schuster, pp. 27, 53.

child's *word* is invoked by one artistic tendency after another as a kind of legitimizing voice of the collective unconscious. There are editors from every conceivable school of writing, who can keep slicing the mountainous piles of children's compositions into separate, packaged visions of the Child.

THE QUESTION OF MANIPULATION

Let us say then, tentatively, that there is no such thing as the voice of the children, meaning a voice distinct from the adults who are presenting it. The next question is, What is so bad about the influence of adult models on children's writing? How else could children be expected to write poems or stories without imitating adults?

The search for a pure "jungle habitat" expression of childhood, unsullied by adult direction, would lead us in circles. In a society where children and adults incessantly interact, either through direct contact or through television, there are no children without adult qualities. So vast is the assimilation by children of the adult's point of view, that if one wanted to start anywhere in a catalogue of elements that might make up a stylistics of children's writing, one would have to list the *incomplete ingestion of adult genres* as one of the foremost characteristics. This faulty imitation, with all its lacunae, accounts for much of the charm in children's writing. I have seen adults delight in a child telling the plot of an underwater adventure movie, smiling at his sudden ellipses and miraculous transformations, when the child would have been just as happy to relate the story in all its clichéd transitions. The little child only knows how to go A, B, D, J, Q, Z and the sophisticated adult says: Marvelous, how dreamlike. Little does he know that most children would love to go A, B, C, D, E, F, G, H, I, J, K, L, M, and so on, to the bitter end.

This is not to discount the factor of originality in children's writing. Some children are very keen on being original. I have come across a handful of artistically conscious, ambitious children who seemed to have embarked on a career in literature astonishingly early. They had no need of coaxing or writing suggestions from me. I considered it my pleasure to know them and to serve them: to collect their writings and see that Xeroxes were made in case the originals became lost, to act as their discoverer and publisher, to make a few suggestions which they listened to with a nice tact, and beyond that, to get out of their way. But these are interesting cases and deserve a special study.

In the end, there is no use regretting a lost state of innocence before the child was taught to write in one style or another. Exposing children to good adult literature can only deepen, enrich, and sensitize their efforts to write. A writer's job—including the child writer's —is to open himself to the world and its influences. And when it comes to writing poetry, why not prepare children for the world they will have to live in by training them to write in an up-to-date style, as one would with the new math or physics?

"Still," an inner voice keeps nagging at me, "there is something ugly about the prospect of a generation of schoolchildren learning to parrot the mannerisms of contemporary writing and to produce works that look, to us, intriguingly advanced, without their really *consciously* understanding what they are doing. We would like to know if these effects were intentional: if the writing came from a place deep within themselves or was merely a case of jumping through hoops set up by the teacher. Did it matter to the child, did he have the proud creative sense of building a world on paper, or did he respond more or less to an assignment cleverly preconstructed to minimize failure?"

The question of manipulation won't go away. The truth is that teaching almost always involves manipulation. To teach means to accept the responsibility of guiding others; the real teacher is one who is reconciled to dirty hands. No matter how antiauthoritarian one would like to be, no matter how much one would like to follow the lead of the children, the adult will always—even through the subtlest approvals: an eyebrow, a frown—be coercing and conditioning his students to perform the way he wants. Nowhere is this coercion more evident than in the teaching of writing. The only consideration becomes, To what degree am I willing to be publicly honest about manipulating, to be clear about it in my own mind, and to accept the burden of this influence?

FINALES AND OPEN FORMS

While I was editing the *Whole Word Catalog,*[8] a compendium of writing ideas for classroom use, I was struck by a peculiar thought. In all these game structures devised to get the imaginations of children rolling—the diagram stories, sestinas, time capsules, bringing rabbits into the classroom, working from photographs or surrealist painting reproductions, the list poems, the rankouts, graffiti, my own gimmicks—there was very little teaching of the way the modern poet actually writes a poem. Which is, to sit down in a receptive state and let one's thoughts move outward on paper, guided by feeling and the charged-particle properties of language.

Pound did not write *The Cantos* by looking at an ambiguous newspaper photograph, nor did Rilke *The Duino Elegies* by starting each line with a color. They had to trust to a train of thought, fractured as this might be; they had to take their skinny souls in their hands and jump. Whatever organizational principles hold together the poems of Rilke, Pound, Garcia Lorca, Vallejo, Eliot, William Carlos Williams, Apollinaire, Roethke, Mayakovsky, and so many others, the wonderful poets of this century, they are of a subtler and less mechanical nature than those we were teaching children to follow.

The fertility of poetry-teaching techniques, and the public enthusiasm for poems that children could be made to write if these methods were followed, seemed to me the obverse of a confession of failure. We were teaching children that poetry could be a fun game. We were not necessarily teaching them how to write poems on their own.

Once I had had this thought I was doomed. In a sense, there was no turning back. I had to rethink what it was I really wanted to teach children about poetry and see if there was a way to impart to them the fundamentals, the discipline of *seeing,* with which they could write any poem at any time.

[8] *The Whole Word Catalog* is available from Teachers & Writers Collaborative. Subscriptions to the Teachers & Writers Newsletter, which has been called "the best source of ideas for teaching writing available in the country," can also be obtained from Teachers & Writers Collaborative (186 West Fourth Street, New York, New York 10014).

I began giving some thought to the characteristic ways kids wrote as compared to the ways I might be pushing them to write. One particular trait intrigued me: the tendency of children to write short stories that ended with a climax or a bang.

Kids' storywriting (and that means their preferred mode of writing, since very few would choose to write a description or an essay on their own) is usually connected by strong physical actions, which succeed each other with the frame-to-frame causality of a comic strip. "The shovel hit him in the head. So he punched the lady in the nose. Then they took him away and locked him in prison forever." Or this climax: "Two men started fighting over the toothbrush. And it broke. After a while the man who didn't have the toothbrush was the stronger. He was pulling so hard that he fell over the cliff. The other man tried to catch a mountain goat to eat but it squished away. So he died of hunger." This apocalyptic tendency could be generously explained as the dramatic gift of children, who have time only for urgent matters. Death, which puts an end to so many children's stories, is seen in their imaginations as the Big Squish, getting underfoot of something bigger.

Yet I still sensed an element of cheating in this sudden *closure* which marked or marred so many kids' stories. It was as if the film had suddenly unexpectedly run out of the projector. Whether the finale was death or "Happily ever after," the endings had the same incomplete, door-slamming quality.

Every teacher knows the relief with which kids end their fantasy stories: "And then I woke up and it was all a dream." The clever writing teacher instructs his students beforehand "not to mention that it's a dream," thereby saving himself the gruesome letdown of having to read that pat ending thirty times, by conditioning them to leave it out. But that still did not get to the source of the problem, which is, Why do the kids so often "kill off" their creations abruptly and prematurely, before allowing the reader to arrive at artistic satisfaction?

We know why that homicide exists in adult writers. An evaporation of feeling for the subject, or a sudden flooding of too much feeling of an anxious nature.

With children I suspect a further reason is that they dislike the mechanical act of writing. If they did not put a stop to their composition, they would find themselves looking into an endless dark tunnel of paper work. The pencil, held tightly beween inexperienced fingers, leaves a blue bump.

Nevertheless, even this mechanical problem could be sur-mounted if they were able to stay pleasurably for longer and longer times in the field of thought. The rush to finish a piece—to "get it over with"—was in itself partly responsible for muscular digital tension.

I wondered if there was a way to lead children slowly into a writing that had no compulsory ending. To connect them with proc-esses and flows that were ongoing, infinite. Their panic before the Infinite was very real; I had it myself. Yet the only way to write good modern poetry, or the sort I liked, Open Poetry, was to take the voyage into openness and to discover the poem in the act of writ-ing it. It was not necessary to start with a plot or a worked-out premise. I wanted to decrease the fear the children might feel in front of the unbounded subject. I would get them to see that exactly what they were thinking and noticing every minute was the inspiration of literature. I would bring in modern writers and read them, to demon-strate how another person's quirky mental processes were valid subject matter, and how much discontinuity was allowable in adult literature. I wanted to make them accept how distracted their own minds were. With this understanding, they could begin to turn that continuous subvocal jabbering—so private, and seemingly useless—to advantage.

Keats speaks of "negative capability" as the rare gift of being able to hold several contradictory possibilities in mind without jump-ing to a conclusion. Schools, with their encouragement of the first student with the right answer, do little to build up a tolerance for this sort of creative tension. The seven lesson accounts that follow show something of my efforts to legitimate uncertainty, and what came of it.

Chapter 15
Lesson One: Stream of Consciousness

I began wih a simple device, the Schizophrenic Class Poem, an idea borrowed from Dick Gallup, in which the whole class takes on the personality of one human being. First we did an old woman. I asked each of them to write a line or two in the voice of an old woman talking to herself. Then we collected these scraps of paper and read them aloud, one after another in random order, as a continuous scatterbrained monologue. The idea was to show that the sudden jumps from one concern to another (brought about by collective authorship) actually mirrored the distracted thought processes of one person.

This proved very popular, I think, because it put such minimal writing strains on each child (a line apiece) and brought the whole class together in a fun activity. They insisted it be done twice more. First they elected to be a "dirty old man," then a policeman. They would have continued doing it with different personae but I felt it was wearing thin and I was anxious to move on to the main course.

I asked the class to write for ten minutes everything that came into their heads—everything they thought, saw, or were physically aware of, like the chair or sensations in their bodies, everything they noticed around the room. I did not want to make it any more specific; I was purposely vague. "I can't tell you what to write because I have no idea what's going on inside your brains. Put down everything you're thinking. Don't censor—whatever comes out, comes out. Your pencil should be moving constantly for ten minutes."

Grumbles. The formality of the time limit seemed a good structural idea, and they caught hold of it. They wanted to be certain what second to start, exactly when the ten minutes were up. "Do we have to do this?" Yes, you have to. There was so much ambivalence in their urge to try it, but resentment against it, that I sensed this was one time it would be better not to give them a choice. I moved around the room checking to see their papers; quiet of an examination. "It's difficult, I know, but give it a try," I said aloud. "Shhh!" a boy behind me retaliated. Toni Farrington came in with a note for Denise Loftin; she stood watching the children writing until I invited her to try it. Then she smiled bashfully and slipped away.

"Aren't the ten minutes over yet?" someone whined.

I was cheating. Fourteen minutes had already passed. "Still one-and-a-half more minutes," I said precisely, looking at my watch.

"My hand's getting tired!" For all their grumbling, they wrote a good deal more than they usually did. Their concentration was palpable. I read their papers aloud, starting with this atypically long piece by Xiomara which caught my fancy. It twittered and jumped like a Virginia Wolfe monologue:

> What pretty shoes Toni has. Toni walks funny. Cheong talks too much. Loftin always has to tell the class the same thing over and over. I wish Phillip would not tell people the project so many times. I wish Lillie and Yolanda would stop talking and Britt and Roberto too. Edith stop playing around with Elisabeth. Roberto laughs funny. Virginia always talking looking but never working. Phillip tells everyone whatever you feel-hear and I write it down. I just heard a funny sound. Phillip just asked Toni if she wanted to try it. David and David are always talking in this class. Pencil always drops. The class seems it could never be quiet in there. Roberto going Hallua or calling Gene. Yolanda fight with Dolores, Lillie talking or changing sometime. Phillip makes me sick because he makes us write too much. Everyone is always handing in their page and I am still writing. Tammy made a very nice design with her name. Christine has to explain everything to me or Virginia. Britt sometimes acts stupid. Phillip always gets pages without names and Mrs. Loftin figures out who wrote it because she knows everyone's handwriting. Everyone always asks me what are you doing. They should know that I am doing what I am supposed to be doing. Tammy always shows me her work it is always good work too. This class talks so much. Dolores and Virginia are too much they always fighting. Of course Dolores is a pain

in the ——. But besides that the class is good. Not everyone
does their homework. I always try to and I usually do. When
I ask how you spell something it takes an hour to get my
answer. Mrs. Loftin every five minutes has to say Keep quiet.
The thing about the old lady and the old man is a nice
experiment.

Xiomara, self-appointed den mother of the class, shows in
this piece how she takes responsibility for everyone's behavior. She
is almost entirely "other directed." If she gives a thought to herself,
it is to assure whoever is listening that she is being good. "They
should know that I am doing what I am supposed to be doing. . . .
Not everyone does their homework. I always try to and I usually do."
Aside from these dips into self-justification, she contents herself with
letting her eye roam objectively and critically over her classmates,
stopping momentarily for a sensuous note. "What pretty shoes Freddy
has." The roving process allows her to share subtle and minute observations of an order that did not usually crop up in her compositions: "Phillip always gets pages without names and Mrs. Loftin
figures out who wrote it because she knows everyone's handwriting."

Some children interpreted the assignment as an opportunity to
suppress syntax and punctuation. Chrysoula responded in this fashion. I wonder where she got the sophisticated idea that thoughts
occur in beeps rather than whole phrases.

> anything that your pencil other time help
> I won't do it I guess Brain Clausen people
> SShSh Go back Oh man look my feet are stiff
> notebook is touching my elbow melissa susan
> Oh brother Phillip why is it spelled Ph not F
> seth fernando said F—you doors slam mouse
> Bill let me see you get the hell out of here
> Karin sat next to me now Charlotte Oh my
> Eve talking Karin might be writing a story
> chair falls hey mouse take that how do you
> get out. Look at maurice My arm Karin bragging
> OWCH My hand
>
> time it been so long I am SSh I am Dead
> hammer I have to lie down Caryn Maurice
> He everyone Richard Help.

Fascinating as some of these free-fall visions were, I found them harder to penetrate and in the long run less satisfying to read.

I was struck by the melancholy cast in some of these meditations. Lillie, a new girl from the South, wrote:

> I am wonder when is I am going to die. people tell me
> that I am going soon and when my aunt died I were
> crying and I felt like jumping into the grave. . . .

Josephine even felt obliged to entitle her stream of consciousness:

My Lousy Days

My sister is a bully and I'm not so happy about it.
No I'm not a bully but when I have to teach you a
lesson I do. Well you are not teaching me anything.
I'm sorry!
It's all right.
Well my times are lousy my friend Jeannie is a good friend.
Well I like her to much I wish she could come to my
birthday party but she can't. to bad. And anyway my
birthday isn't going to be celebrated.
Well to bad again. . . .

The most moving composition, for me, was this poem by Edith:

> Five minutes are too long
> Everybody thinks of something
> Jane reads fast
> I'm hungry my stomach is growling
> I think Christine should know what to do
> Ms. Loftin has a loud voice
> I want to fly. If I can't fly, nothing
>   else should be able to fly.
> Phillip talks too much.
> Jeannie is a chatterbox.
> How does your mouth move?
> Phillip looks funny.
> Phillip interrupts me.

> Nola is stupid.
> I hate myself.
> I hate this school.
> Jeannie cries too easily.
> Jeannie is noisy.
> Jane draws good.
> I can't make up my mind.
> I think Phillip is a squashed tomato.

This felt very much like a poem. The movement from thought to thought was governed by some associative connection; the statements were crystallized into terse language. Each thought fell into a natural poetic line by being presented as something discrete and isolated. But this alone did not account for the stripped-bare starkness of the poem, like the X-ray of a soul.

What seemed to be happening was that each line implicated the speaker deeper and deeper in a series of value judgments which eventually turned against herself. For Edith, the act of thinking is entangled with uneasy comparison to others. (Jane reads fast; Christine always knows what to do.) She can escape from this sense of inferiority for a moment, with an odd speculation like "How does your mouth move?", only to be drawn back into comparisons. Even the lyrical desire to fly is undercut by competitiveness. (If I can't fly, nothing else should be able to fly.) Finally she looks around for others to criticize. (Phillip looks funny. . . . Nola is stupid.) But the judgment of others has an inexorable tendency of reminding you of your own faults—leading her to point the finger home. "I hate myself." This statement, coming where it does, is somehow expected. It awaits her inside her brain like an executioner standing at the end of a row of elms. She need only start thinking from any one place and she will come to that familiar figure with the ax. But she cannot stay there; so she must extend the hate outward, to the whole school. Then to Jeannie, who cries too easily—all those self-pitying, "bad" thoughts she wants to get rid of are projected onto Jeannie. Then a little clearing, an appreciation: "Jane draws good." And the immediate confession, "I can't make up my mind"—because she really can't make up her mind whether to think the worst or best of people—plunking down finally on the victoriously malicious side: "I think Phillip is a squashed tomato." This is possibly the happiest line in the poem,

and certainly the one that she let me know gave her the most satisfaction in writing. For after all, wasn't she getting revenge on the
right one, the one who made her think all these unhappy thoughts in
the first place?

If I dwell on this piece by Edith, it is partly because I have come
across so many responses like it (maybe none quite as honest) in
train-of-thought writing. That same phrase, "I hate myself," turned
up often. Or "I want to die" or "I'm dead." This was particularly
striking in the case of certain popular, affable children whom I had
not suspected of hating themselves. It may seem naïve of me to say
that, if one believes that everyone goes around hating himself. Deep
down I wonder whether self-hate is that universal. To some degree
it must be, which explains why people confess it in their writing. But
I also think that the mere act of making their thoughts conscious to
themselves aroused an anxiety in the kids that got *worded* as self-
condemnation. (Something like Heisenberg's theory of indeterminacy
is at work here, in which the recording agent alters the properties
of the thing recorded.) Part of their self-doubt rose from the artificiality of the assignment. "Write down your thoughts for ten minutes," which on the face of it seems a reasonable enough request,
is utterly self-contradictory, not to mention exhausting, like a cat
trying to catch its own tail. All stream-of-consciousness writing is
affected by this epistemological quandariness.

The recurrence of such phrases as "I hate myself" may have
been a defense against the puzzling, difficult task, a curtain dropped
whenever the writer came to a place where his thoughts were what?
taboo?—possibly, but not necessarily forbidden, maybe so picayune
that it caused pain in tracing them out. The exasperation of tiny steps.
The microscope at the child's disposal was not yet fine enough to
catch those squiggly nuances, which made him frustrated. And so he
offered something big, I hate myself, as a sacrificial victim to cover
all those uncertainties—from precisely the same impulse that made
other children kill off their fictional characters suddenly or send them
off to happiness rather than enlisting them in the labyrinths of narration.

Chapter 16
Lesson Two: Going Mad

I was still troubled by some of the raw distress that had surfaced in the children's writings, but for that very reason I could not let it go. We would have to get past that self-consciousness about "negative feelings" sooner or later; one solution was to carry it to extremes. The next week I was reading to Clausen's class a section of Mayakovsky's great poem, *A Cloud in Trousers*—the part where he is so nervous waiting for his fiancée that his nerves begin to race around the room and his heart catches fire:

> I'll pump barrels of tears from my eyes.
> I'll brace myself against my ribs.
> I'll leap out! Out! Out!
> They've collapsed.
> But you can't leap out of the heart!
>
> Mama!
> I can't sing.
> In the heart's chapel the choir loft catches fire![1]

I doted lovingly over that last metaphor, and then asked them what they thought of the poem. Ricky said he thought the guy was crazy. This good American explanation had been offered many times before, and usually in a smart-aleck spirit that I chose to ignore. But this time I leapt on it. What does that mean exactly, that someone is crazy? I got them together for a discussion about crazy people they saw in the streets and buses. How did crazy people act? They talk to themselves. Don't you talk to yourself sometimes? What made it acceptable for a five-year-old to talk to his toys while a fifty-year-old

[1] *Modern European Poetry*, edited by Willis Barnstone, Bantam, p. 404.

talking to the lamppost might be put away? Lots of kids freely admitted they still talk to objects. I said that was what writers do. David
—bright little bugger—asked, "Hey, where's all this leading to?", thus
forcing my hand. I told them I wanted them to write from the point
of view of a person who had gone crazy or was just then losing his
mind. How do you think a person "goes crazy."

"We don't know!"

"How do you think it starts? Use your head."

"You don't use your head, dummy; you *lose* your head."

"All right, we're going to try it. I want everyone to line up against
the wall." There was a perceptible gasp. After they had been made
to stand up, I gave them these instructions: they were to stroll around
the room in a dignified manner, very proper and respectable, like
the mayor of a town, and then become seized by a fit of craziness. I
demonstrated by choking myself and clawing the air. Then, before
anyone could see them having an attack, they were to make a supreme
effort and pull themselves back to normal. Then back to strolling
through the square. Then . . . another attack. They could express
the craziness in any way they felt like; the hard part was to wait until
they actually felt a little craziness stirring inside them; not to force it,
but to wait for it to bubble up to the surface.

I put the lights out and gave them the signal to start.

Monte Clausen and I were poised like lawmen to break it up in
case anything got out of hand. What transpired was an indescribable
mixture of bedlam and canny restraint. Clausen quipped: "The frightening part is that it doesn't look too different from the way this class
usually behaves." The routine mode in this class is that someone
comes behind another kid, gives him a shove and acts innocent, walking away. Richard and Sammy preyed and pushed as usual. The more
mild-mannered kids like Tristan were seen bouncing their bodies
against the closets. Eve and Nola were having a great time falling
off of chairs. Vernal was howling; Fernando was trying to sideswipe
his enemies; Debbie was doing a whirling dervish. I called a halt
and stressed that they should keep to themselves, not bother others.
They tried it again with more of a sense of enforced isolation, es-
trangement.

I had not known what to expect, and as I watched I was both
relieved that no accidents had happened and also, I admit, a little
disappointed that it did not feel more abandoned. As a theatrical

event it suffered from the same paradoxical stalemate that occurs in all participatory Living Theatre-type overtures, when the audience is invited to "get liberated."

Several kids continued to walk around with puzzled looks, shrugging their shoulders whenever I caught their eye. Others, with more showmanship, threw fits of theatrical nervousness which stopped just short of surrendering themselves to it. These kids knew exactly how far to go.

Then we did it once more, this time with everyone pretending to have just received news of the worst imaginable. The saddest, most terrible thing had happened. They went around "drenched in grief," crying on each other's shoulder and trying to tell a neighbor about their misfortune, only to find that the neighbor was consumed with his own tale of tears.

I got them quiet once again. I asked them to write from any feelings they had just experienced, madness or sadness; not merely write about the feeling, but write *from* the feeling, from the physical sensations which remained in their bodies. Describe the feeling while it was still alive in them.[2] I wanted them to be very aware of their extremities and their chests, *to make their narration of dramatic states extend from that internal, physiological perception.* My hope was that this linkage with something immediate would lead to a fantasy writing which was less facetious, or "made up," and more authentic. In many cases, that immediacy and a new, deeper resonance of feeling came through.

> It feels like your whole life means nothing to you.
> Sadness fills your heart.
> You don't care what happens.
> Your eyes fill with tears and your nose runs.
> You don't feel like moving from the spot that you
>   heard about.
> That day you will always remember that feeling you
>   had inside you.

[2] This soliciting of creative writing directly on feelings may seem in conflict with my position in a later chapter: "Getting at the Feelings." However, there is a big difference between asking someone to write a composition about that abstract topic, My Emotions, and having him put in touch with the feeling and then asking him to describe that physical state.

Sometimes you have gone crazy.
Your whole life has changed.
Everywhere you go you won't get away from that feeling.
It just seems that you can't get away from it.
Somehow you will always remember that day.
It seems like it is stuck in your mind.
The mind is like a tape recorder.
Don't forget you can't get away from that feeling.

MARK MULL

The Sadness

One day I knew I was a goner. My eye had nervously
fell out. My head was filled with such grief it slipped
away. My heart has stopped pumping because grief struck
it. My stomach felt as if it didn't want anything to eat and
floated away. My ears closed up as if it didn't want to hear
the bad news. My feet stopped stepping, as if the next step
would be a terrible one. My hands had nothing to touch
and they stopped because anything it would begin to touch
would fade away as I would too.

JIM AUERBACH

Matthew was a child who took great delight in puns, wisecracks,
and facetious parodies of popular stories. This piece, according to
his teacher, was a breakthrough, the first serious writing he had ever
handed in.

Insanity

With an open eye nothing can be seen. But with the
closed eye the entire world is open to you.
With the open eye death, destruction, and poverty,
with the closed eye life, serenity and eden.
Hell! no one understands the word as thoroughly
as me. But who am I? A mere speck of dust on this
moth ball we call home. I am insignificant; but
so is everybody. Insignificant is nothing, and
nothing is fantasy.

MATTHEW MANDELBAUM

Caryn would not abandon her third-person sarcasm, but even so her story has charm and an undercurrent of something dark:

> Sarah was going to the store. On her way she had
> a crazy feeling and she didn't know what it was.
> All of a sudden she came up to somebody and said
> "Blah mucka lucka nooka." Then that was when Sarah
> realized that she was going crazy. Sarah tried her
> best not to show her craziness. She held it in for
> five minutes and she made another crazy sound.
> Sarah got so mad with herself and she went up to
> an old lady and said "Chula nala sooney fant."
> The old lady got hysterical and went to call the police.
> The police said "Look lady stop the obscene phone calls
> and if you call again you'll get in trouble." Sarah
> went up to the lady and said "Choo, moo." The old
> lady again called the police and the police came
> there and couldn't believe their eyes so they took
> her to a head doctor and he made her better. The
> way he made her better was that they had so many
> talk sessions that she got sick of him and forgot
> all about her problems.
> > The End
>
> > CARYN SCHWARTZ

"It makes your head feel so funny to do this!" Eve said to me. I looked over her shoulder at her paper. First the narration was cast in first person, then she took back her paper and changed every line to the third person because she said it was too scary to leave it as "I." (Every line but the last, where she slipped):

> *Help! He's Going Crazy!*
>
> His head is whirring
> He feels like a stampede of elephants stampeding
> > over his head
> His stomach is going wild, feeling as if things
> > inside are complaining moving around
> > Groaning, groaning

His eyeballs are rolling, feeling as if everything
    around him that he looks at is against him
Feeling as if he should tear everything apart
His fingers are out of control about to do anything!
His face is all scarred up
His mouth in such a position I feel like Count Dracula

No no no!

EVE

* * *

Afterward Eve and I had a long interesting discussion, which I suppose was triggered off by the writing session. It was three o'clock, time to go, but she had a few minutes to spare. That day, as on every Tuesday, she was wearing her green Girl Scout uniform; her pretty blond hair was pulled back in a ponytail over her delicate, severe face, chiseled like a Cranach miniature.

She said she had a problem: she couldn't stop thinking that, for instance, if she didn't jump over a certain square on the floor, something bad would happen. Or she would look at an egg and see *spots* on it and think it was dirty. Or last night she heard the phrase "kiss of death" on the television, and was afraid to kiss her mother goodnight. Mostly, though, it was making herself do things to avoid bad luck when she knew that was just superstition. "This last year it's gotten much worse. What do you think I should do?" she said with a professional analysand look on her face. This Eve, for all her neurotic obsessing, had a self-possession I could not help admiring, and she carried herself with great poise. Her very confession struck me as an index of her openness . . . which is not to say she isn't in for trouble! Since she wanted an answer, I told her when she was tired of doing it she would stop. "But I've been doing it for so long, practically a million times!" I told her to watch the spots very carefully, or recall what immediately happened to her before she went through one of these head games: whether she was angry or frustrated or whatever. "Most problems are improved by paying close attention. It's like the nun who lived in Japan and who was a very good, religious lady. One day she started seeing snakes in her room. So she went to a Zen priest, who's like a psychiatrist, and he told her to describe the snakes. 'Well they're green and kind of slimy. . . .' 'That's not good enough. I want you to go back and tell me everything you notice about them. Habits, movements, down to the last detail.' The woman went away and did what he said, and by the end of two weeks the snakes had gone away. Because they were unreal, they could not survive that close an observation."

I recount this story not because I'm sure at all that it was the right answer to give, but simply by way of saying that I'm not really certain what kids are, or aren't, supposed to know, and when a child asks you a question you have to give him an answer.

Chapter 17
Lesson Three: Walking Around

A counterweight was needed to introspection: the physical world.

The next week I took a group of Monte Clausen's students, who had signed up beforehand for my workshop, for a little jaunt. I was in fact rewarding them for having faith in me. They brought their bulky coats into the Writing Room; there I spoke to them about the power of looking sharply. I showed them a few of Diane Arbus's photographs from the Museum of Modern Art catalogue and explained her theory that what catches your eye when you pass someone in the street is his peculiarity, his flaw. Everyone has something idiosyncratic that a good photographer knows how to catch. And a good writer. I told them we were going outside—up the street to McDonald's Burger Shop—and I would like them to note down very carefully in "word photographs" anyone or anything that caught their eye. No generalizations, just the facts. "Don't try to make a big deal composition out of everything. These are like quick snapshots, on the run." Every time they had written down one of these descriptions they were to *skip a line* and look around for something else. (I made this last technical suggestion to give an integrity and clarity to each of the observed units, not have them run-on in a mush.)

Of course the main thing was simply to get outside and have a good time and be free. Yet the kids understood that a deal was being made, and they would go through with their part. As soon as we hit the sidewalk, as if prearranged, a grizzle-faced bum came limping by the school. The kids leaned against cars for a writing surface and began taking down first impressions. Then a friend of mine jumped out of her car and gave me a big hello hug. The kids thought this was preposterously funny. "Write it down, why not?" I shrugged. We spent ten minutes merely on the streetcorner in front of P.S. 90, time enough to ensure that everyone took the writing seriously and was not using the stroll to blank out. Then we wandered up the street, pausing before the music store, the Salvation Army thrift shop, the construction workers and the tar. We stopped to look through the grillwork gate of the subway power plant, where commutators converted DC into AC, though all we could see through the interstices was a coal-dark mysterious sheen on machines; trying to retrieve some of that freshness that had been worn threadbare with daily, indifferent passing-by. This ability we were trying to reactivate, to see the familiar with fresh eyes, was that same reverence and excitement that people think envelops children, though often they are no closer to it than adults. Even as we dawdled, I found myself wondering what I was trying to do: to search out the soul of every fire hydrant, or accept its dumb objectness as just what it was, minimal but real? Or was the point to celebrate the ordinariness and very lack of mystery?

Finally we hit Broadway, with bearded ladies talking to themselves and dogs attacking their masters—that big parade of maniacs and newsdealers and shopping carts that I was depending on, and it didn't fail me. We wound up in climactic McDonald's, the kids over several tables, while I got on line to treat them to hamburgers. I was waiting on line some five minutes, and when I came back with the food I saw that everyone had continued writing of his own accord. Fernando, who had started off by dictating to me, wrote an additional page by himself and couldn't stop being proud. Gwen, a lovely reserved black girl who freezes when it comes to "imagination assignments," was filling page after page with beautiful observations.

Meanwhile this guy with dark glasses kept circling around the tables wanting to know what they were doing, very friendly, seemed to have all the time in the world. A little uncertain on his feet (probably stoned). The kids told him. He liked the way Eve described it and told her, "Say, you got a beautiful mind." He read a few papers and said to his friends: "They got it all down. Check it out. These kids is beautiful." Someone pointed me out to him and he said, "You're the teacher, eh?" with a broad smile. We shook hands.

Eve pointed out a funny phenomenon to me. On top of the garbage receptacle was a garland of plastic flowers. In fact McDonald's wouldn't have anything as gauche as a garbage can lying around; it was more like a wooden speaker's lectern with decorous slot and a wreath of flowers to further sublimate its function.

I include a few of their pieces (there were many other good ones):

Old man walking down the street. Just looked in a
trashcan. Walks funny and slowly. I see him from
the back only see he has a beard gray haired.

Little red car makes a lot of noise. Left rear
lights blinking, waiting for light to change.

Man with mustache staggering from side to side
might be first man.

Lady just came out of car and kissed Phillip.

Black Junkie reading newspaper has hat. He stopped
in front of car. Acts like newspaper's too heavy
for him. Small and plump.

The sidewalk we're on is damp but it's nice.
Gives you a gloomy quiet feeling. Uphill

We stopped in front of music shop. See sign that says

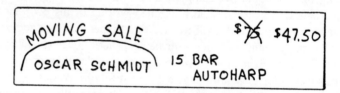

Small silver metal Christmas tree. Has blue round ornaments.

Dog in front of McDonald's. It's a black and white
German Shepherd. It jumped on its old grey-haired
master when he unleashed the dog. Master wore
regular black suit and hat

Guy two tables in front of me who looks like Commissioner
Gordon on TV's BATMAN.

Negro man with an Afro was friendly in McDonald's.

Theatre has The Cabinet of Dr. Caligari

AARON RICHARDSON

This is a man he's walking down the street and as he's
walking he looks in the garbage can he is limping he goes
across the street to get look like he's getting ready
to fall down

this is a lady with a cart in the street
She looks like she is asleep and is smoking
She is holding her self up by the cart

By the Bus Stop she looks just like a dummy
She is small but she is a lady

this is about Garbage it is open
and it is smelling bad and everyone
is walking from it

I heard a baby crying in McDonald's
for his Mommy he was getting very pale

I saw the Guard in McDonald's looking
at a pretty Girl his eyes were rolling

the orange soda tastes like water
it look real good But it tastes yuk.
But I am thirsty

and I saw a woman scolding her baby
because he would not put on his glove

GWEN LEWIS

I deposited Clausen's kids in time for their end-of-day meeting
and sat down on the floor next to Gwen and Eve. The returning kids
were buzzing with excitement and a sense of privilege; the ones who
hadn't signed up naturally felt cheated. Ricky said: "We got milk
shakes and french fries and hamburgers. . . ." Gwen, the eminently
sane one, laughed. "He's exaggerating."

"Now you're in for it," Clausen said to me. "They're going to
expect you to take them to McDonald's after every writing workshop."

I didn't mind. I was overjoyed with the quality, precision, and
sheer bulk of the writing. If handing over a tithe of my salary to Mc-
Donald's was going to turn them into objectivist poets, I was willing
to pay the price.

The behaviorists have their M&Ms; I had my cheeseburgers.

I even toyed with the idea of spending the rest of the writing term on field trips—taking them to the boat basin and Chinatown and having them write on-the-spot notation poems. The success of this first venture gave me the feeling I had stumbled on a rich area. At this point the raw world looked like an awfully good stimulus for teaching the writing of poetry.

The next time I visited their class, I took them into the Writing Room for another briefing. The kids were bunched in their winter coats and anxious to be moving, but they listened. This time, I said, I wanted them to try to put together what they saw with what they were feeling at that moment. To move from the outside world to the inner world of their thoughts and back again.

"For instance, the particular sky on a day like today: the cloud banks that flatten the light in such a way that orange neon Esso signs seem to stick out like knives, and you can never be sure if it's sunny one minute or nightfall the next, and how all that made you feel . . ."

Maybe this was getting a little precious? Nola's frown suggested that thinking about the atmosphere was giving her a headache. We went outside. It was snowing. I took them to Riverside Park, thinking that a little variation, from Broadway to pastorale, would give the exercise novelty.

Under the viaduct with its black walls slimy with bat drippings and echoes and graffiti, they held their noses. "Let's get out of here." I asked them what it was that made them react with disgust (as if I didn't know). Then they found a dead pigeon on the road and we hovered around its crushed wings with what I half-hoped would be meditative fascination. Discovering a dead animal, the subject of a long and academically respectable if dreary tradition of poems. . . . I was beginning to feel uncomfortable with myself for trying to bottle every passing shiver into writing. "Why don't you write about that?" I kept pointing out like a myna bird with one expression. I had become more directive because they were not writing nearly as much as they had the last time. They were having a good time in the snow; why should they write? The world was out there as it always is and I kept trying to get them to trap it between the bars of their lined loose-leaf paper. I found myself making excuses for them: it was not easy to brace a notebook against a wet bench and hold a pencil between woolen gloves with your nose dribbling.

For the thousandth time I was faced with a split in my teaching personality, between the one who enjoyed merely being around kids and watching them relax and the one who craved increased production and was secretly afraid they were taking advantage of him.

When they got to the swings and the seesaws it was obvious which personality would win out. I abandoned my efforts to teach them literature; I released them like sparrows into the frozen air. The boys were chasing each other with snowballs around the swings. Melissa was complaining that her feet were cold.

> I feel a good feeling inside of me, nature and
> knowing that the group likes it just as I do.
> Snow, as much as the beginning of winter should
> have. I see a good deal of snow and buds and
> a subway train. I see a nice monument and
> lots of birds all over. My foot is freezing
> 'cause of leaky boots. A snowed-over baseball
> field.
>
> EVE

> I saw orange beams in a lonely place.
> The stones looked ancient.
> I wish we could get out of here.
> I saw pigeon tracks.
> I saw a dead bird without one wing.
> I saw a path covered with snow.
> It was beautiful.
> The trees look like big hands
> waiting to catch me.
> I saw a train that stopped
> dead on the tracks.
> My hands are cold.
> I saw a man with a paper bag
> on his head.
>
> NOLA

The other papers were half-hearted gestures, soggy concessions with runny ink which I felt guilty about collecting from their pockets. Maybe Nola's and Eve's poems made up for that. The third time around, at the boat basin, the writing was even more perfunctory. I decided it was not worth it to pursue the walking-around motif any further, as long as it aroused in me that conflict.

But each time I tried the walking around with a different bunch of kids, I got excellent results. It seemed to be good for one exposure. I took a group from Mayer's class on a last walking tour. This one encompassed the supermarket and Nedick's and Broadway in the pouring rain. It was a good experience and the kids wrote well. I was a bit melancholy, and inward, as several of the students noted in their papers. I had the feeling I was coming down with a strep throat. The kids wrote with a sympathetic eye for downtrodden humanity. Nedick's is still the last refuge for the rained-on and the spaced-out.

> A person sort of limping sad lonely poor
> How the rain gets my paper
> it makes the red margin soggy
> I see the people going to get a job
> People under awnings
> We passed by the Riverside Theatre
> my boots are wet
> We are going into Nedicks
> I like small places like Nedicks
> because its small it gives good food
> its hardly ever crowded
> Four people get orange drinks
> The orange drink tastes like water
> The food tastes good
> an old man who is sort of poor
> enjoying a lunch french fries a hamburger
> The man eats with a fork and knife
> The man pushes down his fork a weird way
> he pushes the bottom of the fork hard
> It's getting more people now
> Some are waiting patiently and some aren't

MIDORI

Chapter 18
Lesson Four: Eavesdropping

I had some complicated plan which I can't remember now. Denise Loftin's class was in a jumpy mood, but I ignored their signals and went ahead and began reading them some quiet sensory recording poems: *The Young Housewife* by William Carlos Williams, *The Day Lady Died* by Frank O'Hara, and *February* by James Schuyler. All poems with very little attitudinizing, just the bare facts of perception. Someone remembered how last year Denise had sent them into different classes to record teacher-student interactions. "Can we do that again?" I had forgotten what it was I was going to ask them to do, and I said fine, let's split up and eavesdrop. Write down everything people say, without explaining where it comes from. Or else write down everything you see.

I divided the kids into pairs or singles and sent them off wherever they wanted to go: the gym, the bathroom, the kindergarten. A half-hour later they were to return with at least a sheet of overheard dialogue.

"What if we get caught writing it down?" chubby David asked.

"If you get caught," I said, "just tell them you're doing this for a school project."

"Yeah, we'll blame it on you."

"But try not to get caught."

That was the games aspect of it. They understood. They seemed born to spy. They loved to do this because they got to roam around at will.

I took a few kids along with me into that adult inner sanctum, the teachers' lounge. I was curious what the children would pick up on, and I wanted to see how the adults would react to the unexpected presence of children. Of course the note-taking activity was not lost on the teachers, much as I tried to distract them, and they were unusually quiet.

After that we went around to Assistant Principal Glass's office and to the principal's office. Ten-year-old Jonas gives a full report:

> I went to the teachers room and I saw Mrs. Robinson Miss Liu Miss Gonzales and Miss Domingo. We went in and started talking to the teachers then Miss Mitchell came in and Miss Gonzales went out. The teachers looked a little suspicious. Miss Liu had nose spray in her hand. Then Miss Robinson went out. I couldn't hear too much. Then I went to Room 210.
>
> Mr. Glass was in and a lady I didn't know. Mr. Glass and the lady I don't know were talking about teaching. They seemed to be having problems about what their responsibilities were. Mrs. Kaufman said to someone you have work to do. Two kids were sitting on a lady and she was saying ow!!! Then I spied on Mrs. Sarafian. Mrs. Sarafian had a pocketbook I couldn't spy any more. Then I went to Mr. Jimenez. The teachers were suspicious, especially Mrs. Sarafian. Mr. Jimenez looked so serious. He looked as if the world was coming to an end.
>
> JONAS KALISH

Thirty minutes later we reassembled and read aloud the results. There was much giggling. Two things struck me about their response: one was the extreme popularity of the assignment, though it didn't particularly fascinate me. (Months later they were still begging me to go spying again.) The other was its success in drawing out children who did not usually write, like Wendy:

> Ha, Yolanda!
> I'm not going in there
> That's stupid.
> I have to go to the bathroom.
> No, no, be quiet.
> Wait for me.
> My teacher look like a frog.
> I know, I know.
> A yellow ghost.
> Hi Wendy.

Is Candy here? Hi People.
Want to have a date with me?
Hello, girls.
What nice people.
Are you writing me a love letter?
Help! You better not you little monsters.
Fat tail.
I love you.
Hi Wendy. Coming back? Wendy sit down.
Wendy watch me go in here. Bye Bye.
Give me a kiss. Come stupid.

WENDY GONZALEZ

Some kids had gone into the main office, and their transcriptions caught the sparse atmosphere, the forlorn holes in the conversation, and the talk with which the secretaries pass the time.

Main Office

Excuse me
Children out of the entrance
Watch it
What are you girls doing here?
What time is the first luncheon?
Is this going to be the thing for the
     teachers?
And I told you she can't,
She has writing
Typing
She never shows up.
They never even called.

JANE KLINGBEIL

Spying: the Main Office

cough. . . .
     P.S. 90 Manhattan.
     How are you?

We have sheets
    for you. Yeah. Yes.
Hi, can I help you?

He wants me to write a note.

Where's some paper?
How are we going to go?

Our yard is not suitable enough.

I read that we lost our money
    by 83%. We got it? No,
    we lost. Mr. Jimenez, can I have
    some water. Go to your class.

You see Mr. Hardwick?
No He's probably at P.S. 76.

Oh did you see that sale at Macy's
They have bras 99¢

Fantastic.

LIZ ORTIZ

Eavesdropping

Willie this is a joke you know nothing about

Are you in first grade   no I'm in second
said some little Punk.

Did Hazel call you last night no edith
Well erma supposed to call me.

How's your job listed   my new job's o.k.   Look
how much she's getting paid.

She spit right in my mouth
OOOah keep cool

Who Gary yeah

Let me hear her
for Amanda

Slow down
Ahhhh wa wa ha ah

they have a terrible friendship
I hate Chinese and Japanese kids

Oh Chang you dropped your paper

Ladies you have to go outside

My mother finds me every day.

A trip
    Mommy   oh Mommy

SETH

THE PROBLEM OF SELECTION

The children's compositions were beginning to show a wider appetite for the world at large, a receptivity, an ability to see small things. On the other hand, their writing was losing some of its original shape and narrative energy. I could not help thinking that many details in these catalogues were dull random filler that might have been better left out.

They had taken a useful step in locating the ever-present sources of poetry (thinking, feeling, seeing, hearing). But to the extent that they had become mechanical *scribes* of these sources, they were abnegating some of their responsibility for the final work. The kids no longer seemed to be composing their writings as much as "receiving" them like transistor radios. Of course they were merely following my orders. I had told them to write down everything without worrying about continuity. The results in most cases were raw undigested sensory data: as unmediated records of the way children see the world, they were alternately revealing and monotonous.

My objection was not to the uniform flatness of tone. In the long run that might be desirable. It signified an attitude of mind that could be curious without rushing over the side into melodrama. It signified dispassionate science—and I had been looking for a way to bridge the gap between school project writing and "creative" writing. But even as science-lab reports they would have to be boiled down to essentials. It was not easy to convince the kids to work with these papers as first drafts, expanding the good parts and discarding the rest, since their method of collection had induced a suspension of values in which any one detail counted for as much as any other.

How were they to distinguish between the essential and the inessential details?

So the problem of getting children to expand their writing, when pursued successfully, led straight to the problem of selection.

What I wanted to teach them was this: half the trick in writing poetry, or anything else, is passivity—the ability to relax, to entertain an acquiescent, scanning, receiving state of mind. The other half, however, is to keep a vigilant selecting mind in readiness and to know when to *pounce*.

I felt I had gone far enough with the kids in getting them to record passing sensations. Now we needed to investigate what, if anything, held these fragments together. Was there a way of recombining the kids' original narrative thrust with their new attentiveness to minutiae which these exercises in awareness evoked?

Chapter 19
Lesson Five: How Do Things Connect?

Something very powerful happened to me today. I decided to come into Mrs. Loftin's class and teach them "everything I know." That is, I didn't feel like teaching one assignment or another but just speaking from a deeper part of myself about a problem I had come to focus on more and more in the teaching: How can we make sense of all our perceptions? For it seemed to me that "How does a modern poem hold together?" was asking the same question as "How does the modern world hold together?"

I said: "I want to talk to you about a fascinating problem that I've been thinking about. How does a person construct a poem? How does he pick things to put into it? Why this detail and not that detail? Let's say you're walking down the street and you see a man with a limp, then you see a sign, then your tooth starts to hurt, you notice that hail is coming down from the sky. And at the same time there are a million things you're not noticing. We continually have to make choices among thousands of bits of information, just in crossing the street. It's as if you were standing in front of a store with seven TV sets on. Ever done that? Let's say one channel is the weather, and one channel is the way your body feels, and one channel is crowds of people around that you're not sure whether to pay attention to, and another channel is your mother or teacher wanting you to do something. How do you put it together? How does it all make sense? You look at the sky. You look at your shoe. What's the connection between the two?"

"Your shoe is raggedy and dirty," said David, "just like the clouds."

"Like the clouds. Fine. But what about that—birthday cake?"

I noticed a small cake on Xiomara's desk. "And the floor? What's the connection there?"

Pause.

"They both have square tops?" Juliet said tentatively.

Someone else put forward a lame comparison. I realized they thought I knew the answer, and that it was a very empirical I.Q. test answer. In fact I was as much in the dark as they were.

"Maybe there's no connection!" I said, stamping my foot. "Maybe they've got nothing to do with each other. You look at the floor, that's one thing. You look at the cake, that's another. No connection."

"The cake could fall on the floor," said Gene.

"True—the cake could fall on the floor. And then someone could accidentally step on it. That's narrative."

"Someone could pick up the cake," offered David.

"Right, he could pick it up tenderly in his arms, and that would be a whole different relationship, like a romance," I said. "Then he could eat it."

"*You* could eat it!" said Gene. Everyone laughed.

"Okay"—I smiled—"but I think we're getting away from the point. Which is that sometimes we see connections between things and sometimes they stay separate. Period. There's no point trying to force it." I must say, this was a moment of liberation for me. As a poetry teacher I often found myself pushing comparisons, extracting metaphors from people that were forced. No one needs to be trained to make metaphors. A true metaphor is an intuition, a flash of sympathy.

"One way of writing a poem," I continued, "is simply to note down what you see, and if things seem to be like each other, point that out. If not, leave it alone. I'd like to read you this poem about a man walking around and see if it holds together for you."

I read them a translation of Apollinaire's *Tree*,[1] which ends:

> You walked in Leipzig with a thin woman disguised
>   as a man
> Intelligence for that's what an intelligent woman is
> And it's best to keep the legends in mind

[1] *Apollinaire Calligrams*, trans. by Anne Hyde Greet, Unicorn Press, 1970.

Lady-Bountiful in a tramway at night in the depths
    of a deserted neighborhood
I saw a hunt while I was getting on
And the elevator stopped at every floor

Between the stones
Between the multicolored clothes in the window
Between the glowing coals of the chestnut-seller
Between two Norwegian ships anchored at Rouen
I see your image

It springs up between birches in Finland

The beautiful steel negro

The greatest sadness
Was when you received a postcard from La Corogne

The wind blows from the sunset
The metal of carob trees
Everything is sadder than it used to be
All earth's gods are growing old
The universe complains with your voice
And new beings are rising
Three by three

Admittedly a difficult poem. I asked them what they made of it. Did it hold together?

"Yes," said David. "He's remembering different parts of his life."

"What else holds it together as a poem?"

"That's not my idea of poetry!" said Tammy, the rhymester.

"Why isn't it poetry?" I said. She fell silent. "What else holds it together?"

"He's feeling sad. . . ."

"Right! A feeling of sadness goes all through the poem. I'm not even sure what all of it means, but I know what the feeling is. One of the ways of connecting a poem is by having an emotion and pointing that emotion at whatever you happen to run across. A strong emotion is like a ray gun. You point sadness at the blackboard: 'I see the gray chalk disintegrating.' Everything takes on the same emotion in the poem."

"Why don't we act it out?" said Britt, who had already started to mug during my reading. "You read it again and we'll act it out."

I had to laugh at Britt's ability to turn any situation into a spotlight for his acting. "Okay, why don't you act out this shorter one? First listen to it closely and see what you can remember."

I read them Tomas Tranströmer's *After a Death* (which I am told was inspired by John F. Kennedy's assassination):

After a Death[2]

Once there was a shock
that left behind a long, shimmering
                    comet tail.
It keeps us inside. It makes the TV pictures snowy.
It settles in cold drops on the telephone wires.

One can still go slowly on skis in the winter sun
through brush where a few leaves hang on.
They resemble pages torn from old telephone directories.
Names swallowed by the cold.

It is still beautiful to feel the heart beat
but often the shadow seems more real than the body.
The samurai looks insignificant
beside his armour of black dragon scales.

TOMAS TRANSTRÖMER

By now some of the slower kids were becoming dazed from the level of concentration the discussion demanded. Virginia started playing jacks on the floor; Wendy turned to find someone to gossip with. Denise Loftin had gone out to handle some problem with a parent, and discipline relaxed. Ordinarily I would have left it there, but today I cared passionately about what I was trying to tell them. "Listen to this; it's important. It's not only a question of how to write poetry, but how to make sense of your lives."

[2] *20 Poems: Tomas Tranströmer*, trans. by Robert Bly, Seventies Press, 1970.

I asked them to enumerate the objects they could remember from the poem. They were pretty thorough: snow, TV, skis, dragon, armor, telephone directories, drops of rain. Then I read the poem again, this time encouraging anyone who felt like it to pantomime along. Britt hammered up the "shock" by falling on the floor. Dolores kept saying, "When do we get to the dragon part?" After I had finished reading, I asked them to consider what snow, telephone directories, dragons had in common. What was the poem "about?"

No one felt sure enough to answer.

I thought they had been taken very far into unknown territory and deserved a break. I gave them my answer. "The title says 'After a Death.' So someone has died, and everyone is affected by it. The writer is undergoing a kind of shock, which keeps spinning out of him like a comet's tail, and everything he sees reminds him of that shock of death."

Heavy.

I handed out paper and asked them to write. In fact, this part of the lesson was strictly unnecessary because I had only wanted to talk to them, not get them to write. I became timid when I had to explain what I "wanted them to write about," suggesting merely that they pick three things in the room and describe them, and connect the objects with a feeling they were having, or else don't connect the objects at all. Or else (I responded, seeing some of them very confused) just write for five minutes whatever comes into your head.

The results were very strange. About five or six kids wrote beautiful, quiet papers. But some of the most facile and willing writers in this class, like Tammy and Christine, looked desolate. I didn't know whether my delivery had made them lethargic, or thoughtful in a good way—or moody—or whether they felt that way irrespective of the lesson. Tammy, when I asked her to try noting down her thoughts, said she couldn't write a poem without rhymes; she just couldn't! And looked unhappy with herself. Christine said she felt more bored than she had ever been in her life, except for once at camp when she'd had to go to bed at eight o'clock. There was no reproachfulness in her voice, only a statement about the sudden drying-up of the usual diversions of childhood.

Maybe the lesson had gone over most of their heads. I don't care. There are times when you have to teach one for yourself, whether they like it or not!

Jane K. wrote this. Each week her writing gets more forceful.

A Classroom

The coats look like people just standing
in line with their backs turned so that you
don't see their faces. Then the desks look
like straight orderly and dull wooden things,
just waiting for you to push them wherever
you want and to stuff books or papers into them.
And the lights, always standing still
and always bright. Till one day when you
turn them on and they suddenly go off.

JANE KLINGBEIL

And two others:

My Classroom

Xiomara's coat getting pushed back by
the other coats. Like a furry sheep
struggling to get through. Masks hanging
on the wall happy and sad. Bright lights
beaming down from the ceiling. Mrs. Loftin's
high heel shoes reaching up into the sky
like a skyscraper. People laughing and
talking. Dolores putting her hat on her
head and pulling out the part which makes
it look like a beak or the way the front
of a locomotive used to look.

JULIET ELKIND

Lonely Hall

The apartment in the building has 7
written on it. It belongs to me.
Inside it belongs a small kitchen,
no bigger than a 7 foot man.

In this room, there is a color t.v. with
a piano in the back.
The table is a mess. Everywhere you look,
it is full of cosmetics, jewelry and clothing.
Including my mom's pocketbook.
Then, there's a couch with a map over it.
The couch is full of stuffed animals.
The bathroom, where you step into the tub
full of nudity, is small too.
If you step out the place, there is the hall
full of silence.

CECE LEE

Chapter 20
Lesson Six: Portraits

When I was in public school, I paid more attention to my teachers' mannerisms than to the ostensible subject matter. Thinking back to those hours and *years* of sitting behind school desks, I can remember very little of any actual lessons. My world-history teacher was a woman about forty-five, with a habit of incredulously raising her eyebrows at a wrong answer, and an arch, quivering smile: around her mouth were gray mustache hairs that reminded me of a rabbit's. She would raise her arm to scratch her head and I would see the hair in her armpits, fuzzy and intimate. A tuft of down is all I retain from world history. Oh I learned the facts somehow (Charlemagne, the Luddites), but I don't remember the moment of learning them from her. What I remember her teaching me is herself. And the same for the others: the lady with the hairnet who unwrapped her wax paper carrots before reading us Macbeth; the math teacher with the aphorisms who would turn down a request to repeat an explanation by saying, "I don't chew my cabbage twice." My teachers were watched so closely, so microscopically by all of us that one would think the course of study was, Learn this human being by heart.

And then, when I began teaching, I found myself on the other side of the microscope. Children would interrupt in the middle of my discoursing on something—"How come your sideburns are red but your mustache is brown?" Or, bending down to persuade a child who had no desire to write, I would come close to his cheek and he would announce "Your breath smells!" with an unsparingness that quite took my breath away, until I became used to that casual ambush. Certain children, like Gulliver when brought near the faces of his giant hosts with their huge skin pores, had a fastidiousness about adult smells, especially those adults who were giving them orders. We were strutting targets, we adults: our shoes, our hairdos, our habits of control, all learned by heart by creatures smaller than we who were searching for a vulnerability, an advantage to equalize the unfair distribution of power.

But even if they had nothing to gain, they would continue to watch us, fascinated by the sheer carnivalesque balancing act of physical contradictions and quirks which we, as unaware as possible, offered up to them every day.

I told my writing class more or less what I have just said, about studying teachers' looks as a boy, and getting together with my friends after school to trade descriptions of the way the teachers walked or did this and that. The kids immediately began talking about some of the characters they had had in earlier grades. I asked them to concentrate on the physical traits, habits, and peculiarities of different staff members. We decided to do a collaborative portrait (they dictating to me) of their classroom teacher, Monte Clausen, a popular figure, fortunately. I made it clear that we were not in the business of tearing anyone down, but simply, accurately describing the behavior of this person as it manifested itself in physical terms.

Clausen's Mustache

When Mr. Clausen gets mad he turns red as
a tomato.
Also, when he gets mad
His hair sticks up a little bit
When Mr. Clausen talks
his Adam's apple moves around

He looks like an egg with hair on it
He smiles at the woman teachers
He smiles at my mother
He smiles at everybody!

When he's cracking up his mustache wiggles
and his head starts rolling
When he's explaining something to the class
he keeps slurping up his coffee
and it gets stuck in his mustache

Then he licks his mustache to get the
coffee off
I wonder what happens when he brushes
his teeth

When he goes outside and it's very cold
he touches his tongue to his mustache and
it freezes

His mustache hangs over his top lips
like a weeping willow

He's a big softee
When you hug him
he feels like a Teddy bear
But his inside is like cement

Sometimes I go into his class
and I see John hitting Tristan
Then Mr. Clausen says, *Tristan,*

get over here
in a deep bellowing voice
like a grizzly bear.

This poem was so much fun for them to do that they immediately wanted to turn out dozens more on everyone in the school. Group enthusiasm was high while they argued about whom to scrutinize next. I was mistrustful of taking dictation again for them, because of the inevitable influence the recorder has on shaping the poem, so I asked to see what they would do on their own.

They instinctively split into small teams rather than working singly; they seemed to gain strength to say certain things they might not otherwise have dared to write by pooling their observations into one voice. I have seen that happen over and over: for children to discover the power of group opinion as a magical instrument, only to lose sight of it a week later.

I tried the same idea with Denise Loftin's class. This time, as I asked the kids for a subject for a collaborative portrait, Denise did a shrewd turnabout: "Oh no! It's not going to be me. Let's do one on Phillip." She went to the blackboard and demonstrated how well she had learned my techniques for collaborative poem writing—breaking the statements into poetic lines, asking for sharper details—while I sat squirming on top of a desk, under the casual examination of their glances. I was surprised what they chose to notice about me, including mannerisms I had not been aware of: "When he comes in, he just throws his coat anywhere."

Here is one of the less flattering portraits of me:

A Person

Phillip is our writing teacher. Everytime he came
in I get sick. Because he always tell us
write stupid thing like today.
He tell us to explode the word like
it in every corner of the paper. And last
week it is worst than this week. Because
he tell us to go to the street and write
everything we saw and write it down to
a paper. That is very stupid. Now Phillip
said what so stupid. Then he said "You
should try something you never try it before."

SCOTT GEE

Tammy and Christine joined forces to write this:

Toni Farrington has such wiggly hips
she probably spills her soda when she sips
she wears so many bracelets her arms must ache
with those phony eyelashes she really looks fake

she wears rings on her middle finger and thumb
We really think that's dumb
her hair is so frizzy it looks like a mop
We bet she washes it a lot
Ah oh here she
comes
We better run

TAMMY AND CHRISTINE

Tammy was dying to show it to Mrs. Farrington and I had my doubts about letting her out of the room with it. "Are you sure she won't be offended?" "Oh, she won't mind!" Finally I decided it was better to trust the maturity of the adults than to make the kids feel they were engaging in a sinful activity.

The two girls had drawn Magic Marker flowers around the margins of their rather bitchy poem as if to make it "nice." Toni laughed and laughed and promised to frame it. She showed it to a few other teachers, then changed her mind about framing it and hid it in her desk.

A few weeks later Eve showed me a remarkable piece of writing. *Observing Miss Mayer* went on for eight handwritten pages and was the most astute portrayal I had ever seen of an open classroom situation. Here the teacher, Miss Mayer, no longer obliged to lecture the whole class at once, becomes an Argus-eyed overseer, roaming the floor and checking each child's production level. Her dramatic teaching personality combines efficiency with tenderness. "Miss Mayer enjoys massaging Regan's neck and looking over to check on her work." This reflex of doing-two-things-at-once, overlapping the private and the public moment, forces Eve as observer to a frequent use of "while" and other grammatical constructions that suggest the school atmosphere's relentless simultaneity. Excerpts follow:

OBSERVING MISS MAYER

During Class Meeting: During class meeting, very quickly she asks questions and puts a name on the end. Example: "How many pints in a gallon, Jonas." *He* has got to answer no matter if Karen is straining her arm straight into the air. During first period—after class meeting (which is in first period)—Explaining perimeter to Willie and Andrew and Sandra. While waiting for the answer of a question Miss Mayer asked Andrew, she looks down on him. Not head, but eyes. While teaching perimeters, Miss Mayer enjoys her morning coffee. She smiles while Willie answers her question correctly, but in a different way than she expected. —Miss Mayer was looking at Jonas while he interrupted and put her hand on her stomach while saying: Shhhh! As people crowded around Miss Mayer explaining what to do in Sandra's mathbook, she dropped the pencil and uncrossed her legs, picked up the pencil and looked at Jared in a cross way (for what?) crossed her legs and resumed her teaching . . . 2nd period—Still instructing Willie, Miss Mayer accidently wipes her nose with the piece of chalk she was holding and quickly places it down. . . . Miss Mayer takes many comfortable positions, for instance: Placing foot on sill, resting hand on knee or hip etc. (for some reason, all this instructing seems to be math, perimeters, squares etc (and multiplying). While checking Karl's spelling words, she taps her foot for each "You have" (In rhythm) Telling Jonas how to do something in multiplying, she sings: "$10 \times 10 + 10 \times 10 = 100$" etc. Also, while teaching Norma how to do something, she rests her chin on Norma's head—therefore looking over it onto the paper. 3rd period—Meeting Mr. Hardwick—looking over onto papers —and then sitting down to talk about rolls. . . . Miss Mayer enjoys massaging Regan's neck and looking over to check on her work. Right now she is walking around the room checking up on people. Everything is in order so Miss Mayer puts her hand in the gerbel cage and waters them while the other hand is behind. Now Miss Mayer is getting mad at Andrew cause he won't catch on to a math problem. Miss Mayer puts her purse on her shoulder and she's off. In Mr. Hardwick's office Miss Mayer is telling David M., Nina and Noah to write down their thoughts and scrouching down Miss Mayer is talking with her hands, letting them fall, and with an "O.K." sign with her fingers. Now still in Mr. Hardwick's office, Miss Mayer is resting her elbows on her knees smoking a cigarette with Maurice taking down her commands in his mathbook. Again Miss Mayer places her pocketbook on her shoulder walks across the room and puts her arms around Mrs. Trabulski and kisses her and: out of the office. Recess—Miss Mayer walks into Mr. Clausen's room takes a look and goes back into her own. Now she is watching Norma do her mathbook with her chin in her palm. Then a hit on the table for every "good" and a: "Good good good good good good good" came out very quickly. . . . Then she turned out the lights and said, "Shhh! Keep your voices down" and resumed to her helping. . . . Then she walked around her room, wound up a spool of thread, and then again walked back to her seat. Then, after a while, she walked up to the blackboard and started writing evaluation on the blackboard with one hand on the hip. Then she walked into Mr. Clausen's class, up to Mr. Kain's door and down the hall somewhere. I lost her. We will again focus on Miss Mayer on the 4th period—After Spelling Test—Miss Mayer just turned out the lights and reminded of silent work period and now she is walking about the room checking on kids' work. She just walked down an aisle calmly and scratched her back. Miss Mayer is putting names on the job chart with kids crowded all around her. Her tongue is over her top lip as if it was a work of art. She held her hands tight and resumed her Itch itch itch! She just scratched her eye and is walking towards Norma and is leaning over Norma's head and teaching her. Now she is saying Be quiet! She folds her hands. Now Miss Mayer is sitting on the desk eating red hots and sat in her former seat and kids walk up to her asking for help. Again she has her palm against her cheek looking at work. . . . She walked across the room and with both hands on hips bawls out David. . . . Then again walks across the room and with a pencil on her lips looks at a gigantic crossword puzzle. Then Miss Mayer puts her purse over her shoulder and heads for Mr. Hardwick's office. In there she talks with one foot on the desk, one hand in the air and one hand on her stomach. What she's talking about isn't my business. Then Miss Mayer comes back in. . . . Class Meeting—

EVE

What impressed me so much was that the portrait was neither adulatory nor insulting, but clear-eyed. The rhythm and tracking speed of Eve's prose seemed to bring Miss Mayer's movements alive. I guessed it could not have been written without the previous workshop lessons: the walk to McDonald's and the park, the portrait of Clausen, the eavesdropping. It also seemed connected to our talk about seeing spots, in that the close observational procedures had a ritual aspect.

Curious, I spoke to Eve one day at three o'clock. How had she gotten the idea for the Mayer portrait? She said she had wanted to do it for a while. I asked if any of the recording-perception classes had perhaps influenced her. No, she was quite cool on that: "I'd been planning it for a long, long time." Oh well.

I asked her if writing the piece had changed her opinion about Miss Mayer in any way. Again no. She had chosen Miss Mayer because "I'd been thinking a lot about how much pleasanter it is in her room than in my room, where the boys are always disrupting the class meetings. I had originally wanted to follow around one of the boys who fight a lot. But then I thought that since I would have to spend a whole day observing, I would rather be where it was more pleasant."

Had she seen anything new about Miss Mayer?

"The way she's always holding her stomach." What about Miss Mayer in general? "Miss Mayer is just a woman," said Eve, "and so everything she does is like a woman does it. The way she talks with her hands and lets them drop. I couldn't put that into words. It got me so frustrated! I have two thesauruses at home and sometimes I would find the right way of saying it, but I had already written it the other way."

"You can always go back and change it," I said. "But you're right: gestures are the hardest things to put in words."

"You're telling me!"

I asked her if the spots had gone away. She said no, they were still around. Maybe not as bad as before.

Then we talked about Linus and Danny, two clowns in Miss Mayer's class, and how Danny sometimes lost his temper, and how some people were able to be funny all the time and some not.

Chapter 21
Lesson Seven: The History of a Friendship

In the next lesson I was going after some pretty big game. I wanted the kids to write the history of a friendship, from beginning to end, or up to the present time. It has become customary to get children to understand their aggressive feelings by asking them to write about a "fight with a friend or member of your family" or some other incident of stress. What I had never seen done was to ask them to consider a relationship *in time,* with all its fluctuations, betrayals, reconciliations, and shifts of affection. It was even uncertain to me whether some children could see a relationship as a progression. The younger they were, the more they seemed to fling into each other's orbits and snap apart like disinterested electrons. Yet I could not believe no scars were left on the memory.

I began to speak about how, when I was in grade school, I had friends for about a year or two and then the friendship would disappear, and it confused and mystified me. Where did it go? Under the table? It was like the question in that song: "Where Did Our Love Go?" Sometimes there had been a fight. Sometimes there hadn't even been that, but the other person would drop out of my mind or become smaller: I couldn't pick him up on my radar screen any more.

I asked Denise Loftin's class how many thought they had friends. (All raised their hands.) How many had enemies? (just about everyone). How many had enemies who used to be friends, or the other way around? (quite a few more than I had anticipated). In this mechanistic way I introduced the business of shifts of feeling. What happened to the friendship? I asked. Gene told the anecdote of how he had been close to one kid, then one day the kid said, "You wanna swimming pool?" Gene said yeah; the kid took Gene's palm and spit in it. "There's your swimming pool." After that he never quite trusted the kid.

I decided to concentrate on this single phenomenon: the relationship that goes from one extreme to another. It was a good way of demonstrating that friendships do undergo change. And it pointed to a simple truth which I stated aloud: you can be hurt more deeply by someone you care about than by someone who means nothing to you.

There is a feeling you get sometimes when you are talking to a classroom that you have hit a main nerve. A stillness, like an animal holding its breath underbrush. For once everyone was fascinated. I asked if they could remember how any of these friendships had begun. This is an intriguing question, because it presumes a point in time, or a decisive action, whereas many people slide toward friendship by imperceptible degrees. Several children offered stylized beginnings, usually involving a transactional exchange. ("He liked my baseball cards and I liked his comic books, so we decided to swap at his house.") These stories had a patented edge, like the answers married contestants give on quiz shows to "How did you two fall in love?" I suspected that many of their recollections had already been streamlined into myth and overlooked the period of assessment from a distance that preceded the first exchange.

Now that beginnings were out of the way: What happened next? The discussion began going in several directions; we seemed to be submerged in an infinitude of transitions. There had to be some way of organizing this material. I began redirecting the talk with pointed questions: When was the first time you really felt close to this person? Do you remember when you started to think maybe the person wasn't what he seemed to be, or maybe he wasn't a friend you could trust after all? Do you remember what the first argument was about? How did you make up?

Their answers were increasingly interesting and I regret that I did not have a tape recorder to transcribe them. Before the discussion could exhaust itself, I stopped it, to leave some energy for writing. There seemed to be a lot of emotion around visiting the friend's house, so much so that I assigned an alternative topic to write about: going over to a friend's house and what that was like.

The main topic remained: *The History of a Friendship or Enemyship* (a word we invented for the occasion). I said I knew that they were very good at writing about a single incident, a fight, or a celebration—and I drew a large X on the board to indicate that approach—but I wanted to know if they could look at two people in another way, through all the ups and downs of a relationship. I drew a repeating sine curve to illustrate that type of movement.

Again I was asking them to do a difficult (even impossible) task. So I added: "Do the best you can. Maybe you should stick to a few highs and lows to make it easier. You often read the history of a country, but very rarely the history of a friendship. This is the stuff that novels are made of," I confessed.

Everyone tried it. I was very pleased. David came the closest to the analytical circling of a Gertrude Stein novella. But all of the papers had an honesty that gave privileged glimpses of that mysterious subcontinent of children's friendships.

The History of a Friendship or an Enemyship

During the end of the first grade, I got news of someone I knew when I was 6 and up to now he was never really an enemy to me, but a few times I thought he really bugged me, for instance, a guy who sings, and I quote, "I love my cuddly pillow" is pretty dumb, and when it was the end of the fourth grade, or rather the summer vacation, I was so mad that I said that I disliked him so much that I'd rather have never known him! But then again he was my friend and since 2nd grade we were almost always friends. I never really saw him through the summer at any time. I think I liked him most in third grade. The basis of the friendship was because of the things we liked. We both like art and we did it every day. I used to draw all day, picture after picture. He gave me advice, sometimes good and sometimes bad. And sometimes my mother told me to do my own work, then I started to agree with her, and she was right. She knew that I was being led by another person's ideas, and that's how we got to know each other.

DAVID ROMANELLI

The History of a Friendship

The way I met my next door neighbor. Her name is Sandra. It happened when I moved into her building. My friend's named Sandra. It was another girl named Sandra. She lived in the third floor, and I lived in the fourth floor, and my next door Sandra turned around when I said hello to the other Sandra, and my next door thought I was talking to her. So then I started going to her house, and once in a while I started sleeping at her house, She was nice at first, but she thinks she's bad, and sometimes she shows off. Yes, because she has a boy friend, and she's fifteen years old. So she's still the same way, and she's snotty.

VIRGINIA GONZALEZ

The Long Feud (Two Versions)[1]

It all started one afternoon when Christine, Emily and I were walking on Broadway. Emily was supposed to go to my house. When we got to "united" discount store we went in. Christine and Emily lagged behind me. I saw them whispering. Then Emily said "Oh I forgot I have to go to the dentist." EMILY LIED TO ME! I said "Why are you walking with Christine if you have to go to the dentist." She replied "I just wanted to cross the street with her." I said "Why do you have to lie about it Emily?" They stalked off yelling insults at me. I called Kelley and Julie. The next day we started having sides. One side was me, Dara, Julie and Kelley. The other was Emily, Christine, Debby and Nancy. We've started to ignore each other now instead of having to curse at each other. We definitely decided not to fight violently.

TAMMY EINSTEIN

It all started when Emily, Tamar and I were walking on Broadway. Tamar and Emily were going to have a date, and since I live Tamar's way we walked home together. We all went into a store. Tamar walked ahead. Emily and me fell behind. Then Emily said "I'll tell Tamar that I forgot I had to go to the dentist, but I really want to play with you, but I will say that because I don't want to hurt her feelings." Emily told her and Tamar found out the truth. Then we all started yelling at each other. So when Tamar went home she called Kelly, and Julie, and told them all about it. Then Tamar called Emily and bawled her out and Emily bawled Tamar out. The next day Emily told Nancy and me about the phone

[1] [This feud had become a local school legend, like the Hatfields and the McCoys, by the time this lesson was taught. In fact Tammy was reluctant at first to write it down because "everybody in school already knows about it," but I convinced her to preserve it as a part of our folklore.]

call from Tammy. Then we all turned against each other. Dara got
on Tamar's side, and Debby got on Emily and my side. We ignore
each other now except Tammy and me talk to each other as classmates.

CHRISTINE HUNTINGTON

When I Went to Danny's House

When I got in the building it had a guard and it had a very
big mirror and two elevators and when I go in the elevator had two
doors in the back. Then I punched the number B for Basement.
Then I got out of the elevator and said what a mess. Then I went
to Danny and said you have a beautiful apartment Danny. Then
Danny said I know. Then she took out a game and I played with
her. Then I said this house is so beautiful I have to leave good-bye
Danny. Then when I was outside I said That is the ugliest apartment
I have ever seen.

WENDY GONZALEZ

About My Friend Diane in My Last Year School

This is how it started. She told me if I don't give her a dollar,
she is going to bust my _____ for me. And my friends told her that
she better bring 10 dollars to School. And the next day, she did not
bring it.

She told us that her mother wouldn't give it to her. So all five
of us slapped her and scratched her, and the next day she brought
the money and we all got 2 dollars, and we bought us a blimpie and
she wanted some and we told her to go and get some money from
her mother.

And so she went and asked her mother for a dollar. And her
mother slapped her 5 times and told her that she better go and get
that 10 dollars or else she was going to beat her when she got in from
school.

And her mother came to school and beat her with a shoe. And
me and my friends were laughing. And me and her had a fight, and
I won.

I beat her so that she had to go to the doctor, and her mother
told my mother that she had to pay for the doctor. And my mother
told her that if she paid for that doctor bill, she was going to slap
her mother.

And her mother told her that I was not going to the court, so the cops came to my house. And I told them that she started it.
And that
was the end.

LILLIE MAE MCCASKILL

The History of a Friendship and Enemyship

I had a friend with a girl named was Joan. She use to be my best friend. Whenever she was in trouble she always blame it on me. Once we went in the gym she said to me Do you like me when I put you in trouble. But I didn't say nothing and she said Did you hear, and I told her that it wasn't nice to trick people. And suddenly she jumps up and said So you don't like me. And I said That not truth. Cause you get people into trouble. And then she said I am going to be your enemy for now on. You hear me? And she never talk to me for ever and ever and ever and that how she became my enemy. The end.

CARLINE DANIEL

Hector is a friend of my. I know him when I was in fifth grade. One day we were playing punch ball Hector was on my side. When his turn came to bat he hit a base hit I said "Go Hector go!" Then he started running to home plate when he get there he thank me for saying that. Then we start telling jokes. Another week we getting closer and closer. And we still are friend.

SCOTT GEE

* * *

I am not at all certain what was accomplished by these seven lessons. I have no way of knowing what gains in consciousness, if any, took place in the children, or how enduring these alterations were. Short of inventing a new IQ test for poetry and awareness, there is no way for us to measure these changes. All we have to go by are the works produced in class, which are written in circumstances of pressure and distraction, often under the still-fresh influence of the discussion and the teacher.

My original goal was to get them to be able to write poetry autonomously, at home or by themselves, and I don't think I succeeded with most of them. They were still responding to my lead, often giving me what they sensed I wanted. The mark of adult manipulation is very clear: one of the reasons I described these lessons at length was to show, rather than disguise, that influence as it worked its way through the children's writings.

I never managed to bring about a fusion of descriptive and narrative styles.

What I did succeed in teaching them, I think, was to look very closely at small things. Perhaps it will leave them with another attitude toward detail.

V
The Adult in the Child

Everything that came to the children from their parents seemed to come at the wrong moment, from far away, as if produced not by them but by mysterious, unknown causes. It smelled of a great distance and was like the groaning of the folding screens when they went to bed.

These circumstances molded the children. They never knew this, for even among grownups there are few who know and feel what shapes them, forms them and links them with one another. Life lets but a few people in on what it is doing to them. It loves its work too much and talks while it works only with those who wish it success and love its workshop. . . .

To ensure that no dead branches remain in the soul to hinder its growth, and that man does not inject his stupidities into the creation of his immortal being, many things are provided to divert his trivial curiosity from life, which does not like to work in his presence and avoids his scrutiny in every possible way. Among these diversions are all genuine religions, all generally accepted ideas and all human prejudices, including the most brilliant and interesting psychology.

BORIS PASTERNAK
The Adolescence of Zhenya Luvers

Chapter 22
Getting at the Feelings

After centuries of neglect in mercantile America, the inner life is finally getting its due. Every popular magazine, every rock record, every commentary on the American scene contain reference to a hunger for change, away from the "emptiness and sterility," which is said to be the price of our material comfort, and toward a more emotionally meaningful, spiritual, fulfilling, personal life.

Once this hunger was felt, organizations such as Esalen grew up to train leaders who would then impart to groups of people the capacity for heightened sensitivity. Corporations with personnel troubles, racially conflicted high schools, large churches, and drug-abuse programs began to make room in their budgets for sessions which would encourage "dialoguing" and honest expression of feelings.

This "institutionalization of the feelings" took place quietly and almost *sub rosa,* but not without arousing suspicions that it was a way of vitiating rebellion. After all, a corporation might sponsor a weekend retreat or a series of encounter groups between managers and workers; but when they returned to work the hierarchy would remain the same, the assembly line would still be there, and the workers would still have no voice in decisions of production. A worker might have the satisfaction of telling off his foreman within a ritualized setting, but the workplace was a different story.

As corporations go, so go the schools. Space was made in the workaday curriculum for sensitivity, body movement, poetry, and tactile experiences. The sage administrator will render unto Caesar that which is Caesar's: a concession to the inner life, then on to the real work!

Some teachers did make the effort to connect the feelings and intuitions of children with every part of the learning process. But in most cases attention to the interior life tended to be reserved for special occasions, held ready as a treat or a favor. The ghettoization of sensitivity is exemplified by the teacher who asked me at a conference how she could "set up a creativity corner?" When I said with wonder that I didn't understand why she would want to restrict her students' creativity to one small corner of the room, she answered peevishly: "You know what I mean." She was right; I did know what she meant. But I didn't want to know.

Instead of viewing human creativity as the source of strength out of which all learning flows, the average public school sees it as something cute to put on bulletin boards or in assembly programs. This is particularly true of creative writing, which seems destined to be cut off from the rest of the curriculum in spite of the efforts of Sylvia Ashton-Warner and Herbert Kohl and a hundred others to show the organic connection between personal writing and academic skills. Even the name, "creative" writing, implies that it is an afterthought, something extraneous and in addition to "regular" writing —oh, very worthwhile of course, one wouldn't dream of eliminating it—but this very sense of its being worthwhile, this very tolerance which disguises condescension is the "kiss of death." Poetry we won't even talk about: what could be more "worthwhile," more elevated, more isolated from the meat-and-potatoes subjects?

Poetry is the exclamation point one gives to the well-apportioned classroom, the classroom "that has everything." Two sticks of poetry on the walls will do, one in front, one in back, like religious scrolls.

How often have I had to battle that iconic reverence for verse, as something fine and mushy that doesn't mean much but to which one still pays lip service, before I could get poetry and myself taken seriously? Until people see poetry as springing from all of life, they will isolate it in a creativity corner and treat it like a mascot.

* * *

At the heart of poetry is feelings. Some would say regenerated language; both are necessary to make a good poem, but for me a poem which does not deliver the emotional goods is a waste of time. The feelings are the juicy part. I will put up with a lot of obscurity and meanderings if I feel the poet has a large heart underneath: but if he seems crabby, niggardly, listless, desiccated, who has the time? Poetry should replenish.

> It is difficult
> to get the news from poems
> yet men die miserably every day
> for lack
> of what is found there.

WILLIAM CARLOS WILLIAMS

One reason why poetry should have a place in the curriculum is that it is able to turn to use those mysterious, grotesque, creepy, crepuscular, iridescent experiences which the child generally feels he had better leave outside the school door, but which obsess him and rob his attention. The teacher who would like his or her students to write deeply must first persuade the class that these emotions are not only allowed in literature, they are recommended. How to get a child to go beyond the product that one knows is facile and shallow for him—spiritually beneath him? Maybe he was taught to write superficially by an earlier teacher—who knows? It seems pointless to fix the blame, or the original sin, when he first learned to deceive and hide behind written words. Most children (like most adults) are afraid to know what is going on inside them. Sooner or later they would have discovered the knack of literary evasion.

The business of teaching people to write has never seemed to me very far from getting them to acknowledge the true state of their feelings.

Having said this, I am suddenly very leery and I want to retreat, qualify, caution. For we are now in that sticky area where poetry and psychotherapy can become cloyingly entangled with muddy results. (Not to mention the new profession of poetry therapy, which is used in hospitals and which claims to be able to cure insomnia, impotence, and grief!)

Most people would agree that it is a good thing to express feelings in writing. From this follows a series of questions that a teacher might ask: How does one promote a climate of healthy expressiveness so that children will not be afraid to put their feelings into writing? How does one draw the feelings out of shy children? How does one make the strong connection between personal feelings and writing? How does one teach children to make something literarily artistic out of their feelings?

Rather than begin to answer these almost impossible questions, I will mention one way that I think doesn't work, though it is tried often enough. Here a teacher simply assigns the topic: My Feelings. I know one who did this and got results like the following:

> My feelings are sometimes
> Silly
> Sad
> Happy.
> Sometimes . . .
> I don't like my feelings and
> Now,
> I like my feelings.
> Because
> I am writing a story about
> My
> feelings.
>
> ROCIO

I consider this poem a model of the tact with which children handle adult obtuseness. The topic was obviously too vague, and the child responded with brilliant second guessing and a certain charm, though with hardly any self-exposure, while his teacher was delighted that he had written a poem "all about his feelings." Her eyes lit up when she showed me the titles of the other compositions: *Sadness, Who I Am, When I'm Angry.*

The next year this same teacher showed me her list of writing topics. She wanted me to endorse her selection because I was, as she said, "also a firm believer in creative writing." The list assigned a homework entry in the child's diary for every date of the term and included such topics as:

OCTOBER:

2 If I Was My Mother
3 The Sound of the Rain
4 My Neighborhood
5 What I Think and How I Feel About My Name
6 My Weekend
9 What Makes a Human Being Human? Describe and Discuss
10 What Job Do I Want When I Grow Up? Describe
11 What Color Is Friendship? Pick One Color That Comes into Your Mind and Describe Your Feelings
12 My Teacher
13 My Weekend
16 Things That Make Me Mad
17 Things That Scare Me
18 Things That Make Me Sad
19 My Favorite Color. Describe
20 My Weekend
23 Things That Make Me Feel Loved. Describe
24 How Do People Show They Care About One Another? Describe
25 The Nicest Thing That Ever Happened to Me
26 When I Was Little
27 My Weekend
30 Me and Other Children; How I Get Along
31 About Having or Not Having a Pet

This went on for two more pages. I turned to the last entries: Suddenly the Sky Grew Dark, My Weekend, My Life as a Shoe, My Life as a Puppy, The Teacher and the Kid, My Life as a Football, My Weekend, The Accident, Me—1982, What Conversation Did Your Shoes Have Last Night?

I was embarrassed. What a demoniacally mechanical approach to the inner self! Side by side with those old chestnuts about hobbies and weekends (nothing is ever lost), I recognized many "hip" assignments that I had seen or had tried myself in recent years, including the unspeakably cloying "What Is the Color of Love?" (which originated, sadly, in a Teachers & Writers workshop). We were all to blame; we were all responsible for not making clearer the inspiration behind these ideas. They looked so dead, dittoed up and served up as homework topics.

The very idea of preassigned topics for a *diary* was anathema to me. I ventured to suggest that the student be allowed at least to choose a topic out of order when it was more in keeping with his mood that day. Suppose a child was feeling jovial and he had to write about Things That Make Me Mad? If one were truly interested in their feelings, one might get a better picture by allowing them to roam freely over the list . . . or even to write on a subject of their own choosing.

"They can do that during class time," she explained. "This is homework. Allowing them that much freedom of choice would make them confused."

I said nothing more, because I could see she was already offended by my lack of praise. Suddenly the sky grew dark. . . .

I went away wondering to what degree children could see through such transparent attempts to anticipate and to cordon off all the little private corners of their hearts. If I had gotten such a list for homework I think I would have considered suicide. Tonight would a ten-year-old boy go home and stare in desperation at his shoes, wondering what dialogue to invent for them?

Once I saw two prep school kids on a crosstown bus discussing their English teachers.

"She gives us a lot of creative writing for homework."

"Eoyough! I hate that stuff." (Little did they know that one of the arch-perpetrators of CW was sitting nearby them.) "She makes us pretend like we're a chair—"

"Yeah, and you have to write about your moods. . . . Like being dead and how it feels."

"*Eeooooough!* I would never do that."

They continued to swap notes, but I had to get off the bus. In any case, I had heard enough. Just as poetry had become identified in the public's mind with woolly-headedness, so writing about states of feeling was getting a bad reputation as something vaguely shameful and wormy that people tried to pry out of you.

What is so comical is that children generally parade their emotions all day long, stamping out of rooms, weeping, punching a classmate who arouses their jealousy. As a rule they are much less devious in their show of feelings than adults. Yet this cascade of pathos and raging and sudden endearing attachments does not seem to satisfy the teacher with a hunger for articulations about feeling. The childish emotions are not expressed in the verbal language that such an adult will understand, i.e., the language of group therapy where the feeling is mediated or tamed by insight: "I feel very hurt because I feel that you . . ."

So the digging continues. The adult with a psychological bent, wanting to narrow the distance between himself and his charges, will try to initiate the children into the linguistics of emotion. "Of course children are very emotional," he might say, "but they are unconscious about it. They need to understand their feelings so that they can better manage them."

It would be wonderful if such a thing could be accomplished with the delicacy, subtlety, professional knowledge, and concern for the individual that it would seem to require. But all I keep seeing is a wholesale attempt to foist very broad concepts of emotional health on children.[1]

Now that people have discovered they were deprived of a rich, feeling life, it is understandable that they want their children to experience all the variety and ecstasy they missed. But feelings cannot be commanded to perform; nor can they be imported and forced into the diet like vitamin pills. They must be allowed to come out at their own time.

When someone tells a child to write a composition about "My Feelings," he is asking to get a very schematic, abstracted result like the poem cited earlier, which has its own boundaries and conventions belonging to that peculiar hothouse genre that might be called, The Genre of Feelings. With a capital F.

---

[1] Take an example: an educational research laboratory which had had a hand in the development of "Sesame Street" is now designing a new government-sponsored children's television program which will "stress sensitivity and emotions." Apparently the old program was under attack for over-emphasizing "cognitive skills" at the expense of the affective and "social." When I first heard this, I had chills. It was not hard to imagine a cartoon selling the goodness of feeling to preschoolers. What rapacity, and yet what American ingenuity to market anything!

Flora Arnstein describes the reluctance of children to be put on the spot so directly in a fine passage written in 1946:

> I remember an incident of my early teaching days. While I was feeling my way tentatively along various lines, there came the temptation to assign a subject upon which the children might write. If, I argued, the children are stimulated to talk on a given subject, why, instead of expending this stimulus in talk, should they not write? And so we had a short discussion on fear, and I asked the children to write their ideas. The poems that were forthcoming were not particularly enlightening, but just sufficiently so to prompt the insidious suggestion: What a rich source of knowledge about the children, their hidden selves, what a help to the understanding of them it would be if one could get them to write poems that would furnish a clue to their emotional difficulties. My punishment was speedy, unmistakable, and for all time effective. Only one child responded to my request to write upon the chosen subject, sorrow, and she perpetrated the following:

Sad

I'm so sad, sad, sad.
I'd eat if I wasn't so sad.
But I won't eat—not one thing.
I'm so sad.
If I wasn't so sad, I'd play
And run about the streets with the other children,
But I'm so sad, sad, sad.

No commentary is needed other than this: curiously enough, the child who wrote it was the same who had written the one sentimental poem in the class. The question arises whether she was not too accustomed to conforming and catering to the wishes of adults. Her compliance to my request would seem to confirm this supposition.

How much more healthy was the other children's rejection of the subject! Children are not preoccupied with sorrow in the abstract. . . . Moreover, my motivation was not legitimate. However desirable it might be for me to seek to understand the children, the prime reason for their writing was not to supply me with laboratory material.[2]

---

[2] Flora J. Arnstein, *Children Write Poetry,* pp. 112–13.

The problem is not that there is anything wrong with wanting children to write about their feelings: but by inviting children to consider them as large abstractions one isolates Feeling from the concrete contexts that gave it birth and from which all its poignancy derives. To ask a child to meditate upon the idea of Sorrow is strangely enough to draw him far away from the familiar face of sorrow which is the everyday world, and to send him off into a fog (that fog which is so often mistaken for Poetry).

* * *

One more problem needs to be considered: the handling of taboo subjects. You will not notice in that list of diary topics to elicit the feelings any reference to sexual attraction, masturbation, excrement, the pleasures of hurting other people—subjects which occupy a great portion of many children's minds. So fascinating are these concerns that many poets who enter the schools with the purpose of encouraging children to express "whatever's on your mind" have been hit by a tidal wave of toilet jokes, sexual innuendoes, and four-letter words. This is to be expected, and not only because the kids are testing a new adult. What could be a stranger mystery to a child but that a certain act which he performs every day and which he knows everyone else performs every day, cannot be mentioned in speech or writing? Even families that tolerate frankness will have to tell their children not to talk about it in school or in other people's houses.

If a part of the ground had suddenly fallen away, it could not be more mysterious than this conspiracy to shroud commonplace elementary acts in silence. It would be expecting too little of children's curiosity to make them swallow so many secrets without its leaving a trace on their mental lives. No wonder they speak about these things so frequently in the playground or whenever they can come together unobserved. I once overheard a sandbox conversation in which two six-year-olds were talking about their mothers:

"My mother flushes me down the toilet bowl," said one, and the other laughed and said something similar. I had no idea what function this talk had for them, but I knew they could keep it up for hours.

When adults ask children to write about their feelings they usually mean the "acceptable" feelings, like Sorrow or Fear, not the "nasty stuff"; and they don't even have to make the distinction, they can do that with a well-placed frown. Some children will get into trouble by their failure to understand that expressing your feelings means *within certain circumscribed areas*. Cleverer children penetrate the hypocrisy of the code right away, and stay within the foul lines. But they pay a price for it.

There is no more serious threat to the development of authentic writing ability than the habit of censoring one's thoughts. If a child writes something which brings him a rebuke for being off-color, he will not make the same mistake again and again. But suppose he is thinking of these off-color subjects when paper is passed out for free writing? He knows he dare not write what is on his mind; he must invent a screen interest. If he is no good at this sort of pretense, he will decide he "can't write" and will develop into one of those adults who confesses, almost happily, that he can't write to save his life.

Since writing is essentially thinking recorded on paper, and since everyone thinks, how is it possible that many people—educated people—by their own admission "can't even write a letter"?

They must be terrified of committing their thoughts to ink. I have known children who were outspoken enough in discussions but who had a religious fear of writing down what they just said. Writing is, after all, a form of evidence which can be used against you.

This black-and-white evidential character of the written word is by no means lost on schoolchildren. They know the ropes. After several years of schooling, most children will have internalized the voices of censorship to a degree that they protect themselves in advance through *self-censorship*. To the original taboo subjects, they may add fear of sounding stupid or (years later) fear of writing in a bad style; and the picture of self-censorship is complete.

It follows that those who become writers must either be strong enough or naïve enough to override the claims of self-censorship. This may explain the tendency in serious writing to push the moral and formal limits endlessly a little further. Writers have always been drawn to the taboo: aesthetically, to breaking the rules of the form; morally, to exploring shadow areas in human relations and entertaining sympathy for transgressions, and thus expanding the possibilities of moral choice for everyone. The practice of literature is curiously bound up with the forbidden. The very act of making literature seems to require the unlimited freedom to think anything, however dangerous. If writers like myself defend the right of children to express themselves freely, even naughtily, it is because we are backing a principle which we recognize is in our own self-interest.

Anyone who would encourage children to write must face squarely the problem: To what extent is he prepared to allow children to write *whatever* is on their minds? The problem becomes even more complex when it reaches the stage of disseminating the writing. Let us say a teacher allows his class absolute freedom to write anything. Does that mean that everything should be read aloud if there is a class reading, or that everything should be printed in the magazine? Because one thing is certain: the level of administrative anxiety shoots up astronomically as soon as a thing is printed. "What you do in the privacy of your classroom is your affair," the administration might imply, "but that doesn't mean you should let it go home to the parents!"

There is unfortunately no rule of thumb that can be offered to teachers in so many thousands of diverse situations, other than the pragmatic one that every questionable case must be decided on its own merits. My own impulse is to get away with whatever I can, given the local political situation in my school. Since I am opposed to censorship, I see the decision not as a moral question but a political one. How many allies can be mustered among the parents and faculty, what is the temperament of the administration, what is the character of the local community, what is the size of the publication? (A good idea is to bury a risky piece in a hundred pages of stories and poems so that it won't stick out.)[3]

To be a creative-writing teacher with children, one must be prepared to fight a certain number of censorship battles. This seems as much a part of the profession as knowing what a metaphor is. For even if one wanted to avoid any controversy, it is impossible to pre-

---

[3] We did this quite consciously with one child's story, about a girl "with big buns and big titties," in the first issue of *The Spicy Meatball*, which was ninety-six pages long. Someone in the district office still managed to find it and complain, but the controversy was defused when the principal stood up for us. We were taking a chance and we knew it, but we figured it was better to test the water right away. It might have helped us that the magazine was released the last week of school, and whatever flak there was came during the summer.

dict all the ideas and references that a wary eye might find offensive. Once I was called down to the headmaster's office in a private school and reprimanded for mimeoing a poem which contained something about vomit. I had honestly not known that that mundane response to indigestion was on the Dirty List!

In a more tolerant school we were able to get away with "titties" in the first issue of the school magazine, and "piss" in the second. Every year we hope to liberate another contraband item.

It seems to me that many school censorship controversies can be headed off with good tactics and timing, courage at the right moment, and a measure of diplomacy. When a teacher feels that a piece is interesting and effectively written, and that it will mean something to the child to see it in print, he should probably take the chance. However, if the piece does not "sit well" with the teacher himself, it would be foolish to stick one's neck out for an article one doesn't feel capable of defending strongly. One of the most troubling cases is when a child's piece has something in it one personally finds offensive.

This often happens in a second zone of taboo beyond the obvious forbidden subjects. Liberal parents who can deal with childhood sexuality and digestive functions often get upset at the expression of cruelty, bloodthirstiness, or racial prejudice. One can foresee a time when the body will be accepted as natural and beautiful in American schools, while the last outpost of the unmentionable will be hostility.

"Everybody be nice." How understandable a desire that is! Yet it will not recognize what children are really like and what they need. There is a schoolteacher who forbade a six-year-old boy to draw monsters; so the kid started a secret monster club where they talk about and draw monsters.

The violence in stories written by children can be accepted as a drive toward excitement and climax. The cruelty they show each other is harder to take. There are some children who consistently use the shield of freedom granted by creative writing to get back at their enemies. I have stepped in and suppressed the reading of a story about the class's favorite scapegoat—an overweight girl whom everyone loved to stick pins into to see her turn red. The lowness of it sickened me; I had reached my own limits of tolerance. But I could as easily have suggested that the author fictionalize the name and one or two details, and it would have made a good story.

The existence of race hostility in children is more than understandable, given the strong ethnic feelings in this country. Yet most children would not dare record their thoughts on the subject. In one of my writing workshops using stream of consciousness, one sheltered Jewish girl permitted herself to speculate: "Why do Puerto Ricans talk so fast? Why do they all have such loud voices? (no offense)." How many children have similar prejudiced thoughts that are founded in ignorance, but that they are afraid to admit (and possibly have the ignorance corrected) because it is forbidden to speculate aloud on racial traits in the classroom? Afraid to write about the racial gang-ups that they see every day with their own eyes and afraid to confess their own ambivalence, they compete every year in an essay contest for who can write the best paean to brotherhood.

The schools are more interested in moral suasion than in teaching children to think. This is the greatest sin of American public education. It would rather have children parrot current moral attitudes, which are supposed to add up to good citizenship, than to teach them how to think for themselves, by using the evidence of their senses as a starting point, and then analyzing the problem from different perspectives. The moralistic formulas may change; they may embrace progressive views, conservative views, the right, the left, pluralism, the feelings, or that perennially sunny invocation to "smile," but the indoctrinative methods of training good citizens remain the same.

Unfortunately, creative writing has been selected to bear more than its portion of teaching the young to love the Good. Poems are construed into homilies; essays used as sermons.

To summarize: if one wants children to express their feelings in writing, one must be prepared to receive feelings from them which are considered antisocial, as well as acceptable. One must be willing to wade through a great deal of kaka and to have faith that something more interesting will emerge when the scatology has run its course. One must convince the children that the freedom to express their inmost thoughts is meant in earnest.

Chapter 23
The Land of Polka Dots

"I would prefer not to"
Herman Melville
Bartleby the Scrivener

There is a polite, proper, blushing Chinese girl in Mrs. Loftin's class who becomes flustered whenever it is writing time. Her pencils are always neatly lined up on the desk; her shirtwaist is clean and freshly ironed. She sits at the "giggly girls' table," blushing and whispering along with them whenever I come near. I think they think I am very comical, or very ugly, or gross, or sexy. In any case, titillating. I go along with the game up to a point. Then I want them to write.

Each of them has managed to break away at times from that five-headed giggle monster and write stories and poems that are very beautiful—each except Elizabeth. She clings the longest to any rebellion against the writing idea. When she sees that the others have settled down and resigned themselves to trying, Elizabeth opens her neat loose-leaf binder to a clean page and stares.

"Need any help?" I come up behind her.

"No!"

"Do you know what you're going to do yet?"

"I'm going to do what you wrote on the board!" she says, offended. She squints her eyes at the blackboard as if she had not given any thought until this moment to what it was all about, but would now apply herself.

I leave her alone.

Ten minutes later I come back. Still blank.

"No ideas?" I ask with a smile.

"I don't know what to write!" she says crossly.

"Maybe you don't want to do what's on the blackboard. Forget about it. Why don't you just write anything that you're thinking about? I'll help you. You can dictate it to me." I crouch down next to her so as to catch her words.

Most children like the freedom of giving dictation. Not Elizabeth. She will not admit that she needs help nor will she admit what she is actually thinking about. Nor will she even dismiss me with finality; she holds me there, a storm brewing on her tense face.

"I know what," she says finally. "I'll write a story about visiting polka-dot land."

This lets both of us off the hook, temporarily. I leave her to her own devices. When I read the class's papers aloud, I can barely get through hers, it is so forced. "Once upon a time I had a dream that I was in polka-dot land. All the people were made of polka dots. . . ."

I have the impression that she is repeating a composition she wrote last year for her fourth-grade teacher. The tone is recollection, not invention.

The next time she again draws a blank, and resolves it with "A Visit to Lollipop Land." Here all the creatures are made of lollipops. Lollipop heads, lollipop elbows, you name it.

She seems to be operating out of pure panic. I try to lessen the pressure of my presence on her, to be ultracasual, to expect nothing. Some children shrink from any direct approach: you have to wait them out. Yet week after week her writing is vapid and insincere. Her classwork for Mrs. Loftin has the same superficiality. It troubles me. Shouldn't I do something to draw her out more?

On the other hand, of course, not everyone has to be a writer.

A few months later the polka dots return. Something very sad is going on. Elizabeth can't bear to write her true thoughts down on paper. I refuse to believe that she is genuinely obsessed with polka dots on some symbolic level. It seems more likely that one of her former teachers had a penchant for those jejeune flights of fancy that are supposed to decorate the minds of children, like Walt Disney decals, and rewarded Elizabeth for her most innocuous pieces. Now Elizabeth is in a tight spot and tries to make it work again. But the new teacher doesn't like polka dots. Adults are all so hard to please.

She would not be the first one who had been taught the formula: Poetry = The Innocuous. I have seen more than a few children make the instant equation between Imagination and images like pink elephants, chartreuse castles, polka dots, flying candy sticks. If you say "Use your imagination" to such children, they will think you mean the cotton-candy gooey stuff. This is the legacy of certain children's books and television shows which practice moral suasion through the constant diet of only sweet things.

We are faced with a peculiar problem having to do with the exact nature of imagination. Many adults approach imagination as something extraneous to reality, as a holiday from reality. It seems to me, on the contrary, that imagination is *secreted* from reality through meditation on the concrete world. You look at something long enough and something starts to alter. The syrup in the spoon becomes a lake. But this in no way "delivers" you from your circumstances; it may be a way of connecting you even more deeply to the material world that is right in front of your eyes.

Children are presumed to have wild imaginations. (Some do, and some do not.) The adult asks the children to take out their imaginations. The children oblige with ready-made images that corroborate the adult's fondness for the innocent, the picturesque and the happy.

I no longer use the word "Imagination" in my teaching, for this very reason. It has become a dirty word—an invitation for the child to ignore everything that is real to him.

Finally I took Elizabeth aside and gave her my honest opinion. "This is your third story about polka dots. I don't think you care about this stuff. I think you're just grinding it out mechanically. Why don't you try writing what really matters to you? The things you worry about, the things you think of when you're trying to get to sleep. Or fidgeting in class . . . I'd rather you didn't write *anything*, than turn in stories that have so little of you in them. Leave the paper blank if you don't feel like writing!"

Elizabeth frowns. She knows what I'm saying. She doesn't like it much. For a girl like Elizabeth, turning in nothing is an impossible solution: she has been too well-trained not to do the work assigned.

Week after week she complies in her own passively resistant way. She is always dissatisfied with her first drafts. They lay crumpled in her inkwell. Elizabeth spends twenty minutes writing a paragraph, then another twenty copying it in neater handwriting.

At year's end the school magazine comes out. She has nothing in it. She brings herself to confront me, in the lineup before graduation exercises.

"How come you didn't put anything of mine in *The Spicy Meatball?* I guess you didn't think mine were good enough," she answers her own question.

I can barely speak. I mumble my way through it.

At that moment I am wishing I had slipped something, anything of hers into the magazine. But all her pieces were so *lifeless,* and the magazine was overcrowded as it was, and the other editors wanted their students' pieces included, and in the end I thought: Hers are just not good! What's the point of continuing the charade by patting her on the back and advancing her on to the next teacher?

I had failed with her. She stayed as doll-like, as well-mannered, as frightened, as she had been on the first day.

There is finally the issue of privacy. What happens when a child like Elizabeth says: "I don't care to let you into my mind. I know exactly what you want, but I have no desire to show you my insides. I'm shutting the door. Polka dots."

She has every right to say that. And I am duty bound to respect it.

But there is that uneasiness, remembering times that she might have wanted the stone to be rolled away.

Chapter 24
Francis, the Adult in the Child

The first time I noticed Francis—and it wasn't hard to notice Francis, the largest child in Iris Mayer's class—she was bending over a book. She was quite stout, easily forty pounds overweight, but solid, like a writing desk. Her wavy black hair, bobbed in the Spanish style, was parted down the middle. She had good-natured brown eyes and an open, pretty, chubby face that kept drawing me to its ovals. When she looked up from the page, with one of those pensive upturned faces, I could see thoughts traveling calmly across her brow at a not quite childish rate. Then she went back to reading.

She ignored me during the first few writing workshops I gave in her class. I think she felt she was too mature to join in. They were raucous juvenile sessions, and since Miss Mayer's class combined fourth-, fifth-, and sixth-graders in one room, the older children tended to look down on what excited the younger ones.

In the third week I asked her what was up. She confessed that last year she had been very interested in painting and writing, but this year she seemed to want mostly just to do her regular schoolwork. She spoke of her artistic time as something lost in the past. She had a nostalgia for that golden age that reminded me of the way adults speak of children as having more imagination than they. Francis was all of twelve. I told her that I doubted one could misplace the ability to write quite so easily; however, she should do a short piece on how this came about: how her interest had shifted from writing, and what other changes it might be connected to. (I was thinking of puberty, but I didn't dare say it.)

Francis rose to the bait. Her story said virtually verbatim what she had told me. By now I had connected her name with the author of a story in last year's *Spicy Meatball,* by one of Karen Hubert's students, which had impressed me.

I'm very fat and I know because everyone tells me so. But I am the kind of person that does not take everything serious. My sister is fat like me but she has a very different fat than I do. My brother-in-law is very skinny. So I call them fat and skinny. My house is a pig pen. I have a lot of rats. I have two snakes and four bats and one black cat. Sometimes they are a drag. Every day I want a new rat and bat. I like skeletants. I have some ants, not the ant of the family, the ants that itch. Sometime when I want to laugh I throw them on me.

FRANCIS ZERAUS

There are other children who write more brilliantly; but Francis's particular knack is to be able to write always in her own clear voice. "I'm very fat and I know because everyone tells me so." This is exactly the way she would say it aloud. A little defensively, but accepting the situation, as if the fact of her overweight problem had caused her to become more analytical and realistic than others her age. There is that wonderful Gertrude Steinlike sentence: "My sister is fat like me but she has a very different kind of fat than I do."

After she says "My house is a pig pen," there is a pulling back from the pain of honesty and a skid into the cat-bat-rat flippancy which she may have felt is expected of children: "I have two snakes and four bats and one black cat." This is filler. Mechanical enumeration—quite common in children's writing when the first inspiration has deserted. Then the penultimate line has a self-reflexive pun which pulls the reader up short: ". . . not the ant of the family, the ants that itch." Francis saves her story by catching herself in mid-thought. The last line gives a very satisfying closing image. It reconnects to the beginning with the "fat" business, through the monstrous contrast in scale—the tiny ants versus her largeness—and her resolution of the problem by laughing at it.

To me, this story exactly sums up Francis's perplexity of feeling both like a child and an adult.

The next week (after writing about how she didn't like writing any more), Francis asked if she could just look out the window and write whatever came into her mind. She loves to curl into the window sill and feel the radiator heat on her behind. I thought of the Russian cooks in Turgenev's stories who spent hours sitting on top of the stove. From time to time she cast disdainful sidelong glances from her paper to the noisy boys, the way a horse looks at the cows in the field. She showed me the mood piece she had been writing: the first paragraph. Now she was stuck. I gave her an idea for extending it— by describing the people she saw from the window in precise details. She went back to writing and wound up the piece by returning to her inner world. This natural movement from inner to outer world and back to inner is the most encouraging sign one can see in a young writer, or any writer.

New York looks dull but when you sit down and think about it, it's a very busy city. Ever since I've been in New York I've been a very lonely person. I've changed a lot. I guess it's because I've grown up. I understand when my mother says NO, even if she doesn't give me an explanation. It's very noisy in my class. I hate noise it gives me headaches. It just started to rain. I love rain, walking through the rain. Many times I wish I were a bird and just fly away when I want to. I hate having to be tied down some place. That's why I don't like to have pets. There's a lady walking by with a pink umbrella. There's a long hair guy with a bag on his back, a lady with two children. Some men putting in some pipes. A man looking at the thin air. A lady putting down her bag to open her car. There's a lot of smog today. I'd like to be outside today. I already have a headache. My favorite place in the school is on the third floor. You come up from the stairs and go straight down the hall until you get to a wall with a window sill. Then you turn left and there's a window sill. There's where I sit when I'm lonely or sad or feel like daydreaming, or just being alone. There's where I go when I'm out of the room for more than five minutes. A bum just went by. I always see him when I sit on the class window sill. The things that entertain are music, art, dance, movies, tv. I would like to someday be able to go on a motorcycle. My most biggest thrill is to become a fashion designer. I always stare at something and just go to another world, just thinking; you talk to me and I don't even hear you. I always wanted to be a singer, and take designing as something to turn to if singing doesn't go well. But then I stopped lying to myself and told myself that I'll never make it as a singer.

FRANCIS ZERAUS

The piece gave me a thrill when I read it. I love the way it just rolls on and on, from one melancholy perspective to another, with nothing to break the flow. There's so much dignity, so much self-recognition in it. An entire life, practically.

I told her how good I thought her story was. We got on immediately; she was quite open about herself and said among other things that she was originally from Cuba; that her grandmother was very important in her life; that her father wasn't around; and that her mother didn't understand her.

Iris Mayer passed me one day in the halls. I asked her how she thought the workshops with her class were going.

"You've made a real difference with Francis," she said. "Suddenly she's outgoing and wants to do writing and helps the other kids."

That was all she had time for. We were both speeding off in opposite directions. But her remark stuck with me.

I began looking forward to the Monday-afternoon workshop because Francis was in it, and whenever she was absent I felt disappointed. I would duck into Iris Mayer's class later in the week just to see how Francis was doing. It was as if I were falling in love with her. So little is understood about the magnetism between teachers and children that it invites snickering to admit that I found myself drawn to this particular girl student. But it was not like an attraction of a sexual nature. It was rather that I seemed able to be completely myself with Francis; we understood each other without needing to explain much. In her presence I felt that rapport and that warmth which is such a rare thing that who can afford to disregard it, in whatever form it appears?

At the workshops she never wanted to do what the others were doing; she wanted me to suggest a special assignment. "Whatever you feel like," I said. "I don't know how to begin," she said. So we would think of something together. Usually this involved my drawing out her current worries and then asking her to write about them. I would have taken a more indirect, allegorical route with some other children, but Francis had not the slightest trouble writing up her "life problems." Analytical realism was her forte. Action, heroic plot, fantasy—the strengths of so many child writers—these she showed no interest in.

One day she was looking rather blue and I suggested she write about her mother and her. She wrote:

My Mother Doesn't Understand Me

My mother doesn't understand me because she thinks I'm going to be like her, that I'm going to chain myself to my mother like she did. She let my grandmother make all her decisions for her. My mother wants me to be like my sister, a secretary. I don't want to be one but she says alright and then the days go by and she tells me again. I have plans for my life. She made my sister become a secretary but she hated it. My mother doesn't understand me because we don't communicate very well. I guess it's because of the generation gap. My sister is a little different, she says she won't do something and the next minute she's doing it. I'm not like that, my decisions are firm, when I say I'm not going to do something, I won't. My mother doesn't understand me, because when I like something she starts criticizing it. And I hate criticism because no one is perfect to criticize. If I say green she says orange. I have more communication with my sister. We get along beautifully. But I still think my mother is one of the best mothers in the world. I'm so happy today. I think it's the best day of my life. I really have no reason, I just don't know why nothing great has happened to me but I just feel happy.

It really seemed that she had written herself out of a bad mood.

Every time Francis wrote well, the next time she got a little nervous about my expectations. She was afraid of disappointing me—as if performing as a writer was the currency she had to pay to hold my attention and good opinion of her.

I had suggested one day that she might want to write the life story of her grandmother. It was a way of having her combine the factual with more mythical and imaginative materials; of getting her to try her wings more. She liked the idea very much. Then she bogged down.

"How should I start it?"

"Anyway you want. Start out with when your grandmother was a little girl. You can throw in lots of description about how Cuba looked in those days."

"But I don't know what Cuba looked like in 1900!"

"That's just the point. Make it up."

"I don't think I can write it and make it seem real."

"Then write it to sound like a fairy tale."

I was giving her some persistent clues toward a certain kind of story that I liked to read: the family chronicle that mixed realism with fabulistic, folklore elements (*One Hundred Years of Solitude*, for example). Whether she understood what I was after or not, whether she resented the manipulation or not, the struggle still stood: to write down the whole life of her grandmother. Surely there was something unfair about the project. And underneath that question was another doubt: What would happen if she couldn't do it? Would I stop liking her?

I didn't quite understand this pressure on her until we met in the hall a few times and she immediately threw out an apology for not having finished the grandmother story. She had connected my mere presence with something she had to do. I hated to see myself turning into a symbol of coercion in Francis's eyes.

I told her it really wasn't that important to me whether she finished the story or not. I had only given her the idea as a suggestion because she asked for one. And if she never wrote another word in her life, I would still enjoy her company.

There. I could not have said it more plainly.

Nevertheless she continued to regard the grandmother story as something she had contracted to do. From time to time she showed me a few lines and asked me if it was on the right track. I said yes, keep going. I was determined now that it would be her story without any more input from me.

After Christmas vacation she handed me a typed copy of the completed story; and we both breathed a sigh of relief.

The Life of Maria Peldorno (My Grandmother)

Once upon a time there was a second youngest child born to a middle class family. She was a very pretty girl when she grew up. When she was thirteen she started to work. Her father didn't object to the fact of her working so he let her. She had two sisters and five brothers. She didn't have a mother at the time she started to work. Her mother had died when she was five. She was born in Cuba. In those days Cuba was different. Castro wasn't in command. Cuba was a very nice place to live in. There was no violence it was peaceful until Castro came along. Getting back to the life of Maria Peldorno. She worked in a beauty parlor. She started out by cutting men's fingers. But with time she got better. She was a girl that went dancing three times a week. She was very active. She met her husband one day she went to his dentist office. He had a very beautiful dentist office. She had gone to clean her teeth. Then he started to go where she was working to get his hands done. So they started to date. With time they got married they had a few fights. One time they had a fight because he was gambling and she was home with dinner ready so she went to get him. When he got home he didn't like what she had cooked so she sent him to a restaurant and she never cooked for him again. Time went by they have a little girl named Lidia. They raise the girl in Cuba the girl was sent to the best schools. Time goes by very fast when the girl was seventeen her father dies. Maria is left alone. The girl gets married the same year her father died. Time goes by. Then Castro started to take over Lidia leaves Cuba but leaves Maria and her first daughter. About a year later Maria comes out of Cuba with her granddaughter. When they all meet Lidia had another daughter that with time Maria had raised. Time goes by Maria gets old she has raised a daughter and two granddaughters. Now she is a sick old lady on welfare. She is happy. She is 62 years old now.

The story was more ambitious in narrative scope than anything Francis had done previously. From her first piece to this one, there was solid growth. Not only was it good, but she had managed to finish a story that took several sessions to conceive. She had "fulfilled her obligations." Now we could settle down to being friends again.

She told me she was mostly bored to death after school. She would sit in her room and do nothing. Had she any friends? A few, but most of the kids were too bratty or silly. I asked her what she thought of this kid or that one—I went down the list of my favorites. It was fascinating to find out how one young person made distinctions about the others, since to me they were all "bratty," sensitive, and full of potential. Francis had a cavalier way of dismissing with a word: Tammy was a "snob," Roberto a "creep," Nola and Melissa were "still playing with dolls."

Whom did she like then?

She named two comrades, one a stranger to me, the other, Hannah. Hannah was one of those children who seem so much wiser, sadder, and more complete than any adolescent, because their faces reflect the burden of understanding all adults and remaining loyal to childhood at the same time.

"If you have two good trusty friends, what are you complaining about?" I said. "You're ahead of the game!"

That didn't matter; she still felt bored. Always this word to describe it. I watched her chasing little Noam around the room or squirting water from the fountain. In times like these she had a sunny happy-go-lucky disposition that gave the lie to her famous "boredom." I even suspected that the boredom was a pose, copied from the adults around her because she wanted so much to be thought an adult.

But no: it was quite real. Most likely boredom was the term she used to describe the slow tapping of her soul, drop by drop, into a thicker substance.

Francis, stay with that dreary isolation. It may be something very fortunate that is preparing for your awakening. (How not to make people afraid of boredom?) Some people are fortunate enough to live through the crisis of solitude in their early years. Bad turns and the opinions of others can never wholly dominate them afterward.

I remembered how often at her age I used to lie on my bed with a book, holding it as if it were my life raft. "Do you read a lot?" I asked Francis.

"Not so much. I can't find any books that interest me. *Diary of Anne Frank* I read twice," she confessed. "And *I Never Promised You a Rose Garden.*"

I understood the genre. "I'll find you some books," I promised.

That night I searched my shelves for something to give her. It had to be something magnificent, something she could sink her teeth into. I was impatient with the idea of finding a book pitched at a sixth-grade-vocabulary level; it seemed condescending. In the end I opted, bizarrely, for *The Best Short Stories of Dostoevsky,* because he was the first writer who had changed my life. And because I hoped his loud, quirky narrative voice would appeal to Francis and show her more dramatic possibilities for her own writing.

I doubt that it altered her life. She said she enjoyed it, though.

One day I was talking to Francis and the fact that she had lived in Florida emerged.

"Did you like Florida?" I asked.

"No," she said in that tone of blasé negativity that she and I both found amusing. "It was completely dull. My mother and I lived in a hotel and on Saturday nights we would go down to the lobby and play checkers. I almost yawned myself to death."

"I have heard that Florida can be dull," I said, "but I should think the Cuban population has made things livelier."

"Oh, they're worse. Cuban families don't let you go anywhere on a date without a chaperone. I couldn't even sneak off to the bushes if I wanted to."

"Francis!"

"Well, it's true." She went on about hotel life, and her account was a masterpiece of accumulated details on sloth, which reminded me of Ring Lardner's Floridian tales. Finally I couldn't restrain myself and said the inevitable (which made me feel ashamed, like a vulture picking at conversations), in a clear but hurried voice—

"You should write a story about that."

"Oh, sure. It would put all my readers fast asleep," said Francis. "I wouldn't even be able to finish it."

"Not necessarily. You described it so juicily, you might get a kick out of remembering it all. Boredom is a classic subject for literature. If you write about boredom in a lively, entertaining way, it can be wonderful."

She was not convinced, but I saw she was thinking it over.

"You know, truthfully, it astonishes me," I said, "that with all the boredom that children have to put up with, and some children have very boring days that seem to last forever, all they ever write about is horror creatures and excitement."

"That's not so surprising," said Francis.

"Right. But you can break the trend. *Boredom in Florida*—think of the title!"

"That does sound pretty good," she laughed. We talked for a while longer; I was unwilling to leave since we were having such a good time. Eventually the lunch bell ended it for us. "It was good talking to you," I said earnestly. "I really enjoyed myself."

"I didn't. All that yakking gave me a headache," Francis cracked.

That was the difference between children and adults.

Chapter 25
June Diaries

Roberto told me his love problems today. First he liked Julie, but then her mother nixed it. "That was a long, long time ago." Then he had a crush on Consuela. "First she said she wouldn't go with me, then she said she would, then she said meet me in the yard. Then she told me she couldn't go with me! All because another guy got there first. And I know the guy too—Luis. I spied on them in Riverside Park. Consuela and Luis were making out—I punched him and his eye got all puffed out."

"Is this true?"

"Yeah, I spied on them," he said, evading the part about whether he'd hit Luis.

"Why did you hit Luis?"

"He stole my girl!"

"She wasn't yours."

"It don't matter. I'm going out with someone else now."

"Who?"

"Everybody know—Dolores."

I was profoundly jealous. I asked him if he liked any other girls in school.

"Tammy—but she got her nose permanently stuck in the air."

"Doesn't Dolores have a strict mother?"

"What her mother don't know won't hurt her."

"Do you go out with her in the night, or just during the day?"

"Day and nighttime too if I feel like it!"

Later that afternoon he was mooning around. He begged to be given a part in the videotape we were shooting. Big, handsome, sulking boy, subdued as I had never seen him.

We were walking up the street carrying equipment when he said: "And then another bad luck. Dolores got to quit on me. Do you know anyone who likes me in this school?"

"I like you."

"No I mean a girl! You ain't a girl."

"Did you ask her why?"

"They never tell."

"Why not?"

"Because she afraid I'm gonna hit her. They never tell you the reason. One time a girl quit on me and I smacked her cross her face."

"Roberto! . . . That's not the way to treat a woman."

"I wouldn't do it again."

"You might be scaring them away—!"

"Dolores isn't scared of me."

"What then?"

"I know the reason. She like another guy more. Scottie! What does that guy got that I don't got? And Scottie told her fifty times that he couldn't stand her. Now what kind of sense does that make— he don't even want her and she runs after him."

I felt so much sympathy for Roberto. He feels a woman's love is his due and he doesn't know how to conjure it. He wants to rip it out of her.

Sometimes when people hear what we're doing at P.S. 90, they say, "Gee, I really feel cheated. When I was going to school it was horrible. But now they have all these fun things to do—boo hoo! I want to go back to second grade!"

The truth is, it's not that different. There are still bullies, two-faced friends, disappointments, betrayals, confusion. Growing up maintains its own sluggish, melancholy tempo. Of course we can make things easier; we can take away some of the adult-inspired cruelties, but before we get carried away with our own propaganda about reforming the schools, we should keep in mind that the way of childhood is hard.

JUNE 9

It was such a hot sunny day, temperature reached 95 degrees, I wanted to beg out of the writing workshop, but Iris Mayer said

"You're taking them this afternoon, aren't you?" so I figured what the hell. How badly can it flop?

There were mostly fourth- and fifth-graders—the seniors were at graduation practice. Noam was plucking a guitar and I realized he could play quite well, so I put away my idea for the lesson and took them into the Writing Room to write songs.

The first song we wrote was a 1950s rock-and-roll takeoff about soda fountains and motorcycles. It had a catchy refrain that went:

> Bubble gu-um in my ponytail
> Bubble gu-um in my ponytail
> Bubble gu-um in my ponytail
> Bubble gu-um in my ponytail
> Bubble gu-um
> Bubble gu-um
> Bubble gu-um
> Dadadadadadada

The rest of it was even less distinguished.

The next song went to the tune of "Greensleeves":

> My father died when I was three
> My mother died along with he
> I sat and sat up in a tree
> My grandmother didn't think it was good for me
>
> Bad luck was always around
> Even when I went to town
> My father was square and I am round
> I got on a plane that was China bound. . . .

And then a stanza about China. We were having a good time. We sang each stanza several times, then they said, "Let's sing it for the whole class! Sing it for Miss Mayer!"

We went back to their home room; it was 2:15 and Iris Mayer was getting ready to take them down to the sprinkler, reminding them that no one could go in the pool without a bathing suit. In the confusion of everyone getting on line there was no time to do the songs.

Monte Clausen sent me down with a few late stragglers to the park. There at the bottom of the hill was a scene that made my heart joyous: sprinklers and kids getting wet and tossing water on each other in an orgy of splashing.

I remembered how much fun it had been for me as a child to go into the wading pool under the bridge.

One of the younger teachers was there, wrapped in her own thoughts. Eve was wandering around talking to herself, her sun dress looking spotless. I said to another teacher, Miss Brooks, "What a nice day," and she agreed.

"How do you like it, Iris?" I asked.

"I don't like it. It's awful. The boys are splashing the girls and Willie is beating up everyone and there are too many kids and I hate it when Clausen leaves me with both classes. As far as I'm concerned, this is a complete waste."

Not wanting her to cloud my good spirits, I moved away. "Hold these for a minute, please." I left my books—and ran into the pool. Clothes and all. I ran around in a circle seeing no one I knew but getting cool. It felt terrifically relaxing. Willie dumped buckets of water on my jeans and I made as if to strangle him. Then I ran out of the pool and up to the benches where I shook out my saddle shoes.

"You're such a kid. When are you going to grow up?" said Iris, not really nastily but indulgently.

"It got me cool, didn't it?" I said. I sat panting and feeling the heat coming back as the water dried off my shoulders.

JUNE 12

Monday and Tuesday at the Print Center, we had some kids helping us collate *Spicy Meatball* #3: Juliet, Edith, Elizabeth, and Jane. They did an amazing amount of work. Larry Zirlin, the printer, kept coming down to the basement and marveling: "I swear, this place looks more and more like a sweatshop. Do you girls know about the child-labor laws?"

"We do," said Edith, making a sassy face.

"What does he pay you?"

"We each get an ice cream cone."

For lunch, Sue Willis invited us—the girls, Larry, and me—over to her house and laid out a huge spread of cold cuts. I was so dazed from three days' collating that all I could think of was, "Boy, this salami sandwich tastes good. Boy, this whole wheat bread tastes good." Truly mindless. Edith and Jane had giggling fits when they learned that Sue was not the only occupant of her large apartment; she shares it with her BOYFRIEND!

The girls were terrific collators. They had worked out an ingenious assembly line which was so rapid—each feeding the next a few pages—that we managed to finish all thousand *Spicy Meatballs* by 2:30 Tuesday.

Larry helped us lug boxes to the car. You could tell he was exhausted and happy to get rid of *Spicy Meatball* for the next six months —at the same time perhaps a little sentimental about the whole job ending.

We drove up to school for distribution. We handed it out to all the lower grades, but the upper-grade classes were still in the auditorium for graduation rehearsal.

GRADUATION DAY

In front of the auditorium, the sixth-graders were lined up, nervous and yet well-behaved. Girls had their hair done up in ringlets— Wendy Gonzalez had achieved the pinnacle of her *virtu,* in sidecurls and a full-length dress. Lots of turquoise formals. Yolanda was wearing a cute white mini-communion dress. Vicky, later to be given the Best Female Athlete award, had on checkered shorts! Roberto was wearing a grown-up wine-red sports jacket and kept flipping his tie self-consciously in imitation of the Oliver Hardy gag. Francis Zeraus was very jolly and becoming-looking in a pink pajama suit. We winked at each other.

I went out into the kindergarten yard for a breather—the equivalent of a smoke, if I smoked—and stood in the weather for some minutes. Little tiny girls were having a jump-rope contest. They were so young that they wore a perplexed dazed smile when they lost (that is, when the teacher told them their turn was over), as if they didn't yet understand the concept of failure. I came back and the graduates were still lined up, but by this time the parents had filled the auditorium and I took a seat in the back row next to two teachers, Janet Brooks and Charles Pepper.

As the graduates filed in and circled around in an elaborate figure eight, each one adjusting to the embarrassment of being on display in his own fashion, Janet and I kept remarking how beautiful these kids were. Comments from other teachers ran the same. It was a long-delayed release of love for the children—a rare opportunity for the teachers to see all the kids physically in front of them without having to control their behavior, letting loose a wave of pent-up pride, nostalgia, and affection. I, for one, insisted that this class was much more exceptional than the last graduating class, in terms of strong personalities; but it was probably that I had had a chance to work with them for two years, whereas the others had been my students for only one.

The speeches were short. The ceremony had a peppy beat. Addresses were punctuated with popular songs sung by the graduates, accompanied by a good mixed (adult-child) band. Several of the speakers paid tribute to *West Side Story* as one of the high points of the year. I was starting to get butterflies in my stomach as I looked down the program card to my act, which was coming up. It had been listed as a surprise, and no one knew what to expect.

It was something Britt and I had cooked up between ourselves. Britt would come out on the stage first, looking tough, bored, and hoodlumish—a bit like his dice-rolling portrayal of Riff in *West Side Story*. Then once he had set the scene, I was to enter as a doddering old man and start singing in the corniest, hammiest voice imaginable, "You'll Never Walk Alone." What better song for a graduation? Britt was to play against me: ridicule me, scoff with disbelief, steal the scene in any way he could think of. I was to go on earnestly, pretending I didn't notice. Then when I came to the high note, the generation gap would be triumphantly bridged: I would lift him onto my shoulders (this was the risky part) and we would sing the last chorus together.

"How much time do you want to take before I come on?" I whispered to Britt.

"Fifteen minutes," he answered.

Even Marcel Marceau has trouble holding people for fifteen minutes. How good does this kid think he is? I suggested more like two minutes.

"Okay, two minutes."

"Are you nervous?" I asked.

"Why should I be," he said, "after all the films I've been in and stuff?"

We both went backstage. A minute before he was supposed to go on he came up to me and confessed, "I don't know what I'm supposed to do." I realized he had blanked. "Maybe if I had something to work with—like this bat," he said, picking up a baseball bat that was on the floor.

"Fine," I said, "use any prop you want. Just don't hit the distinguished guests onstage or do anything that looks disrespectful."

When he entered onstage, he started doing a pantomime of hitting a baseball and watching it travel. Then he did that again. He was having trouble thinking of something else. He seemed stuck. I decided it was time to come out. I started my song in the wings, and advanced on Britt with almost a menacing quality—"Walk on through the wind, walk on through the rain!"—I was singing so loud that I had the peculiar sensation that my voice was detached from me. My voice and I were two different entities, my voice spreading out like a cloud over the audience, and I standing onstage, wondering just like everyone else where this noise was coming from. Britt did a beautiful job of undercutting me, and when it came time for the double-decker part he got up on me without a hitch, riding on my shoulders like a man on a camel, to the thunderous approval of the graduation audience.

The teachers clapped me on the back as I made my way toward the rear of the auditorium. The skit had been a sunny diversion for everyone. Then the graduation exercises settled down again to more sober matters. Diplomas were handed out; awards awarded. Francis won the art award; Britt took dramatics. Dolores made a farewell speech in Spanish. How sorry I was to say good-by to them was something I could barely face. I saw so many kids I loved who were going to graduate. Roberto, Gene, Luis, Britt, Willie, Dolores, Gregory, Xiomara, Yolanda, Virginia, Francis, the three Davids, Liz, Maria, Marissa, Tammy, Robin, and the ones I had never really gotten close enough to know—Lillie, Claire, Kelly. If only there was some way of leaving them back! Then we could have a fantastic repertory company; oh, what shows we'd put on!

Chapter 26
Conclusion

My thinking about education has undergone a very noticeable shift from the first days I came into P.S. 90. Then I was more concerned with releasing children's imaginations. By now I almost take it for granted that, in a relaxed supportive atmosphere, that expressiveness of theirs will surface. Now I would say my main thrust is teaching the discipline of sticking to something. Building, finishing on a promising start are the skills I want most to give students. And beyond that, an understanding of how continuity operates: how far one can follow out a strand, and when it is necessary to abandon it and start a new one, and whether, at some later point, it is possible to combine the two strands.

The development of the Writing Team had the sharpest influence on me as a learning experience in this regard. The strength of the team has been from the start its willingness to explore different artistic media and not get cornered into selling one form above all others. If a child did not want to write (and why should every child want to be a writer?), we would do theater and video acting with him; if he was more of a visual artist, we would put him to work painting scenery or drawing cartoons; if he jumped around a lot, we would use him as a dancer or a stunt man. Somehow we always felt sure that the creative spark was the same and was entitled to come out in whatever form it wanted to shine. This point of view placed an obligation on us to expand ourselves and learn how to try other media than the ones in which we were trained: how to operate film equipment, direct plays, choreograph, make scenery. And this has been one of the blessings of the job, that it has given us the opportunity to learn new techniques along with the children.

For me, one of the greatest satisfactions has been in watching the growth of the other members of the Writing Team. I realize that my account has been lopsided in the direction of early troubles. I have not known how to describe the later part of our learning to trust each other and work together with great joy—a joy that has meant so much to me in my own life but that is embarrassing and gushy to tell to strangers. It is easier to write about conflicts than to find the words to explain the quiet, dependable way the team operates now. We have been together for three years. Karen Hubert has been doing brilliant, original work in the systematic mining of narrative genres (adventure, horror, love, detective stories). Sue Willis has done exciting projects such as her course in linguistics for children, or the one around medieval themes, teaching the children Chaucer and doing an Everyman play, a Dance of Death, and a street carnival. Certain videotapes which Teri Mack has made with her students, like *How to Live Without a Father,* have gone deeper in feeling and content than any others I have seen by children. To write about all their projects would have made this book overly long; my hope is that some of the highly original experiments the other Writing Team members have done will also receive the attention and public recognition they deserve.

The videotape program has grown considerably since the first year. Parents picked up their children's interest and attended training workshops taught by Teri Mack. Now a cadre of parents, teachers, and paraprofessionals is well-versed in the equipment and able to go out on "shoots," relieving some of the pressure on the Writing Team to tape every event.

As the videotapes made by children continued to accumulate, I became aware of a sameness or repetitiveness which bespoke the excessive influence of action television. It seemed to me that before we could go on filming, the children needed a better groundwork in the culture and grammar of film. So I began giving a weekly course last year in the History of Films, in which I lectured about film aesthetics and then showed movies. Some of the films were obviously a little steep for the kids (fourth through sixth grade) but I wanted to get beyond the *Red Balloon* children's programming and find out how they would handle a meat-and-potatoes, non-condescending film-history course. They saw *Potemkin, Passion of Joan of Arc, Intolerance, The Gold Rush, The General, Cabinet of Dr. Caligari, Nosferatu, Man with a Movie Camera, Zéro de Conduite, Citizen Kane, The Bicycle Thief, Stagecoach, Singing in the Rain, The Big*

Heat, The Checkers' Speech, Pull My Daisy, Rebel Without a Cause and several others. Their responses continually surprised me. They loved *Singing in the Rain, Rebel Without a Cause,* and *The Gold Rush,* as would be expected. But they also adored the slow-moving, elegiac *Nosferatu* and *Cabinet of Dr. Caligari,* and liked *Joan of Arc* and *Potemkin,* while they detested *Citizen Kane* and *Zéro de Conduite.* Out of the intensive study of silent movies came an enriched appreciation for the beautiful image, the art of lighting, and mimed acting, which then filtered into their own films. One of the side effects of the course was a turning away from videotape toward Super-8, which was better suited for capturing silent-film images.

On the strictly literary front, *Spicy Meatball* has continued to be published twice a year. However, we became aware of the need for another publishing outlet to handle material that was too long for the magazine. Faced with the development of longer works by children (some novella length) or collections of stories and poems by gifted individual children, we decided to start a small press to release these separately. The Seventy-Five Press was begun in order to issue limited-edition booklets of high-quality children's writing. Each of these booklets would have the same page size and format, in 350 copies apiece.

The first two books to be selected were Alissa Kwitney's collection, *A Huge Lion of a Book* (her title) and Aaron Richardson's science fiction rewrite of Wells's *The Time Machine.* The two authors were given a book-signing party. The "cocktail party," with fruit punch and cookies baked by the authors' mothers, was a lovely event in which adults and children, invited by the writers, mingled and drank, while the two ten-year-old authors sat at adjoining desks signing autograph copies. It was not much different from a downtown publishing party, with the difference that at this reception some of the guests actually opened the books and read them on the spot.

Since then the Seventy-Five Press has issued more than eight booklets, including a bilingual collection of writings by Spanish-speaking children, translated by themselves; Hannah Brown's *The Harry Sneedless Stories,* and Matthew Goodwin's adventure novella of eight people trapped in the Himalayan mountains, *Survival!*

In case one gets the wrong idea that P.S. 90 is blessed with exceptional numbers of talented children, I can only say that there are good writers in every grade school in the country. The point is to find them and give them their deserved exposure in print. The discovery of talented products by children creates a burden to bring them to light. But there is no getting around that burden.

What is true for our own work is equally true for the children's. They need to learn how to see and respond to the desirable burden which good, unfinished work places on people. A piece of promising work cries out for completion. It seems to have a will of its own and to want to reach the deepest life available to it, like a river cutting its own channel. Each task whispers in the ear, suggesting an organic curve to pursue. You can either ignore that appeal (but at the risk of dulling your inner voice), or obey, which generally means more labor.

The job is going well when it casts up new problems for exploration before the old ones have been quite concluded. It may seem at first that the work has a frightening propensity to open outward in all directions, without ever diminishing. But each succeeding step narrows the problem slightly, just as a nineteenth-century world-embracing novel consents to letting its loose ends be tied together in the final chapters, not without evoking a melancholy for that early stage when everything was possible and open.

In any case, it is impossible to overstress the importance of building habits of work completion at an early age. Whether one approaches this from the scientific area, by bringing experiments to some conclusion, or the artistic area, by taking theater games to a point where they can be presented onstage before an audience, the value of following through the work and sharing the information with the community is universally applicable. If children can be further involved in the reproduction and display of their efforts, it will give them one more reason to complete them in the first place.

I must take pains to differentiate here between a mechanical obsession with the completion of all tasks—from eating every pea on the plate to forcing oneself to finish a dull book, which has a neurotic basis and often grinds down the spirit—and the ability to finish what one actually wants to finish. The most important discipline we can try to teach young people is how to identify and stay with things they want to investigate, but which they are inclined to drop too quickly because of fear of failure. Here the teacher can be very helpful in remembering just those activities which had excited and attracted the child at one point, and giving a supportive but insistent *nudge* to encourage the child to see it through to completion.

We all know people with talent, intelligence, and obvious ambition who have a mysterious inability to finish things that are very important to them. Even in their hobbies, a lethargy overtakes them when it comes to following through on something which at first they had raved about: learning an instrument, building a model boat, working in the darkroom, studying Japanese, writing an article. Since these people are sometimes our closest friends, or ourselves, it would be worth while to look into the reasons for this sudden abandonment of a promising start.

On the one hand, the person decides he "just hasn't got it." In a private moment between himself and himself, he comes to the conclusion that he has exaggerated his aptitude, or desire, for the thing. "I don't have anything to say, so why continue the farce of writing an article?" He levels a judgment on himself at an early snag and finds himself wanting.

Or in some cases the person may realize, correctly, that he had placed more importance on a little hobby than he had originally admitted. Writing an article for a local paper was to be the start of a journalistic career; learning Japanese masked glamorous fantasies of becoming a United Nations interpreter and getting out of a dead-end job. The hardships of early practicing reveal to him how far he is from true professional mastery—the top of the field, which is his real dream. In coming to a better understanding of the motives behind the initial enthusiasm, he feels ashamed of his overreaching tendencies and lets the project deflate.

But neither of these barriers—the negative judgment leveled on one's ability after first difficulties, or the discovery of unrealistic personal fantasies—would be enough in themselves, necessarily, to force a person to give up. Most people *do* sense that no matter how unprofessional their workmanship is, there is some satisfaction to be felt from the mere act of assembling pieces into a finished whole, in seeing something they made take shape before their eyes. I think what prevents some people from making that final push is not so much laziness, as unwillingness to experience the pleasure it would bring. The inhibitions against pleasure go very deep. To finish an activity would be a form of release. There are artistic and vocational types of frigidity, as well as sexual.

The child who crumples up her story and throws it into the wastebasket—often if you pull it out of the garbage after she leaves, you find the writing was not bad at all, in fact very promising. What is operating here if not a fear of having to compete at a higher level? A fear of success?

The problem, restated, is how to teach whole experiences, how to teach an appreciation of beginning-to-end. Promising starts, no matter what anyone claims about doing something for the sake of doing it, produce more satisfaction when seen through to completion, and then seen by others. And children know very well when something is for real, or when it is for "a taste of the process."

I remember in the fifth grade being called to the back of the room to do something with litmus paper. Every one of us had to have his turn doing this thing with litmus paper, and if you did it one way, it turned blue and another way, pink. Shortly afterward I was completely in a fog about what I had "learned"; all I could remember was waiting my turn in a circle and feeling pushed. But from the school's point of view the learning-by-doing law had been respected: I had had my litmus paper experience.

Learning by Doing is a credo so deeply absorbed into the American educational ideology that it has become axiomatic, like the law of gravity. It has had the effect of making activity appear to be a positive good: so long as the kids are busy doing something, the quality and meaning of the experience are to some degree assumed. Learning by doing has a good deal of common sense behind it. Where the thinking goes wrong is in forgetting to ask (as in our national involvement in Vietnam): What are we doing exactly? Why should I do this? How does my little job connect to the other parts of the process? Who is going to use this thing I am doing, and toward what end? Learning by doing, while good as far as it goes, is short on preliminary analysis and shallow on ethics, and it lacks historical perspective.

I will give another example, closer to home. When she first began working with Teachers & Writers, Teri Mack went into a classroom to introduce the kids to videotape. She would be working all year long with this class and wanted to give as many of them as possible a sample exposure to videotape. She played a game called Hot Camera: each one of them was to hold the camera and say or film something which showed his personality, then pass it on like a hot potato. In this way, Teri would get to know something about each child, and the children would get a feel for the camera.

This was the plan. What happened was somewhat different. The children ran around, grabbing for the microphone; they did not use the opportunity to reveal anything about themselves. A large group drifted away, bored with waiting their turn, and the others became increasingly wild. Teri wisely called a halt, saying it wasn't working. She asked the class why they thought it had gone wrong. The teacher's explanation was that the children were naughty. "You must learn to co-operate with each other." Teri, with typical conscientiousness, took the blame on herself for not providing enough direction.

It seemed to me that both were wrong: Teri might have given much more direction and the results still would have been unsatisfying, because the original idea was weak. No child is going to be fooled into thinking that he can really express his personality in a few seconds with everyone else breathing down his neck, waiting to grab the camera away from him. To operate a camera for a half-minute is a pseudoexperience: not enough time to begin to master it, but just enough to reassure the adult that at least the child has been "exposed" to it, has gotten a taste of it.

A taste for poetry, a taste for ecology, a taste for videotape, a taste for litmus paper, added up, gives a taste for randomness and fragmentation.

This is good preparation for a future life in corporate America, where you are not asked to know any more than is necessary to carry out your end of the operation. It is also good training for a leisure life which involves the restless, often senseless, sampling of pleasures and one-shot pseudoexperiences.

What do I mean exactly by a pseudoexperience? When a person does something to acquire it in his personal dossier, to step into someone else's skin for a moment by proxy, and "steal" that other person's life, or life style, the experience has a false note. I once heard a true story about a woman who picked up a man in the street for $2.00 because she wanted to know what it felt like to be a prostitute. She told this to a much older woman, her friend, who said: "My dear, you still have no idea what it is like to be a prostitute. I knew many of those women in Paris, and they are out there every night; those women work very, very hard."

The distinction is one of depth, commitment, and responsibility for one's actions, which gives a certain dignity to any work. Holding the camera for a moment was a trivial pastime: the children could see that *nothing was at stake,* so they responded by not taking it seriously. If they had been presented with a more mature task, such as having to produce a videotape for cable television within a month's time, and asked how they should go about it, these same children would probably have responded thoughtfully and intelligently. Planning a stage set or a magazine may have inspired the same thoughtfulness. I find children to be very attracted to work processes which take a fairly long time to complete and thus can gather momentum. They like to hang around printing shops. They like to feel connected to the bigger world, the world of work, production, manufacture. I will go so far as to say that they often hunger for work. But that work must be serious, whole, and useful, and preferably require a measure of craft. Of course they resent the *busywork* of satisfying an endless stream of workbook demands, all of which come from outside authority. They are such adept shirkers of other people's assignments that their thirst for work of their own tends to be overlooked. But give them a job which is seriously going to amount to something, or which they have chosen to do through their own interest, and they can work at it all day. Then the myth that children have short attention spans is shown up for the oversimplification it is.

*   *   *

A year after *West Side Story,* we had a reunion party for the cast. They had all gone their separate ways, to different junior high schools, and so the party was a good chance for everyone to see old friends. Some of them had returned often to visit P.S. 90, and you had the feeling that they missed the more childish, safe environment of their grade school. Britt had, in a sense, never left. He still comes by about once a week to borrow the videotape equipment for the dramas which he continues to produce, direct, write, and star in—now without any adult assistance. Willie got into some disagreements with the teachers at his Catholic school, and for a while was seen rather too often in the halls of P.S. 90, talking earnestly with the littler kids and being an older brother to them. But what had happened to the others? I was dying to find out.

They began arriving at three o'clock from all corners of the city. They kept their coats on, a new mark of dignity. Everyone was pleased to see each other and yet they seemed embarrassed. After two exchanges they ran out of things to say—they whom you could not get to stop talking in the old days. The girls and the boys had as if by sign gravitated to opposite sides of the room; that was also something new. I kept offering everyone potato chips and cookies and soda; and then, at a loss for what to do next, I put on the videotape of their *West Side Story*—the evening performance. The kids watched with breezy, off-and-on interest. Thank God for Virginia, who kept commenting and talking about the show and laughing and giggling. Virginia hadn't changed one bit. Gene had longer hair and looked more in pain. Roberto was turning into a moody, touchy, James Dean sort of youth. Dolores managed to let me know she had lots of boyfriends—"too many! I'm always thinking about *boys* and I'm forgetting to do my schoolwork."

She had to leave early. Luis, who seemed chastened, commented to me in a low voice: "Dolores doesn't look so jacked-up as she used to be. I like her better this way—not so jacked-up." I was surprised by his observation: whatever he meant by "jacked-up," I'm not sure, but she looked just as manic to me as ever.

Throughout the playback of the performance, the kids had been more or less irreverent toward it, but when the videotape ended, they responded in a very unexpected way. Several kids started organizing support to do *West Side Story* all over again. Yolanda, Virginia, Luis, and Britt were the most vocal.

"Are you crazy?" I said.

"But I thought that was why you called us together," said Luis.

"No, I—thought it would be nice to have a reunion, that's all."

"Come on, Phillip, *West Side Story* was the most fun I ever had in school. I don't hardly get a chance to have any more fun any more," Luis complained.

"No, no, no, no . . ."

Yolanda said: "We could do it between ourselves in the church basement. How many want to put it on?" They took a vote, which was confusing and inconclusive.

Britt had the final word, half-campy, half-serious: "We got to do it *one more time*. Once more to hear the people shout, '*West Side Story! West Side Story!*'"

The party broke up. Scottie had shocked me the most. He had a deep voice and a mustache and I couldn't put the two changes out of my mind.

They had gone away, fragile children.

They came back a year later, biceps bulging, looking streetwise, manly, restless.

Sometimes I think I am growing old in this job. If they could have grown so much, certainly I must have been here a long time. I have taught the younger brothers of students I had had several years ago; I have seen whole families march across the grades, have had a chance to compare and make those spurious psychological explanations of particular children in terms of their home lives (sibling rivalries, broken marriages) that are the delight of teachers everywhere. When you encounter, as your students, different scions of the same family tree—cousins, brothers, sisters, parents—then you really begin to develop a different attitude toward teaching. You begin to feel the history of the community passing through you.

By now, people take me for granted in the school. I no longer think of myself as such a specialist—or so special. I am one inch away from being a classroom teacher.

Almost all books on personal teaching experiences gravitate toward leaving. The teacher is discovered doing things that raise the ire of a certain part of the community; his fraternizing with students provokes gossip; the principal will not renew his contract; or the grant runs out; he leaves, sadder and more prepared, perhaps to try somewhere else where the air is freer.

God protect me, I am still hanging on. The tragedy has not yet struck. If the lack of a denouement leaves this book incomplete, I accept the dramaturgic flaw. My prayer is to stay at P.S. 90 for as long as possible. Don't even ask me to predict when that will be. With so much that is constantly being ripped away from us, please, let me hold onto this life a little longer.

Appendix
A Little Anthology
of the Spicy Meatball

Appendix

A LITTLE ANTHOLOGY OF THE SPICY MEATBALL

Note: I have selected the stories and poems in this collection from among the first five issues of *The Spicy Meatball* and the Seventy-Five Press. Naturally, any writings that already have appeared in other sections of this book have been excluded here. Some of these pieces came from lessons given by other team members; some came from my workshops; a number were submitted by classroom teachers who were doing their own creative writing at P.S. 90, or by children working independently. Thus, in no sense can it be assumed that these are all the products of my teaching method or that I mean to take credit for them. But they do reflect the spirit of *Spicy Meatball.*

The Stars

Tea
Coffee
Milk
Chocolate
The kids
Were
Playing
And
Screaming
All day
My husband
Was sleeping
And weeping
All day
That's what
Happens
In the
Planet by
The Stars

RHONDA TUCKER

Eric's Story

The earth is a puzzle that God is making
and he lost some pieces of the puzzle,
and he lost four corners of the puzzle, and
he made it a circular puzzle because of it—
it has green purple, red blue, and he
called it earth. Now the rest of it was
all black, and he called it space, and on
this puzzle that he built he saw the
puzzle was real, and he said, 'I want some
life on this planet' so he made humans and
animals and plants and my grandma Rose, so
that is the end of my story.

ERIC STREICHER

I Am Tonya

Who am I really? But the world does not answer.
Am I Jewish, Protestant, Catholic? But the world is
silent. Am I religious? But what does the world say.
It is silent. Am I yellow, pink, blue or green? I look
all around. I see hate and love. What do I say to
this religious thing? I am silent. I ask my mother.
"Wait till you grow up to find out what you want
to be." Shall I be a Protestant, Baptist, Methodist?
I may never know.

TONYA PENDLETON

I am a parent. I have trouble with my boy Thomas, and a
girl Cynthia. Cynthia came in today, crying. Jason (the
boy next door) had hit her. Jason came in, his face pale.
He had a bloody bruise on his forehead. Thomas had hit
him. Thomas had hit him because he loved his sister. I
told him to go to his room because he shouldn't hit anyone
no matter what they did. Thomas blushed and went to his
room. I asked why they had hit each other. I was very
surprised to know all of this was over which of their
dogs were greatest. I called Jason's mother. She gave him
a spanking in front of Cynthia, found out what it was all
about and left. I said that she and father would talk this over.
Well, it was finally decided that they wouldn't go out for
a week, no T.V., and no dessert. The kids went to bed
crying. Kids!

TONYA PENDLETON

The First Time

I look at myself in the mirror
I am beautiful
But do you think so?
It's your opinion that matters.
I dab some lipstick on and walk
outside. There you are a handsome
brute
Suddenly we are dancing.
I'm floating across the floor. . . .
It's all over. The night was much too
short for me.

TONYA PENDLETON

Just Get Up And Run!

KATHY: Cindy, have you ever felt like just running?

CINDY: What do you mean, Kathy?

KATHY: Like just dropping all your responsibilities and going some place where there were none.

CINDY: Yeah, I guess you mean like not doing school work, not doing what your mother says and stuff like that.

KATHY: I wish I could, but for some reason I wouldn't. I can't explain why; I'd sort of be afraid of what's ahead and some other things. I just have it trained into my head that that's impossible, but it really isn't, is it, Cindy?

CINDY: No, it's not.

KATHY: I wish I could do it.

CINDY: Why?

KATHY: My life has been so screwed up for the past couple of weeks. I'm twelve. My family isn't poor or anything. I just can't get my school work done. School isn't hard, it's just a pain. Plus my older sister is going away to high school and I just can't talk to my mother.

CINDY: I guess that I feel that way, too. My mother makes me spend most of my time studying, but I don't seem to learn half as much as I do walking the streets, thinking things out. I don't know what stage my life is in and I don't know where to go next.

KATHY: That's the state I'm in.

CINDY: Why can't we run away?

KATHY: I guess it's so old fashioned we don't think about it.

CINDY: If we were to plan a real complicated one, just to have an adventure and make them worry, do you think it would work?

KATHY: Yes, I think it would!

CINDY: We would have to plan long and carefully, but maybe we could make it.

SUSAN WARD

Lightening

I see a streak of lightening
I see many of them
   but this one is spectacular
   it's streaking down so excellently.
   and its shape is The excellent shape,
   it's yellow as a bee and as violent
      soon it will disappear, what a short
      life lightening has but it sees
      the world, lightening is so rapid
      And when the rain pours it flies
how spectacular to fly the devils fly with
      lightening. And sometimes Ride
      I see one riding mine

KARLI DWYER

The Sparow

ONe day in pine hill I was walking to shul
And I saw a bird. it was on its tummy. I turned it over and its tummy
   was bleeding all
over. I put it gentley on some grass and went to shul. I prayed and
   prayed for the
bird there. when we went back from shul I looked for the bird. it was
   not there!
I belive god made him well again. after a few years I knew he was
   dead,
but I think he comes back from heaven to sing to me because I
   always hear a sparows
call in pine hill. I hear it from dawn till dark. once I went to
   bed crying,
but I smiled to hear the sparows call again.
he still sings to me every time I come to pine hill.
say what you might, but this is true.

ALISA KWITNEY

The Dog of God

"God," said an angel, "you are not happy.
So to make you happy, Milord, a party."
"BUG OFF!" shouted God. "It is (true)
but I am only lonely." "A WIFE!" shouted
the angel. "AY! A wife makes you sick!"
shouted God with anger. "A dog?" said
the angel. "O . . k . . a . . y . ," answered
God, not really sure.

So an angel went to earth and got a dog.
Then a burst of thunder came and God got
sick and God started a long long sleep.
Ever since then man ruled. But God gave
a present to all dogs . . . Dog is God
backwards, so if you see a dog run
backwards, bow.

ALISA KWITNEY

The Kidnappers

It was just about dark when I heard something in the kitchen.
I tried to tell Mommy, but she was too lazy, and said, "Look here,
stupid, if you wake me up I will never get back to sleep. And
furthermore, you got ultrasonic hearing 'cause I don't hear a thing.
Zzzzz zzzzz." Well, I thought, w . . w . . wel . . l . . l I . . I . . yikes,
crooks! I will walk into that room. Clip clop . . . mmmm Mom!
 Crooks,
call the police! Hurry up! No time to waste! Don't let them get away!

Mom yells: "You stupid inconsiderate dummy! You sleep wrecker,
 you! Now you can't sleep in my bed!
"Help, protect me from the bandits, Mom!"
"Oh, go play in the gutter!"
"Mom, aren't you going to save me from those stupid kidnappers?"
"No, stupid, so go back to sleep. You bother me any more,
 froggie face, and you won't be able to sleep in my bed
 for two whole months."
"What a crabby grouch."
"Just for that, you can't sleep with me for two whole months, like
 I said."
I go into the kitchen. "Yikes! Help! Kidnappers!"
One of the kidnappers was very long and skinny and had little bugs
behind his ears. The other one was very fat and very short and
his nose stuck out like the Empire State Building. The skinny one
grabbed me. And put me in a car with mosquitoes, bugs,
insects, and spiders crawling over my head. Cockroaches
crawled all over me. And I thought, I wonder what Mom will
think. They wrote a note to my mother that looked like this:

> Excuse me, dear, dear, dear lady:
> But—but we gotta your child. You
> want her back? So pay us 2,000
> dollars in golden cash.

My mother paid the money, and they brought me back. And a
spider made a nest on my head and the fat guy, I could
lie on his nose. Soon I got back to tell you this story,
but when I got back, my mother said, "Why didn't you
tell me there were kidnappers?"

ALISA KWITNEY

The truth is love and friendship
But that is scarce for me
That is plain to see
Where do you find it?
In a plattered plate?
Or in a tin can?
I think you find it scarce.

ALISA KWITNEY

Who like a topless belly dancer
The belly dancer moves a lot
She wear a bikini and fringe
The belly dancer clothes are
red black brown green purple
A lot of nasty people are looking
The belly dancer has long
hair and people like to
see her hair when she moves.

ILEANA IZQUIERDO RAMIREZ

They Are Calling

They are calling Nan come at once
But I do not answer. It is not that I
don't hear I am very sharp of ear
But I am not Nan Go and wash. But I
don't go yet their voices are quite clear
I am humming but I hear But I am not
Nan I am poet They are calling Nan come
to dinner! And stop I stop humming I
seem to hear clearer now that dinner's
nearer Well just for now I am now and I say
Comming

YVONNE VENTURA

Lose the Noisy World

Stop bothering me.
Go away.
Leave me alone.
I'm choking.
Get out of
me. I'm in red.
    Oh cross me
out of the
world. So green
less, so leaf less,
soon to be a
Nothinbody. A horse
person   a quieter

Joining the Horse People

Now! now,
now I'm a horse
person . doomed to
nays and wos.
Hard metal in my
mouth. Kicks in
my side. I hate being
a   horse person.
    THE
    HORSE
    thing

                              LISA RIPPS

This girl who was very smart
The girl was very nice but sometimes
    got too tart
This boy really liked her but she
    thought he was a brute.
He loved to secretly watch her
    undress until she was in her
    birthday suit.
And finally she was in peril
That this hoodlum fellow might rape her
Or her good friend Merrill
So she married this man
And after their child was born, he
    robbed her bank account and ran.
Their son joined the Peace Corps
Not like his father
When he came home he was most
    respectable.
He also married a girl who was quite
    eligible.
As the murmur within her body said
    you're getting over the fence,
She went to the country to die in
    silence.

DEEDEE FISHEL

President James Macmillan Thinking to Himself

I felt pressure in my last election when what's his
name ran against me. I only won by a margin so
I was elected. And that was a month ago.
And since then I've been going to a million meetings.
And making speeches.
But it really is not that bad.
I feel like I'm a big man like Wilt Chamberlain when
he was on the Lakers.
Now my security guards are out to lunch. And I'm
all alone locked up in this room.

STEPHEN WEISS

Fantasy

I sit in the snow.
I make a snowball.
I look at it, round and symmetrical.
I look at my fingers,
Curving around the snowball.
I throw it.
It explodes in a flurry of color.
Explodes, staining the world with its color
The snow is psychedelic!
My snowman is on fire!
The trees blend with the sky.
The world spins before my eyes.
Green and blue snow falls from
the purple and orange clouds.
I get up and walk home on the purple sidewalks
Looking at the red streets.
But where is everyone?

There is a clap of thunder, like a giant
animal roaring.
There I am, back in the snow.
I sit in the snow.
I make a snowball.
I look at it, round and symmetrical
I look at my fingers, curving around
the snowball
I throw it. . . . .

PERI DWYER

Simplicity

The girl walks slowly
She kicks her bookbag ahead
It is blue and black

No Name

Quiet in the class
The reading test will begin
My score will be high

Compliance

people speak of me
They want me not to have ears
I pretend not to

PERI DWYER

I Wish I Knew

I wish I knew
What to do
I go outside
feeling fine
But,
I wish I knew
what to do

I play all day
feeling o.k.
But,
I wish I knew
What to do

Play only babies
but,
My friends and I
Act like ladies.

I WISH I KNEW

JANICE BRODIE

Black Mama

Black Mama are you going to
work to day

Yes dear

Black Mama are you going to
earn us some money

Yes dear

Black Mama are we going to move out
of this dump

Yes dear

Black Mama are we going to move
to White country

No dear we're going to be free

JANICE BRODIE

Dear Lady

You are stink in the lunch and your hand are stink. And you are
skinny. Every time you give bread the bread are stink Boom Boom
Lady you are stink and stink and very stink and every time they tell
you to give something and you didn't give nothing and stink stink
stink oh Lady you know what you did to us. When we said to give us
something you didn't not give us nothing you are stupid.

BERTHA TAILLEFER

Repeating Poems

Oh ishcabibbel rainy days are no fun.
Why be so fussy, Caryn?
Because that's the way I am.
Oh.
Why be so fussy Caryn?
Because I am.
Oh.
Good-bye, I am going roller skating.
Because I am.
I'm going to study in my room.
Good bye, I'm going roller skating.
Oh ishcabibble rainy days are no fun.

I am going to writing class, Mr. Clausen
O.K., but be back soon.
Sue, should I take a pencil and paper?
Yes, you should.
O.K., be back soon.
I'll try to.
Yes, you should.
O.K.
I'll try to.
Yes, do that.
O.K.
I'm going to writing class, Mr. Clausen

CARYN SCHWARTZ

Most marvelous music maker
At all times
Though
The
Horrible
Eky
Water falls on the piano.

Matthew has
A
Nice
Diddle-
Ee-do
Life
Because he has
A
"U" in his
Marvelous name.

MATTHEW MANDELBAUM

Wait, that tastes good. It's already
in flight, just a little music,
a stamping, a humming, girls you warm
you silent girls dance the taste of the
fruit experienced.

ANTONIO TRINIDAD

Hi Langston Hughes

There you lie in your lonely coffin
But not for long.
I sit here on a grey stone.
Talking with you.
To keep you company.
What do you want to talk about?
It is getting late. I have to go now.
Bye.

TRACEY BRODERICK

TALES OF HORROR

The Thumb

How can one live with a thumb which is terrifying to mankind? I'll tell you this story which will give a chill to your spine.

My, how old a woman can be without age. Rain fell upon her head with tiredness she walked trying to find some shelter. The houses passed her like forgetness leaving her alone in the world.

I'm not going into that house she said, when she passed the house of death. Old Mr. Greenwich lived there. No one knew how he could live in a house so dark to the eye.

No shelter left to go to, only that forbidden place. She walked toward it with life walking away from her. She knocked twice . . . twice and at last she heard someone.

"Come in," said the dark shaped figure. "I saw you by the house lots of times, I was wondering why you didn't come in." She stared at his left hand. Why didn't he have a thumb, where had it gone?

She walked through the dark halls. Suddenly he turned around and his thumb grew from its knuckles and she saw him nearer until he had killed her with a shocked experience.

JOSEPHINE TAVERA

Swamp Thing

One night two boys were near a swamp. Suddenly something began to rise from the swamp. It was a giant. One of the boys said, "Hey Charlie, come over here." He said, "Just a minute!" "Charlie, come quick, help!" "Pete, what's wrong? He . . . e is dead." Charlie called the police. Let's have your story son. You say you found him dead, right. He called you but you told him to wait. Then he screamed. Well son, you could go now.

That night a car was going by the swamp. The man turned his steering wheel and the car went down the cliff. Here's a special news bulletin: a car was found in the bottom of the cliff near the swamp. The news chief heard. Two things happened that night and I'm going to see what's going on there. Well it's night time chief. Let's go to the swamp. Here we are chief let's look around. Chief come over here look it's the swamp monster don't shoot him I understand his problem he doesn't know what he is. This is the end of swamp thing shoot him! That's the end of him.

STANLEY LOYOLA AND LEE ROSS

A Soggy Eyeball Smashed
Against the Window

One morning I woke up. I looked
out the window and saw a soggy
eyeball smashed against the glass.
I almost threw up. There it was,
a soggy eye running down the glass
of my window—it stopped. I called
my baby sister. She pulled it apart
and started to suck on it. She said
it was very good. Then I threw up
on it.

SCOTT HILL

A drop of blood is yuk.

LISA M. OJEDA

The Over Relaxest Man

There was once a man who was very
relaxest. It is nice to be relaxest
but the way that this man was relaxest
was crazy. You see, he was so relaxest
his tongue started falling off. And as
that happened, his eyes started rolling
down his chest. After his ear fell off
he wasn't relaxest any more.

DONNA BEASLEY

Mad

WHEN I GOT MAD AT MY SISTER
I RAN OUT OF THE HOUSE AND GOT ON
MY BIKE AND WENT TO THE BEACH TO SWIM THEN I
WENT TO
THE BIG HILL THAT YOU ARE NOT SUPPOSED TO GO
NEAR
I WENT UP ANYWAY WHEN I GOT THERE THERE WAS A
PLACE WHERE THEY
USE TO BURN PEOPLE I CLIMBED UP ON IT THEN THIS
BIG BIRD
FLEW OVER ME THEN I I THOUGHT TO MYSELF
THAT IF I WAS WATCHING
T.V. I WOULD SAY THAT IS NOTHING TO BE SCARED OF
BUT RIGHT THEN IT WOULD BE SCAREY.

MAJA ANDERSON

TREE OF POSSIBILITIES

Hubert received a draft notice. He was
1) A strong American who was willing to fight.
2) Scared to go into the army and hated America.

1) Hubert rode to his draft board proud and
   3) did not pass his physical
   4) passed his physical

2) Hubert was worried to go
   5) so he burned his draft notice and became a conscientious objector
   6) but he went anyway and passed his physical

3) Hubert's pride was hurt and disgraced.
   7) But he pulled himself together and became an ALL AMERICAN CONSTRUCTION MAN.
   8) So he became a rebel

4) Hubert loved army life but when he saw someone spit on the flag he died of disgust.

5) Hubert went to court and did not have to go to the army on the basis of him being a conscientious objector.

6) Hubert was captured by the enemies and told them all he knew. Then he was killed.

7) Yes, Hubert was there when all those good American construction workers rioted those radical students. He was hit over the head with a wrench. He did not die but he became a radical.

8) Yes, Hubert was there when all those nasty American construction workers were there. He got hit over the head with a wrench and became a construction worker.

GINA DEMETRIUS

Sue is in the bath tub.
1) She could drown
2) She could get out and dry

1) She's laying there. Her mother and father walk in and pump
the water out of her. The next day she is buried.
3) She could come alive again
4) She could rot and turn to bones

2) She would stand up, get out, put the towel over her and rub
herself dry.
5) She could get towel cloth all over her
6) She could get an infection from rubbing too hard.

3) The next day she would dig herself out of the coffin, and
out of the ground, go to her mother and be alive again.
7) She could get hit by a car while going home
8) She could make it home safely and her mother would
scream.

4) She would rot in a few days, her bones would lie there like
only her bones were buried.
9) Archaeologists could find them and they would be a
great help to history
10) They could stay there and the worms would chew
them. Then they would all be gone.

DAVID REBHUN

BEING ALONE

When the clock is alone it stops working
When the policeman is alone he breaks rules
When the hot dog man is alone he eats the hot dogs
When the most important man is alone he starts cheating
        people
When my brother is alone he calls his girlfriend
When I am alone I start eating
When a person is in the class alone they mess up the room
When the president is alone he starts drinking

XIOMARA ROMERO

I'm Alone

I like to be alone, alone every day
I scratch my feet when I'm alone
I scratch my head
And I play
I scratch my head and think
I remember everything
My grandmother, I saw her buried
It took a long time
Then I remember my grandfather
When I was a little baby he used to diaper me
And he would always buy me stuffed animals
Then I remember my father
He used to murder me every day
When I told lies.

BERNARD SHEPHERD

If I was in a house by myself
Then I looked at a picture
Then also I look again
Then I said that eyes are looking
        at me
Every day
Every day
She don't stop looking at me
They are big, but not very big
Her eyes try to say
I do not hear but my self.
I am waiting and you never can.
You have me because I love you.

ANTONIA IZQUIERDO

Two by David Chalat

The day has come
I notice something
Night has fallen
My sheets are white as a glow passes over
I see my mind
The emotion that I have
The boundaries of my mind which interlock
The walls of knowledge
Which feed luminous sounds to my brain
But now the day has come
I notice something
The night has fallen.

I'm in my room
    Watching the tube
        look a man is flying
    look a plane is swimming
A mortal person dives through the screen
A turtle vomits out hatred
I see a baby drink the hudson
I saw a man piss in the gutter
The liquid like a river disappears

"Nothing"

I'm sitting here doing nothing just rotting away trying to write something. But now and then I get an Idea but I turn them down and scrap them. I am trying to write something that gives me an idea but I just scrap it again and again. "I just can't think of anything," I say to myself, and go on again—but I finally got a good idea and try to write a little and presto!!! here is where I am up to writing all of this B_____T!!!

I can't	I'm
do any	just plain
old thing	bored

My mind is wiped clean by this idiot who comes here once a week and sucks my head clean of ideas by putting my ideas on paper and printing them and handing them to other students for their knowledge enlargement.

The End

MATTHEW JOHNSON

ABOUT LOVE

McGovern and Mona

This is Mona   She daydreams alot and she
loves McGovern   so she day dreams
about McGovern
She is thinking
that she's dancing
with George McGovern.

Mona   Mona   Mona!
She really really
loves him
WOW!   She looks
in the Love Machine
What does she
find she finds
it's him man is
she glad.

She's dreaming that
McGovern carries her. She's
happy.

She smiles so
happily   She is so
glad she screams
    out   *McGovern*

McGovern   *McGovern*

McGovern   and she
screams   I'm the
luckiest person in
the world

Mona is day dreaming that McGovern
kisses her. She wants
it to come true
but she knows that
it won't she says
Oh   McGovern!   Oh
McGovern!
          Kiss me
                    Kiss me

MELISSA KRANTZ

The Coffee Shoppe

Marion sipped her hot coffee sitting in a restaurant booth
alone. She did not see the figure standing beside her.

"May I join you?" he asked.

Marion turned around. "Of course."

He was tall, dark eyed and extremely handsome, she figured. She noticed how low he had buttoned his shirt.

"My name's Justin Barnes. Perhaps you never noticed me.
I play the oboe in music class. Pretty lousy, though," Justin said
with a grin as he started to stare into Marion's eyes.

"Sorry. My name's Marion. Marion Lase."

"Are you French? Marion Lase sounds like a French name. French names like yours are beautiful," he told her as he kept looking in her eyes.

"It is French. My father is French, and my mother is an American," she answered.

When they came out from the coffee shoppe, there was something different about them. They walked out hand-in-hand.

Justin gave Marion a lift home. He then said to her, "I'd like to see you tomorrow. Dinner, maybe? My treat."

"I'd love to!" Marion replied.

"Great. Pick you up at 8:00," Justin told her and left her without her objecting. Marion sighed. It was a soft sigh, with a fragrance of love about it. It was her first dinner date. She was 18, and never had she met a boy who made her smile so. Perhaps it was true. Maybe she was in love. She was sure it wasn't infatuation.

At 8:00 the next day, Justin arrived in his blue Chevy promptly. He took Marion to an unfancy but delicious restaurant. While they were at the table, comfortably seated, Marion asked him a question.

"How old are you, Justin?"

He laughed. "Well part of me is 80, my heart is 20, and my brain is 4."

Marion grinned. "No, really."

He lifted his eyebrows slowly. "Twenty. Why?"

"Oh," she answered. "I'm just curious."

They had dinner and patted their stomachs. Justin looked firmly into Marion's face. It wasn't just a look, but it was a stare. And his lips were not turned up or down. Marion noticed how serious he looked, and she was almost about to laugh. But she didn't, as he started to speak in a low voice.

"Do you love me?" he asked, placing his hand in hers, studying her carefully. He watched how she crossed her legs, and held her fork in her slender, long polished fingers. Her eyes opened showing off her long lashes. Her hair fell before her ears, but Marion didn't bother to push it back. She was startled at Justin's question and didn't know what to say. She knew whatever she said would probably be stupid.

"Well, yes, I guess I do, Justin," and found nothing else to say but to wait for Justin's reply. He didn't say anything, so Marion spoke again.

"But after all, we just met."

Justin took his hands off hers, and ran his fingers through his hair.

"Even so, Marion," he began, "I feel a sort of 'thing' for you. I've always loved you, even before you knew me. I'd see you at lunch with your girlfriends, and I followed you to the coffee shoppe when you were alone, so I could get a chance to talk to you."

Marion shivered. She thought to herself, "This guy's really got something over me. He's making me feel creepy. And I mean I'm really getting the shivers. I love him, but I'm scared to love him, really."

When they were driving home, Marion noticed that this was not the way.

"Justin, are you heading for the park?" she asked suspiciously.

"It's the best way to see the moonlight," he answered. He then stopped the car in front of the park. "When I said 'I love you' I meant it. Now that we're even, it shouldn't be too hard to . . ." he said and stopped. He reached over to kiss her, but Marion backed away. "Please, Justin, don't!" she cried. But he couldn't be stopped. Marion jumped out of the car and took the bus home. There she cried for hours.

The next day, she was nowhere to be found. But there was someone at the counter. Marion. She sipped her hot coffee in the coffee shoppe. And somehow, she felt two eyes perplexed on her.

CECE LEE

"*Let Me Die* . . ."

Linda Rogers was combing her hair. "Tomorrow's the last day. I commit suicide," thought Linda. "But why Linda?" she asked herself as she put down her comb and strode into the bathroom. "I know why I wanna kill myself . . . because of Jeff!" She banged her fist down on the marble. "Ouch!" she screamed, "Why did he leave me? . . . Oh Jeff don't you see I love you . . . I need you too . . . or I used to!"

She went into the kitchen and fixed herself a piece of toast. She began to butter her toast as she thought of Jeff. She scraped off some of the butter and said through a mouthful of toast, "Why wait till tomorrow? Okay! I will kill myself today . . ." She went to get her butcher knife and thought aloud, "I want this to be public . . . I want Jeff to hear about this and think, "Why didn't I stay with Linda? . . . Or this wouldn't have happened!" She laughed gleefully. She put down her toast and put on her best clothes. She wanted to die beautiful. She went to the roof (29 floors high) and stood there for twenty minutes. A woman across the street called the firemen. Linda heard the sirens and jumped. Right into the fireman's arms. "Let me die," she shouted over 16 times and fainted. They put her in hospital. She fell in love with the fireman and is happily married.

MELISSA DeSOTTO
ALLY VEGA

My most valuable possession is my television set. Sometimes my t.v. blinks out on me while I'm watching something great. One time I was watching the N.Y. Knickerbockers with ten seconds left in the Knicks trail 102 to 103. I was going crazy when Earl Monroe shot my t.v. went on the blink. I kicked the television like crazy. My t.v. has scratches, bumps dents and the color is fading away.

Even my brother beats it up. He throws his candy, soda, apples, and cotton balls are all stuck in the tubes.

GEOFFREY KING

I am a person who lives in New York.
I feel happy because I am back in school.
My heart beats really hard when you put on your furry coat.
I start laughing when you put on your sun glasses.
I also get scared when you look sick, like now.
Don't ask why.

MARGARET VARGAS

One day a man whistles at a woman, a big woman. He likes
to whistle a lot and a lot she likes it too. A whistle gets two
kisses. He whistles and whistles, kiss and kiss, a happy ever
after.

CLARET FARIAS

The Teacher That Bought the Vase on Lexington Avenue

Once there was a teacher whose name was Ms. Slax. She taught
in a school called "The Henry Kissinger School." Everyone
there, including the teachers (especially the men), thought she
was the prettiest woman in the school. It was true, too! She had
wavy, red hair that she washed twice a week, a perfect figure,
and really beautiful clothes. Anyway, all the men in the school
(including the principal, Mr. Simon Peabody) kept sending her
bouquets of flowers. They were crazy over her! But poor Ms.
Slax! She was running out of vases to put all the flowers in!
First she used up all her vases, then her glass glasses, and finally,
paper cups! "Oh dear!" she sighed, "I've used all my vases,
glasses, and cups! And just got another bouquet! Oh dear!"
Then she had an idea. "I know what I'll do!" she cried! "I'll
go down to Lexington Avenue and get a new vase!" And that's
exactly what she did.

As she was strolling down Lexington Avenue, she met Mr.
Charlston, a teacher in her school. "Why hello, Mary!" he said.
Mary Slax was her name. "Please, Ben, don't call me Mary," she
said. "Very well, Ms. Slax, if you say so!" he said. Ms. Slax

smiled. "Where're you going?" Mr. Charlston asked. "I can't tell you," she replied, and went on her way. Mr. Charlston looked after her, scratched his head, and sighed. Then he turned and went his way.

Ms. Slax stopped in front of an antique shop. There were no vases in the window. "Oh dear," sighed Ms. Slax, and walked on.

Finally she came to a store called "Wilson's Vase and Pot Store." "Oh good!" exclaimed Ms. Slax. "I think I found what I've been looking for!" Then she opened the door and went in. The shop was a very big. There were billions of shelves, with billions of pots of all kinds sitting on them. And, of course, vases of all kinds, shapes, and sizes. "Oh, this is just what I've been looking for! I'm so glad I've come!" she looked around. There were so many vases to choose from! Then a man came out from behind a counter somewhere and came up to her. He thought she was pretty, too. He had a long, black moustache that he twisted thoughtfully and slick, black hair. It was clear to see that he was italien. "Ah, Miss, may I help you?" he asked with an italien accent. Ms. Slax turned around. "Oh, why y-yes, you can!" she stammered. She had been startled. "What are you looking for, Miss?" inquired the clerk. He was liking Miss Slax more and more, and feeling glad that he was a bachelor. "Perhaps," he thought, "she will come out with me tonight!" Ms. Slax replied, "Oh, I'm just looking for a nice vase to put some flowers in." She did not say just where she had gotten them from. "Ah yes, a vase. Does madame want any particular pattern?"

"No, not really."

"Hm-m-m-m." He twisted his moustache. "Let me see. Ah! I know! Come over here, madame, over here." Oh how he liked Ms. Slax! And, Ms. Slax was beginning to, well, admire him too! "Sir," she asked, "how should I address you?" He turned to face her. "Just call me Antonio, Anthony for short. What should I call you?" Ms. Slax was so surprised that at first she didn't answer. Then she said, "Just call me Mary." The very name she had told Mr. Charlston *not* to address her by! "Very

well, then, Miss, ah, Mary, I have just what you want, I think."
By now he was head-over-heels in love with her. And she with
him too! Well, Antonio showed her a vase, a really beautiful
one, with porcelin with tiny roses and daiseys painted on it.
"Ohhhh!" exclaimed Ms. Slax when she saw it. "I want it! I
want it!!" she exclaimed. "Oh, I do!" And so she did. And . . .
as Antonio was wrapping it up, she asked, a little shyly, "Would
you like to come to dinner with me tonight?" Antonio looked
up and smiled a white-toothed smile. "If madame will have me,"
said he.

It was the beginning of a wonderful friendship.

YVONNE S. KINGON

DREAMS

When I Had a Dream of a Love Story

One day I was downstairs eating breakfast. My boyfriend
came in and he kissed me and said let me have some coffee.
Ok I said I made it I said and he said I need $30. I said what
for Johnny oh for something Rhoda that was my name. I gave
him the coffee and did not give him the money and he left and
I went down stairs and I started to cry and then I woke up
and it was a dream.

AND that goes to show you never trust nobody not even
your own boyfriend.

The End

By you know who
DOLORES VELEZ

Yo me levanto por la manana y me lavo
las manos, me limpio la cara, me bano
y me duermo y al estar dormido sueno:

Que hace 3 dias vi un enorme Angel y
que lo haber visto en una llama de fuego
y al des patarme vi sui no era realidad.
Si you fuera Angel estaria en el reino del
cielo pero como no soy Angel estoy en
el reino de la eternidad.

I get up in the morning and I wash my
hands. I clean my face and I bathe and
I go to sleep and when I go to sleep I
dream:

That 3 days ago I saw an enormous angel
and that I had seen it in a flair of fire and
when I woke up I saw that it wasn't reality.
If I were an angel I would be in the kingdom of heaven but since I am not an angel
I am in the kingdom of eternity.

CARLOS B. CASTRILLO

My Dream

I only have good dreams. Once I had
a dream about a candy store—a man
came in and robbed it. My mother
owned it. She got killed in the rob-
bery. So I ate all of the candy in the
store and bubble gum. I ate the
french fries and the hamburger and
some of the frankfurter. She had
heroes and stuff like that. I became
so full I had to have my stomach
pumped. I kept on spitting up. The
doctor said I should've came earlier
because I need my tonsils out. I said
"NO" I ate enough candy and stuff
like that. He said I can die if I didn't
have it out. I said let me die, let me
die. They said, "No We try to
succeed in every patient." I said don't
try to succeed in me. They said if it
was up to me I wouldn't but it's not up
to me so goodbye. They came in later
—I was laying there pretending I was
die. They put me in a casket. I was
buried alive

The End

P.S. I'm glad it wasn't true—the
only part I wish was true is the part
about the candy store and about the
hamburgers and stuff.

JACKIE DEAS

Dream

I had a dream I am not going to tell you
cause it is none of your business.

BLUE SKY

TO DIE

When you die
You say
I worked hard today.
And you lie down
And then you're gone.

SARA LOEB

Death in Light

When you die, an invisible shell of
your body lifts your mind high into
the air, but low enough to touch the
ground. Your mind sees, not your eyes.
And you feel that you're sliding down
a slide of water into the sun.

MARK FRIEDBERG

What It's Like to Die

It looks like everything is going black
It feels like everything in your body
Has gotten a traffic ticket
And has to get off the road.

NICHOLAS BUNIN

My Feelings of Death

Would you like the feeling of death
in you? It is disgusting for people to
have it. It is ugly to me and to others.
It would be good to live forever, but it
is impossible because death is in its way.
Too, it is a beautiful thing to live
forever.

JOSÉ QUINTERO

The Cold Night

I watch a
        movie about
PT 109 and I was
Kennedy. Boy and
I went
        to the tub and
I turned the water
        on   It flooded out
        of the tub. And
        I got my
        gun and

        bang bang bang

My coffin was
        the refrigerator.

End

PAUL FELDMAN

In the city, it was filled with millions
and millions of water. Me and just
one more person were the only ones living.
That other person was a salesman. He was
Downtown, and I was Uptown. He was trying
to sell the dead people some hair tonic. He
will sell it to any person, just for some money.
We met at the middle of the city. He tried to
overload that junk hair tonic on me, but I don't
want any. Just me and him. At midnight he
started to die. In the morning I just let him
float away. Then I started to feel sick. I
tried to stay alive, but then it happened.

BRUCE LEVY

Emily Dickinson

When she was one year old, she was an actor. She used
to be the best star of all. I met her one time in a restaurant.
It was called the Emily Dickinson. She was married to a big
man, strong, handsome, but stupid. Oh yes, I know you out
there are wondering what happened. Well, let me tell you. She
was talking about Love to her husband. I was on the other side.
She said Kiss me Kiss me, but her husband said No. She said
Kiss me please. I couldn't stand it. She just kept on saying Kiss
me. So I up and said, Why don't you kiss her? The husband
said: She has hot lips. So I went home and went to bed.

BRITT WILLIAMS

MIXED FEELINGS

I
(grouchy & mean)

The morning is the worst time of the day especially on school days!

I can't stand brushing my hair, it's so knotty.

I think babies are big mouth brats, all they do is make trouble!

Popsicles are so drippy and sticky all they do is make a big mess!

I hate to read, it's so boring, all you do is read and turn the page.

I
(sweet & corny)

I love the morning because it's the start of a new day.

Brushing my hair is so much fun, I could brush it all day.

Babies are so cute. They are so little and harmless.

In the summer all I can think of is nice delicious, breathtaking popsicles.

I think my favorite subject is reading. It's so very exciting and interesting.

CHRISTINE HUNTINGTON

I have a pair of Ice Skates, that I
love so much that one day when I was
skating, I said to myself, boy, I love
these skates. Then my skates started
to love me back. I was hopeless. My
skates stuck with me everywhere.
They ate with me, slept with me, and
made me go anywhere they went. They
made me skate every day to make me like
them better, but instead I hated them.
Then one night when the skates were asleep
and I was awake, I untied the shoe laces and
the skates slipped off my feet. I was re-
joiced, but before I could celebrate, I had
to show my revenge. Then, I took my knife
and killed them. I was free, FREE! The
next day I threw a party. It was great, and
I was free.

MATTHEW GOODWIN

Mixed Love

I love you as a drunk likes his beercan.
I love you because you are so beautiful but dumb
It makes me feel superior
I love the way you brush your hair like a witch
I love your dandruff, it makes you look like
White Christmas
I like the way you do the hippo walk
I love you like an old man loves a bikini
I love you like the moon likes the night
I love you like a hammer hits a nail
You and me are like hamburger and tomatoes
I love you as Nixon kisses Agnew
I love you like a kid loves Sesame Street
I love you like a cookie monster likes cookies
I love you like a peach, it tastes wundervar
Ah, ecstasy of it all!
I love the sun as I love myself
My name is Jamaica
I love you like the crust in my underwear
I love you like California loves Reagan
I love you like a pencil likes this writing paper

CLASS 6-326

My Father

My Father is a man of many problems. He is also a very good father in many ways. To try to make an attempt to change a lot of the things that make his life not as good as it would be, he goes to a group called Primal Therapy. This kind of therapy is much more strange and unusual compared to regular therapy. Regular therapy is sitting down on a nice comfortable couch and calmly discuss your problems. But Primal Therapy is where you yell and scream out until your guts pop out. This method is to yell out all the hatred that is deep down within yourself. This Primal Therapy has helped my Father considerably over the last six months.

My Father is also a very well coordinated man. His favorite sport is tennis. He also plays basketball, football, and baseball. While he was growing up he was extremely miserable. My Father had very strict parents. His favorite sport when he was a kid is basketball. My Father's name is Richard Hoffman. He stands 6 foot 3 and weighs 195 pounds. He's 42 years old. His occupation is a school teacher. He admits that he's not perfect, but then who is?

JED HOFFMAN

Father

He has a little hair and is also very
funny. He talks a lot and sometimes
when I have trouble understanding a
word he goes through a big thing. Like
when I didn't understand the word
biology it took him 15 min. to explain.

DENA LEVINE

Mi mamá y mi papá estan peleando. Yo y mi mamá estábamos haciendo un bizcocho para mi cumpleaños. Y después vinó mi papá y cogío la máquina de batir el bizcocho. Mi papá cogío la máquina y la tiro en el piso de la cocína. Éstrelló la máquina y chocó con la pared de la cocína. Estábamos haciendo un bizcocho para Carlos Maysonet.

CARLOS MAYSONET

My mother and my father were quarreling. My mother and I were baking a cake for my birthday. Later, my father came home and took the hand mixer. He took the mixer and threw it on the floor of the kitchen. The mixer smashed up and hit the wall. We were baking a cake for Carlos Maysonet.

CARLOS MAYSONET

My Cousin

My cousin's four years old,
And what I see about her,
Is that she won't cheer up,
Unless you crowd around her.
When my cousin talks about certain people,
It seems to make her smile,
But after she does that,
She bucks her teeth for awhile.
My cousin's cute and nice,
But there's one thing about her,
Whenever she gets attention,
She always wants to go further.
There's something about her,
She's very very kind,
But when someone talks about her,
She really blows her mind.

NANCY STADE

Jamaica

When I was a month old my mother and father sent me to Jamaica and I stayed there till I was 3 years old. When my mother and father came to bring me back I did not know who they were. I had a Jamaican accent. We stayed there for a few days. One day we went to the beach. And there were almonds there. I was picking them off the tree and eating them. My mother said don't eat that and I said don't worry mammy it's an almond.

TRACEY BRODERICK

Un día cuando mi papa vinó con un perro bien, perro bien, grande yo dije: "¡Ay! ¿ahora que vamos a hacer con el gato?" El me dijo: "Lo tenemos que votar." Y yo le dije: "Papi, ven acá que el perro y el gato están peleando!" El gato está más bravo que el perro. "Papa! Corre, Papi, corre antes de que el gato se trepe en los tubos!" "Mira, Papi, ya se trepó el gato." Nosotros no sabemos como el gato se trepó en los tubos. "Vente, Elsie, ayúdame a cogerlo." "OK Papi, ya voy, ya voy." "Elsie, tu lo coges por ese lado y yo por el otro. "Elsie, Elsie, ayúdame que ya lo tengo!" "OK, Papi, aqui vengo." Ahora tenemos que votar el gato afuera para que se vaya para siempre. "Ay, Papi, tengo ganas de llorar." "Bueno, ya como tenimos un perro te vas a gustar mas que el gato." "Bueno, es verdad, Papi."

ELSIE CRUZ

One day when my father came with a very, very big dog, I told him: —Ay! Now, what are we going to do with the cat? He told me: —We have to throw it away. I told him: —Daddy, come here, the dog and the cat are fighting! The cat is wilder than the dog!
—Daddy, run! Run, before the cat climbs on the pipes! Look, Daddy, the cat is already on the pipes!
—Come on, Elsie, help me to get him.

—Okay, Daddy, I'm coming. —Elsie, you try to catch him by that side and I try the other. —Elsie, Elsie, help me! I caught it! —Okay, Daddy, I'm coming. —Now we have to put the cat outside so he runs away forever. —Ay! Daddy, I feel like crying! —Well, as we have a dog, you are going to like him better than the cat. —Well, it is true, Daddy.

ELSIE CRUZ

DESCRIPTIONS

"The Hotel Room"

In a certain hotel room, 209 to be exact, two people were moving in. When they opened the door they shuddered with disgust. There on the wall just barely hanging was a lamp light with a dim light which cast just enough light to put the room in an erie spirit. The shade was tattered on one side, and had a huge coffee stain on the other. The striped wall paper which was supposed to cover the wall was coming off in strips. The stuffing of the couch was coming out, and where it was not, springs were breaking through the upholstery. The window was streaked with an egg and some other unpleasant stuff. Brawled out on the floor were newspaper, evidently left from the last people that were there. The newlyweds ran down the stairs and left.

GINA DEMETRIUS

My Block

Dirty on the sides
  Broken in the
  Middle of the
  Block
    And
     Dark at
  Evening

    Light in the
     morning
  Light
   Light when
  it's sunny

  clean when it's
morning

    The scratched
  Mail Box the
    Distance

  of the other
 Box up the glaring

    street few
  people in the
     neighborhood
    today in the
    very few times

 you   ever
   see
    the Block
  in Distinction.

       DAVID ROMANELLI

My Job

My job is deliver laundry and I go to an apartment. You could smell the stink when you were outside the door. When I go in I saw about 20 cockroaches on the sink and some on the rugs. And on the cup. Then I saw the house so dirty get paper all over the floor. The chair all full with coats. And get food on the floor so the cockroaches could eat. Then I go out I take a good fresh air. And the man said "Do you like the smell in there." I said, "I hate it but maybe you like it." Sometime I pick up laundry in her apartment and I bring the laundry back to the laundry. And my grandmother opens the bag and cockroaches are coming out. And I think that is the stinks and dirtys house I ever saw in my life.

SCOTT GEE

A Teacher and a Student

TEACHER: Richard can you do the Math?

STUDENT: Yeah I can do it. Do you think I'm dumb?

TEACHER: Well, you act like you can't do it. You sit there like a dummy.

STUDENT: You're the dummy 'cause you won't help me.

TEACHER: How do you expect me to help you. You are always out in the hallways.

STUDENT: While I'm at Mr. Johnson's room I'm working down there and you're sitting up here talking. You should mind your own business.

TEACHER: Don't get smart with me. I'll send you to the principal.

STUDENT: I hope the principal drops dead.

TEACHER: Your report card will drop dead when your mother sees this report card.

STUDENT: How do you know that I might not tear it up in front of your face?

TEACHER: I'll give it to your sister.

STUDENT: So? I don't care. When my mother puts it away I'll tear it up.

TEACHER: I know what's on your report card.

STUDENT: How you going to tell her when she don't come here. I'll get you fired.

TEACHER: I'll suspend you till your mother comes to school.

STUDENT: So I'll come to school anyway. Why don't you mind your own business?

TEACHER: So, you mind your business you troublemaker. That's why I separated you from everybody else.

STUDENT: So listen Teacher I still got friends at free play and listen here Teacher don't get snotty!

TEACHER: The first chance I get I'll get you out of this room but no one wants a troublemaker.

STUDENT: So I kick everyone's butt in the school.

TEACHER: No you won't 'cause if you do the principal will kick you out of this school.

STUDENT: I'll kick the principal's butt out of this school.

TEACHER: O yeah?

STUDENT: O yeah! ! ! ! ! ! ! ! ! ! ! ! !

GEORGE McGILL AND SIMON SUMPTER

THE HARRY SNEEDLESS STORIES

by HANNAH BROWN

(This collection was originally published as a
Seventy-Five Press book)

The Plight of Harry Sneedless

Harry Sneedless was a quiet man. He had short mouse-gray hair
a mouse-gray moustache and tortoise shell glasses. His favorite
colors were mouse gray and a dull light blue. He owned a three
room apartment furnished in his favorite colors. He lived with an
odd light blue cat named Irving. He owned a Xerox shop and worked
in it six days a week. There you have a portrait of Harry Sneedless.

Harry Sneedless had no friends, save for one in a small town
in Iowa. For some unexplainable reason the landlady was attracted
to him. She tried to invite herself over twice, but failed. This made
her very suspicious of him. She suspected he was a criminal. She
went to the police and they became very excited and raided his house
when he was at work. When he got home he was puzzled.

The police said that he would have to come to the station for
questioning. Still puzzled, he went. The police officers questioned
him. Much to their embarrassment, he did not seem to be a criminal.

Then they had a psychiatrist talk to him. The psychiatrist found
him normal, contented, happy, and ordinary. If you are any or all of
these things, everyone knows there must be something wrong with
you.

So they told Mr. Sneedless to get all his things and come back
to the police station. He took his cat, his clothes, some books, and
some souvenirs of trips.

When he arrived at the station, he was put in a waiting police
car and taken to an institution.

Irving

"This is no normal cat!" said one expert to another.

The second expert, gray and wrinkled, looked up. "How do you
come upon that?" he asked.

"Well, it's blue," he said. His name was Max. The ancient one's name was Mr. Herbert.

"Oh, I hadn't noticed," Mr. Herbert said.

This tiring conversation took place in the examining room of the I.F.P.W.H.S.W.W.T. The Institution For People Who Have Something Wrong With Them. This is the institution to which Mr. Harry Sneedless was taken. The two men were examining Irving, Mr. Sneedless's blue cat. Irving was as ordinary a cat as Harry Sneedless was a man. Irving was content to sit in Harry's lap listlessly as Harry dozed and dreamed of things that never were and never will be.

The institution officials were afraid if they took Irving away from Harry Sneedless that he would become neurotic. Irving spent most of his time with Harry. Sometimes he wandered around the institution. This was fun, because people said things like, "Now I'm seeing blue cats! I must be a' going Freddy! Well, it has been a nice world. . . ."

Sometimes people yelled, "Get away, cat!"

Irving helped keep Harry from being too lonely. Since Harry Sneedless was normal, he had nothing in common with the other patients.

"How are you?" asked Mr. Herbert.

"I am fine," answered Harry.

"How do you like it here?" asked Max.

"It's allright, but I'm bored. I liked it before. With my little Xerox shop. Why did you take me away?" asked Harry.

"Because you need a rest," said Mr. Herbert.

Harry Sneedless became more and more bored. He wrote stories, read books, played with Irving. But Irving did do something. He started a diary. And now I turn the narration over to Irving.

(Excerpts from Irving Sneedless: Diary of a Blue Cat)

10/11/72

Things are so boring. I went to the library today. They kicked me out. This place is a prison. The people who run this place should be in it! The food is rotten. I keep getting Nutritional cat food. Harry has been slipping me some of his bacon and eggs for breakfast. Poor guy, Harry. He misses the Xerox shop. So do I. For both of our sanity, I'm going to bust us out!

A [1]Day in the Life of Harry Sneedless and Irving

Harry Sneedless woke up and got out of bed. So did Irving. Harry Sneedless began to get dressed. Then, Harry combed his mouse-gray hair, trimmed his mouse-gray moustache, shaved, and brushed his teeth.

Then he went to the kitchen to make breakfast. Irving was sitting on the table waiting for him. Harry made himself some coffee and a hardboiled egg. He gave Irving some slightly watered-down dry cat food. When they were done eating, Harry washed his mouse-gray coffee cup, his dull blue plate, and Irving's mouse-gray saucer.

He said good-bye to Irving and left for work. He walked the two blocks and arrived at work early. While waiting for a customer to come, he Xeroxed some manuscripts and put some papers in the sorting machine.

A customer arrived. He wanted 20 pages Xeroxed 5 times and sorted. The man wanted it ready by Friday. Harry would be paid on Friday. Agreed. The man left.

Then the store became very busy. There were lots of things to be done.

At 12:30 Harry closed the store and had lunch. He always ate lunch at home, so he could be with Irving. He made himself a can of soup. He gave Irving some shrimp flavored cat chunkies. Then Harry relaxed and read the *Post*. He got up and washed out his soup bowl and his coffee cup. He said good-bye to Irving and went back to work. From 1:15 to 2:00, the small Xerox shop was open for business. From 3:00 to 5:30, it was closed. Harry Xeroxed the things customers had brought in through the whole day.

At 5:30 he went shopping. He went to a small grocery store. Sale! Hamburger Meat! a sign read. Harry bought hamburger meat. He also bought some toothpaste. He walked the one block, and arrived at his dull blue and mouse-gray apartment.

Irving welcomed him. He gave Irving some catfood. Harry was thirsty, so he drank the cola. He made himself a hamburger. He put

[1] Harry Sneedless was released from the Institution after 6 months.

some A-1 Sauce and some onions on it. He made himself some coffee. He and Irving ate dinner and watched the news.

For dessert, Harry had an apple. He read a library book for about an hour. He did a cross-word puzzle for a while. He was humming out loud, and Irving was purring blankly. Harry Sneedless, the one and only.

Murry

A cockroach scuttled through the dark hall. All its life this cockroach had been fairly ordinary. Still it had been slightly different. It had always been afraid. Afraid to steal food, afraid to run out, and play in the rug. He had lived his life listening to taunts of other cockroaches. But he was meek, and afraid. But today was different.

The cockroach's name was Murry. He had always hated the other cockroaches. They teased him and beat him up. If he hadn't left, he would have gotten himself a nice job stealing food, and he would have played in the rug. But he left. He left all the other cockroaches behind. He was very solitary, and wanted to be alone. Suddenly he picked a door and went in.

This was Harry Sneedless' apartment. Harry was at work. Murry walked over the woodwork. He noted the furniture and liked it. He headed towards someplace, hoping he would find the kitchen. He found the kitchen and he found Irving!

Irving was Harry's blue cat. Irving was asleep on the linoleum. Murry was shocked. But he soon realized Irving was asleep, and he might as well make the best of it.

Murry discovered a rug in Harry's bedroom. He lived there. For a few weeks he led an extremely boring existence. For lack of something to do, he began a journal. He wrote with a pencil stub on the back of the rug. Even Irving was boring. He didn't chase Murry. Murry began to look forward to writing in his journal.

One day when Murry was writing, Harry pulled the rug and began to shake it out. He saw Murry writing and found the journal. He read it with amusement. Harry felt he *had* to tell someone. Foolishly, he called his landlady and told her.

"He's gone loony he has!" she said. "Again! Cockroaches writing! Poppycock!"

Harry was excited at finding a unique cockroach. But his ecstasy was broken into by a knock on the door.

"May we come in, Mr. Sneedless?" said a voice.

Harry and Irving heard it and were instantly afraid. Harry ran to the door and bolted it. Murry sensed something was wrong and became alarmed. It was Mr. Herbert and Max from the Institution! Suddenly they realized it. They were a trio and the Institution was the enemy!

The Escape of Harry Sneedless

Murry was frightened. Harry was frightened. Even Irving, shrewd as he was, was frightened. For Mr. Herbert and Max were at the door.

"Mr. Sneedless, are you home?" asked Mr. Herbert. "Come on now, I won't hurt you. Mr. Sneedless, if necessary, I will break down the door!"

Harry Sneedless, quiet as he was, became resourceful in the face of crisis. Mr. Herbert and Max were at the door. They wanted to take him back to the institution. The institution! They knew he was not crazy. He must not be taken back. He was propelled by desperation. Murry was afraid because he knew Harry and Irving were afraid. He understood that what must be done must be done quickly. Harry opened the window. Irving got ready to follow after him. Frantically Murry climbed on Irving's back.

But Harry didn't jump. He climbed the fire escape. Irving quickly followed. Harry closed the window behind them. When they got down, Harry picked up Irving and Murry. Harry hopped on a bus. It was going uptown. He got off at 121st. Then they went to a movie. It was a cowboy movie. They all fell asleep.

The next thing they knew the matron was tapping Harry on the shoulder. "Hey, buddy, ain't you leavin'? The picture's over."

"Oh yes, Excuse me," said Harry, and left. Irving perched on his shoulder, with Murry in his fur. Murry was no longer afraid, he was too busy enjoying the ride. He had a few pieces of popcorn in the theatre, but Harry and Irving were hungry. They stopped in a crummy coffee shop and sat down. He ordered two ham sandwiches, and gave one to Irving. Ordinarily Irving would have turned up his nose, but he ate a little. Murry finished it off. Harry also had a coffee. Then they all got on the subway. On and on the train rode.

Harry awoke to find a man reaching into his pocket.

"Oh, sorry, man, I didn't mean to wake you. Stay loose," and the man got off the train, and walked away with some of Harry's money in his hand. Harry stared at him in bewilderment. Deciding he had nothing to lose, he got off.

He walked onto the street, and breathed in the fresh air. He came to a supermarket that was stocking its shelves. He went in and bought Irving some catfood. Harry and Irving both knew well that Murry was along. They sat on a park bench. Harry poured out some catfood, and Irving ate. Murry picked up crumbs and chewed them vigorously. Harry looked around. He felt at peace, and no longer hurried or frightened. He thought of nothing, neither the future nor the past. In the morning air, he watched the daily ritual of stores opening. Harry tapped his fingers to the rhythmic crunch, crunch of Irving chewing catfood. He sighed and looked up.

"We've got to find him," Mr. Herbert said to Max. "We've got to."

"But why?" asked Max.

"Because we've got to, that's why!" replied Mr. Herbert with emphasis. "He ought to be locked up. They let that mad man loose against my better judgement. He's a born troublemaker. I've never liked him. The ruckus he stirred up with his landlady. Well!"

"What did he do?" asked Max.

"Skip it," Mr. Herbert sighed.

That night Mr. Herbert was having dinner with Mrs. Herbert, who was Harry Sneedless's landlady. He said to her, "How do you think we can find Sneedless?"

"Well," she said, "You could put a check on all grocery stores in Manhattan, and ask if any catfood had been sold to men with blue cats."

"Beautiful!" he cried. "I'll do just that tomorrow."

It began to rain. Harry saw no point in sitting on the bench any longer, especially since Irving detested rain, and Murry might drown. He went into a bookstore. He bought a dull over-dramatic novel. Then he took his 35¢ and got on the subway train, to see where fate would bring him. Again he slept. As he was asleep, the train left many, many stations behind.

When he woke up he was on Fulton Street. He got out and
walked around. Harry didn't like the smell of fish, but Irving did.
Boxes with fish heads were littered about. Harry gave a fish head to
Irving. He ate it up quickly. Now, how about for some food
I like, thought Harry. He went into the cafeteria at the South Street
Seaport. He had coffee, fish sticks, and french fries. Murry also had
some.

"Well, hello," said a man.

"Hi," said Harry.

"My name is Menhegler Virbitz. An ole seafaring lad am I."

"I'm, uh, Harry Sneedless," he said. Was this man a spy for the
institution?

"I run a tugboat from here to Queens. Sometimes I carry passengers. What do you do?"

"I'm unemployed. I used to have a Xerox shop. Let me tell you
about it." So Harry told him.

"And you think they'll follow you?" asked Menhegler.

"Yes."

"Well, I can help you hide from them. You can sleep in my
boat. I'll teach you how to handle it. I'll give you room and board.
But you'll have to work. O.K.?"

"Yes, but—"

"But what?"

"What about my cat?" asked Harry.

"Take him along. He can eat mice. Come on now. You look
tired," Menhegler said. He led Harry to the tugboat. It was very plain,
and had a gassy smell. Harry began to feel queasy. He wondered how
he could spend the night there. Menhegler showed him two small
rooms, a tiny kitchen, and a bedroom. Menhegler unfolded a cot
and indicated Harry was to sleep there. Harry quickly fell asleep.

"Yes," the man was saying, "We do sell catfood. No I don't
recall a man with a moustache and a blue cat. I'll tell you if I see him,
though."

"Nope. But if I see him, I'll give you a ring," the saleswoman in
the next store said.

Again and again Mr. Herbert got the same answer. He was following his wife's suggestion and trying to find a store that sold catfood, where Harry had bought some. He drove his car to the next
supermarket. He had a carphone and it rang. It was Max. "Mr. Her-

bert, Waldo said he just found the store. It's on 124th and Broadway. Come now!"

Meanwhile Harry was being awakened at 6:00 A.M. "You've got to clean the place. It's a pigsty. Come on." Harry was not used to such requests at that hour, but he figured he'd better get used to it. Murry and Irving were pleased with their new surroundings. Menhegler prepared to go to Queens, and pick up supplies for the cafeteria, also to buy some instant coffee and some muffins for himself.

It took Harry all day to clean the tugboat. He took only one break. Then after making many trips back and forth, they had dinner. Harry had grown accustomed to the slight rocking and felt queasy no longer. He made hamburgers in tomato sauce for dinner, and coffee and muffins. Harry was already sick of muffins. He was tired, that night. He thought cleaning the tugboat was much harder than running it. Until Menhegler started teaching him the next day.

"Well," said Mr. Herbert, "This doesn't get us any closer to what we're looking for. Where do we go from here?" he said after he arrived at the supermarket. They talked for a while and decided to put an ad in the paper. The ad read:

ANYONE

who knows anything about the whereabouts of Harry Sneedless please call
this number—(212) 333-6598. Suspect
is around 5'9" middle-aged, medium
build, grey hair, moustache, glasses.
He has a blue cat, and carries it with
him.
LARGE REWARD!

It is doubtful many people read those ads. But one of the few people who did was one of the few people who knew where Harry was. His business was going bankrupt. He needed the money.

"Hello," he said. "Is this 333-6598?"

"Yes. Do you have information?"

"Yes. I know his whereabouts. Come to this address." He gave an address and hung up.

Harry, Irving, Murry, and Menhegler were eating their once a week lunch in the cafeteria. The owner of the cafeteria came in.

"Hello," he said. "It's nice to know you have regular customers when business is so bad." He signalled and Mr. Herbert and Max walked in. It was the cafeteria owner who had finked!

Harry, Irving, and Murry froze. Murry jumped into Irving's fur. Harry grabbed Irving and ran.

"Don't worry, we have all the street exits covered," said Mr. Herbert calmly.

But Harry didn't run for the street exit. He ran for the tugboat. He had been learning for about a week and a half. He could just barely handle the boat. He jumped into it. By now Mr. Herbert and Max saw that he wasn't running for the exit. Harry had a good head start. Mr. Herbert, Max, and the other two men ran after Harry. They jumped into a small speedboat. The two men tried to start it.

"Dammit! Get moving!" cried Mr. Herbert.

The men started the motor. It was sunny. The dirty water churned. On sunny days it didn't seem *that* bad.

"Can we overtake him?" Mr. Herbert asked one of the men.

"No, but we can crash into him. That will jam the motor. Or we can try to hook the ropes onto him," the man said.

Harry really was doing pretty well, considering his experience. But the two men were very fast, and so was the boat. They crashed!

But they had already reached the dock in Queens. Harry grabbed Irving and Murry, took a deep breath, and jumped out of the boat.

The Revenge of Harry Sneedless

Harry jumped onto the docks and landed with a crash. Irving clung to Harry, and Murry clung to Irving. The jump had been quite a shock to Murry, but Irving, who knew Harry's mind as well as he did, knew it was the only thing to do.

Mr. Herbert and Max were hoping and praying that Harry was injured, and wouldn't be able to run. But the only injuries he suffered were a sprained ankle and the shock of the other boat crashing into him, and his leap onto the dock. Despite their hopes, Harry jumped up and ran, limping slightly because of his ankle.

"After him!" yelled Mr. Herbert. But the crash had not only jammed the motor of the tugboat but also the motor of the boat Mr.

Herbert and Max were in. When Mr. Herbert saw that Harry was escaping and that he could not be pursued, he went into hysterics. Harry Sneedless had $3.00 in his pocket. He knew he couldn't hide all his life. He would have to get a job and stay hidden. Then he'd have to decide what to do. How could he hide? Many people must know his description. He knew he would have to disguise himself. Irving was very conspicuous. He felt everyone knew who he was, as he walked down the street. Then he found what he had been looking for. A discount center.

He bought a small towel, a pair of cheap sunglasses, a large cap, and a poncho. He wrapped the towel around Irving and Murry, so he appeared to be carrying a small baby. He put on the poncho and the cap. The sunglasses were large, but they had plastic frames. He put these on top of his other glasses since he needed them to see. Harry hoped this would be a sufficient disguise.

Now he needed a new name, and a story for not having I.D. His name couldn't be Joe Smith or anything like that, he thought. William Abott. He was from Omaha. He had a friend named Murry Irving. He had been robbed. His luggage, wallet and I.D. had been taken. He had no way of getting home. He decided to search for Murry. He decided to get a job.

Not the most convincing story, but it would do. But Harry knew he couldn't hide under a fake identity forever. He carefully looked for a subway station where he could sneak under the turnstile. He sat and thought. He decided. Then, he fell asleep.

He woke up. It was 5:00 A.M. He got off and walked to a newspaper stand. He found an old paper lying on the ground, and looked at the want ads. As he thumbed through the paper, he noticed a picture of himself. Only now it was not an ad but a story in the newspaper. He quickly looked away from that section.

WANTED: Messenger—Researcher for
"Plant Life" magazine. Must be
responsible. Call (212) 999-9395
and ask for Mr. Froggitz.

That looked like a good job to Harry. He decided to wait until 8:00 to call. At 8:00 he went into a phone booth. He dialed 0.

"Hello, may I help you?" asked the operator.

"Yes, I just put 5 dimes in a phone and I didn't get them back and I can't get through," said Harry.

"Very well, sir. I'll connect you."

"The number is 999-9395," Harry said.

The phone went click.

"Hello, may I please speak to Mr. Froggitz?"

"Speaking."

"I'm applying for a job. You know—with 'Plant Life,'" said Harry.

"Very well. Come over. Good-bye." He hung up. "Oh, Matilda, oh! Only 3 applicants. Oh Matilda, why?" Mr. Froggitz cried to a green snake plant, whom he referred to as Matilda. There was a knock on the door. "Come in," said Mr. Froggitz.

A man entered. "Are you Mr. Froggitz?"

"Yes."

"My name is Fritz Shnoogle. I applied for the job. Let me tell you about myself. I was worm editor for 'Insects Everywhere' magazine. I was laid off. So was the lady bug editor. Now, Mr. Froggitz, I was close to these worms. I was close to the greenery they lived in. I loved the whole job. And then I was fired. Ah, well. So, I have decided to work here. I only ask one thing, sir, that I be allowed to keep worms in the plants in the office," he said.

"Well," said Mr. Froggitz, "You'll get every consideration. Who's next, Matilda?" he said across the plants.

"I am," said Harry. "My name is William Abott." He told his story.

Perhaps there is a certain understanding between people who have never wanted anything nor gotten anything out of life. It can't be said that they understood each other, neither of them had ever made an attempt to understand anyone, but perhaps they sensed they were somehow alike. Or maybe it was just a trick of fate that Mr. Froggitz hired Harry.

As the interview was drawing to a close, Mr. Froggitz looked up. "Matilda," he said, "Is there anyone else waiting?" He got up and walked to the door, and looked into the waiting room. "No, he didn't show up, Matilda. No. Pity. And such a good job, Matilda. Well," he said, turning to Harry, "You're hired. Payday is Friday. Come work for me tomorrow. The pay is $125 a week. Good-bye."

As Harry left, he could hear Mr. Froggitz moaning, "Oh Matilda," through the closed door.

Harry slept on the subway that night. He was tired of it. The rattling and rumbling annoyed him, and the hard seats made him ache. But there was no place else for him to go.

Today is Thursday. Tomorrow is Friday. Tomorrow I will have money. I won't have to sleep on the subway. Maybe I will leave town, Harry thought. Then a line of T.V. dialogue came to him. "The airports and bus terminals are the first places they'll check."

So Harry decided to stay and work. A plan, rare for a man like Harry, began to take shape.

He went to work the next morning and found it easy. He had to leave Murry and Irving in a locker with the door slightly ajar. At 5:30 Mr. Froggitz presented him with a check for $125. He took Irving and Murry out of the locker and went to look for a small hotel. He found one. He bought some food and another shirt. The money he had left over he saved.

It went on this way for a month. Then Harry knew he had saved up enough money. He knew that this was the time.

"How does it work?" asked Harry.

"That's complicated," said the man. "I'll show you how to set it off."

The man's name was Jerigilah Lemmington. Harry was buying a bomb from him. He had simply looked up his name in "The Stink" a revolutionary newspaper under "Bombs and Weapons."

"I don't want to *kill* anyone. Do the $20 bombs kill?" asked Harry.

"They can. But the $15 bombs won't. How about it? They'll create a disturbance. You can be sure of that," he said.

"O.K. I'll take ten. Put them in a big crate," said Harry.

He made more preparations. The day drew closer.

There was a knock on the door of the institution.

"Who is it?" asked the receptionist.

"Arnold Glotz," said Harry. "You may not remember me. I'm the one from the N.A.P., one of the organizations that help to make this lovely institution able to work."

"What's the N.A.P.?" asked the woman.

"The National Organization of Philanthropists. Now you see I'm assigned to see that everything is A-OK around here. You know, we have to see that the patients have T.V. privileges and that the doctors have Reader's Digest. So I wish to have a little tour, tell the philanthropists all is well, and leave."

"Well, Mr. Glotz, I'll have someone conduct the tour," said the woman.

"No need. I'll wander around at random. I wouldn't want to trouble you. Thank you, and bless you, my friend," said Harry.

He studied himself in the mirror for a moment. The fair skinned complexion looked all right. So did the fake beard, the fake blond moustache (over his own) and the fake nose. He also had on a fake toupee and numerous pimples. Not to mention elevator shoes. He had also looked up a disguise man in "The Stink." No one except Irving would have guessed it was Harry.

He walked on. He looked into offices. Some were empty, some were occupied. He planted bombs here and there, choosing the right places. He also cut off the water from the sprinkler system.

He came back to the receptionist's desk. "Everything is fine, the patients are wonderful. I've never seen them look so happy. And call me when any of the doctors run out of Reader's Digest. Goodbye, See you next year," said Harry. He left and hid in the woods and waited.

Five thirty. Harry had to get into the place. He was sorry he hadn't brought Irving, who could triumphantly witness the destruction of the institution. The patients would be in the dining room now. He climbed in through a window. The bombs began to go off. Bombs were exploding everywhere, filling the air with smoke and fire. Terrifying loud noises filled the air. The institution officials were in a panic. Some passed out, some sobbed hysterically, and some prayed. But most of them ran around shocked. The patients also had mainly the same responses. But some of them had been there so long they just sat and stared. They didn't care anymore.

He quickly went into the file room and set fire to all the records that the psychiatrists kept of their patients' case histories etc. Then he unlocked the dining room doors. He waded through the smoke, down the corridor. He grabbed the loud speaker.

"Patients! You are free! You are liberated! Run! Run! Flee! You are free! Free! FREE! Liberated! We have won! You are free!" he said.

The patients quickly grasped what Harry had said. Pushing

back the guards, they ran. They were stunned to see a bus waiting for them.

"Get in, get in!" cried Harry.

The patients, or rather the fugitives, climbed in. Harry drove them to the bus terminal and told them they were free, and could go home. The patients sat in silent awe of the man who had freed them.

"Don't worry, They won't get you. You *are* free," Harry assured them. The patients went home. Harry drove the rented bus around the streets then he returned the bus to the rent a car company. He returned to the hotel. He would be William Abott for one more night.

Harry waited fretfully for the news the morning paper would bring.

"Bombs Planted In Mental Institution. Police Search for Culprit," Harry read. He found out that Mr. Herbert and Max both had nervous breakdowns. They couldn't give the names of the patients who had escaped. They couldn't even tell what had happened. Wilfred Mukoy a guard did give an account of what happened.

"Well I was standin' atta dorr, when I heard these noises. An' then they sounded closer, if you know what I mean. Then I realized they was bombs. Well, I never seen anything like it since I was on the national guard. Then there was this voice a comin' over the loud speaker. I can't rightly remember what it said."

And the receptionist, Helena Gargol had said, "A man from the N.A.P. came. He said his name was Arnold Glotz. He could have planted the bombs." She gave a description. There was a small scandal with the N.A.P. who withdrew their funds. Now even if Mr. Herbert and Max regained sanity, there would not be enough money to reopen, or pay for the damages.

Harry called Mr. Froggitz, and said he had found a job tending sheep in a New Jersey farm that had a more promising future.

"Oh Matilda," cried Mr. Froggitz. "What's Fritz Shnoogle's number?"

Harry took Irving and Murry and went home. He was William Abott no longer. He testified in court that he had been followed and pursued by Max and Mr. Herbert for months. He claimed that his business had been hurt severely. He also said he had suffered severe mental anguish from it. When the matter of the other patients who had run from the institution was questioned, Harry said, "I'm sure they have all gone home. I'm sure they were all quite sane. I know some of the people and perhaps they needed some help, but they certainly didn't belong in a place like that. Since it has been shown that Mr. Herbert and his assistant were not sane, and they had complete control over who was admitted to the institution, I think that the patients who were admitted should be released. They were not capable of judging who should be put in and who should be kept out."

So, Harry went back to his apartment, and his Xerox, his mouse gray and dull blue furniture. Irving and Murry came with him. Perhaps, somehow, Irving knew what had happened. Even if he didn't, he knew what had happened to Harry. He knew that Harry had become different, and had acted as only a person in desperation can. Harry had done something he never believed he could have done before, and never thought he could ever do again.

The End

Afterword

Afterword

Being with Children was my attempt to portray everyday life in the classroom. But the only way I could think to portray that life was to focus on extraordinary moments and challenges. Certainly my mere presence in the elementary school as an artist-in-residence who was supposed to function as a "change agent," so to speak, meant that I was altering the very quotidianness of the situation I was hoping to describe. And yet, everyday life sweeps all before it and in time, normalizes for good or ill, the novelty of the intruder.

Above and beyond describing intended innovations, I wanted to show the weight of the constant elements: the play between adults and children (or children and children) and the environment (physical, bureaucratic, historical) of the institution. Indeed, if I could be said to be putting forth any method in this book, it might be summarized in two words, *relationship* and *environmentalism*. The first term refers to a desire to ground my teaching in an awareness of the individual characters of my students and colleagues and the nature of the contact between us; the second, to an insistence that good teaching is not a curricular stencil that can be imposed over any situation, but must flow from an analysis of the local situation and an experimental response to it.

These ideas, which may strike the reader as mild platitudes to which no one could take exception, actually continue to be resisted at all educational levels. In 1983, eight years after *Being with Children* first appeared (and long after it had gone out of print), a writer for *Language Arts,* John Rouse, contrasted it with a newer book, *A Celebration of Bees,* which purported to offer a method of poetry-writing that would be "just about 100% effective" for seven- or eight-year olds, junior high school students, college students, or adults. "A sort of one-size-fits-all approach," is the way Rouse characterized it. At the risk of sounding self-serving, I will

quote the concluding summary of John Rouse's piece, because it says better
(if more immodestly) than I can the reasons why the *Being with Children*
model was not widely taken up:

> So here we have two very different ways of working with children—one
> methodical, the other experimental. One looking back to what has already
> been seen or felt, confining expression to the descriptive, the other looking
> ahead, trying out possibilities of feeling and form. One relying on a high
> degree of control, the other chancing the unexpected. And these approaches
> must have very different effects on children, on their habits of perception, of
> feeling and thinking—on their developing selves, in short.
>
> We can see this in the poems they write. Those done as experiments, in a
> classroom where anything can be said, express the self-confidence and humor
> of their writers with a variety of forms and subjects. Reading them we come to
> know these children as real individuals to whom things matter. But those
> poems written in accordance with the Method are blandly uniform and
> impersonal. For the Method deals with children in the abstract, requiring
> them to set aside their individual interests in order to conform to a procedure
> and fulfill their production quota. Years of such training would produce people
> adaptable to whatever mechanistic demands were made on them—people
> capable of doing any dirty work while retaining their innocence, since they
> feel apart from what they do and therefore clean. People who sustain them-
> selves in their loss of possibility with sentimental illusions that help them
> manage their self-pity and suppressed anger. They *need* the release given in
> the sentimentality and violence purveyed by the mass media.
>
> The Method, in other words, tends to produce people who feel very
> much at home with things as they are. And that is why methodical, unpoetic
> methods have always dominated writing instruction: they have a social utility.
> Certainly Lopate's experience in P.S. 90 cannot represent any general trend in
> our educational system, where the tenure of poets must always be uncertain,
> their place marginal. The future of writing instruction is better represented by
> *A Celebration of Bees* than by *Being with Children,* although there is no doubt
> which book teaches us more about children and writing.

I would not want to suggest a simple opposition between a pedagogy
of relationship/environmentalism and one of curricular method. There can
be no teaching without some sort of curriculum, and certainly I put
forward in *Being with Children* my own curriculum ideas, not only in
"Seven Lessons" but, more casually, throughout the book. However, the

very casualness with which these ideas were strewn indicated my discomfort with following a system, any system, in teaching writing or film. Whether this was the mark of the amateur, pedagogically speaking, or the defensive posture of another sort of professional identity (poet), there is, I know, a certain part of my brain that shies away from systematization and rigorous intellectual method, preferring the freedom of the improvised experiment. For someone like me, children were the perfect coworkers, because they too shy from abstraction while throwing up endless clues, wants, and taunts inviting immediate response.

When I wrote *Being with Children,* fifteen years ago, my idea was to organize it in such a way as to put the reader through the same sort of experiential maze that I myself had undergone. After I turned in the manuscript, my publishers felt that the *West Side Story* section was so appealing that it ought to be moved forward, perhaps even start off the book as an audience-grabber. This I resisted. I wanted to show how one gropes one's way uncertainly into an environment as complex as a grade school, and how it is only after becoming familiar with the personnel and the kids that one can undertake so large a project. If such a measured presentation meant that the beginning was slow, I said, so be it. I now realize that to some degree they were right, it does bog down a little in the early chapters, where we keep meeting new characters without the benefit of a strong propelling action. But I still feel strongly that *West Side Story* belongs where it is.

On rereading this book after all these years, I've sometimes winced at the confessional exposures of myself and others, and might wish that I had exercised more restraint then. But it's too late now (and not entirely cricket) to sanitize one's literary past for self-protective purposes. *Being with Children* is certainly a young man's book, and reflects the energy and almost manic outgoingness of that period in my life. What surprises me most is how many literary modes exist side by side in this one volume: personal and impersonal, narrative, descriptive, didactic, polemical, case history, diary, even a "novella" (the *West Side Story* production) smack in the middle. At the time I remember telling myself that since I did not have the courage yet to tackle a novel, I would secretly make *Being with Children* into a sort of non-fiction novel, with characters, dialogue, and dramatic scenes. In a sense, too, I was already experimenting with that spectrum of essayistic discourse—the jigsaw puzzle, one-man anthology approach I later used in my essay collections, *Bachelorhood* and *Against Joie de Vivre*—designed to show off my variety and perhaps make the best of my scatteredness.

Being with Children was meant to be viewed in the same line of autobiographical educational accounts as those predecessors who had been inspirational to me: Herbert Kohl, Sylvia Ashton-Warner, John Holt, James Herndon, Jonathan Kozol, and George Dennison. At the time, I thought I was a latecomer marching along in a fine parade. I did not quite grasp that the parade had ended. Between the year *Being with Children* was published—1975—and today, there have been scarcely any *experiential,* first-person accounts of teaching (and these few tended to receive scant attention in the media). Certainly there continues to be a steady stream of how-to method books, quick-fix panaceas, armchair jeremiads by academics about the sorry state of classical learning, and so on; but that earlier genre, which I am tempted to call the "educational romance," has slowed to a trickle. Why should this be so? The challenge that the art of teaching poses is no less engrossing and complex to newcomers entering the field than it was to the above-mentioned chroniclers, so why should they be silent about their experiences?

I'm not sure why. I can only speculate that it has had something to do with market saturation (the reading public is first fascinated and then bored with reading about the problems of children, blacks, women . . .); or with back-to-basics testing anxiety, which has put the classroom teacher on the defensive, forcing him or her to swallow expressions of self-doubt and threatening away the messy, experimental voice of personal accounts; or with a larger sense of contemporary disenchantment vis-à-vis work (there is not much writing about anyone's job and workplace as a major source of engagement and satisfaction); or even with a certain professionalization of educational discourse, similar to the way that the early anthropologists who were so much like adventure writers—novelistic in their reports— were succeeded by others who tended toward more cautious, theory-laden, or quantifiable approaches. Whatever the reasons, I wish the old experiential approach would stage a comeback. Education plays too large a part in our lives, both as national employer and as shaper of future generations, for society to ignore the individual voices and personal maps of articulate teachers as they thread their way through a new, different classroom universe.

*   *   *

Being with Children ends with a prayer that I stay on at the school for as long as possible. In fact I lasted five more years. They were very productive years for the Writing Team and for myself, during which we continued to help children write, shoot films, and put on plays, while also building a school radio station and teaching the kids to make their own comic books. My own pedagogic ambitions culminated in a full-scale production of Chekhov's *Uncle Vanya* with fifth and sixth graders. After ten years at P.S. 90, however, I had run out of fantasy projects and seemed in danger of repeating myself, coasting. Also, being a writer-in-the-schools paid so poorly, and there was nowhere to go beyond the first rung. In the face of federal cutbacks and institutional resistance, I realized that it would always be a start-up job at best, intended for young, enthusiastic, emerging artists who could live with the small wages in return for the experience, then depart when they became better established—which was now my situation. Too, the morale at P. S. 90 had been affected grimly by several losses: first its popular young assistant principal, Claude Hardwick, died of cancer; then Stanley Riegelhaupt (the teacher with the loud voice) committed suicide;* the city's fiscal crisis had wrought havoc with the school personnel; and one by one my old gang, the teachers who'd been my pals, was drifting away, some burned out, others lured by higher-paying jobs in law or computers or counseling. It seemed the right time to leave. So I took a university post teaching creative writing to graduate students.

But I miss the kids. Their excitement, their funniness, their capacity to surprise. No other job has ever used me—used me *up*—so fully. I look back on those years at P.S. 90 as a golden decade, the one period in my life when I could be a hero in my own eyes. I was socially useful, serving the community and breaking new ground educationally (or at least it felt that way at the time).

Recently I paid a nostalgic visit to P.S. 90. It seemed a tiny bit quieter than in the raucous open-corridor days, but I was happy to see it had remained a very stimulating learning environment. The principal, Ed Jimenez—"still crazy after all these years," as the song goes—could barely contain his excitement about a new program he had snared for the school, Paideia, which taught philosophy and moral values to school-

---

* Editor's note: Both the *Uncle Vanya* production and the suicide of the schoolteacher are treated extensively in Phillip Lopate's new essay collection, *Against Joie de Vivre* (Poseidon).

children. I watched him (with a twinge of envy) lead a group of kids in a lively, probing discussion of a book they had read. Then he went on to praise the Teachers and Writers Writing Team, which I had started almost twenty years earlier at P.S. 90 and which is still going strong ten years after my departure. It is, in fact, one of the main selling-points that he uses to encourage parents to enroll their children in his school.

I am glad to say that my old organization, Teachers and Writers, is thriving as never before. It has a whole new batch of dedicated writers and artists operating in the New York City schools, as well as regional projects in Texas and the Midwest, and an impressive catalogue of books that were generated largely from its own workshops. In an era when the teaching of writing is in danger of being systematized to death, the Teachers and Writers approach remains flexible, humane, and aesthetically sophisticated.

As for the kids themselves, I followed many of them up to a point, then lost track over the years. The last I saw of Britt, he had gone into the Army; he looked very handsome and upright in his uniform. Francis and I corresponded for years, until the link became too attenuated. Hannah Brown, author of *The Harry Sneedless Stories,* has become a writer in adulthood; she lives in Israel and still looks me up whenever she is in this country. A few of the boys, I heard, got involved with drugs and petty crime: stealing wallets, that sort of thing. I once saw Dolores in the 72nd Street subway station. She didn't notice me. Then again, maybe it was only someone who looked like an older version of Dolores, who may no longer bear any resemblance to the way she appeared as a child. Wherever they all are, these once and no longer children, I wish they could realize at least subliminally how much they helped me to grow up, and how vivid they remain inside me still.

Acknowledgments

The hardest decision I have had to make in writing this book has been whether to use the real names of teachers and administrators in the school where I have taught. My affection for them as people and for the reality of the events and locales was finally outweighed by the concern that some of the things I wrote might personally embarrass them. In order to leave the names real I would have had to remove most or all of the "negative" judgments I made, which would have created a falsely saccharine picture of school life. To me, there is no loving people truly without seeing them fully—that is to say, with both positive and negative qualities—but I also realize that it is one thing to accept criticism from a friend, another to see your name and character bandied about in print. The sole exception to this rule of confidentiality has been to give credit to the child writers for their stories and poems. My sharpest regret is still that I have not been able to honor my friends at P.S.— by name; but they know who they are, and they know what my huge debt is to them.

I would also like to thank the following people for reading the manuscript in its various stages and giving me suggestions and first aid (without them I would have gone crazy): Richard Elman, Robin Glass, Maxine Groffsky, Karen Hubert, Ann Lauterbach, Betty Ann Lopate, Carol Lopate, Leonard Lopate, Ezra Millstein, Liz Newstat, and Bill Zavatsky.

I am especially grateful to my editor at Doubleday, Sally Arteseros, and to my agent, Wendy Weil, for guiding me so capably and patiently through this first book.

I owe more than I can say to George Romney for his gentle strength and example.

Xecopy Express on West Sixty-seventh Street has been very good to me.

To the other members of the Writing Team, Sue Willis, Teri Mack, and Karen Hubert—thank you.

Most of all, I would like to thank the leadership of Teachers & Writers Collaborative—Steve Schrader, and, before him, Marvin Hoffman and Martin Kushner—for giving me this chance.

P.L.

About the Author

Phillip Lopate is the author of *Bachelorhood, The Rug Merchant, Against Joie de Vivre,* and *Confessions of Summer.* He is on the selection committee of the New York Film Festival, and is a recipient of Guggenheim and National Endowment for the Arts fellowships. His works have appeared in *Best American Essays, The Paris Review,* Pushcart Prize annuals, and other publications. Mr. Lopate is an Associate Professor at the University of Houston and also teaches at Columbia University's graduate writing program.